PRAISE FOR CHARLES J. GIVENS AND

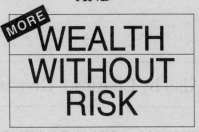

MORE WEALTH WITHOUT RISK

Also by Charles J. Givens

FINANCIAL SELF-DEFENSE:
How to Win the Fight
for Financial Freedom

The indispensable companion to
MORE WEALTH WITHOUT RISK

UPDATED AND EXPANDED
FOR 1995 AND BEYOND

MORE WEALTH WITHOUT RISK

How to Develop a Personal Fortune
Without Going Out on a Limb

CHARLES J. GIVENS

POCKET BOOKS
New York   London   Toronto   Sydney   Tokyo   Singapore

In view of the complex, individual, and specific nature of financial matters, this book is not intended to replace legal, accounting, or other professional advice. Laws vary from state to state and the reader is advised to obtain assistance or advice from a competent professional before making decisions about personal financial matters.

The author and publisher disclaim any responsibility for any liability, loss or risk incurred as a consequence of the use of this book.

POCKET BOOKS, a division of Simon & Schuster Inc.
1230 Avenue of the Americas, New York, NY 10020

ISBN: 0-671-69403-0

First Pocket Books trade paperback printing April 1995

10 9 8 7 6 5 4 3 2 1

POCKET and colophon are registered trademarks of Simon & Schuster Inc.

Cover design by Barry Littmann
Front cover photo by Debra Lex

Printed in the U.S.A.

To
Chuck and
Rob,
my sons,
Julie Anna, my daughter,
and
Adena, my wife,
my greatest supporters

You will see all the elements of our secrets. The conclusion will be yours to draw. We can help you learn it, but not to accept it.

The sight, the knowledge, and the acceptance must be yours.

Ayn Rand
Atlas Shrugged

CONTENTS

PART I

PERSONAL FINANCE STRATEGIES

PART II

TAX-REDUCING STRATEGIES

PART III

POWERFUL INVESTMENT STRATEGIES

Preface

MY STORY

Charles J. Givens

While I was still a young man, my father died. Even after owning his own successful business for years, he died absolutely broke. There wasn't even enough money to pay his funeral expenses. I will never forget wondering, "How, in a great country like America, can anyone work so hard an entire lifetime and end up with nothing?" With half-formed tears I promised myself that that would never happen to me. No matter how long or hard I had to search, how many books I had to read, or how many people I had to ask, I was determined to find the answers. I wanted to be rich, and nothing was about to stop me.

What I learned about money over the next 15 years enabled me to build my personal and business fortune. The determination and single-mindedness of purpose paid off. If you read the financial articles in *USA Today*, *Newsweek*, *People*, *The Wall Street Journal*, *Money*, or *Venture* magazine you know the story. I feel fortunate to have been able to share my strategies and encourage others through such great talk show hosts as Oprah Winfrey, Bryant Gumbel, Phil Donahue, Sally Jessy Raphael, and Geraldo Rivera.

I have found that there is no downside to having a lot of money. Money is freedom, and freedom is the ability to do whatever you want when you want to do it.

The path I followed in building my wealth was certainly not the easiest. Every possible mistake was made for one reason—no one was around to show me how.

At age 25, I created a Nashville music business conglomerate, Colony International. At 27, I was broke. No one had ever told me that I, and not my insurance agent, was responsible for being certain that I had enough of the right kind of insurance. My soon-to-be-completed—and opened—recording studio and office building burned to the ground, taking with it all my business records and dozens of valuable master tapes on which I never collected a dime.

During the next four years I moved from the bottom to the executive suites of Genesco, a major apparel conglomerate, by designing management computer systems in an era when computers were new and computer professionals almost nonexistent. The job gave me the leverage to use borrowed money to finance my way into stock market wealth. New companies, new issues, and new profits to borrow against. Then in 1968 the market turned. No one had ever told me that stocks can go down. Instead of continuing to follow my own instincts and common sense, which had created the paper fortune, my emotions led me to a group of vested, fast-talking stockbrokers. "Here. You watch my money," I said, almost relieved. Well, they must still be watching it, because I never saw another cent. I traded my new burgundy 1968 Cadillac for a mortgaged Volkswagen, sold my house to pay off the margin calls, and left corporate America and Nashville with a bankroll of only $200 in my pocket, representing my entire first 30 years of living and working.

My third million-dollar idea was the creation of a luxurious yacht club. Cashing in a $3,000 insurance policy, I put a 60-day option on a beautiful estate previously owned by a Pittsburgh steel magnate on the banks of the Indian River in Florida. With no extra money and no income, the next few months were financed by a wallet full of credit cards.

The $50,000 required to close on the property was obtained only at the last possible minute. Everything seemed to be working. Plans to convert the estate to a yacht club were drawn up, and soon the club would be finished. No one, however, had pointed out that it was probably better to complete the docks before the club. The government of the state of Florida decided to prohibit dredging in the river while a long-term ecological study was finished. No docks—no boats; no boats—no yacht club. The trustee for the project neglected to make a mortgage payment, and the third mortgage holder foreclosed. It was all gone in one day. Three times in eight years I had created a million-dollar idea starting with nothing. I could make money, I just didn't seem to be able to keep it.

Beginning in 1971, through a combination of leveraged business and real estate investments, I managed to build and keep the fortune I now enjoy. In 1986 *Success* magazine chose for the first time the 20 living Americans who they felt had started with the least chance, made the biggest mistakes along the way, and built the biggest fortunes. I was very honored to be one of those 20. Why is that important to you? Because when it comes to money, yours or mine, I know what I'm talking about. If I tell you a strategy will work, you can bank on it. You can use these strategies to open financial doors never before available to you, to compress the time it takes to build your dreams. Most importantly, enjoy every moment of the journey as I have learned to do. That's what separates the real winners from the losers.

This book is simply a composite of the money strategies I have discovered over a lifetime of personal financial experience. You will find them both easy to understand and easy to apply.

Making financial decisions is like standing in a room full of doors, knowing that behind one is the financial reward you seek, but behind the others are financial perils you seek to avoid. Without additional knowledge your alternatives are not appealing. Through trial and error you may make a choice detrimental to your wealth, or you could refuse to choose at all as most do, letting fear create financial stagnation. An unseen third alternative is the one you have chosen through this book—making your financial decisions by knowing in advance what lies beyond each door, a form of X-ray vision that will connect predictable financial results to your choices. You cannot fail in a plan that allows you to choose results instead of only the processes or paths to be followed. That, my friend, is the power you now hold in your hand.

Without knowledge, personal and business financial decisions are made with an ounce of logic peppered with a pound of emotion. Money does not behave according to the rules of common sense. Instead, wealth building has its own set of principles—principles that work, work all the time, and work for anyone. These principles, or money strategies, add to your wealth, compress time, and endow you with what most refer to as the Midas touch.

I feel fortunate to have financial success coupled with good people to run my businesses so that I can afford to devote most of my time to teaching my strategies. It was for that purpose that I created my nonprofit educational foundation in 1975. Today, it has grown into the Charles J. Givens Organization with over 600,000 members worldwide—families who depend on us for all their financial help and advice. It was also for that purpose that I have written this book. My money strategies are safe, practical, and can be applied to every aspect of your financial life. Better yet, you don't have to be a financial wizard to put them to work for you.

INTRODUCTION

When TV interviewers ask me what qualifies me to teach people about money, my answer is simple—"Because I have a lot of it." To build a $100-million fortune in less than 20 years took learning just about everything there is to know about money. Much of what I learned formed the foundation for my wealth-building success, and this is what I'm about to teach you. What took me years to discover, you will learn in the next few hours and apply for the rest of your life. The knowledge will increase your awareness, but the application of that knowledge will increase your wealth!

Budgeting is not a wealth-building strategy. In fact, nowhere in this book is budgeting even mentioned as a path to financial success. Budgeting requires sacrifice, seeing yourself doomed to your current income, payments, taxes, and premiums, and then spending what little is left without any hope for a better future. Budgeting will not create long-term wealth any more than fad diets create long-term weight loss. All you end up doing is criticizing yourself for your failure to exercise discipline.

Your objective is to create more money to spend, not to relegate yourself to spending less. Creating more is what my strategies will do for you—more money to do and have the things you want for yourself and your family right now. No waiting.

> ### Strategy #1
> **IF YOU WANT TO LEARN ABOUT MONEY, LEARN FROM SOMEONE WHO HAS A LOT OF IT.**

You will never get better at tennis by sitting around talking to the clerk who strings tennis racquets at the sporting goods store.

You will, however, advance your game with lightning speed by spending time on the courts with a pro.

The only money pros in this country are those with self-made wealth, not those who talk about it for a living, like many stockbrokers, financial planners, insurance agents, college finance professors, and financial writers for magazines and newspapers. These folks all have a place to go and a job to do, but that job is not going to build your wealth and give you control over your financial future. Using the strategies in this book will.

Most financial people, whether well meaning or not, usually have one thing in common. They are struggling to pay bills, struggling to get out of debt, and are hoping for a financial miracle just like you. In other words, they are basically broke, and broke people are obviously not qualified to give financial advice. No matter how many years of college, no matter what the three-letter "Big C" designation after the name (CPA, CFP, CLU),* almost all so-called financial professionals are doing no better with their money than you are!

Someone once said that some financial people are called brokers because they are usually broker than you are. Now don't get me wrong, broke and homeless are not the same for the purposes of our discussion. To be broke, all you need to do is have the ability to spend money faster than you can make it. You can achieve "brokeness" on a $25,000-per-year or a $150,000-per-year income. Wealth is not defined by your income—only by your outcome.

Wealth is not what you make it, it's what's left over.

You can easily be broke while putting on the appearance of financial success: a home with a big mortgage, two new cars in the driveway encumbered with five-year car loans, and a lavish lifestyle with a mailbox full of overdue credit card bills. All of them eat into your wealth, they don't build it. The purpose of building your wealth is to have more left over, enabling you to live out your dreams instead of just paying your way through the month.

To build wealth, you have to find someone who will lead by example and teach from experience, instead of depending on traditional textbook approaches. I suppose you could say that as long as you keep reading this book, you have chosen me as your guide for what heretofore has been the often confusing,

---

* CPA—certified public accountant
  CFP—certified financial planner
  CLU—certified life underwriter

complicated world of money-making and dream-building. I won't let you down.

What I am about to teach you is more than a good strategy or two, or even a hundred. It is a way of life, a total way of thinking that always leads to financial victory. In life there is always limited time, but your experiences and dreams are limited only by your knowledge and willingness to apply what you know. You have in your hands half of the knowledge you will need for lifelong financial success. The other half is in *Financial Self-Defense*, a book that should reside on your bookshelf in plain sight next to this volume. Together they will give you the optimum strategies for just about every financial decision you'll ever have to make. But for now, you've got plenty to get you started.

The wealth-building strategies in this book will not turn you into an instant millionaire, but use them in a coordinated plan and you will automatically and systematically enjoy one or two million extra spendable dollars over your lifetime. Going beyond that, if you choose, will require starting your own supersuccessful business, but you can easily accomplish the first million or two with knowledge and time, and without sacrifice, simply by living the strategies in this book.

So, let's begin.

Part I

PERSONAL
FINANCE
STRATEGIES

Chapter 1

DEVELOPING YOUR FINANCIAL BLUEPRINT

I expect to spend the rest of my life in the future, so I want to be reasonably sure what kind of future it is going to be. That is my reason for planning.

Charles Kettering
Industrialist
1950

OBJECTIVE ————————————————————

TURN DREAMS INTO REALITIES.

There are three strategies we were never taught in school:

- how to run a successful marriage
- how to raise successful children
- how to build wealth successfully

The purpose of this book is to show you how to overcome the third of these educational gaps—how to build your wealth quickly and easily by making your financial decisions correctly and with confidence.

Everyone with self-earned wealth will tell you that money is not complicated. The confusing trade terms, buzz words, and complex explanations that are thrown around by investment counselors and financial people are not necessary. They just muddy the waters and sometimes hide the fact that the so-called experts don't really know what they're talking about.

In the course of my life, I have discovered a success principle that has enabled me to accumulate tens of millions of dollars while maintaining a constant state of happiness, emotional balance, and zest for life.

3

Strategy #2
ACHIEVE SUCCESS IN ANY AREA OF LIFE BY IDENTIFYING THE OPTIMUM STRATEGIES AND REPEATING THEM UNTIL THEY BECOME HABITS.

Success with money, family, relationships, health, and careers is the ability to reach your personal objectives in the shortest time, with the least effort, and with the fewest mistakes. The goals you set for yourself and the strategies you choose become your blueprint or plan.

Strategies are like recipes: choose the right ingredients, mix them in the correct proportions, and you'll always produce the same predictable result: in this case, financial success. The success strategies for managing money and building wealth are called Money Strategies.

As you learn to use Money Strategies as a part of your day-to-day life, financial frustration and failure will become a thing of the past. Why, then, do so many people find it so difficult to accumulate wealth and, more importantly, to enjoy the journey? There are two reasons: not being clear about what they are after and not knowing the strategies for achieving it.

The starting point in any plan is where you are right now. Where you are is where you are. Your first objective is to accept yourself and your current status as an O.K. place to be without making excuses as to why you don't know more or aren't doing better. Excuses become the limiters that turn realistic dreams into idle wishes. Lack of action and the lack of a willingness to change are almost the only things in life that create frustration and depression.

When it comes to excuses for not taking financial control, I hear them again and again:

"I can't even balance my checkbook." "I don't want much."
"I'm too old." "I'm too young."
"I'm too broke." "I'm too tired."
"I can't get my husband (or wife) to listen." "I'm too dumb about money."
 "I'm too busy."
 "I'm too scared."

Excuses do not produce results. You can find unlimited excuses for failure, but no one ever makes an excuse for success.

Now figure out where you want to be—your goals in life—and write them down. Your written plan sets the tone, speed, and most importantly the direction for your life. If you've ever attended a rousing motivational lecture, you were probably struck by the spirit, humor, and drive, but walked out of the room thinking, "Now, what the hell am I supposed to do?" Enthusiasm, but no direction.

Direction can turn the power of a light bulb into a laser beam. Lasers are nothing more than sharply focused light. Lasers have the power to cut through steel and destroy missiles in space. Same light as the light bulb—just focused and directed. Clearly establishing objectives and choosing your direction will turn the power of your mind into the laser beam it was meant to be, drawing to you the opportunities, people, and knowledge you will need, allowing you to cut through the obstacles along your success path.

Power to accomplish also lies in knowing how to compress time—to do in one year what it takes everyone else ten years to accomplish. The strategies in this book are powerful time compressors.

Success also requires an understanding and use of the Momentum Principle.

Strategy #3
SUCCESS REQUIRES FIRST EXPENDING TEN UNITS OF EFFORT TO PRODUCE ONE UNIT OF RESULTS. YOUR MOMENTUM WILL THEN PRODUCE TEN UNITS OF RESULTS WITH EACH UNIT OF EFFORT.

Direction and control begin with a written plan spelled out in two parts. Part A lists "dreams"—what you are after both financially and personally. Part B lists your "strategies"—the specific financial and personal road map that will take you from where you are to where you want to be. By clearly defining your direction, and by adopting the correct money and attitude strategies for control, you will automatically establish the shortest possible route.

When I was 18, I sat down with a pad of paper and, without totally realizing what I was doing, wrote an action blueprint for my life. I called it my dreams list. The exercise will do the same for you, clearly defining at one time and in one place your goals, dreams, objectives, and even your fantasies. Choose a totally quiet spot where you will not be interrupted. At the top of the pad of paper write the following:

DREAMS LIST

If I had unlimited . . .

TIME
TALENT
MONEY
ABILITY
SELF-CONFIDENCE
SUPPORT FROM FAMILY

Here's what I'd do . . .

Relax and let the ideas pour from both your conscious and subconscious. Don't evaluate your potential for achieving each item you write. What you will write will excite you, motivate you, inspire you, make you laugh, and, most of all, define desires and dreams that all too often are ready to surface but are held back by the complexities of daily living. Write it all down no matter how silly it seems, no matter what it costs. The ideas will come slowly at first, gaining speed as you leave behind the realities and limits in your life.

My first list was 181 dreams long, of which 175 have already become reality. Since that time I've added dozens of others, as you will probably find yourself doing.

All of us at any age have dreams, and the first step of turning dreams into reality is to get those dreams out in front of you where you can see and feel them.

Having taught my students this dreams list strategy for over 12 years, I have seen some truly wonderful things happen that might never have occurred otherwise.

A 66-year-old Ph.D. spent his birthday hang gliding with me off the huge sand dunes at Kitty Hawk, North Carolina.

A 14-year-old boy started his own successful business.

A 45-year-old, recently separated housewife with no previous sense of adventure rappeled straight down a 200-foot cliff, then rode a zip line 60 feet in the air, 300 yards across a valley at 40 miles per hour hanging from only wrist straps, resulting in more self-confidence in two days than she had achieved in her entire lifetime.

Through the dreams list strategy a 35-year-old mother swam and played with dolphins at Kings Dominion Park in Virginia, a dream she had had since she was a child.

A 28-year-old European immigrant, who barely spoke English, built a $5-million fortune in five years starting with a $6-an-hour job. I will never forget the tears of joy in his eyes as he sat in my office in Orlando telling me the story of his success and the part my strategies had played in his life.

Once you have made your list with no limits, choose those objectives that are the most important to you. Some will be individual objectives, others will include and require the support of your family. Encourage your spouse and children, if you have them, to create their own lists.

After you define your dreams, the things you want to do, places you want to go, what you want to be and accomplish, the next logical step is to build your road map—your strategies list. The rest of the chapters will show you all of the safe alternatives for creating the wealth to live out your dreams.

Chapter 2

BECOMING YOUR OWN FINANCIAL EXPERT

Go out and buy yourself a five-cent pencil and a ten-cent notebook and begin to write down some million-dollar ideas for yourself.

Bob Grinde

TAKE CONTROL OF YOUR FINANCIAL FUTURE.

The two most important words in managing money and building wealth are "take control." No one will ever watch your money or your financial future as well as you—no broker, financial planner, or insurance agent. Control begins with your written plan and is exercised through your choice of money strategies. The correct strategies turn wealth building, like walking, into a series of small, easy-to-accomplish steps.

Unless you were fortunate enough to be left a million dollars by a rich uncle, you must begin by learning to transform your income into wealth. There are only three types of money strategies needed to transform income into wealth, but you must use all three—none is optional. Omitting any one from your plan would have the same effect as removing a leg from a three-legged stool.

PERSONAL FINANCE STRATEGIES

Personal Finance Strategies are those day-to-day personal and family decisions you make unrelated to your job, taxes, or investments. Personal Finance Strategies enable you to save money as you spend it. The objective of Personal Finance Strategies is to increase your spendable income each year by thousands by getting rid of financial waste.

Personal Finance Strategies will:

A. Cut the cost of your life insurance by up to 80%.
B. Cut your automobile, mortgage, and homeowner's insurance premiums by up to 50%.
C. Cut your lifetime mortgage payments by up to 50%.
D. Cut your MasterCard and Visa interest up to 40%.
E. Turn your home-equity or insurance-policy cash values into income or wealth.
F. Restore your credit in 60 days.
G. Get your kids through college free.

TAX-REDUCING STRATEGIES

Income taxes are the biggest expense you'll encounter in life, bigger than the mortgage on your home or the cost of getting your kids through college. You can never build any real wealth without first getting your tax life under control.

One-third of all the wealth you will or won't accumulate is dependent on whether you have a good tax plan. My experience in working with over 600,000 families during the past 15 years indicates most families are paying twice as much in income taxes as necessary. Why? Lack of a good tax-reducing plan. Your objective is to pay no more than 5% of your income in taxes.

The biggest taxpayer in American history was Elvis Presley. I remember from my days in the Nashville music business how Elvis prided himself on the massive amount of taxes he paid. He had no tax plan, no tax shelters, and got little or no tax advice. He was also in a unique position. He couldn't outspend his income; money literally came in faster than he could get rid of it. After the excessive income and estate taxes were paid, and because of pitiful planning, Elvis's estates was incredibly small, the government got it all.

You, on the other hand, are probably having no difficulty in outspending your income, and if so, a good tax plan will begin to plug the dike. Every dollar you save in taxes is one dollar added to your tax-free wealth. Under the new tax laws, $1,000 of additional tax deductions will save you approximately $300 in taxes.

There are two steps in reducing your taxes:

A. Make money you spend tax deductible as you spend it.

There are 75 strategies that will turn your personal expenses into tax deductions; you can make your vacation, education, automobile, videotape recorder, money you give to children, club memberships, interest on loans, and entertainment tax deductible. A good tax plan will make up to 60% of your income deductible as you spend it.

B. Use the power of retirement plans and investment tax shelters.

Tax-free compounding is one secret to financial success. Retirement plans and tax shelters give you the power of tax-free compounding.

POWERFUL INVESTMENT STRATEGIES

Investing money and saving money are not at all the same strategies. Savers are those that earn less than 6% per year and do little more than make financial institutions wealthy. Successful investing, on the other hand, requires knowledge and not risk to accomplish the following three-pronged objective: to earn 15% per year safely, with no commissions, and no taxes.*

How can you safely earn 15% a year in a world that expects only 7% from banks and bonds? By using any of what I consider the ten best investment opportunities in America—those that you won't find advertised in the financial pages or sold through brokers and financial partners. All are uncovered in Part III, Powerful Investment Strategies:

1.	Asset Management Accounts	Chapter 29
2.	No-Load Mutual Fund Families	Chapter 31**
3.	Mutual Fund Margin Accounts	Chapter 32
4.	Self-Directed IRA and Keogh Accounts	Chapters 18* and 33*
5.	401(k) and 403(b) Employer Retirement Plans	Chapter 18*
6.	Tax-Sheltered Mutual Funds—Self-Directed Annuities	Chapter 34*
7.	Discounted Mortgages	Chapter 35
8.	Tax Lien Certificates and Liened Property Sales	Chapter 36
9.	Reinvested Home Equity	Chapter 9
10.	Your Own Home	Chapter 9

Paying unnecessary fees and commissions on your investments is like throwing $20 bills into the fireplace to heat your home. You'll get the job done but the method is extremely

*Past experience is no guarantee of future performance.
**Requires use of the Money Movement Strategy (Chapter 30)

ineffective. You cannot be splitting your money with everyone else and expect to have much left for yourself. By learning to work directly with financial institutions, you can eliminate the middleman, the commissioned salesman, and keep 100% of your money working for you. On October 19, 1987, the stock market and most investors' stock portfolios dropped by 20%. The one-day drop shocked the world and crowded other news items from the headlines. Yet every day millions of investors turn over billions of dollars to investment salesmen, and experience a one-day drop in their investment capital of 8%. Although no headlines are made, paying commissions is the same kind of investment loss.

To start your Wealth Without Risk program you need only income. It doesn't matter whether you have $1 or $100,000 in your investment plan. Making big money does not take big money, only knowledge and a little time.

WHERE THE MONEY GOES

It might surprise you to know that the average couple in America earns about $41,000 per year and lives paycheck-to-paycheck with little hope of breaking the cycle. Here is a chart that shows you where the money typically goes.

AVERAGE FAMILY INCOME $40,000*

Household Expenses

Food	5,000	
Clothes	900	
Utilities	1,900	
Household	2,500	**Household**
Car	800	**$11,800**
Gifts	500	
Pets	200	
	11,800	

Insurance

Car	1,200	
Life	1,100	
Children	300	
Health	900	**Insurance**
Disability	300	**$4,900**
Credit Life	350	
Mortgage	600	
Homeowner's	450	
	4,900	

Taxes

Federal	4,000	
State Income	1,200	**Taxes**
Social Security	2,800	**$8,000**
	8,000	

Payments

Mortgage/Rent	10,000	
Car Loan	3,900	**Payments**
Credit Cards	1,500	**$16,400**
Personal Loans	1,000	
	16,400	

For Self

Fun	500	**Self**
Vacation	1,000	**$1,500**
	1,500	

No Savings	
No IRA	TOTAL
No Investments	**$42,600**

NO MONEY LEFT OVER.

*From USA Today study and Charles J. Givens Organization study

Remember, real wealth is not how much money you make but how much is left over!

Now here is a chart showing where the money goes before and *after* Money Strategies are used.

USING THE CHARLES J. GIVENS
PERSONAL FINANCE AND TAX STRATEGIES

Family Income—$42,600

	Before	After	Difference
Insurance	4,900	1,120	3,780
Taxes	8,000	3,900	4,100
Credit Cards	1,500	700	800
TOTAL	$14,400	$5,720	$8,680

New money for investments, fun, vacations:
$8,680

After applying just the Personal Finance and Tax Strategies the couple now has $6,180 extra tax-free dollars to spend and invest—each year. Same income, but a new lifestyle and outlook for the future. You will save thousands each year in all of these areas by using the Personal Finance and Tax Strategies. Coupled with powerful investment strategies, you will automatically and systematically achieve your objective: Wealth Without Risk.

Chapter 3

AUTOMOBILE INSURANCE—CUTTING YOUR PREMIUMS 50%

By promoting insurance on the basis of what people think about uncertainty, instead of what they would be correct in thinking, by exploiting the fallacy that one buys insurance to collect for a loss instead of showing that the purpose of insurance is to avoid uncertainty, we have invited a plague of problems upon the insurance industry.

Henry K. Duke
Letter to *Harvard Business Review*
1955

OBJECTIVE ──────────────────────────────

SAVE UP TO 50% OF THE COST OF YOUR AUTOMOBILE INSURANCE WHILE MAINTAINING NECESSARY COVERAGES.

Salesmen will try to sell you a dozen types of automobile insurance coverage. Half no one needs yet everyone buys; the other half, everyone needs but few know how to buy. This chapter will clear up the mystery of what you need, what to avoid, and how to save hundreds to thousands of dollars per year in the process. Have your current automobile insurance policy in front of you and make notes on the items you wish to change as you read this chapter and learn the correct strategies.

Auto insurance laws were enacted to protect innocent victims of accidents from serious financial loss. Most states require that registered car owners carry liability and sometimes a few other coverages. The minimum amount of insurance required in your state, however, has little to do with the amount of insurance you actually need or want.

Automobile insurance is one of your biggest expenses in life. You'll find you can cut your premiums up to 30% to 50% with knowledge and a basic understanding of what each type of automobile insurance covers, choosing insurance by knowing your actual chance of collecting or paying a claim, and picking far less expensive alternatives for many of the coverages that you do need. In this chapter we will examine the ten most common automobile coverages to determine those you do need or must have and those that waste your money. They are:

bodily injury liability	comprehensive
umbrella liability	collision
property damage liability	medical payments
no-fault insurance or PIP	uninsured motorists coverage
death and dismemberment	road service and towing

HOW YOUR AUTOMOBILE INSURANCE PREMIUMS ARE DETERMINED

TYPE OF COVERAGE

There are ten major automobile coverages to pick from to include on your policy. Some you need, some you don't. Those you need fall into two categories:

- insurance needed to protect you financially
- insurance required by your state

The two categories are usually not the same.

Other forms of auto insurance should be covered better and more cheaply by using insurance coverage on policies other than auto policies. If you are covered in two policies for the same risk, you have duplicate coverages and are wasting big dollars. We will identify the coverages you do and don't need and show you how to eliminate duplicate coverages.

AMOUNT OF COVERAGE

Most of the ten types of insurance coverage you find on your auto policy have limits. A limit is the maximum number of dollars the insurance company will pay in one accident for the damage done. Some limits are fixed by the insurance company or the value of your car and are stated in the policy. These fixed-limit coverages include:

- comprehensive and collision (the maximum is the value of your car, although you choose the deductible)

- no-fault insurance or PIP
- road service and towing

All other coverages give you the choice of the maximum the insurance company will pay. The higher the maximum the greater your yearly premiums. These optional-limit coverages include:

- bodily injury liability
- property damage liability
- umbrella liability
- medical payments
- death and dismemberment
- uninsured motorists coverage

Even though you choose a maximum, the insurance company will pay only the actual damages. Death and dismemberment is the only exception. You often choose from two or more maximum limits, but as with life insurance, the full amount is paid out.

Choose limits that are too high on any of these coverages and you throw premium money away on insurance on which the statistical chances of collecting are far too remote. Choose limits that are too low and you end up underinsured or unprotected against a potential real risk. In this chapter you will learn to choose correctly.

In addition to how much and what kind of coverage you choose, five factors relating to where you live, how you drive, and what kind of car you own also affect the premiums you pay.

RATING TERRITORIES

Premiums are higher in cities, where population density and traffic congestion are high, and lower in rural areas. The company's accident experience in your area also determines your rates. Your premiums from company to company for the same city can vary as much as 100% because of different accident ratios. That's why it pays to shop.

DRIVER CLASSIFICATION

Age, sex, and marital status are all factors used in determining your insurance premiums. Those over 25, women, and married people have fewer accidents and the lowest rates. Males under 25 who are unmarried and the principal drivers of a car have the greatest statistical chance of accidents and therefore the highest rates.

DRIVING RECORD

Those responsible for accidents or who have been convicted of driving violations tend to have a greater statistical chance for future accidents and therefore pay higher premiums—much higher premiums.

USE OF CAR

Those who drive to and from work have a greater chance for accidents than those who use a car for pleasure only. Premium categories are usually:

1. No commuting   —lowest premium
2. Less than ten miles to work   —higher premium
3. More than ten miles to work   —still higher premium
4. Business use   —highest premium

TYPE OF CAR

Expensive cars cost more to repair and therefore cost more to insure.

Strategy #4
CHECK INSURANCE RATES ON AN AUTOMOBILE BEFORE YOU BUY.

Because some cars are more expensive to replace or repair, insurance companies assign code numbers (1–21) to each model. The higher the code number the more your car costs new and the more expensive your collision and comprehensive premiums will be.

A damageability rating is assigned to each model of car based on the sticker price and how easily that model is damaged in a collision and how much it costs to repair. Damageability ratings can significantly raise or lower your comprehensive and collision premiums, so check the insurance rates before you buy.

For example, if a model is initially rated a 7, its sticker price is between $6,501 and $8,000 (see the Automobile Insurance Sticker-Price Code Numbers that follow). The rating is then upgraded by +1 or more if the car is more expensive to repair than other cars costing the same amount, or lowered by −1 or more if the car is less expensive to repair. This means that while the car's sticker price could be between $6,501 and $8,000, its damageability factor may make its cost of repair like that of a car that initially costs $8,001–$10,000, and your premiums will be as much as 20% higher.

AUTOMOBILE INSURANCE
STICKER-PRICE CODE NUMBERS

These code numbers categorize your car by sticker price. The higher the code number the more expensive your comprehensive and collision premiums.

Code Number	$ Sticker Price
1	0– 1,600
2	1,601– 2,100
3	2,101– 2,750
4	2,751– 3,700
5	3,701– 5,000
6	5,001– 6,500
7	6,501– 8,000
8	8,001–10,000
10	10,001–12,500
11	12,501–15,000
12	15,001–17,000
13	17,001–20,000
14	20,001–24,000
15	24,001–28,000
16	28,001–33,000
17	33,001–39,000
18	39,001–46,000
19	46,001–55,000
20	55,001–65,000
21	Above 65,000

Note: There is no code 9 in the rating system.

Strategy #5
SHOP AROUND TO SAVE 25% ON AUTO INSURANCE PREMIUMS.

Automobile insurance companies in most states set premiums based on the amount of claims paid in each area. Auto insurance rates in the same area may vary as much as 100% from company to company. According to an independent study, fewer than one in four drivers will get more than one quote before buying auto insurance, a major financial error. When your policy is up for renewal, get several quotes. Shop around. You will be amazed at the differences in prices.

Automobile insurance rates are not fixed by state law, as

most people falsely assume, except in two states, Texas and Massachusetts. Ironically, Massachusetts has about the highest auto insurance rates in the country. So much for government control. In these two states you will save big money by carefully choosing your coverages instead of choosing a company because it has lower rates.

Twenty-two states require approval of the state insurance commission before maximum rates can be raised for each coverage, but you'll find big differences in rates in these states just as you do in the balance of the states that require no maximum-rate approval of any kind.

Some of the companies that seem to have lower rates in many areas are Geico, USAA, State Farm, Travelers, and Liberty Mutual. Many agents, to make shopping more difficult, will not quote over the phone, but don't let that stop you. Let your wheels do the walking.

Strategy #6
CUT THE COST OF INSURING YOUR DRIVING-AGE CHILDREN BY INCLUDING THEM ON YOUR POLICY.

Buying automobile insurance to cover your teenage children or other young drivers can drive you to the poorhouse. Insurance rates for those 16 to 25 are astronomical in comparison to the already high rates for everyone else. Generally you can save big money by using these simple strategies:

- If you are paying the auto insurance premiums, do not allow the car to be titled in the name of the child. Include your child as an additional driver on your policy.
- If your child wants or buys a car in his or her own name, make the purchase conditional on the child's getting his or her own insurance, a lesson in reality.
- If your child is away at college without a car, some companies will give you a bigger discount on your family auto policy because driving opportunities for your child will be significantly reduced. Be certain to ask.
- Use all the strategies in this chapter to reduce the overall cost of your policy 30–50%, which will also drop the extra premiums for a young driver by the same percentage.
- Carry higher deductibles to reduce the cost of coverage, but get your child's agreement in writing to be responsible for paying any nonrecovered deductible of up to $500 to $1,000 for an accident caused by him or her.

- Carry at least a minimum of $100,000/$300,000 of liability no matter how little your net worth.
- Don't teach the child to drive yourself. By having him or her take an accredited driver training course, some companies offer a discount.

AUTOMOBILE LIABILITY INSURANCE

Two kinds of liability insurance are a must on your automobile policy both financially and legally—bodily injury liability and property damage liability.

Bodily injury liability insurance covers injury you might do to people in other cars, pedestrians, and passengers in your own car. You and your family members are also insured while driving someone else's car, including a rental car. Bodily injury liability covers damages plus your legal defense costs up to the limits stated in the policy, whether determined by out-of-court negotiation or by a jury. You choose two limits on a policy: the maximum the insurance company will pay one injured person and the maximum the company will pay to everyone injured in an accident. Most states require that you carry at least $10,000/$20,000 limits, meaning $10,000 per person and $20,000 per accident. (Property damage liability is discussed in Strategy #11.)

As you build your wealth, you may be seized by the fear, as have many who have gone before you, that some unscrupulous attorney may attempt to redistribute your wealth in an actual or threatened liability suit for damages you do with your car. I once asked an attorney at a cocktail party, "Why did you choose to limit your practice to automobile liability claims?"

"Because that's where the big bucks are," he said, snickering. "A good trail attorney can manipulate the emotions of a jury into almost anything, and I'm a good trial lawyer." That is precisely what is wrong with the court system in America. A trial has become a group of 12 people trying to decide who has the best lawyer.

What are the real chances that your wealth and your future can be almost instantly wiped out in a personal injury suit that resulted from something you did or actually didn't do with your automobile? The answer to that question determines how much liability insurance you need.

The most important and most overlooked factor in determining what insurance you need, as well as what coverages are truly good values, is the reasonable estimate of your chance of ever collecting or having to pay a claim. Remember, all insurance is a bet, and with insurance you always lose something. The minimum you can lose is your premiums. Whether your insurance company pays a claim or not, in this case a liability claim, you still lose the premiums. Your insurance premiums are therefore a guaranteed loss—the higher your premiums, the greater your guaranteed losses. However, if you have no insurance or too little insurance, the elimination or reduction of the guaranteed loss of premiums is offset by the increase in risk that you could personally be liable for a large claim that would eat into or eat up the net worth that you have built.

With liability insurance, your objective is to buy enough insurance so you can be reasonably certain that the premium and not a claim for damages is your maximum potential loss. You don't want to have to kick in where your insurance leaves off. Financial success requires that you minimize or eliminate all potential losses.

Your strategy is to balance the two—to have enough insurance to protect against the real risk while not overpaying premiums in order to protect against some imagined or statistically improbable risk.

Insurance companies do not, and in most cases will not, let you know your real risk or your lack of it. If you were given a probability chart with your actual statistical chances of having to pay a claim, your decision would be easier. For instance it would be ridiculous to spend any amount of money, no matter how small, to insure against a risk that had only a 1 in 1 million chance of occurring each year, whereas it would be imperative to insure against any expensive potential peril that had a 1 in 2 or even a 1 in 10 chance of occurring in a single year. No matter how simple this principle sounds when you read it, it is obvious that most people have no concept of statistical analysis, considering the number of lottery tickets that are sold. A big lottery jackpot typically has odds of winning of 1 in 10 million. Yet people line up to spend $1 to $100 on $1 tickets. If you truly understand the mathematics of risk, you will never again buy a lottery ticket, not for a dollar, not for a dime, not for a penny.

Lottery tickets are like insurance premiums; they are a guaranteed loss, except for the states or other lottery operators, who have a built-in guaranteed gain. If you don't understand the mathematics of winning, your mind will trick you with statements made from emotion, such as "Well, somebody's got to win" or "It's only a dollar." Over your lifetime those beliefs, which translate into hundreds of continual incorrect financial

decisions, can destroy your chances of making and keeping any
real wealth.

The same "loser" mentality is reflected in most people's
insurance policies. Emotionally your mind wants to insure
against every possible calamity to matter how remote, as long as
the premiums are affordable. That mentality is exactly what
insurance companies count on to sell you sometimes overpriced
insurance on which you have virtually no chance of collecting.
I have yet to meet an individual or family that purchased
automobile or life insurance based solely on the statistical
chance of collecting rather than the emotion generated from
visualizing the pain and trauma of the possibility of even the
remotest loss. Therefore, I have yet to meet someone whose
insurance plans couldn't be vastly improved by using my strategies.

There is, on the other hand, a separate group of people who
have gone entirely in the opposite direction, those who refuse to
admit the possibility of any potential risk, buying only the
amount of insurance required by law or, worse yet, none at all.
This group usually includes those living so close to the paycheck-to-paycheck wire that their only concern is financially
surviving the month. To take such a short-term view of a financial plan is just as dangerous to your financial future as over-
spending to cover all imagined risks.

This lack of concern for real risk is evidenced in the number
of renters who do not carry any form of tenant's insurance to
cover what few personal assets they do own, such as clothes,
furniture, stereos, and TVs. One break-in or fire and all that's left
is the monthly payment on the loans or credit cards you used to
purchase those possessions.

How much liability insurance is enough? If liability insurance
were free, the answer would be "There's never enough." Liability insurance, however, is not free; the more you buy the more
you pay. Your objective, therefore, is to balance the premiums
you pay against someone else's chance of collecting from your
policy or attaching your personal assets—without wasting
money.

The good news is that your chances of being involved in an
automobile liability suit with an adverse verdict for over $1
million, or even $100,000 for that matter, are remote, so remote
that only under certain unique circumstances is that risk worth
insuring against. Yet everyone reads or hears about one or two
big jury awards. What you don't hear about are the millions of
folks who were not sued, or the small percentage who were sued

but whose settlements were almost insignificant compared to the picture that lurks in the minds of most drivers.

My goal was to get a clearer picture of liability awards, but where to begin? Because claims information is a closely guarded secret of each insurance company, my researchers had to use indirect but reliable sources to get you the inside story—the court records themselves. I sent my research staff to south Florida, which is nationally known as the "sue-happy capital of America," to scour through 15 months of court records to determine the true level of jury awards and settlements in every automobile liability suit for that period.

Remember that anything settled out of court would not normally appear in the records, so only the biggest of liability awards and uninsured motorists claims contested by individuals or their insurance companies are shown in court records. Here is a surprising synopsis of the results of our investigation:

- Even though there are more than 2 million drivers in the area, only 342 cases went to trial in the entire 15-month period, including 15 cases of DUI (driving under the influence of alcohol or drugs).
- Even after the cases were tried and juries made their awards, the average settlement was under $25,000.
- Million-dollar or more settlements were rare and were incurred primarily under two conditions:
    The defendant was a company whose employee caused the accident. (In Florida, companies are held totally liable for damages caused by their employees in auto accidents.)
    The defendant was convicted first of DUI, driving under the influence.

Strategy #7
IF YOU OWN A COMPANY WITH COMPANY CARS AND TRUCKS, CARRY A MINIMUM OF $500,000 TO $1 MILLION OF BODILY INJURY LIABILITY INSURANCE.

Although the average court award to an individual from an individual defendant in an automobile liability suit is less than $25,000, our research does show that awards increase dramatically if the vehicle at fault is company owned. Even though it is an absolute failure of the American court system that awards are often increased when the injuring party has an apparent ability to pay or has a big insurance policy, rather than the award's being determined by the actual extent of the damage or liability, that's the way the system works for now, and we all have to live with it.

Listed below are representative examples of jury awards from south-Florida courts when vehicles owned by a company were at fault in a personal injury accident. These awards averaged 10 to 20 times higher for the same type of accident than when the defendant was an individual.

AUTOMOBILE INJURY JURY AWARDS

Sample of the huge awards made by juries in liability court cases in which the defendant was a company

Jessen vs. Jameco (also DUI)	$1,000,000
Harris vs. Winn Dixie	700,000
Dunleavy vs. Florida Power	295,000
Peel vs. American Sightseeing	240,365
Luecke vs. General Container	224,000
Duke vs. Southern Bell	87,700

Your strategy is clear. If your self-owned business owns company vehicles driven by you and/or others, carry a minimum of $500,000 to $1 million of bodily injury liability insurance, even though liability insurance on company-owned vehicles is much more expensive. The good news is that this strategy does not apply to part- or full-time home-based businesses that use the family car infrequently as a business car.

Strategy #8
IF YOU DRINK AND DRIVE, BUY ALL THE LIABILITY INSURANCE THE COMPANY WILL SELL YOU.

The largest jury awards are made to plaintiffs injured or killed in automobile accidents in which the defendant was driving under the influence. There is little tolerance in this country, nor should there be, for those who choose to risk others' well-being while driving drunk or on drugs. The jury awards seem to be at least 1,000% or 10 times higher against drunk drivers and are normally way beyond the limits of any liability insurance.

Here are some awards from south-Florida cases. Remember, the average award against an individual who is not intoxicated is under $25,000. If these statistics aren't enough to cause someone to give up drinking, that person is a candidate for a residential detox treatment center.

AUTOMOBILE INJURY JURY AWARDS FOR DUI CASES

Sample of the huge awards made by juries in liability court cases in which the defendant was convicted of driving under the influence (DUI)

Grant vs. Brutz DUI	$7,000,000
Colonna vs. Sysomboune DUI	6,525,000
Talvera vs. Smith DUI	1,400,000
Meigs vs. Sutlif DUI	1,000,000
Owens vs. Mercak DUI	499,500
Lykles vs. Nobil DUI	200,000

Strategy #9
BEGIN WITH ENOUGH BODILY INJURY LIABILITY INSURANCE TO PROTECT YOUR NET ASSETS.

Theoretically, if you injured or killed someone in an accident that was your fault and a jury awarded the injured party or the heirs an amount greater than the amount of liability insurance you carry, the plaintiffs would have a right to claim just about all the net assets you own, including:

- bank accounts
- savings and investments
- home equity (except in a homestead state such as Florida)
- jewelry and other personal assets
- your estate if you died in the accident

You might be forced into bankruptcy, and only the assets protected by your state law from bankruptcy creditors would remain yours. The truth is, if your liability insurance covers at least your net assets, your chance of paying an amount above your insurance coverage is remote.

If it is your net assets that are at risk, then the absolute minimum amount of bodily injury liability insurance you want to carry is equal to the amount of your net assets. As often happens in court, the defendant, or in this case the driver at fault, is required to produce a statement of assets and liabilities, also known as a financial statement, and juries, which do not normally think in terms of complicated formulas, will often award at least the amount of the defendant's net assets whether or not they are covered by insurance. Out of all the court cases during a 15-month period in south Florida, in only one case did the court award include a required extra payment by the defendant in excess of his insurance limit.

> ### Strategy #10
> ## IF YOU USE THE FAMILY CAR FOR PART-TIME BUSINESS USE, CHOOSE THE BODILY INJURY LIABILITY LIMITS FOR AN INDIVIDUAL.

The extra-large jury awards for company vehicles involved in accidents seem to apply to light- to heavy-duty company trucks and cars with permanently mounted business advertising signs. If you follow my tax reducing strategies in Chapter 25 for creating your own small business, you will use your personal automobile at least part-time in your business, generating hundreds in extra deductions. From an insurance perspective, treat the use of this automobile as personal and insure it using the personal bodily injury liability limits indicated in Strategy #9.

> ### Strategy #11
> ## CARRY A MINIMUM OF $50,000 OF PROPERTY DAMAGE LIABILITY, OR A MINIMUM OF TWICE YOUR NET WORTH.

The second form of liability insurance that is an absolute necessity both financially and legally is property damage liability insurance. Property damage liability covers damage you might do with your car to someone else's car or property. Family members and others driving with permission are also covered by your policy for damage they might do while driving your car.

You choose the maximum amount the insurance company would have to pay in any one accident to fix all the other cars except yours. You can choose limits usually between $5,000 and $100,000. Doing more damage than $50,000 would be extremely unlikely, although remotely possible if you destroyed a new Rolls-Royce or exotic car.

If you are living paycheck-to-paycheck and have few assets, your state's minimum required limit may be the best value for you. The money saved by reduced premiums can go toward building your wealth. If you are somewhere in between, a good rule of thumb is to carry property damage liability insurance of up to twice your net worth to a maximum of $50,000.

Your property damage liability insurance kicks in only if the accident is proven to be your fault. If so, your collision insurance pays to fix your car. If the accident is the fault of another driver, his or her property liability insurance pays to fix your car.

Strategy #12
BUY $1 MILLION OF UMBRELLA LIABILITY COVERAGE FOR UNDER $200 PER YEAR.

The more assets you accumulate the more important personal liability protection becomes, but you can easily end up overpaying for liability insurance by taking high liability-limit coverage on both your automobile and homeowner's policies.

Instead of raising the limits on both automobile and homeowner's policies and paying double premiums, you can buy an inexpensive "supplemental umbrella liability policy" that covers all your possible personal liabilities. You can buy $1 million of protection with an umbrella policy for under $200. You must ask for umbrella liability insurance by name. Since the commissions paid to insurance agents for selling these policies are so small, your agent may neglect to mention it. Some companies also allow you to cover rental property liability in your umbrella policy for slightly higher premiums.

Before selling you the umbrella liability supplement, most insurance companies require you to:

1. Carry a minimum limit on your homeowner's and automobile policies, usually $100,000/$300,000. If your current limit is only $50,000/$100,000 for instance, your basic policy limit will have to be raised first.
2. Place both your automobile and homeowner's policy (if you own your home) with the same company.

When you need higher liability limits based on the strategies just discussed, ask for umbrella liability insurance. Umbrella liability is one of the few truly good values in insurance. Most companies offer umbrella liability if you ask. If yours doesn't, consider changing companies.

COMPREHENSIVE AND COLLISION INSURANCE

Comprehensive and collision insurance pay for damages done to your car. Comprehensive insurance pays for damage or losses due to theft, vandalism, fire, glass breakage, falling objects, explosions, or other damages that result from anything other than collision with another vehicle or object. You choose a deductible ranging from $0 to $1,000. The higher your deductible the less your premiums.

Your collision insurance covers damage to your car in the event of an accident with another vehicle or object no matter who is at fault. If the other driver is at fault, your insurance company will pay you first and then seek reimbursement from the other driver's insurance company. Your insurance company will pay you for the full damages done to your car in the collision minus your deductible. When your insurance company collects damages from the other driver or the driver's insurance company, you will be reimbursed even the amount of your deductible. If the damage to your car is significant, it is the insurance company's option whether to repair or replace your car and where it will be repaired. Deductibles you can choose usually range from $100 to $1,000.

Strategy #13
RAISE THE DEDUCTIBLES ON YOUR COMPREHENSIVE AND COLLISION COVERAGES TO $500 OR MORE.

The best and quickest way to save money on collision and comprehensive insurance is to raise your deductibles. With a simple phone call to your agent, you can save between $25 and $250 per year depending on the number of cars you own, the types of cars, which company you insure with, and your driving record. The worse your driving record, the more you will save. If you have young drivers on your policy, this strategy is likely to save you a bundle. (Also see Strategy #6.)

The deductible is the amount you agree to pay before the insurance company has to kick in. Most policyholders opt for the lowest possible deductible—usually $100—on automobile comprehensive and collision coverage. Lower deductibles may make you feel good, but they do you no good. Each year, less than 10% of all automobiles will be involved in accidents or losses, and only half of those policyholders will have to pay any deductible themselves.

Begin with the increased deductible with which you feel most comfortable, $500 or $1,000. As your assets and income increase, increase your deductibles accordingly. Increasing your auto insurance deductible to $500 will reduce your comprehensive and collision premiums as much as 40%. Increasing the deductible to $1,000 will cut those premiums up to 60%. The better your driving record the less you are paying for low deductibles. If your driving record is poor, you can be paying $100 or more in extra premiums to insure only an extra $400 potential loss that may never happen. Premiums paid for low deductibles are one of the worst insurance values.

The following two strategies will show you why low deductibles don't make sense.

Strategy #14
NEVER FILE AN INSURANCE CLAIM FOR UNDER $500.

Smart policyholders don't file small claims. File one or two small claims and your insurance company will raise your premiums next year by as much as 25%, or worse yet, cancel your policy. Save your insurance claims for the big dollar amounts and save big premiums by becoming responsible for payments of any amount of repairs up to $500 or even $1,000 yourself.

Strategy #15
NEVER PAY OUT MORE IN PREMIUMS THAN YOU CAN COLLECT IN DAMAGES.

You pay so much extra for lower deductibles that, over the course of your life, even if you are a lousy driver, you could not collect in damages half of what you're paying in premiums. Lower deductibles waste dollars. Remember, insurance is not free. Collecting on a claim from an insurance company is not a gift. The insurance company's cost of processing even the smallest claim is over $400 just for the administrative expenses and paperwork, and these costs are added to the premiums you and other policyholders pay for lower deductibles. That's why insuring the cost of repairing the first $1,000 of damage to your car costs about the same in premiums as the cost of insuring the next $10,000 of repairs.

Strategy #16
SUBSTITUTE A NO-FEE CREDIT CARD FOR THE FEAR OF BEING SHORT OF CASH TO REPAIR YOUR CAR.

For some the concern is, "What if I am responsible for a deductible or can't collect from the other driver and don't have the extra money to fix my car?" Remember first of all that with a $500 deductible your total risk is only an additional $400 greater than with a $100 deductible.

Your best "no-cost" repair insurance for the extra money if you are short of cash is a non-annual-fee MasterCard or Visa that is never used for purposes other than emergencies or unusual one-time expenses. With a $1,000 to $2,000 limit, you have emergency cash available, but unlike insurance premiums, the credit card costs you nothing unless you use it. (See Chapter 10 for credit cards with no yearly fees.)

Strategy #17
WHEN THE VALUE OF YOUR CAR DROPS BELOW $2,000, DROP THE COLLISION AND COMPREHENSIVE COVERAGE.

Remember, if your car is damaged, you cannot collect more than what your car is worth no matter how much insurance you carry or how much in premiums you've been paying. When your car is older and not worth much, it no longer pays to carry comprehensive and collision coverage at all. Thieves don't tend to steal old cars; the penalty is no greater for stealing a new car. When you look at the amount of premiums you pay plus the high deductible, it doesn't make sense to carry comprehensive and collision insurance on older, less expensive cars.

When it comes to damages, older cars are often just as expensive to repair as new ones. Therefore, the premiums for comprehensive and collision insurance will seem outrageously high for less than $2,000 worth of total insurance. They are. Plus by following these strategies you would be carrying at least a $500 deductible anyway, making your maximum real coverage on an older car not worth the money.

Strategy #18
DON'T BUY EXTRA GIMMICK COVERAGES SUCH AS TOWING, CAR RENTAL, AND AUDIO EQUIPMENT.

The premiums for extras on an auto policy cost you more money than you could ever collect. Towing and car rental coverages cost $20 to $80 extra per car per year, and yet only a small percentage of policyholders will ever file a claim on either. The high premiums charged to insure a few hundred dollars of audio equipment also make a poor investment. However, do insure your car phone or audio equipment when the total worth is over $1,000.

Strategy #19
PREDETERMINE HOW MUCH AN ACCIDENT OR A TICKET WILL RAISE YOUR PREMIUMS.

You'll also be shocked at the different practices auto insurance companies have affecting policyholders who get ticketed or are involved in an accident. Some will raise your rates 25% after only one occurrence, others will cancel your insurance altogether. Because these policies and practices are predetermined by the insurance companies but not advertised, your insurance company knows what it will do if you get a ticket, a specific number of "points," or have an accident that is or isn't your fault. Call your insurance company now and ask its policies. Make a note in your insurance file, or if possible get the answers in writing. It could save a lot of hassle later on. When shopping for insurance, be certain to ask these questions of each company and use the answers as one factor in determining which automobile insurance company you choose. Choose a company that won't brand you a loser just because of one bad experience.

Strategy #20
ASK FOR THE BASIC AUTOMOBILE INSURANCE DISCOUNTS.

There are numerous discounts offered by auto insurance companies to those who fall into special groups. When buying auto insurance be certain to ask; the agent may not bring them up. A combination of these potential discounts can save you big dollars each year.

Discount For	Amount Saved
1. Multicar—more than one automobile insured by the same company	5–15%
2. Driver training—take a state-certified course	5–15
3. Good driving record—no tickets	5–15
4. No claims against your policy	5–15
5. Antitheft equipment—alarm or systems that disengage the ignition	5–15
6. Senior citizen	5–15
7. Antilock brakes	5–15
8. Passive restraints—air bags, automatic seat belts	5–15
9. Annual mileage less than 10,000 miles	15–20
10. Multipolicies—all policies including homeowner's and auto at same agency	5–15

If you qualified for all the discounts, it almost looks as if your auto insurance would be free. Of course that's not the case, but it can get a lot less expensive. If you ask for all of the discounts you are entitled to, your premiums may drop 25% or more. It pays to ask.

Strategy #21
DECLINE OR REDUCE THE PREMIUMS FOR NO-FAULT INSURANCE BY SUBSTITUTING BETTER, FULL-TIME INSURANCE COVERAGES.

The state-by-state creation of the no-fault insurance laws has created a boondoggle out of what could have been a beneficial, time-saving, premium-lowering insurance concept. "No-fault" in its purest sense is a great idea. Here's how it is supposed to work. In an accident, each driver's losses, including automobile damage and medical expenses, are covered by his or her own insurance company, regardless of who is at fault. Think of it—no more expensive lawsuits, no staggering attorneys' fees, no multiple years of legal battling, no wildly differing potential outcomes created by emotionally charged juries.

Unfortunately, the concept hasn't worked well. By the time these good ideas were turned into law by state legislators, each with his or her own agenda, no-fault has in many states created a legal mess without solving many of the problems for which it was intended. The concept failed mostly because state legislatures are crammed full of attorneys who just didn't have the heart to restrict or eliminate automobile liability lawsuits and potentially cost themselves or their fellow attorneys fees. Why is it that only attorneys seem to be able to get off from work long enough to become politicians?

No-fault laws affect all of the major coverages in your policy including:

- bodily injury liability
- property damage liability
- comprehensive
- collision
- medical payments
- uninsured motorists

There are now six different major types of no-fault laws among the various states categorized by the amount and type of insurance required, and whether the state's no-fault laws give the right to sue in addition to collecting damages under the no-fault statutes. Without the elimination of lawsuits, "no-fault" laws have in many states caused increased instead of reduced premiums. It's sort of like giving your teenage son the keys to your car, but telling him not to drive it while you're gone for a few days. More than half the states have yet to pass no-fault laws, so they at least still have the chance to create something workable right from the beginning.

The real unanswered question concerning no-fault is: If the purpose of no-fault insurance is to reduce premiums paid by policyholders by reducing the expenses of the insurance companies, why then do you have to pay an *additional* premium, sometimes called PIP (personal injury protection), in order to get the coverage? In many states the payment of extra premiums is required. In others the coverage and extra premiums are optional.

In reality, PIP insurance, whether required or not, is just another form of medical payments coverage, which is to a large extent a duplicate of your family's health and hospitalization policy. In addition to your own medical expenses, PIP covers reimbursement for lost income, which should instead be handled by using the disability income strategies in my book *Financial Self-Defense*. Although the medical expenses of other passengers in your car are covered by PIP, they are also covered under their own health insurance policies and by the liability portion of your auto policy, so why pay the extra premiums to insure risks that are or should be covered elsewhere?

The other downside to PIP as a substitute for health insurance is that it isn't. You are paying premiums for medical coverage limited to $5,000 to $50,000, depending on the state in which you live, with the average being $10,000. Where any premium expense is required by law, you can expect the premiums to outweigh the benefits. Your health plan at work or your personal health policy covers you and your family up to $1 million.

Usually you can't collect for the same injury twice, so why pay the premiums twice? Your strategy is to eliminate or reduce the premiums on all duplicate or unnecessary automobile insurance coverages. You reduce premiums with no-fault by declining the coverage when it is optional. In some states, such as Florida, where the PIP coverage is required, you can reduce premiums by asking for up to a $3,000 deductible. See *Financial Self-Defense* for a complete list of PIP states and options.

Strategy #22
BUY COVERAGES THAT INSURE YOU 24 HOURS PER DAY AND DROP HIGH-PRICED PART-TIME INSURANCE.

The question when it comes to life, health, and disability insurance is not whether you need it, but instead what is the best and least expensive way to buy it. I am often asked this logical question: "If a person does not have life, health, or disability insurance policies, shouldn't he then carry the extra insurance on his auto policy like the medical, life, and funeral expenses covered by no-fault, PIP, medical expenses, and uninsured motorists?"

The answer is neither yes nor no. Yes, it's better than no insurance, but no, what you really need is the right insurance. The solution is to begin immediately to get the coverages you really need using the strategies in this section, a process that can take as little time as a few days.

The problem with including health and life insurance on your auto policy is that they are single-risk coverages. In other words, you are covered only when you are driving your automobile. If you are in your car two hours or less a day, that is the only time your insurance is in effect. You are not covered for accidents or losing your life the other 22 hours! Since auto accidents represent only a fraction of your health and life risks, you want one life insurance policy and one health insurance policy that cover you 24 hours per day 365 days per year including, but not limited to, the time you spend in your car.

By choosing the right full-time policies at the minimum costs, you have both the coverages and the huge premium savings you need. Refer to Strategy #57 for assistance in planning your insurance strategies.

Strategy #23
DROP DUPLICATE COVERAGE AND PREMIUMS PAID FOR MEDICAL INSURANCE.

Medical payments coverage pays for medical expenses such as doctor and hospital bills caused by a car accident to anyone riding in your automobile, including you, your family members, and nonfamily passengers. You and family members are already covered for medical bills under your hospitalization policy, and others riding in your car are covered by the liability portion of your auto policy or by their own hospitalization policy. Typical premiums for this coverage are $40 per year for $5,000 of insurance. You cannot collect twice for the same medical expenses, so if you have hospitalization insurance, medical payments coverage is a complete waste of your money. If you don't currently have a hospitalization policy, your objective is to get one as quickly as possible—one that covers you and your family 24 hours per day, not just the few hours you drive your automobile.

Strategy #24
DROP OR REDUCE UNINSURED MOTORISTS COVERAGE BY SUBSTITUTING BETTER COVERAGES.

Another kind of insurance that contains coverages that should be carried in a different form in other policies in your insurance plan is uninsured or underinsured motorists. Uninsured motorists is a coverage that seems to get insurance agents and personal injury attorneys all emotional. Insurance is just insurance. Because you are the one who must pay the premiums, your insurance decisions should never be emotional but mathematical.

Uninsured motorists coverage is really backward liability life insurance. Instead of you paying premiums to cover damages you might do to another driver or his or her property, you pay premiums to cover damages someone else might do to you. Who would pay the money if the other driver didn't have enough insurance? Your own insurance company, the promotional literature claims.

The truth is they may or may not. And then who is going to determine what the insurance company owes you—you? Not hardly. For instance, your insurance company may make you a modestly small offer. Rest assured it won't get emotionally charged up about what you've gone through like a jury might, and the claims adjuster knows you'll probably settle for almost any amount to avoid the threat of a prolonged court battle for which you would have to hire your own attorney to fight your own insurance company. Your insurance company, which is supposed to take your side, can suddenly become your worst enemy.

If you're buying uninsured/underinsured motorists coverage so you can collect quickly and easily from your own insurance company, why then does it seem that so many claimants end up having to hire and pay an attorney and spend years attempting to collect the money for them? Many auto insurance policies have an arbitration clause that says if you don't think your insurance company made a reasonable offer under uninsured/underinsured motorists coverage, you can't even go to court to settle the dispute. You must submit to claim benefit arbitration and pay for your own arbitrators out-of-pocket.

The best way to determine the necessity of uninsured motorists coverage is to see what potentially can be covered. The policy states you are covered for the amount of liability of the other driver. Liability if a case goes to court can include:

- your medical expenses and those of passengers
- death or damage to someone in your car caused by negligence of the other driver
- pain and suffering
- lost wages from work
- money for other related damages

As you can see, coverage for all damages to you but the pain and suffering is a duplication of coverage that can be found in a group health policy, your life insurance policy, and a disability income plan if you choose to have one. Damage to nonfamily members riding in your car is covered by your liability coverage or their medical or life insurance policies.

Pain and suffering is an outdated law concept that has made attorneys rich, jammed the court systems, and played on the

emotions instead of the logic of jurors. Money doesn't pay for
pain and suffering because pain and suffering is not a financial
loss. There is a lot of pain and suffering during everyone's
lifetime, both emotional and physical, but that does not necessitate spending money on auto premiums in a vain attempt to
combat it.

You don't buy insurance to cover the pain and suffering
caused by a relationship that breaks up, or the trauma of losing
a job tied to your feelings of self-worth. You don't buy life
insurance to eradicate the emotional pain caused by the loss of
a loved one. You buy life insurance to replace lost income.

Why then would it make sense to pay extra premiums to
cover pain and suffering related to or caused by an automobile
accident? Once you are willing to forgo collecting for pain and
suffering and are willing to accept the reimbursement of the
financial costs of a loss, uninsured motorists becomes a case of
duplicated, better-to-be-insured-elsewhere coverage and requiring the premium that can be eliminated.

Every other month or so I get a letter from a personal injury
attorney who questions why I would recommend dropping this
coverage, with a typical comment being, "I've seen clients who
wouldn't have collected a dime had it not been for their UM
coverage." The reason their clients would not have collected a
dime is not related to the value of the UM coverage. It is because
they have not used the right strategies to make sure they were
covered by the right amount of the right kind of life and health
insurance to begin with.

Remember, the reasons for replacing uninsured motorist coverage with other forms of coverage is a very logical move for the
following reasons:

- Uninsured motorist coverage only covers you during the time that
  you are in your car or, in some cases, while you are a pedestrian.
- Uninsured motorist only covers you if another "driver" is at fault.
- Uninsured motorist coverage is reduced or eliminated by any amount
  that you collected from the other driver.

As you can see, the strategy is both logical and easy to use. If
members of the media want to overpay for insurance, mortgages,
automobiles, etc., let them. Remember how many times I've
said, "Financial journalists are basically well-meaning, but often
broke, living paycheck-to-paycheck like most other Americans,
with little or no actual knowledge about money." That lack of
knowledge is showing in what they write.

UNNECESSARY AUTOMOBILE INSURANCE COVERAGES

There are lots of coverages on an auto policy for which you are paying duplicate premiums, for which you can be insured better by other full-time policies, or that you don't want at all.

Before eliminating any kind of insurance, first check to be sure the insurance is duplicate coverage AND is not required by your state laws. Here is a list.

Coverage	Where You'll Find It in Your Auto Policy	Your Substitution
Funeral Expenses	No-fault, Uninsured Motorists	Term Life Insurance
Death and Dismemberment	Death and Dismemberment	Term Life Insurance and Health Insurance
Medical Expenses (you and your family)	Uninsured Motorists, No-fault, PIP	Health Insurance
Medical Payments (nonrelated passengers in your car)	Uninsured Motorists, PIP, Medical Payments	Your Liability Insurance, Passenger's Health Insurance
Lost Wages	Uninsured Motorists, No-fault, PIP	Disability Plan
Loss of Life	Uninsured Motorists	Life Insurance
Pain and Suffering	Uninsured Motorists	No Insurance
Consortium (loss of companionship due to death of a spouse)	Uninsured Motorists	No Insurance

---

Strategy #25
NEVER BUY INSURANCE TO COVER INSURANCE DEDUCTIBLES.

Some insurance salespeople are using a new ploy to confuse those who are successfully implementing the Charles J. Givens insurance strategies. We will call it the "Don't you realize your deductible isn't covered?" deception. This sales pitch typically shows up with automobile medical payments, PIP, and rental car collision damage waiver (CDW) insurance.

Here's how it works with medical payments insurance. You are at your automobile insurance agent's office redesigning your policy according to the strategies in this chapter. "I want to drop the medical payments coverage," you say. "I already have a hospitalization policy at work, and this coverage is a duplicate."

"Oh, no, it's not," says your agent with apparent alarm. "If you were injured, you would have to pay the deductible out of your own pocket, up to hundreds of dollars."

Your first reaction may be, "Oh, my gosh, I didn't think of that!" However, what the agent indicates as a concern is instead a part of your premium cost-cutting plan. Your strategy is to cut insurance costs by raising your deductibles (see Strategy #13). Why then would it make sense to spend money buying insurance specifically to cover those deductibles that are already saving you money? In the case of medical payments coverage, the premium versus risk factor would make this insurance one of the worst you could buy. Since you would already be covered by your hospitalization insurance for every cost except the deductible and your share of the co-insurance you would be paying full automobile medical premiums solely for the coverage of a few hundred dollars of potential losses. Your automobile insurance company has limited its risk to only the deductible, while continuing to collect the same amount of premiums from you as it does from someone who had no other insurance at all. Don't fall for it.

Strategy #26
BUY A SEPARATE SIX- OR NINE-MONTH POLICY TO COVER MOTORCYCLES, MOPEDS, OR SNOWMOBILES.

Motorcycle insurance (including mopeds, snowmobiles, and other miscellaneous vehicles) is similar to auto insurance, even though motorcycles are not classified as automobiles by insurance companies.

Most states requiring auto liability insurance also require motorcycle liability coverage. You should have liability coverage for your motorcycle. A car owner may insure a motorcycle with an endorsement to his auto policy. You are not automatically covered for your motorcycle through your basic auto policy.

Motorcyclists can get coverages for bodily injury and property damage liability, medical payments (usually limited to $500), uninsured motorists coverage, and collision and physical damage coverage. Use the same strategies for your motorcycle as you would for your automobiles. You probably do not need coverage for other passengers since they are covered by both the liability portion of your motorcycle policy and their own hospitalization insurance.

Many insurance companies offer six-month and nine-month policies to motorcyclists and snowmobilers who garage the equipment for the winter or summer. Ask your agent; it will save you money.

Strategy #27
REDESIGN YOUR AUTO POLICY BY CHOOSING THE OPTIMUM COVERAGES, ELIMINATING DUPLICATIONS, AND MINIMIZING PREMIUMS.

Use the form that follows to redesign your automobile policy for lower premiums. Part 1 gives you a synopsis of the coverages you need and those you should consider dropping or changing; Part 2 will help you analyze and redesign your auto policy. On the form, list the liability limits and coverages you now have on each automobile that you own along with any changes you wish to make using the insurance strategies in this chapter. If you have more than two automobiles, make a copy of the page. Contact your insurance agent and make all of the changes, noting the changes in your premiums. Don't expect enthusiasm from your agent, who stands to lose commissions from your changes. It's your money. Fight for it.

Also use copies of the form when getting auto insurance quotes. Most automobile premiums are stated on policies as six-month premiums. If you pay every six months, you must double the premiums shown to obtain the yearly figures. Conversely, you will save twice as much per year as shown on your six-month policy.

REDESIGNING YOUR AUTOMOBILE INSURANCE POLICY
Part 1

Coverages You Need

Liability
  Bodily Injury   Covers damage to other people.
  Property Damage   Covers damage to other people's property.
Comprehensive   Covers damage to your car by fire, theft, or
                            anything but collision.
Collision   Covers damage to your car by collision with
                            another car or object.

Coverages to Substitute, Drop, or Minimize by Following the Previously Discussed Strategies

No-fault (PIP)	Covers medical, funeral expenses, lost wages, and other basic auto insurances.
Medical Payments	Covers medical and funeral expenses.
Uninsured/Underinsured Motorists	Covers medical expenses, funeral expenses, and pain and suffering, substituting for the liability of a noninsured or underinsured driver.
Emergency Road Service	Covers towing and roadside service.
Car Rental Expense	Covers rental car if yours is damaged.
Death/Dismemberment	Covers death or certain combinations of injuries.
Specialty Coverage	Covers audio equipment, glass breakage, etc.

In some states, some of these coverages may be required by law. Check your state rules through your insurance agent. A complete list appears in my book *Financial Self-Defense*, Chapter 8.

REDESIGNING YOUR AUTOMOBILE INSURANCE POLICY
Part 2

Enter the limits you have and premiums you currently pay from the declarations page of your current policy in columns A and C. Call your agent if you have any questions.

Enter the new limits you have determined and the new premiums you are quoted in columns B and D.

Coverages to Reorganize

Coverage	A Current Limits	B Your New Limits	C Current Premiums	D New Premiums	Strategies
Bodily Injury Liability	/	/	$	$	Choose limits based on Strategy #9
Property Damage Liability					$50,000 maximum or twice your net worth
Umbrella Liability					Buy if you need higher limits
Comprehensive Deductible					Increase to $500 or $1,000
Collision Deductible					Increase to $500 or $1,000

Coverages to Substitute, Drop, or Minimize

Coverage	Current Limits	Your New Limits	Current Premiums	New Premiums	Strategies
Medical Payments					Substitute the coverage in your health and life policies
No-fault (PIP)		-0- or state min.		-0- or min.	If required, check on a possible deductible
Uninsured Motorists		-0- or state min.		-0- or min.	Substitute the coverage in your health and life policies
Emergency Road Service		-0-		-0-	Pay the rare road service or towing bill yourself
Car Rental Expense		-0-		-0-	Use your second car, get a ride to work, or rent a car yourself
Death/ Dismemberment		-0-		-0-	Substitute the coverage in your health and life policies
Specialty Coverages (check your policy)		-0-		-0-	Drop

TOTAL PREMIUMS $ _____ − $ _____ = $ _____
                 (CURRENT)   (NEW)   (TOTAL AMOUNT SAVED)

To save even more money, shop around for better rates, ask for all possible discounts by name, check first on what a company will do if you get a ticket or have an accident—your fault or not—and get an insurance quote before you buy any car.

Chapter 4

AVOID RENTAL CAR INSURANCE RIP-OFFS

It was beautiful and simple as all truly great swindles are.

O. Henry
"The Gentle Grafter"
1908

OBJECTIVE ————————————————————————————

SAVE HUNDREDS OF DOLLARS AND AVOID UNNECESSARY HASSLES WHEN YOU RENT A CAR.

Travel anywhere by plane these days, for business or for pleasure, and chances are you will end up renting a car when you get there. And as if the expense of renting a car was not enough, the rental car companies have been able to turn unnecessary insurance gimmicks into a billion-dollar income center, all at your and other car renters' expense. In this chapter, I will show you the winning strategies whether you are renting a car at home or abroad, and how to save hundreds in the process while avoiding unnecessary hassles.

By advertising low daily or weekly rates, and adding on huge unnecessary insurance premiums, the rental car companies create huge profits from the confusion and fear of their customers. It has been estimated that rental car companies rake in over $1 billion a year just from the add-on insurance. The four main add-on rental car insurance premiums are: collision damage waiver (CDW), personal accident insurance (PAI), personal effects coverage (PEC), and liability insurance supplement (LIS). Others seem to appear periodically. Although extra insurance coverages are supposedly optional, the rental car company will do everything within its power to see that you end up buying them. All of these insurance coverages are either unnecessary because you are already covered on other policies or incredibly overpriced for the insurance you actually get.

Here are typical daily and weekly premiums:

		Daily	Weekly
1.	Collision damage waiver (CDW)	12.00	84.00
2.	Personal accident insurance (PAI)	3.00	21.00
3.	Personal effects coverage (PEC)	1.25	8.75
4.	Liability insurance supplement (LIS)	4.95	34.65
	TOTAL	$21.20	$148.40

Strategy #28
DECLINE ALL EXTRA INSURANCE COVERAGES WHEN YOU RENT A CAR.

COLLISION DAMAGE WAIVER (CDW) INSURANCE
Year after year, rental car companies require that you become liable for more of the damage caused by a collision or rollover of a rented vehicle. Your deductible for damage to a rental car ranges from $3,000 to the full value of the car. The rental car company, of course, will offer you collision damage waiver insurance for about $12 a day to cover your deductible.

Here is what they don't tell you. Even without the CDW insurance, you are already covered by the rental car company for fire and theft, and under the "Occasional Driver" clause in your automobile policy, you may already be covered for collision damage for the same limits and deductibles as on your personal auto. Some personal policies even cover the rental car deductible. Even the deductible you might have to pay would be reimbursed to you by your insurance company if it collected from another driver who was at fault.

PERSONAL ACCIDENT INSURANCE (PAI)
Personal accident insurance is nothing more than an expensive life insurance policy with medical payments. The policy states, "This coverage pays for death directly caused by an automobile accident independent of all other causes." Never take the insurance. You would be paying the equivalent of $1,000 per year for a $175,000 life insurance policy that covers you only a few

minutes a day—while you are driving the rental car. The actual value of the insurance is less than $50 per year. You are already covered for medical payments by your hospitalization policy.

PERSONAL EFFECTS COVERAGE (PEC)

Personal effects coverage is insurance that covers loss or damage to your personal property in the rental car or hotel room while you are renting the car. Coverage on one major policy is limited to $525 for you and your immediate family members.

Again, an absolute waste of money. The exclusions—what they won't pay for—are almost comical: teeth, contact lenses, furniture, currency, coins, tickets, documents, and perishables or mysterious disappearances. What in the world is left? Your own homeowner's policy may already give you similar coverage when you are away from home. Check with your insurance agent or read your policy.

LIABILITY INSURANCE SUPPLEMENT (LIS)

When you rent a car, your automatic liability coverage for injury or death to others is the bare minimum required by the state. For an extra $4.95 a day, the liability coverage is increased to $1 million or more. You don't need it. Your auto insurance policy already covers you up to its current limits, and by getting the "personal umbrella liability" policy described in Chapter 3, you are covered for up to $1 million of liability at a fraction of the cost of the rental car insurance.

You can pay as little as $100 a week to rent a car, and as much as $120 for additional unnecessary insurance coverages. The discount rental car companies in resort areas, such as Florida, are the most misleading in their advertising. Because they advertise rental rates as low as $99 a week, vacationers end up at the counter only to be threatened into accepting the "optional" insurance.

Rental agents are often paid bonuses for selling the extra insurance, and sales pitches are somewhere between aggressive and obnoxious. Some companies require a deposit of as much as $750 if you don't take the CDW. You may end up taking the insurance just because you're afraid the deposit would put your Visa over the limit. Plan ahead and you can avoid the hassle.

Strategy #29
CHARGE A RENTAL CAR ON A CREDIT CARD THAT COVERS THE DEDUCTIBLE.

One of the new, truly valuable credit card services is automatic coverage of the rental car deductible when you charge the rental on your credit card. The American Express personal platinum card covers the first $50,000, and a Diners Club card covers the first $25,000 of damages. MasterCard and Visa cards also cover the deductible up to $3,000, and there is no additional cost to you.

American Express corporate cards do not cover the deductible. If you own your own business, your business insurance carrier may be able to add the rental car deductible coverage for you and all your employees to your business policy for a fraction of the yearly cost of buying it at the counter.

Strategy #30
CHECK THE COVERAGE IN YOUR PERSONAL AUTO INSURANCE POLICY FOR THE "NON-OWNED VEHICLE" OR "OCCASIONAL DRIVER" CLAUSE.

When it comes to your money, never assume anything. Although you are probably covered by your own insurance policy for collision or comprehensive damage done to a rental automobile whether or not you are at fault, take a few moments to get out your policy and check once and for all.

Here are two clauses from an actual auto insurance policy. Yours should look similar if you are covered. Your coverage, however, can be limited by the policy.

COVERAGE FOR THE USE OF OTHER CARS
The coverages in this section you have on your car extend to a loss to a newly acquired car, a temporary substitute car, or a non-owned car. These coverages extend to a non-owned car while it is driven by or in the custody of an insured.

RENTAL CAR DEDUCTIBLE AMOUNT EXPENSE
Pays any collision or comprehensive deductible you may be legally responsible for should you have an accident in a rental car.

Be certain that an extra premium is not required on your policy to put one of these coverages in force. The non-owned car in this case can be a rental car. Make a copy of the first page of your policy (the declarations page) and the page or pages containing a statement of your coverage for a non-owned automobile similar to those above and keep them with you whenever you travel. Should the need ever arise, you can prove on the spot that you are already covered.

Some insurance companies have now limited the amount they will pay for a rental car deductible to $400. Not a lot if your deductible amount was $3,000. Of course, in this case you can buy additional insurance on your policy, called coverage R-1, that will pay the full amount of any deductible for which you were legally liable on a rental car. This extra premium should only be paid if you are a frequent renter of cars. Or better still, cover the deductible by charging on a credit card that offers the benefit.

Strategy #31

NEVER LET ANOTHER PERSON DRIVE YOUR RENTAL CAR UNLESS HE OR SHE IS ADDED TO THE CONTRACT AS AN ADDITIONAL DRIVER.

One more warning. Any insurance you have and even the CDW insurance from the rental car company is invalid if someone else is driving your rental car who is not listed as an additional driver on the rental application and/or is not listed on your personal automobile insurance policy. To be listed as an additional driver, the other person must have his or her name and driver's license number added to the rental contract. With some companies spouses are automatically covered, but you must ask. You may list more than one additional driver if necessary.

Your attitude may be that since you rented the car, you can let anyone you choose drive it, even if he is not added to the rental contract. You're correct; that is, until the other driver is in an accident with the rental car. Then all bets are off. No one, not your insurance company, the car rental insurance company, and more than likely not the driver, will want to pay, leaving you holding the bag. Your strategy: never let another driver not listed on the rental contract drive your rental car, not even a family member.

Adding an additional driver is easy and takes less than 30 seconds. Adding a driver used to be free, but some companies are now charging $1.50 for each driver added. The additional driver must simply show his or her driver's license.

Strategy #32
DON'T FALL VICTIM TO THE "YOU MUST PAY NOW" WRECKED RENTAL CAR DEMAND.

So what happens if you wreck a rental car and you didn't take the CDW insurance? Can you stay in control of the situation and minimize the extra problems? The answer is yes—if you know the strategies. Here is what you do if the accident is not your fault and the damage is caused by another driver:

- Call the police immediately no matter how small the damage.
- Get a copy of the police officer's report for your insurance company or find out where to get one.
- Demand that the police officer give the other driver a ticket no matter how remote the chance of conviction. The middle of an accident scene is no time to be a nice guy or gal from a legal standpoint. If the other driver receives a ticket, your insurance company and the car rental company will be forced to go after the other driver or his or her insurance company instead of putting the pressure on you. A ticket also prevents the other driver or his or her attorney from later turning the tables on you by claiming the accident was your fault. Remember, there is nothing "fair" about the American legal system.
- Report the accident to your rental car company and immediately ask for another car to drive and you will get it.
- Fill out your rental car company's accident report.
- Ask for a written estimate of the damage from the rental car company, preferably before you leave town, but don't delay your trip.
- Get extra copies of the rental agreement for your insurance company and/or credit card company that covers the deductible.

Only the major rental car companies such as Avis, National, or Hertz will normally not demand that you pay the deductible instantly. Most all other companies and even some franchises of the big guys will. Since the rental car company already has your credit card number, it will normally put a "hold" on your account for $1,000 to $3,000 to cover the deductible, then send in a credit card slip showing "signature on file."

Your strategy is clear. Refuse to pay and refuse to sign a charge slip for the deductible. There is no debtors' prison in America. I have heard of instances in which the accident victim was told that if he didn't pay right then and there the police would be called. The police have no jurisdiction over a civil financial dispute and would only laugh if called. But when you aren't sure, it is easy to be intimidated by veiled threats.

If the car rental company wants to collect from you personally, force it to go through the entire legal process. If you had no insurance of your own and were responsible for the deductible yourself, could the company win? Probably, but to collect $1,000 to $3,000 would cost at least that amount or more in legal fees. Remember the most important principle of American justice: attorneys always get their share, even if their share amounts to more than the money in question.

If you ask the car rental agency not to put a hold on the funds in your credit card account, your request will fall on deaf ears. In that case, your strategy is to call your credit card company and dispute the hold. You may have to talk to a supervisor. Tell the credit card company representative that you are already insured and that the representative is welcome to call your insurance agent. You will get your way as long as you are willing to push until you do. Once the charge slip has been run through, you have the right to dispute the charge until the matter is resolved with the car rental agency to your satisfaction. Of course, if you have a $500 deductible, or any deductible, you will have to pay that amount yourself if, and only if, the accident was your fault.

MasterCard and Visa will at your request take the amount off your bill until the matter is resolved. American Express will leave the charge on your bill while working with you to resolve the problem.

Strategy #33
WHEN YOU RENT A CAR ABROAD, TAKE THE COLLISION DAMAGE WAIVER (CDW) INSURANCE.

The major exception to declining the rental car collision damage waiver (CDW) insurance occurs when you rent a car abroad for vacation or business. There are two reasons.

First, the chances of damaging a rental car abroad are five times greater than when you rent a car in the United States. The United States is the only country in which I've ever driven that teaches people defensive driving. In most other countries, drivers believe in offensive driving, which makes a novice American driver feel as if he is slipping into an unwanted slot in the Monte Carlo Grand Prix. In most countries, local drivers do not recognize lanes, lights, or speed limits, and gridlock is so abundant that metal-to-metal distances are often no more than two to three inches from car to car.

Bombay, India, has the wildest drivers in the world. Thousands of cars zoom along bumper to bumper and fender to fender at speeds seldom less than 60 miles (100 kilometers) per hour, resembling a flock of birds instantaneously changing direction every few seconds.

In many parts of Europe, from Spain to Italy, you will be pushing it along the freeway in your four-cylinder rental car at 75 mph, feeling free of the 55 to 65 mph U.S. interstate restrictions, only to be passed as if you were standing still by one after another $75,000 Mercedes doing close to 100 mph. Believe me, in this case the $15 per day for the insurance is a good bet.

Don't let these descriptions deter you from renting a car and driving abroad, although the total rental cost of $150 to $400 per day might. Driving in most countries can be an exhilarating, adrenaline-pumping experience not to be missed. There is a second reason, however, to take the CDW insurance. Many emerging nations have not yet accepted the "innocent until proven guilty" concept. Damage a rental car in one of these countries and the car company will demand immediate payment for the deductible if you didn't take the insurance. It doesn't care when you explain about your personal insurance policy and credit-card-provided deductible coverages. In addition, most U.S. insurance policies do not provide any coverages for an automobile driven abroad whether it's yours or the rental car company's.

Instead of just putting a hold on your credit card account, the car rental company may ask you to sign a credit card slip for an astronomical estimated car repair bill or even to sign one or more blank forms. You may even have to produce an additional credit card to cover the loss. Immediately your card or cards can be up to their limits, putting a serious financial damper on the rest of your trip.

What happens if you refuse? In many countries your right to leave the country may be denied or your passport temporarily placed in custody until the account is settled. The same thing can happen with a disputed hotel or restaurant bill. Although there is no real personal danger in such a circumstance, you quickly discover you do not have a winning hand to play. The whole process is a time-consuming nuisance.

Having spent the equivalent of several years of my life in over 100 countries, I've seen and experienced it all, so in this case playing to win means you take the CDW insurance.

Chapter 5

GETTING CONTROL OF YOUR HOMEOWNER'S POLICY AND OTHER INSURANCE

Keep the home fires burning.

Ivor Novello
Composer
(1893–1951)

OBJECTIVE

LOWER THE PREMIUMS ON YOUR HOMEOWNER'S POLICY WHILE GETTING RID OF POOR-VALUE COVERAGES AND GIMMICK INSURANCE.

Homeowner's insurance is to your house what auto insurance is to your car. In your policy you can buy coverage for damage to your home, contents, property, yourself, your family, and even insure against liability claims by someone who gets hurt on your property. As with auto insurance, not all coverages are either necessary or good values. With your increased insurance experience gained from working with your auto policy, let's check out, redesign, and reduce the premiums on your homeowner's policy. Get out your homeowner's or tenant's policy so that you can check coverages and make notes on the policy of those you want to change.

Strategy #34
**TAKE ONLY THE COVERAGES YOU NEED ON YOUR
HOMEOWNER'S POLICY.**

The risks inherent in owning a home are called perils. These perils have been divided by the insurance industry into 18 categories. The amount of premium you pay for a homeowner's policy is determined by the number of these perils you wish to cover. All the coverages deal primarily with:

• your home
• other buildings on the property (e.g., detached garage)
• your personal belongings
• living expenses for temporary relocation

There are six major types of policies, known as HO-1 to HO-8, and the perils covered by each are shown in the chart on the facing page. The advantage of an HO-2 is the coverage for frozen pipes and water damage. This policy is the best value for those living in climates where pipes do freeze. Others living in warmer climates can get the best value from HO-1, which costs less. The best value in a policy, if minimum premiums are the goal, is HO-1—particularly if you live in an area where the pipes don't freeze. As with any insurance, it is a good idea to reduce premiums by not taking coverages for events that have only a remote chance of happening. Even if you should have to pay a small claim or two during your lifetime for perils not covered, your premium savings are worth it.

HO-5 covers all possible perils except flood, earthquake, war, and nuclear accident. Some policies cover damage to property of guests, others do not. The HO-4 renter's policy covers only personal property. Condominium owners can purchase a special policy HO-6 similar to HO-4 to cover personal property or damage not covered by the condo master policy. In Texas only, policies are labeled A, B, or C and require careful reading to determine what is covered.

Mobile-home owners pay more for homeowner's insurance because mobile homes are more vulnerable to the elements. Older homes are expensive to insure. If you have a unique older home, you can save money by asking for an HO-8. The HO-8 covers repairs or actual damage but not replacement since the cost of replacing some older homes might be astronomical.

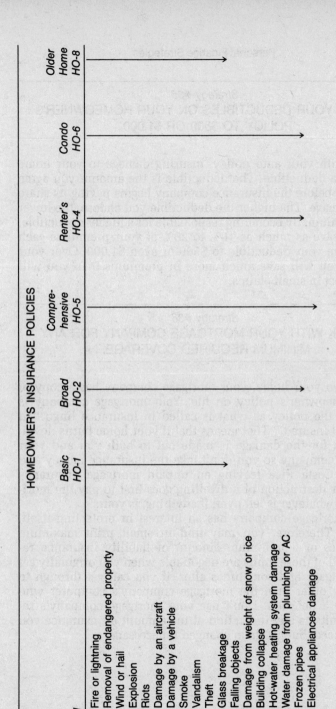

HOMEOWNER'S INSURANCE POLICIES

Peril	Basic HO-1	Broad HO-2	Compre- hensive HO-5	Renter's HO-4	Condo HO-6	Older Home HO-8
1. Fire or lightning						
2. Removal of endangered property						
3. Wind or hail						
4. Explosion						
5. Riots						
6. Damage by an aircraft						
7. Damage by a vehicle						
8. Smoke						
9. Vandalism						
10. Theft						
11. Glass breakage						
12. Falling objects						
13. Damage from weight of snow or ice						
14. Building collapse						
15. Hot-water heating system damage						
16. Water damage from plumbing or AC						
17. Frozen pipes						
18. Electrical appliances damage						

Strategy #35
RAISE YOUR DEDUCTIBLES ON YOUR HOMEOWNER'S POLICY TO $500 OR $1,000.

Just as with your auto policy, insuring damage to your home includes a deductible. The deductible is the amount you agree to kick in before the insurance company begins paying its share of the damage. The higher the deductible you choose, the lower your premium. By becoming responsible for a higher deductible, you can save as much as 10% to 20% of your premiums each year. Raise your deductible to $500 or even $1,000. Over your lifetime you will save much more in premiums than you will ever collect in small claims.

Strategy #36
CHECK WITH YOUR MORTGAGE COMPANY FOR ANY MINIMUM REQUIRED COVERAGE.

If you own your home, your mortgage company has a copy of your homeowner's policy on file. Your mortgage company is listed on the policy as what is called in insurance lingo "an additional insured." That means that if your home burns down, the check for the damage is made out to both you and your mortgage company so you don't take the insurance money and retire in Costa Rica leaving an unpaid mortgage. Insurance money for destruction of a dwelling goes first to pay the mortgage, and whatever is left over, if anything, is yours.

Your mortgage company has an interest in protecting itself, not you. Therefore, you may find in small print maximum deductibles or a minimum amount of liability insurance required. All of these limits are negotiable when you originally get your mortgage and sometimes after, if you can get through to somebody other than the mortgage company's computer who can make a decision. Don't use your mortgage company's required limits as any indication of the amount of insurance you actually need, but get them changed if necessary.

Strategy #37
DECLINE THE ADDITIONAL OPTIONAL COVERAGES ON YOUR HOMEOWNER'S POLICY.

Additional coverages you can choose as options to your homeowner's policy fall into the following six categories. None are a good value for the premium charged.

1. Removal of debris.
2. Damaged-property removal.
3. Fire department surcharges—up to $250.
4. Temporary repairs to prevent further damage to property.
5. Trees, shrubs, and plants—covered up to $500 or a maximum of 5% of the dwelling insurance. Since windstorms are excluded, this insurance is of little value.
6. Stolen credit cards—up to $500.

All these are risks for which you are better off accepting the responsibility yourself without paying extra premiums.

Strategy #38
PURCHASE A PERSONAL ARTICLES "FLOATER" TO COVER EXPENSIVE PERSONAL ITEMS.

Your basic policy limits what you can collect for theft or damage of personal items. Usually your basic policy covers personal items for 50% of the amount of insurance on the house. If your home is insured for $90,000, you might have $45,000 of insurance on personal property. Check your policy now. Some policies specifically exclude jewelry, furs, or other items, or limit coverage for specific expensive items. You can insure expensive jewelry, furs, and other personal property with a personal articles "floater." As your wealth increases and your personal assets increase, make certain your insurance is increased yearly or with each new acquisition.

When you or someone in your family buys or receives as a gift an expensive piece of jewelry or fur, immediately notify your insurance agent. You will normally be required to have the piece appraised either by a store you choose or one chosen by your insurance company. Send a copy of the appraisal to your insurance company and store one in your safe deposit box or away from your home. With some policies *all* new expensive items must be appraised to be insured. Take a picture of the item and store it off site. You can collect only on what you can prove you have lost, not necessarily on what you actually lost.

Strategy #39
VIDEOTAPE YOUR VALUABLES FOR INSURANCE RECORDS.

That's right, you can only collect for what you can prove you lost, and once an item or its purchase records are gone, you may not get an understanding claims adjuster. The best way to provide an acceptable insurance record quickly and inexpensively is to use your video camera to create a record of furniture, knickknacks, artwork, clothes, stereo and video equipment (including model and serial numbers), musical instruments, and everything else of value. While you are taping, verbally record the value of the asset and where and when you bought it. Put the videotape in a safe deposit box along with receipts. Records won't help if they are lost in a fire or burglary along with the assets. If you don't have a video camera, use your slide or Polaroid camera and a tape recorder.

Strategy #40
BUY REPLACEMENT VALUE COVERAGE, NOT MARKET VALUE COVERAGE, ON YOUR HOME AND CONTENTS.

Here is a simple, inexpensive strategy that can save you thousands that you might otherwise lose.

You can choose from two different types of insurance coverage on your home and its contents—replacement value or market value. Replacement value coverage will pay whatever it costs to replace an asset that is lost, destroyed, or stolen. Market value coverage will pay only the current value of the asset after age and wear and tear are deducted. If your five-year-old $1,000 video player is stolen, the replacement value coverage will pay you $1,000, but market value coverage may net you only $200 since your video player is now considered used and abused. Surprisingly, replaced value coverage costs only about $10 more per year.

Make certain your fire insurance is also replacement value coverage and not a market value policy. The value of your home may fluctuate with real estate market conditions, and a market value policy could pay you less than the replacement cost.

Ask for an appreciation clause in your policy that will automatically raise your coverage limits each year for anticipated inflation without the necessity of checking with your agent.

Strategy #41
CARRY AS FIRE INSURANCE AT LEAST BUT NOT NECESSARILY MORE THAN 80% OF THE REPLACEMENT COST OF YOUR HOME.

Fire insurance rates are set by considering location, distance from the nearest fire hydrant and fire station, the type of construction, and the age of the home. These are factors over which you have little control. You can, however, control the amount and kind of insurance you buy, which controls your premiums.

Carry enough insurance to cover at least 80%, but not necessarily 100%, of the replacement value of your home. With most but not all homeowner's policies, you are automatically covered for up to 100% of a loss, as long as the policy is written for 80% or more of the replacement value of your home. Never underinsure because if coverage is less than 80% of replacement cost and you have a loss, the policy will pay only a percentage of the loss. Never overinsure because you're paying premium dollars on which you can never collect. If your $100,000 home is insured for $200,000 and is a total loss, you can collect only $100,000, even though you have been paying premiums on $200,000 of coverage. Check your policy to be sure of the specific rules, and if appropriate, save money by reducing your coverage.

Strategy #42
BUY A SPECIAL TENANT'S POLICY, HO-4, IF YOU RENT A HOME OR AN APARTMENT.

The tenant's policy (HO-4), designed for those who rent an apartment or house or own a cooperative apartment, is a must. This policy insures household contents and personal belongings against all of the perils included in the broad form (HO-2), plus additional living expenses if the property becomes unlivable due to fire or other damage. The policy does not include fire or other damage insurance for the building since you do not have a financial investment in the structure. Tenant's policies usually provide a minimum of $4,000 coverage on personal property, and a minimum of $800 for additional living expenses. If you have more than $4,000 of personal property, be certain to add extra personal-articles insurance. It is not expensive. Tenant's policies also provide liability coverage for injuries, property damage, and legal expenses in case someone is injured or someone's property is damaged on your premises.

It is amazing how small a percentage of those who rent homes, condos, or apartments actually carry tenant's insurance and how often they are shocked when they discover that their landlord is not responsible for loss or damage.

Strategy #43
PROTECT YOUR RENTAL PROPERTIES WITH AN OWNER'S, LANDLORD'S, AND TENANT'S POLICY (OLT).

An owner's, landlord's, and tenant's policy protects someone who rents a property to others. OLT policies cover the liability arising from the ownership and maintenance of rental properties. OLT policies are relatively inexpensive and can be added as a supplement to the fire insurance policy on a rental home you own or sometimes to your homeowner's insurance policy.

Strategy #44
DROP OR REFUSE TO BUY THE "BIG SIX" INSURANCE GIMMICKS.

The first two steps in getting control of your insurance plan are redesigning your automobile and homeowner's policies for better protection for far less money. Your next step is to identify and eliminate hundreds of dollars you are wasting every year on six forms of gimmick insurance that are attached to policies or purchases sometimes without your knowledge or because you were mentally and emotionally coerced into taking them.

- Credit Life Insurance
- Credit Disability Insurance
- Mortgage Life Insurance
- Automobile Service Contracts
- Extended Warranties on Appliances and Electronics
- Chargegard

These insurances duplicate what by now should already be covered by your life, health, and disability plans, or they cover repairs to your automobile, electronic, or appliance purchases that can almost always be done for far less money than the cost of the insurance. Go through your car loan papers, mortgage papers, purchase agreements, and credit card statements, and when you find any of these forms of insurance, drop them, asking for a refund. And from now on when you are offered these insurance gimmicks, refuse them no matter how good the salesperson's story sounds at the time.

1. Credit Life Insurance—overpriced insurance that pays off a consumer loan if the borrower dies. Protects the lender more than the borrower.
   Substitute: your term life insurance policy.
2. Credit Disability Insurance—overpriced insurance that makes payments on a consumer loan if the borrower is permanently disabled. Protects the lender more than the borrower. Few ever collect.
   Substitute: your savings, investments, or disability plan.
3. Mortgage Life Insurance—overpriced insurance that pays off a home mortgage if the borrower dies. Protects the mortgage company more than the borrower.
   Substitute: add the payoff amount of your mortgage to your term life insurance policy.
4. Automobile Service Contracts—overpriced extended warranties on a car that go into effect only after the manufacturer's original warranty runs out. Structured to produce almost 100% profit for the dealer and insurer.
   Substitute: a moonlighting mechanic who does your auto repairs for $7 to $15 per hour.
5. Extended Warranties on Appliances and Electronics—overpriced repair contracts that kick in only after the manufacturer's warranty runs out. Structured to produce 80% or more profit for dealers and insurers.
   Substitute: an occasional repair bill paid out of your pocket.
6. Chargegard—overpriced credit life and credit disability insurance on credit card accounts.
   Substitute: your term life insurance policy and disability plan.

Be sure to read my book *Financial Self-Defense*, Chapter 7, "Get Rid of Hidden Insurance That Is Costing You $2,000 a Year," for complete strategies on how to find and cancel these insurance gimmicks, along with an in-depth look at how they have been robbing you of hundreds or even thousands every year of your adult life.

Strategy #45
ALWAYS BUY OPTIONAL FLOOD INSURANCE IF YOU LIVE IN A FLOODPLAIN.

Hurricane Hugo made victims out of many homeowners a second time when they were informed they were not insured for flood damage. Flood damage is excluded from most homeowner's policies, and should you ever have damages from a flood, you don't want to learn that fact from your insurance company claims adjuster.

Flood insurance is available from your homeowner's insurance company as an option if you live in a floodplain. The federal government is actually the guarantor of the coverage through your insurer. If you don't live in a designated floodplain, your chance of a flood caused by nature is almost nonexistent.

Designated lowland or coastal areas of the United States are labeled floodplains by the government. In those areas there is a far greater incidence or risk of flood damage, and if your home is sitting in one of these areas, proper financial planning makes flood insurance a must. I have owned only one of my hundreds of rental homes in a floodplain, and sure enough, one year I had significant flood damage that was repaired by the government-underwritten flood insurance I carried.

If your home is in a floodplain and you have a mortgage, the decision is not a big one. Your mortgage company will normally require that you buy the optional flood insurance as part of the mortgage agreement. However, once your property is paid off, it will be up to you to see that your investment is protected; no one is there to do it for you.

Strategy #46
VERIFY THAT YOU ARE INSURED UNDER THE REGULAR FLOOD PLAN, NOT THE EMERGENCY FLOOD PLAN.

The original government flood insurance program in general use prior to 1984 was called the Emergency Flood Plan. The problem was that the maximum coverage was $35,000 for the house and $10,000 for the contents—not much protection if your home is worth two or more times that amount. After 1984, many states adopted the Regular Flood Plan, which covers up to $185,000 for buildings and $60,000 for contents, a much more realistic amount.

If you already have flood insurance, check your policy immediately to be certain you have the Regular Flood Plan protection. If you are unsure, call your insurance agent now. Read the policy carefully for what is and what is not covered by the insurance. For instance, to have full replacement-cost coverage on the contents of your home, you must occupy it 80% of the year, an exclusion that would affect anyone owning a second home in a designated floodplain, such as our home on the ocean in Ponce Inlet, Florida.

Chapter 6

BETTER LIFE INSURANCE FOR 80% LESS

Insurance—an ingenious modern game of chance in which the player is permitted to enjoy the comfortable conviction that he is beating the man who keeps the table.

Ambrose Bierce
The Devil's Dictionary
1906

OBJECTIVE

CUT THE COST OF YOUR LIFE INSURANCE UP TO 80% WHILE INCREASING FINANCIAL PROTECTION FOR YOUR FAMILY.

Life insurance is a plan whereby you pay money to the company while you are alive and the company pays your chosen beneficiary when you are not. The longer you live, the more the insurance company profits. Life insurance is a must for anyone with family responsibilities and little personal wealth. Because it is misunderstood, overused for underprotection, and sold through marketing gimmicks with little real value, life insurance can also be detrimental to your wealth.

First, here are a few terms that you must understand in order to take control of your life insurance costs.

DEATH BENEFIT. The amount of money that will be paid to the beneficiary if the insured dies; the amount of life insurance. Also called the face value of the policy.

PREMIUM. The amount you pay to the insurance company. Life insurance premiums can be paid in one lump sum (single premium), one check each year (annual premium), or periodically by quarter or by month. Premiums can be for insurance only or partially diverted into investments, prepaid policies, and retirement plans.

POLICY TERM. The period during which the life insurance is in force. The term can range from one year to a lifetime.

FEES AND COMMISSIONS. Charges for administrative and selling expenses levied by the insurance company against your premiums or cash value.

SURRENDER CHARGE. The amount of money the insurance company keeps if the policy is canceled. Surrender charges apply only to policies with investment plans such as whole life and universal life and can run into thousands of dollars.

Let's begin with the basics. How much life insurance do you really need? To determine the amount of life insurance you need, you must first determine if you need life insurance at all.

Strategy #47
IF YOU ARE SINGLE WITH NO DEPENDENTS, DON'T BUY LIFE INSURANCE.

Billions of dollars of life insurance in force today is on the lives of single people with no family responsibilities. Who would get the insurance proceeds, the dog or goldfish? Life insurance should be used only to prevent a financial hardship that would be created if the insured dies. If you are single, invest your money for use while you are living.

Some singles list their parents as beneficiaries. Unless your parents are your dependents, you are wasting your money. If they were to lose you, getting a lump sum of cash won't help reduce the hurt. Use your life insurance premium money for living.

Strategy #48
DO NOT BUY LIFE INSURANCE ON CHILDREN.

The purpose of insurance is to protect against the loss of income or financial assets. Although your children may be an emotional asset, they are certainly not financial assets unless you have secured them high-paying jobs in television commercials.

Parents buy life insurance on children because they are told by a salesman that it is the loving, responsible thing to do.

Insurance on children is a life insurance salesman's dream. The pitch goes something like this: "Because you love your children, you will want to buy life insurance on them, won't you?" If your answer is no, then it sounds as if you don't love your kids. If you love your children, why would it help to collect large sums of money if they don't live? It wouldn't. All life insurance belongs on the lives of income-providing parent(s), not the children.

Another ridiculous salesman's pitch is that if you insure a child while he or she is young, it guarantees the child's insurability later. There is a 99% chance that if a child reaches 18, he or she will be insurable anyway, so why spend money insuring against an improbable event?

Life insurance is also sold as a method of financing college. Whole life insurance, as a method of providing a $5,000 college education fund for your child, is far too inefficient to be called an investment and should not be considered. A $50,000 life insurance policy on a one-year-old child will cost $250 per year and be worth $5,000 when the child reaches college age. By the time the child reaches 18, your cash value would be $5,000. Two hundred and fifty dollars per year invested correctly in a mutual fund family could create a college fund of $40,000, in the same amount of time. I have never yet met a family who paid for a college education from life insurance on children, even though tens of thousands have fallen for the bait.

The same reasoning applies to your spouse. If your spouse is responsible for a significant amount of family income or takes the place of paid child care, he or she is a financial asset, and inexpensive term insurance makes sense until the kids are grown. If your spouse does not work or take care of children, or intends to work only part-time, your spouse is technically a financial liability and insurance is both unnecessary and financially foolish.

Strategy #49
AS YOU GET OLDER, CARRY LESS LIFE INSURANCE.

As you get older, your responsibilities usually decrease and so does your need for life insurance. Your objective is to become self-insured—to build enough wealth that you will have no need for life insurance at all. The insurance salesman will incorrectly tell you the older you are, the more insurance you need. Why? Because in sales school he was taught that the older you get, the more money you will have that could be spent on life insurance premiums. Remember the purpose of life insurance is to replace income from a job you would no longer have if you were retired. As you get older, more of your income should come from non-job-related sources, and if you saved/invested correctly, the investment income will continue even after you are gone.

Strategy #50
SEPARATE YOUR LIFE INSURANCE FROM YOUR INVESTMENTS.

Strip away all of the sales gimmicks and what you have left are only two basic types of life insurance policies: life insurance with a savings plan, and life insurance with no savings plan. Your strategy: never use life insurance as an investment. Let's first look at those policies that combine insurance and a so-called investment plan.

WHOLE LIFE INSURANCE

Whole life is a plan in which your money goes into a "hole," never to be seen again. Whole life was the first major life insurance/investment combination and has literally cost millions of people unnecessary billions of dollars since its inception.

Only in the last few years has it come to light that "whole life" is not an investment at all. Your cash value is really the property of the insurance company and makes the insurance you are buying overpriced by up to 600%.

Whole life policies usually have level premiums (equal yearly installments) and claim to build tax-deferred cash value. That claim is misleading. When you die, your entire cash value somehow disappears into the coffers of the insurance company. Your beneficiary receives only the face value of the policy or the cash value, whichever is greater, but not both.

Let's say at age 35 a father buys a level-premium whole life policy with a death benefit of $100,000. After paying a premium of $1,300 each year for 20 years, he has accumulated $35,400 of cash value. If he dies, you could expect his beneficiary to collect $100,000 plus the $35,400 cash value, a total of $135,400. However, the beneficiary receives only $100,000—not $135,400. The so-called investment is no investment at all, but only his heirs will discover the deception when the insured is gone. (See following chart.)

If the insured decides to borrow the $35,400 of cash value, they've got him again. His death benefit is reduced by the amount he has borrowed plus interest owed.

THE DISAPPEARING CASH VALUE

At age 35, a father buys a whole life insurance policy under the following terms:

$100,000	Death benefit (face value)
$1,300	Yearly premium
$35,400	Cash value after 20 years

At age 55 he dies.

What he thought his family would receive:		What his family actually received:
$100,000	Death benefit	$100,000
35,400	Cash value	0
$135,400	TOTAL	$100,000

The cash value of $35,400 becomes the property of the insurance company. Whole life is therefore an overpriced term insurance policy.

On a term insurance policy the amount paid to your heirs is the death benefit, the same as in the whole life example above. Whole life is therefore just a grossly overpriced term insurance policy.

The truth about whole life insurance is often enshrouded by appealing promises that turn out to be marketing hot air. Here are a few you will hear and why they are misleading.

"YOU CAN BORROW YOUR CASH VALUE."

If you need money, you can borrow your cash value at a low interest rate like 5 to 8%. What a benefit! The insurance company is charging you interest on your own money that you overpaid in premiums. If you die before the loan or interest is paid back, it is deducted from the proceeds.

"YOUR POLICY WILL EVENTUALLY BE PAID UP."

Most everyone loves the idea of a paid-up policy; at a point in time that means no more yearly premiums. In reality, a paid-up policy is created only by overpaying your premiums. The overpayment will eventually be used to pay your future premiums. Therefore, all paid-up polices are just prepaid policies.

"YOU'LL BE EARNING INTEREST."

One of the biggest financial revelations of the century was when someone discovered that whole life policies were paying an average of only 1.3% interest. Worse yet is the fact that you never receive it. Through a slick maneuver, the insurance company has found a way to pay all of the interest, not to the policyholder or beneficiary, but to itself. The interest earned is added to your cash value, and the cash value, remember, becomes the property of the insurance company, unless you surrender the policy or live until it matures.

"YOUR INSURANCE POLICY IS A TAX SHELTER."

Another myth is that somehow life insurance enjoys some special tax status. For instance, you are told you can borrow money from your insurance policy tax free. You can borrow money from anywhere tax free—from a bank, through an equity loan on your home, or from your brother-in-law. There are no income taxes on borrowed money.

You are told that insurance proceeds, at the time of death, are income-tax exempt. After death, there is no income tax on any part of an estate. Insurance proceeds and the rest of the estate are subject to estate taxes.

"IF YOU BUY LIFE INSURANCE WHEN YOU'RE YOUNG, IT WILL COST LESS."

It is true that yearly premiums are less when you are younger, but only because you will pay greater total premiums over a longer period of time. The same faulty reasoning would apply if an automobile salesman told you, "Finance your car for five years, instead of two. It costs less." Actually, the car, like buying insurance, would cost far more. Only the monthly payments would be lower. The only reason to buy life insurance when you are young is financial protection for your family.

"I'VE GOT A WHOLE LIFE POLICY THAT WILL GIVE YOUR HEIRS FACE VALUE *PLUS* THE CASH VALUE."

Yes, you can buy a whole life policy that pays both. The gimmick? The premiums are much higher than the already overpriced regular whole life policy. How much higher? You guessed it. By an amount that with minimal interest is necessary to pay the heirs the extra cash value.

UNIVERSAL LIFE INSURANCE

"Earn 6 to 8%, guaranteed" claim the never-ending parade of universal life ads. Universal life is nothing more than a term life insurance policy coupled with an investment plan. The investment can pay fixed interest rates or, in some cases, can be self-directed into mutual funds. However, only the amount of premium above the cost of insurance, fees, and commissions goes into the investment. Universal life insurance makes a poor wealth-building, wealth-protecting plan for many reasons.

Here is an example that will illustrate why. A 45-year-old man buys a universal life policy combining a $100,000 death benefit with an investment projecting a yearly return of 8% for 20 years. He pays $2,000 in premiums per year or $167 a month. He is paid the 8% only on the money that goes into the investment, that is, what is left from the $2,000 premiums after the fees, commissions, and, of course, the cost of the insurance itself are deducted. In a typical universal life policy, the first-year fees and commissions alone can amount to $600. He loses 30% of his $2,000 to fees and commissions before he earns a dime on the investment portion.

Let's say tomorrow afternoon you stroll into your bank and put your $2,000 into a certificate of deposit. "No problem," the new accounts officer tells you. "By the way, there is a $600 charge for opening the account." How quickly would you be out the door, into the parking lot, leaving only a trail of dust behind you? Losing the money to a life insurance company makes no more sense than losing money to the bank. The actual yearly investment return is less than 6% for the first ten years. Each year in a universal life policy, the hidden cost of the insurance increases, further reducing the amount that goes into the investment, but you never see it happening because your premium remains the same. A high surrender charge penalty is the insurance company's method of attempting to make it impractical for you to change your mind and drop the policy. Those companies that charge the least in front-end fees usually have the biggest surrender charges. You get nailed one way or the other. "Well," you might respond, "at least 8% is a fair return when money market rates are 4 to 5%." Is it? More fine print states that the 8% interest rate is guaranteed for the first year only, and then the interest rate you actually receive can drop to as low as 3%. Some guarantee.

SINGLE-PREMIUM WHOLE LIFE INSURANCE

Single-premium whole life insurance is sold primarily as a tax shelter, not as insurance. The concept is simple enough—you deposit a single payment of between $5,000 and $500,000 into a plan that combines a whole life policy with an investment. You are supposedly able to accumulate earnings over the years, which can then be borrowed with no taxes, to be used as your income during retirement. There are six major drawbacks.

1. You are buying the wrong type of life insurance—whole life.
2. You must buy insurance to qualify for the investment, so less than 100% of your money is invested.
3. There are heavy front-end commissions and fees, big surrender charges that reduce the investment benefit, or you receive 6 to 8% per year on an investment that should pay you 10 to 12%, based on the return the insurance company is getting on your money.
4. There is a better tax-sheltered investment, often available from the same insurance companies, called an annuity. The annuity earnings compound tax free as long as the money is left invested. The best tax-sheltered annuities are those that offer mutual funds as investments (see Chapter 34, "Self-Directed Annuities").
5. You are told the major benefit is that you may borrow money tax free from a single-premium whole life policy. The truth is you may borrow money from anywhere tax free. There is no income tax on borrowed money.

TERM INSURANCE—THE RIGHT INSURANCE

Term insurance is pure insurance, no frills, no bells and whistles, no savings plan. Term is the least expensive life insurance, often 70% to 80% less than the insurance-plus-investment policies. Term pays salesmen far less in commissions and therefore is seldom offered if you don't ask. Because whole life and universal life insurance policies, as we have seen, contain poor investments, term insurance is the life insurance choice of all knowledgeable insurance buyers. That leaves you with only two major decisions: determining what is the best kind of term insurance for you and then finding it at the best price.

There are three types of term insurance:

ANNUALLY RENEWABLE TERM (ART)

You buy a policy for one year at the end of which you receive a renewal notice for the next year's premium. The younger you are, the lower the rates begin, increasing each year by a few dollars. ART is usually the least expensive and the best value of the three types of term insurance if your need for protection is one to four years. The insurance is guaranteed renewable every year as long as you pay your premium. As you get older, your life expectancy decreases, so the yearly premium increases.

DECREASING TERM
With decreasing term, your yearly premiums remain the same over the term but the amount of your insurance decreases. Decreasing term is used for both mortgage insurance and credit life insurance and is overpriced by up to 400%.

LEVEL PREMIUM TERM (LPT)
You choose a policy period, five, ten, fifteen, or twenty years. Both your premium and the amount of the insurance remain constant over the entire period. The longer the term chosen, the higher the yearly premiums. The advantage of a good level term policy is that your premiums remain constant each year—no increase. The disadvantage is that your level term premiums are higher in the first few years than the premiums on an annually renewable term policy, but they are lower in later years. If you are struggling financially, you may need lower ART payments, but level premium term insurance with its fixed yearly premiums over the term is often the best choice of term insurance for most families.

Some level premium policies require that you requalify after each term, others are guaranteed renewable.

Strategy #51
BUY ENOUGH TERM INSURANCE THAT, IF INVESTED AT 12% PER YEAR, IT WILL REPLACE CURRENT FAMILY INCOME.

The purpose of life insurance is to keep your family financially alive if you die. The optimum insurance plan is to buy enough insurance so that if the amount received by your family is invested at 12%, your family will have the same income as before. In other words, the interest income from the investment would replace your former income, which your family could no longer get. The amount of insurance that if invested at 12% would replace your job income is exactly 8.5 times your yearly salary. If your salary for instance is $50,000, the 8.5 times multiple would mean that you would have a term life policy for approximately $425,000.

If you are short of cash, living paycheck-to-paycheck, there is a second alternative, the minimum plan.

Studies have shown that it could cost your spouse and children as little as 50% as much money if you are gone to maintain the remaining family members' lifestyle. Many of your current expenses could be eliminated—expenses such as club memberships, family vacations, and entertaining. Therefore, the minimum amount of life insurance you would carry would replace 50% of your income if invested at 12%. That amount would be 4.25 times your income.

Refer to the Life Insurance Planning Chart that appears on the next page. Locate your approximate current family income in column A. In column B, you will find the amount of insurance that if invested at 12% would replace 100% of your family income. Columns C–J show you some sample low premiums of guaranteed level term rates available to purchase the amount of insurance you need. Later in this book, you will learn how to invest with a safe annual return of 12% and more.

The thousands of dollars you save by buying the right amount of the right kind of term insurance should be used during your lifetime to build your wealth, not the insurance company's.

Strategy #52
BUY ANNUALLY RENEWABLE TERM (ART) INSURANCE AND SWITCH COMPANIES EVERY FOUR YEARS.

Your objective is to buy the least expensive life insurance that provides the greatest financial protection. The ART system is one way to accomplish that goal.

Insurance companies, believe it or not, often offer the first three or four years of annually renewable term insurance at less than competitive rates—the way a grocery sells a carton of milk at a loss just to get you in the store. If companies offer the first few years of ART for less than competitive rates, why couldn't you just change companies every three or four years to take advantage of a new set of lower rates? You can and that's the basis of the ART system.

The rates for the same person at the same age are dramatically different between companies. The rates vary as much as 30%.

Some companies have rates as much as 100% more than others. You begin this strategy by picking the company with the lowest initial premiums for your age, but be sure to compare rates based upon three to four years.

LIFE INSURANCE PLANNING CHART

(A) You or Spouse's Current Income	(B) Approximate Amount Invested at 12% that would replace Income 100%	Yearly premium* cost for first 15 Years of amount of insurance shown in column B							
		(C) Age 25	(D) Age 30	(E) Age 35	(F) Age 40	(G) Age 45	(H) Age 50	(I) Age 55	(J) Age 60
$20,000	170,000	210	210	217	271	370	543	805	1230
25,000	210,000	243	243	251	318	439	653	976	1501
30,000	250,000	275	275	285	365	508	763	1148	1773
35,000	300,000	316	316	327	423	594	900	1362	2112
40,000	350,000	357	357	369	481	681	1038	1577	2452
45,000	375,000	378	378	390	510	724	1107	1684	2622
50,000	420,000	415	415	428	563	802	1230	1877	2927
60,000	500,000	480	480	495	655	940	1450	2150	3470
70,000	600,000	562	562	579	771	1113	1725	2649	4149
80,000	675,000	624	624	642	858	1243	1932	2971	4659
90,000	750,000	685	685	705	945	1373	2138	3293	5168
100,000	850,000	767	767	789	1061	1546	2413	3722	5847
125,000	1,000,000	890	890	915	1235	1805	2825	4365	6865
150,000	1,250,000	1095	1095	1125	1525	2238	3515	5438	8563
175,000	1,500,000	1300	1300	1335	1815	2670	4200	6510	10260
200,000	1,750,000	1505	1505	1545	2105	3103	4888	7583	11958
300,000	2,500,000	2120	2120	2775	2975	4400	6950	10800	17050
400,000	3,400,000	2858	2858	2931	4019	5957	9425	14661	23161
500,000	4,200,000	3514	3514	3603	4947	7341	11625	18093	28593
750,000	6,250,000	5195	5195	5325	7255	10888	17263	26888	42513
1,000,000	8,400,000	6958	6958	7131	9819	14607	23175	36111	57111

All rates are guaranteed 15-year level term. *Rates shown are for a preferred-risk non-smoking male in good health. Female rates are equal or less.

If you stay with the same company, no matter which one, notice that your premiums go up each year.

The downside to the ART system is that you normally must get a new physical every time you apply with a new company, so excellent health, occupation, and habits should be considered.

$100,000 ART INSURANCE COMPARISON CHART

A	B	C	D	E	F	G
	Federal Kemper	Federal Kemper 1st yr.	First Colony	First Colony 1st yr.	Jackson National	Jackson National 1st yr.
Age	1st 10 yrs.	premium	1st 10 yrs.	premium	1st 10 yrs.	premium
29	($115)	$115	$133	$133	$149	$149
30	120		142		155	
31	129		153		161	
32	136	115	163	134	169	149
33	144		172		177	
34	(157)		190		185	
35	168	116	204	(136)	193	151
36	186		218		204	
37	200		233		218	
38	215	117	250	136	234	(158)

Note: Columns C, E, and G show your first-year premium if you bought the policy at the age indicated on the left. Columns B, D, and F show your premium at each age if you kept the same policy since age 29.

Had you remained in Federal Kemper for ten years, your tenth-year premium would be $215 (column B). By using the ART switching system as illustrated, your tenth-year premium at Jackson National would have been $158 (column G), a savings of $57 or 26% for that year alone.

You may wonder, "If you can save that much money by changing companies every few years, could you save more by changing every year?" Yes, however the extra $10 to $20 per year saving would not be worth the extra effort of the paperwork and medical exam. Plus, as you might suspect, no company we know of will let you.

Buy the new policy before you cancel existing policies to make certain you are still insurable. The final step is canceling your existing investment insurance and reinvesting the cash value. The choice is yours. You can use your money to make yourself or the insurance company wealthy, but not both.

ART is not only the right kind of life insurance if your need is a guaranteed short period of one to four years, but it's also prudent if you expect a change from a hazardous occupation or sports activity that is preventing your purchase of "preferred rate" level term.

ART could also be utilized by a person who quits smoking for the one to two years they are waiting to qualify of a nonsmoker level term.

Strategy: Replace your existing whole life and universal life policies with term insurance.

There is only one valid financial reason for buying or keeping whole life or universal life policies at any age: your health has deteriorated and you are no longer insurable. You are always better off with term insurance and investing the difference yourself while you are insurable, reinvesting your cash value in self-directed, tax-deferred annuities. Refer to Strategy #54 for details.

Never replace a policy until a new policy is issued. The strategies to replace whole life, universal life, single-premium life, and other cash-value policies, which attempt to combine investing and life insurance protection, are prudent for the majority. The strategies of replacing various types of term insurance with new policies that will provide either the same amount of life insurance protection for less premium, or more life insurance protection for the same premium, are mathematically intelligent decisions. But you should never quit paying for any insurance policy that you may replace until a new policy has been issued by the new insurance company and it has accepted your premium payment. It is vital that you do not go one minute without the insurance protection you need. It is better to pay one month's premium to two companies for double protection than to risk a loss while not insured.

Strategy #53
DON'T CONVERT YOUR COMPANY LIFE INSURANCE TO A PERSONAL INSURANCE POLICY WHEN YOU LEAVE A COMPANY.

When your company offers you a health insurance policy as a company benefit, a nonoptional life insurance policy is normally included in the package. Including life insurance is one way an insurance company can add almost guaranteed profits since the mortality rate, or number of insured that will die each year in any large group of people covered by life insurance, is fairly predictable. Total payments of doctor and hospital claims for the same group of insured people, however, are not predictable. The amount of insurance can range from $5,000 to $50,000. Often managers or executives are covered with up to $50,000 of life insurance as a company benefit since the company-paid premiums are not taxable to the insured on up to that amount of coverage.

If you are like the average employee who changes jobs seven times during a working career, chances are you will be faced with hidden health and life insurance decisions when you leave a job. By federal law, whenever you leave a company with 20 or more employees, whether your departure is voluntary or you are terminated, you must be given the option of converting your company health insurance policy, including the life insurance, from a company to a personal policy for up to 18 months. The difference is that when it becomes a personal, not a group policy, your rates go up astronomically, and your company stops paying any of the premiums unless you had something in your employment contract to the contrary. One of the best ways to cut these huge personal health premiums is to drop the unnecessary or poor-value coverages, like the life insurance. When you convert a policy, the only reason you should consider keeping the life insurance is if you are in poor health or otherwise uninsurable.

The overpriced life insurance should be dropped for two important reasons. First, the life insurance usually goes from term insurance into very expensive whole life insurance on the personal policy. By keeping it you would be violating one of the important strategies discussed earlier—never buy low-benefit, high-priced whole life. Since most people never read the health insurance conversion terms, but only gasp at the new premiums, this insurance company gimmick goes unnoticed! You are paying whole life rates, but the insurance company knows you will probably drop the policy within a year, losing all the premiums, including cash values.

Second, you want only one life insurance policy on yourself and at the lowest possible term rates—one policy whose face value is enough to cover everything from loss of income to the payoff of your mortgage or other debts, as determined by you. Following the strategies in this chapter will help you obtain that one optimum policy.

Strategy #54
USE THE LIFE-INSURANCE-TO-ANNUITY TRANSFER RULES TO TAX-PROTECT INSURANCE CASH VALUES.

When you drop a whole life or universal life policy for any reason and receive the cash value, you are subject to taxes on the earnings but not on the original principal amount you paid in. If you have a significant amount of earnings or taxable cash value, transfer the money into a self-directed tax-deferred annuity. The tax laws allow a tax-free exchange. Your cash value is now yours and is tax protected. The best annuities are those that offer mutual funds as investments. There is no "rollover" provision for cash values. (See Chapter 34, "Self-Directed Annuities.") See Strategy #57, #2.

Strategy #55
BORROW AND REINVEST YOUR LIFE INSURANCE CASH VALUE.

A second alternative, if your health makes you uninsurable, is to borrow the cash value of your current whole life policy at 5 to 8% interest and reinvest at 15 to 25% using the investment strategies in the investment section of this book. Borrowing your cash value is a tax-free transaction except in some single-premium life policies.

Under the new tax laws, interest paid on borrowed insurance money is not deductible if used for personal reasons, but you can deduct the interest if the borrowed money is used as investment capital, or for business expenses.

Strategy #56
DON'T GIVE LIFE INSURANCE PROCEEDS TO YOUR HEIRS IN A LUMP SUM.

Write your will or trust so that life insurance money is invested according to your instructions, and not given to family members in a lump sum. Only then can you be certain that the money will last until the kids are grown and continue to provide for your spouse. After the kids are grown, you can have the principal split among your family members. In eight out of ten cases studied, lump-sum insurance proceeds left to families were totally gone in one to five years through unintentional mismanagement or poor financial advice. You will find a complete explanation of how to accomplish this and the paperwork for an insurance investment trust in my book *Financial Self-Defense.*

Strategy #57
REORGANIZE YOUR TOTAL LIFE INSURANCE PLAN.

Now you're ready to make your move to straighten out your lifetime life insurance plan. Here is how:

1. Determine the amount of term insurance you need using Strategy #51.
2. Call The Insurance ClearingHouse at 1-800-522-2827. The Insurance ClearingHouse is an organization I personally set up with Buddy and Jo Hewell, the Charles J. Givens Organization's insurance consultants, to help you put together a better term life insurance plan without having to listen to the all-too-frequently misleading insurance sales pitches. Buddy and Jo Hewell, the directors of The Insurance ClearingHouse, are licensed to do business in all states except North Dakota, and they will help you find a policy at good rates. Although it was created primarily for Charles J. Givens Organization members, there is no charge for this service to you as a reader of this book. The expenses of The ClearingHouse are paid by commissions received from the insurance companies with which the policies are placed.

Buy insurance as if you expected to die tomorrow and invest as if you expected to live forever. The majority of your financial plan, therefore, should be devoted to living.

REORGANIZING YOUR TOTAL INSURANCE PLAN

The strategies for insurance that you are learning should be used together to create one comprehensive, low-cost insurance plan. A typical family of four can easily pay as much as $5,300 on the myriad of apparently logical insurance options (see column A, following page). By using the life insurance and casualty insurance strategies in Chapters 3–6, they cut their insurance costs to $1,850, a savings of $3,450 per year.

Using column C, write in your current insurance premiums. As you use the strategies in these chapters, enter your new reduced premiums in column D and total to determine your overall yearly insurance savings. Over the next 20 years you will save 20 times that amount!

	Typical Family		You	
	A	B	C	D
Type of Insurance	Before	After	Before	After
Life Insurance on Children	200	0		
Universal Life Insurance	1,500	0		
Term Life Insurance	0	300		
Credit Life Insurance on Loans	200	0		
Automobile Insurance	1,100	600		
Specialty Insurance	200	0		
Mortgage Insurance	600	300		
Hospitalization Insurance	600	300		
Homeowner's Insurance	300	200		
Rental Car Insurance (vacation)	100	0		
Umbrella Liability Insurance	0	150		
Disability Insurance	500	0		
Other				
TOTAL	$5,300	$1,850		

Chapter 7

GIVE YOURSELF CREDIT

'Tis against some Men's Principle to pay interest, and seems against others' interest to pay the Principle.

Benjamin Franklin
Poor Richard's Almanac
1753

GET CONTROL OF YOUR CREDIT BUREAU FILE AND ESTABLISH GOOD CREDIT HABITS

The bank must have slipped because it issued me my first credit card just before Christmas in 1965. The timing couldn't have been more appropriate. As in other gift-buying seasons, I was flat broke. I immediately charged $300 for a magnificant Tyco "HO" gauge miniature railroad layout, a present for my boys—in one thousand easy-for-a-child-to-assemble pieces. Ever since my mother sold my prized Lionel train set to get money for food, I had dreamed of the day when I would have sons of my own old enough to help me disguise my desire to recreate my youth.

Because I wasn't a child, I was in the attic until 6:30 A.M. Christmas morning putting together the Ping-Pong-table-sized train layout. Time was running out, along with my alertness and patience. The airplane glue, with its high concentration of acetone, put a smile on my face, but made me feel as if I were putting all those little plastic pieces together with gloves on. No matter. Rob, age three, and Chuck, age four, were elated; Dad was exhausted. It was my Christmas "biggy" and I had pulled it off. Pride lit up the room as chemical smoke poured from the tiny engine, puffing its way through plastic towns, switches, and papier-mâché mountains.

By three o'clock in the afternoon, I was asleep on the couch while the train in the playroom began a perilous journey. Waking to the sound of a hammer striking metal, I stumbled into the garage to see Chuck, still in his blue Christmas robe, dismantling the expensive, heavily financed engine into a hundred pieces. Resisting the temptation to faint, and holding back the tears, I screamed, "Chuck, what are you doing?"

"Dad, this is so neat. I just want to see how it works."

How can you get angry with a curious four-year-old? The train was gone, like so many Christmas toys, in a few, short hours. But the payments continued through the following Christmas. That was my first lesson about credit. Payments can continue long after the enjoyment is gone.

There seems to be no end to the young couples I meet who have managed to create, quite unintentionally, the same kind of credit dilemmas, by charging when cash is short and hoping the money will be there when each payment comes due, stacking one monthly payment on top of another until nothing is left for the necessary expenses.

There are three uses of credit listed here from worst to best.

THE THREE BASIC USES OF CREDIT

Worst—to purchase *perishables,* such as meals, gas, groceries, airline tickets

Better—to purchase *depreciables,* such as automobiles, furniture, clothes

Best—to purchase *appreciables,* such as mutual funds, a home, or other investments

---

Charging perishables is the least desirable and most misused form of credit. It gets you into credit trouble with nothing to show for it. One month after you charge an expensive meal, your minimum payment covers the potatoes, the next month the steak, and in a few months the dessert. While buying this month's food, you're still paying for last month's feasts. Payments linger long after the goods or services are gone.

Purchasing depreciables on credit is not quite as bad. These are goods and services that will never again be worth what you paid for them, although their use and enjoyment will at least last as long as the payments. A better use of credit, yes, but you end up stacking long-term payments on top of long-term payments that can eventually bury you.

The best use of credit by far is borrowing money at a low rate and investing in appreciables with a higher rate of return, or in something that will grow in value. In other words, making money work for you. Appreciables include a home with a mortgage, margined mutual fund shares, rental real estate, and a leveraged business or IRA. Leverage is the use of borrowed money to make money—often called using OPM (other people's money).

Financial success requires practiced discipline, and there is no better way to practice than with credit management. It is not necessary or wise to cut up your credit cards as some would have you think. Developing discipline is the answer, and the following strategies will get you started—painlessly.

Strategy #58
PAY OFF CREDIT CARD PERISHABLE PURCHASES EVERY MONTH.

With credit cards it is all too easy to let the money you owe on perishable purchases pile up month after month until you are swamped in debt. On your credit card statement is a box called "new purchases this month." The minimum you can pay if you ever want to get out of credit card debt is what you owe for your new purchases for the month plus the minimum required payment.

Pay off the credit card perishable purchases you make this month with a check next month when you receive the bill. Never wait until you think you have the money—that time may never come. If you charge $100 for gasoline and meals, pay $100. Begin now.

Strategy #59
DEDUCT A CREDIT CARD CHARGE IN YOUR CHECK REGISTER AS IF YOU MADE THE PURCHASE WITH A CHECK.

Count the money gone—it is. Every time you make a credit card charge, enter the amount in your checkbook as if you had written a check for the goods or service. Circle the amount of the charged item to differentiate the charge from a purchase by check and enter "C.C." in the check-number box to indicate a credit card charge. Deduct the amount of the charge from your bank balance. Although the money is still in your account, you have virtually set it aside for payment on your credit card bill when it arrives. At the end of the month, the circled items represent everything you charged on all credit cards. The money has already been deducted from your bank balance and is available for payment.

Think of it. No more statement shock. No more frustrated remarks like, "I couldn't possibly have charged that much this month." As you deduct each charge in your checkbook, you will become more aware of what you are really spending. The plastic fantastic has no mercy, but credit cards cannot control your financial life unless you allow them to.

Strategy #60
DEVELOP A POWERFUL CREDIT PROFILE WITH THE "BIG 8."

To develop a positive, powerful credit profile, qualify yourself in as many categories as you can based on the chart on page 83. The more categories under which you qualify, the easier it is to get credit when you need it.

Your credit profile, good or bad, will determine how easy or difficult it is to get bank loans, auto loans, personal loans, credit cards, or any other form of financing. Your profile can also determine what interest rates you pay, higher or lower, and in some cases will also be a determining factor in whether you get a certain job or even an applied-for larger life insurance policy. A positive, powerful credit profile does its own explaining so that you don't have to. Your objective is to consciously and constantly upgrade your credit profile.

You can survive in America if you have poor credit—or, worse yet, no credit—but poor credit is a definite handicap to wealth building. It is easier to play the piano with all ten fingers than with bandaged thumbs.

You must be willing to go public with who and what you are, no matter what the so-called offshore promoters tell you about privacy.

THE "BIG 8"
ELEMENTS OF A POWERFUL CREDIT PROFILE
(In order of importance)

1. A positive, up-to-date credit report
2. A home with a mortgage
3. An American Express card and/or Diners Club card
4. A job you've held for a year or more
5. A current or paid-off bank loan
6. A MasterCard or Visa card
7. A department store credit card
8. A telephone in your name

Going public is accomplished by making available your financial statement, your tax returns, and your credit bureau data. The first two you furnish, the third will be obtained from the credit bureau by prospective employers and lenders.

Loan and mortgage applications are usually approved or rejected based on a point system. One to six points are assigned to each item in eight different categories. If the number of points you score overall exceeds a certain total, determined by the lender, your loan is approved; if less than the required total, your loan is automatically rejected.

Following is a model of a credit-scoring process taken directly from the procedures book of a finance company that will let you score yourself (page 84). About 18 points is the minimum score required to pass the credit test. The more you score the better your chances.

Owning a home with a mortgage shows stability and scores more points than most items on a credit application. It does not matter if you were required to qualify for the original mortgage, or if you simply assumed a no-qualifying FHA or VA mortgage.

An American Express card has almost as much clout in the financial world as a mortgage. To qualify for the card, you must show an income of over $15,000 a year and pay the balance each month. Diners Club finishes a close second to American Express. Diners Club reports on its cardholders to all major credit bureaus; American Express does not. The American Express green card is good; the gold and platinum even better. Always list your American Express or Diners Club card number first on any credit application. Pay the fee; your credit profile is worth it. If your application is rejected, file a new one every six months until they give you a card, or have a cardholder, such as your parents, issue an extra card on their account until you can qualify on your own.

A current or paid-off bank loan, a MasterCard or Visa, and a department store credit card are indications that others have been willing to extend you credit. If you don't have these credit references, it will pay you to get them whether you need the credit or not.

Your payment habits, good or poor, are shown on your credit report.

Factors	Points	Your Score	Factors	Points	Your Score
Marital Status			*Monthly Loan &*		
Married	1	____	*Credit Cd Pymts*		
Not Married	0	____	Zero to $200	1	____
			Over $200	0	____
Age					
21 to 25	0	____	*Credit History*		
26 to 64	1	____	Loan—Most Banks	2	____
65 and Over	0	____	*Residence*		
Monthly Income			Rent Unfurnished	1	____
Up to $600	1	____	Own Without Mtge	4	____
$601 to $800	2	____	Own With Mtge	3	____
$801 to $1,000	4	____	Any Other	0	____
Over $1,000	6	____	*Previous*		
In Addition			*Residence*		
Phone in Your			0–5 Years	0	____
Name	2	____	6 Years and Up	1	____
Checking or					
Savings	2	____			

Strategy #61
CHECK AND CORRECT YOUR CREDIT BUREAU FILE ONCE A YEAR.

The credit bureau is the first place your potential creditors and employers will check. A positive, up-to-date credit file is your responsibility, not that of the credit bureau. A positive, up-to-date credit bureau file is something you create, not something that happens automatically. You have more control over your file than you may think.

All credit bureaus are governed by the Fair Credit Reporting Act passed by Congress in the mid-seventies. In a congressional subcommittee on credit bureau abuses, a story came to light of a man who lost his credit, job, wife (from the pressure), and finally took his own life because of totally incorrect information in his credit file, which he was unable to have removed. With the advent of new laws, the credit power is now in your corner.

My organization conducted a credit bureau accuracy study in 1979. To our surprise, we discovered that 24 out of 25 credit bureau reports contained incomplete or incorrect data. Wait until you see yours! One report showed a man married to his first wife, whom he hadn't seen in eight years, and working for a company that had been out of business for six years.

Every credit bureau, by law, must give you a complete, accurate report of everything, including your credit history and a list of every potential creditor and employer who has been given information from your credit file during the past year. Knowing what others know about you is half the battle.

To obtain a credit report, you are required to identify yourself by completing a mail-in form, or appearing at the credit bureau, and paying a nominal charge of about $10. If you live in a city of over 300,000 people, there may be two or more credit bureaus you will want to check. Look in the yellow pages under "Credit Reporting Agencies."

Credit reports are easy to read once you get the hang of it, and most come with explicit instructions. If you still have trouble, the credit agency is required by law to spend time with you at its office explaining your report.

The credit bureau uses a rating system with the letters O, R, or I, followed by a number from 0 to 9. O is a 30-to-90 day "open account." R represents "revolving accounts" such as credit cards and department store accounts, and I is used for "installment credit," such as an automobile or furniture loan. R-1 is the best, R-9 usually means the account was written off by the creditor because of a bankruptcy. Your goal, of course, is to get all of your accounts to R-1 or I-1 status. When you do, the credit world is yours. A few prompt payments will usually upgrade any account. Refer to the sample credit report (page 90) and code explanation (page 86).

CREDIT REPORT CODES

The following codes are used on a standard credit report like the one shown on page 90. When you receive a copy of your credit report, use these codes to determine the reported status of your accounts.

ECOA DESIGNATORS

The Equal Credit Opportunity Act designators explain who is responsible for the account and the type of participation you have with the account.

J - Joint—Husband and wife are jointly responsible

I - Individual—Only the person whose name is on the account is responsible

U - Undesignated–No other designation was reported

S - Shared—An account on which two or more people who are not spouses are responsible

M - Maker—The borrower on a loan or mortgage

C - Co-Maker—A co-signer on a debt who becomes responsible if the debtor defaults

A - Authorized User—An authorized user of an account in someone else's name

T - Terminated—Account closed

Letter Codes

Type of Account	Credit Report Code
Open Account (90 days)	O
Revolving—additional charges can be made at any time up to the credit limit	R
Installment (fixed number of payments) used for fixed amount accounts for major purchases like furniture or automobiles	I

Number Codes

Current Manner of Payment	Payment Code
Account too new to rate or credit has been approved but not used	0
Pays account as agreed—the best rating possible	1
Pays 30 to 60 days late or one payment late	2
Pays 60 to 90 days late or two payments late	3
Pays 90 to 120 days late or three payments late	4
Pays later than 120 days	5
Filed Chapter 11 or other form of bankruptcy	7
Repossession—item purchased or secured was repossessed because of payment default	8
Bad debt; placed for collection—account was over 120 days past due and given to collection agency or attorney for collection	9

"Type of Account" and "Current Manner of Payment" are shown together in the "Credit History" section of a credit report under present status; e.g., "R1" means "revolving account, pays as agreed."

Credit reporting agencies do not evaluate your credit file, but make the information available to credit bureau members, who may be banks, mortgage companies, department stores, or other issuers of credit.

There are several strategies that will help you control your credit file. To order copies of TRW, Equifax, and CBI credit reports, you can call 1-800-876-9771.

Strategy #62
CORRECT ALL PERSONAL DATA ERRORS ON YOUR CREDIT FILE.

Included in your personal data are your address, Social Security number, employment history, income, and telephone. This part of a credit file is the easiest to correct, but often the most inaccurate. Since 24 out of 25 credit files contain errors, check even the most obvious entries.

Strategy #63
HAVE THE CREDIT BUREAU REVERIFY AND CORRECT ANY INCORRECT CREDIT DATA.

Your credit files may contain information about late payments that weren't late or bad accounts that are not yours. Request that the credit bureau reverify the incorrect data. The credit bureau has 30 days to check and correct the file. Check to be certain the corrected data is entered into your file.

Occasionally, your creditor's records are wrong and the reverified data will remain incorrect. If so, you will begin to get the runaround. Contact the creditor yourself to correct the errors and furnish canceled checks or other necessary information supporting your position. Obtain from the credit bureau a consumer dispute form like the one shown on page 91 and list all disagreements with the information in your file.

Strategy #64
HAVE ALL MISSING POSITIVE CREDIT DATA ADDED TO YOUR CREDIT FILE.

You will be surprised when you see your credit file at how much data and how many accounts are missing. Although there is no law or rule that you are required to supply any negative credit data about yourself, you have the right by law and the duty to yourself to have all the positive data and accounts added to your file.

Supply the credit bureau in writing with a list of all charge accounts, credit cards, loans, and mortgages you have kept current. Include the account numbers. Include loans that have been paid off or accounts no longer in use. The credit bureau must, within 20 days, verify the information you have supplied and add it to your file. Recheck your file after 60 days to be certain it includes the new data.

Strategy #65
ADD THE REST OF THE STORY TO YOUR CREDIT FILE.

You have the legal right to add your side of the story to your credit file, that is, why your payments were late, or that credit information in your file is incorrect and is being reverified. Add important information such as the fact that you were unemployed during the period when the payments were late or the fact that you moved and the bills went to the wrong address. One failure of the credit reporting system is that your file often shows how many times you have been 30, 60, or 90 days late in paying, but does not show how long ago. Add to your file the fact that all late payments were prior to a certain date, why they were late, and the fact that payments are now current. Your side of the story can make a difference to your potential creditors and employers.

Strategy #66
HAVE THE CREDIT BUREAU REMOVE ANY DEROGATORY INFORMATION OUTSIDE THE STATUTORY LIMITS.

Negative information can remain in your credit file no longer than seven years, except for bankruptcy, which has a legal credit file life of ten years. You have the right by law to a credit file that does not contain information older than these statutory limits. The credit bureau will remove older data but often only if you request it.

Strategy #67
USE SMALL CLAIMS COURT TO RESOLVE CREDIT DISPUTES.

What if you follow these instructions but can't seem to get a creditor to supply correct information to the credit bureau? Take 'em to court—small claims court, that is. For a small filing fee and without an attorney, you can, in most states, file a suit claiming damages from the incorrect information. You won't have to go to court since it would be far less expensive for the creditor to straighten out the error than to pay an attorney to fight your claim.

Strategy #68
IF YOU ARE REFUSED CREDIT, FIND OUT WHY.

If you get turned down for a loan or mortgage, you have the right by law to know why, and finding out is in your best interest. You must, within ten days of receiving the notice stating denial of credit, contact in writing the company that rejected you. The lender must tell you specifically why your application was denied. You can then decide if you should reapply with the same lender supplying new or corrected data or apply somewhere else.

Credit Report

NAME AND ADDRESS OF BUREAU MAKING REPORT CBI ATLANTA	__ in file __ single ref. __ trade __ EV&T __ Full __ Pres. Res.		
REGIONAL CENTER 3660 MAGUIRE BOULEVARD ATLANTA, GA	date rec'd. 09/22/91	date mailed 09/22/91	CBR rpt. inc. verified yes X no

CONFIDENTIAL REPORT	inquired as: **Joan Adams**	in file since 07/13/84
Report on (surname) **Joan Adams**	ss #: **265-71-4112**	spouse's name

Address: **100 Blue Lk. Dr.** city: **Atlanta** state: **GA** zip code:		resid. since	
Present employer: **Surprise Gift Shop**	position: **MGR**	mth. inc. **$1,755**	since 1984

Date of birth **12/15/55** number of depndts.		owns	buying X	rents	
Former address city state		zip code		from	to
Former employer: **1741 Riversedge Dr., Atlanta, GA**	position held	mth inc.		from	to
Other employers	date verified	position held	mth inc.	from	to

Credit History

firm—	code	date rptd.	date opd.	credit limit	term mths.	act. bal.	pres.	times	ecoa status	act. number rev'd.
Freedom	447ON119	08/91	09/90	2000	61	2027	R1	10J	I	3000436618
Barnett	497BB108	08/91	01/91	13,000	230	12k	I1	07I	I	7099-33280185
GECC-RC	906FF278	08/91	02/91	1,800	79	1626	R1	05I	C	CC735464-W21381
Robinson's	906DC86	07/91	12/90	195		178	R2	05I	I	10627305
Visa	491ON24219	08/91	05/91	1,500	64	1344	R1	01I	A	4060950001048946

Public Records and/or Summary of Other Information

Inquiries—

Con SVC	447AA36	09/22/91	1st at MES	458BB2852	05/14/91
Navy-VISA	491ON24219	05/05/91	GECC	404FF304	03/01/91
Barnett BK	447BB2575	01/14/91	MD Nat BK	801BB1845	01/13/91
Chrysler	447FA50	01/13/91	Don Mealey	447AU348	01/13/91

CONSUMER DISPUTE FORM

_____ _____
Area Code   Telephone No.

Personal Identification (Please Print or Type)

Name _____
        (Last)   (First)   (Middle Initial)   Suffix (Jr., Sr., etc.)

Present Address _____
                    (Street)   (City)   (State)   (Zip)

Former Address _____
                    (Street)   (City)   (State)   (Zip)

Date of Birth _____   Social Security Number _____
              (Month)   (Day)   (Year)

I RECENTLY RECEIVED A COPY OF THE REPORT CONTAINING MY CREDIT HISTORY, AND I DISAGREE WITH THE FOLLOWING INFORMATION:

CREDIT HISTORY

Name of Business	Account Number	Specific Nature of Disagreement

Public Record and Other Information Court or Business	Case Number	Nature of Disagreement

Other: (i.e., information from other credit bureaus, etc.)	Item	Nature of Disagreement

I understand that the information I have disputed will be rechecked when necessary at the source, and I will be notified of the results of this recheck.

_____   _____
              (Signature)   (Date)

Strategy #69
TO GET CREDIT AS A SMALL BUSINESS OWNER, INCORPORATE AND LIST YOURSELF AS AN EMPLOYEE.

If you've ever owned a business, you know that credit is tough to get until you can show substantial income, assets, and longevity. List yourself as an employee of the company instead of the owner and have your accountant verify your income with the lender. An alternative is to incorporate your business. For less than $50, plus the state filing fees, you can incorporate your small business without an attorney by contacting your state corporation commission for the forms and instructions. You then pay yourself a big salary and deduct your expenses as employee business expenses, furnishing copies of W-2 forms instead of tax forms to a prospective lender. Give the lender the phone number of your bookkeeper, accountant, or other involved persons to verify your employment and salary. If you want the credit, you must learn to play the game.

Strategy #70
WHEN BORROWING MONEY, NEVER TAKE "NO" FOR AN ANSWER.

Because one store, bank, or mortgage company turns you down doesn't mean everyone will. Make obtaining credit a game and say to yourself, "I will not be denied." I once saw a now successful young lady get turned down by five banks in two days for a $2,000 business loan. The sixth bank said yes. Where would she be today if she had given up after five banks?

Use your good credit to build your wealth. Work on overcoming the stigma of poor credit in the shortest time possible, but most of all, put your credit profile and credit power where they belong—in your own hands.

Chapter 8

CREATIVE CREDIT REPAIR

That which is creative must create itself.

John Keats
Poet
(1795–1821)

OBJECTIVE

GET CONTROL AND REPAIR YOUR CREDIT WHEN LIFE THROWS YOU A FINANCIAL CURVE.

If you want to build and maintain a powerful credit profile, credit control is the key. Unfortunately, no matter how well you plan, there will be events in your life that will throw you into a tailspin. The level of financial success you attain in life will have little to do with how successfully you deal with success, but a whole lot to do with how you deal with the rough spots.

Strategy #71
WHEN IN A FINANCIAL HOLE, PROTECT YOUR ATTITUDE EVEN MORE THAN YOUR CREDIT.

Life can create lots of different financial traumas, such as:

- letting thousands every year trickle away due to financial ignorance
- bankruptcy forced by overindulgence in debt
- layoffs, terminations, or company closings
- a business that doesn't pan out
- big losses in lousy investments

- huge, unexpected medical bills
- a costly divorce
- bailing children out of trouble, financial or otherwise
- a spouse who has to quit work

Almost all of us will experience one or more financial traumas during our lifetime. For that reason, even more important to protect than your credit is your attitude. If you become negative, start asking, "Why me?" and play the "If only this hadn't happened" game, rest assured it will take you twice as long to recover than it will if you accept where you are and approach your future with an "I will not be denied" attitude. Your mind is the only thing over which you can exercise total control, and during times of stress, your mind is the most important thing to control. It will work for you or against you. It's your choice.

Strategy #72
WHEN THE BILLS LOOM LARGER THAN THE AVAILABLE CASH, USE OFFENSIVE, NOT DEFENSIVE, STRATEGIES.

When there is more debt than money, most people want to hide, even to the point of not answering the phone for fear of another call from a creditor. Or they let the bills and overdue notices go unopened. There is a better way.

First of all, in debt as in sports, you gain an advantage by knowing what the opposing team is up to. Take advantage of the knowledge contained in calls and mail. Creditors will advise you of their every pending move in the hope that it will somehow inspire you to bring your account current. No need to wonder and worry.

Second, go on the offensive. When you know a payment is going to be late or you are laid off and will miss a couple of payments, call each of your creditors and tell them you'll be late and why. Be direct. Talk with integrity and don't make excuses or act wimpy. At the end of your explanation, use those magic words, "I need your help," and ask how you can work out the payments without damaging your credit rating. Local department stores, furniture stores, and appliance dealers with which you have accounts will almost always work something out with you and will promise not to give you a bad credit report. They want your business when you are back on your feet.

Credit card companies are not always so willing to help.

Remind them that about once a year, usually at Christmas, many credit card companies offer the "you can skip next month's payment" plan and ask if you can use that offer now. If you aren't getting anywhere with the account representative, ask for the supervisor, who has more authority to make special deals.

In the early seventies, when I ran my own consulting company, it would be either feast or famine. If you own your own business, you know what I mean. One month there were tens of thousands in the checking account, and a couple of months later the credit cards were maxed out and the bank account was drained. Every time I got in a bind, I went on the offense, and every time my creditors would pull me through. Each week I was behind I would call and give them an update. I bugged them, instead of the other way around. They trusted me because they knew I was neither what is known in the credit world as a "deadbeat," someone who doesn't pay, nor a "skipper," someone who leaves town owing money.

Be aggressive; when you're overdue, don't make your creditors call you. You will produce far better results than if you attempt to hide. Most importantly, when you're behind in payments, promise only what you can deliver and deliver what you promise. Miss a promised payment date and any trust you've built is instantly gone. Occasionally a credit card company will ask you to send in your credit card when your account is overdue, but it will often reissue the card as soon as your payments are caught up.

Be aggressive. Damage control is the key.

Strategy #73
DON'T LET THE CREDIT DOCTORS OPERATE ON YOUR WALLET.

You can hardly turn on the television today without seeing an ad claiming that your credit can be repaired—immediately— good as new. However, often you must first call a 900 number that will charge you $3 per minute or up to $35 for the call, just to give you the information.

If it's such a good deal, why do you have to pay big bucks for the call, you may ask. To pay for the expensive television time is the answer. But you don't stop paying there; you're just getting started. The next level of credit repair from your 900 call might cost you $200 to $1,200 if you fall for it. These high-priced credit doctors can do absolutely nothing more than you can do yourself with the credit repair and credit-file control strategies in this chapter.

Stay away from the mass-marketed credit repair clinics. At this point, they don't know anything you don't know despite their wild and bizarre claims.

Strategy #74
CONTACT CONSUMER CREDIT COUNSELORS WHEN YOU ARE DEEP IN THE DEBT DOLDRUMS AND DON'T SEE A WAY OUT.

Are there any good guys in the credit repair business? You bet there are. Often the legitimate organizations can help by working with both you and your creditors to come up with an agreement until you can get on solid footing. You must, however, know how to find them.

These credit repair organizations are nonprofit and are listed in the phone book under Consumer Credit Counselors. To find one in your area, check your phone book first, or write or call for a list of more than 400 offices:

National Foundation for Consumer Credit
8611 Second Avenue, Suite 100
Silver Spring, MD 20910
800-388-2227

These offices provide one-on-one financial counseling, educational programs, and debt management programs. The educational programs help people learn how to manage their money and use credit more wisely. The debt management programs attempt to negotiate lower interest charges or have them waived entirely as debtors pay off their debts by putting money monthly into a trust fund from which creditors are paid.

Strategy #75
TO GET OUT OF THE LATE-PAYMENT CYCLE, DO WHATEVER IT TAKES TO INCREASE SHORT-TERM CASH FLOW.

Miss a payment and the past-due notices and evening phone calls begin flying. It is, first of all, embarrassing to be behind on payments, like breaking a promise you made. Even worse, you wouldn't be late at all if you weren't already having trouble juggling your cash flow. Now, here come the pointed fingers from the collection departments attempting to make you feel like an unworthy, worthless person—all over a few bucks.

Late-payment problems can mushroom into major financial headaches and dilemmas such as these:

- Once you're behind in mortgage payments, your mortgage company won't accept less than the full amount due. You cannot just pay the current month's payment or a partial payment.
- The late charges can be staggering. The automatic late charges on a mortgage or rental agreement can be $50 to $100. On most credit cards the late charges are $15 to $20 per card per month. Quickly, the late charges add up to the level of another major payment in an already depleted budget. All money you pay is first applied to late charges before anything is applied toward the regular payments for principal or interest.
- Credit card companies react quickly and will ask you to stop using your cards or even cancel them, requiring you to change instantly the way you handle your money.
- You begin operating your checking account so close to the wire that a check or two bounces—twice—causing $40 to $100 in late fees, and before you can catch the problem, more checks bounce, which drains additional capital from your already empty account. You end up owing the bank money just to bring your checking account back to zero.
- You use your limited cash to pay bills other than utilities and then come home from work to find the electricity, telephone, or water to your house shut off, plus a notice of the fat reconnect charge required to restore the service.
- Get behind just three payments on the car, appliances, furniture, or other "secured" item, and the repossession team comes to carry it away, normally while all the neighbors are working in their yards.
- Your credit report suddenly begins to look as if it's been run through a shredding machine, preventing you from borrowing any money to get yourself caught up and out of the hole.
- Your telephone becomes the vehicle by which your creditors scream at you and dole out veiled threats.
- Your attitude suffers and you become depressed and short-tempered, and the rest of your personal and business life begins to suffer on a grand scale.

This is not a Stephen King horror novel you are reading. It is my estimate that more than 60% of all families go through part or all of this scenario one or many times. For some, it becomes a way of life, but it does not provide for much of a life.

The way to break the cycle and get some temporary relief and financial control is to increase your cash flow. Here are the strategies that will help you do just that over the short run. None are permanent solutions; they are onetime, short-term, cash-flow-increasing strategies that can help reverse the debt-payment dilemma. Discipline and planning and the right strategies are required in the long run.

STRATEGIES TO INSTANTLY INCREASE SHORT-TERM CASH FLOW
Check Those You Can Use

___ Check for old insurance policies with cash values. You want to get rid of these policies anyway.

___ Check the equity in your home (if you own one). A home equity loan could pay off your debts, consolidate the bills into one lower monthly payment, and best of all, you can claim one-third of the interest as a tax deduction. Get the loan before late payments show up on your credit report.

___ Borrow enough short-term money from relatives to keep you from getting behind and being assessed late charges or bad-check charges, which would throw you further into the hole.

___ Get involved in a small business in which you have little or no investment but from which, with a little tenacity and talking to enough people, you can immediately get some extra income.

___ Use every cash-saving strategy in this book including insurance and tax strategies.

___ Temporarily increase your allowances on your W-4 at work to increase your take-home pay. (See Strategies #191 to #195.)

___ Put in every hour of overtime you can if you get paid for it.

___ Get a second job for a few months until you are out of danger.

___ Borrow from your 401(k) or similar retirement plan interest and penalty free. (See Strategy #170.)

___ Use the hardship rules to withdraw money penalty free from your retirement plan. (See Strategy #169.)

___ Use a commercial debt consolidation loan only as a last resort. If you don't get the loan, the credit check may cause your credit file to be updated, uncovering all of the late payments, which up to that point were not even reported to the credit bureau.

Strategy #76
HAVE THE CREDIT BUREAU REMOVE ALL UNAUTHORIZED OR OUT-OF-DATE CREDIT INQUIRIES.

More and more often, I hear about people who were turned down for a loan, credit card, or other credit, not because their credit record wasn't good but because there were too many inquiries from merchants or prospective lenders into their credit file.

For the past few years and from now on, all major credit reporting agencies list on your credit report every merchant, lender, or prospective employer who has requested a copy of your credit bureau file. The result? If you have had too many inquiries during the past few months, you are denied credit. Why? Because it seems to a prospective creditor as if you:

- have gone charge-raving mad, or
- are desperate for capital and are looking everywhere, or
- are attempting to obtain as much credit card credit as possible by getting a dozen to a hundred different MasterCard and Visa cards.

The importance placed by creditors on the number of inquiries into a file began with the airing of a television commercial selling a course on how to get an unlimited number of credit cards. In those days of no cross-checks, a person with decent credit could apply at the same time to 20 different MasterCard/ Visa franchises and receive a full line of credit of, say, $2,500 from every one!

Someone could create an instant credit line of $50,000, whereas his or her income and credit file might support only $5,000 of debt. The idea of the program was that the borrower was to get a cash advance for the full amount, use the money to buy real estate, and resell at a profit before the payments came due. The problem, of course, is that real estate is seldom easy to turn over quickly at a profit. Hundreds who used the approach couldn't pay the money back and ended up filing for bankruptcy, costing the credit card companies untold millions. Since then, most issuers of credit have become squeamish about issuing credit to anyone with lots of inquiries made over a period of a few months, and they don't have or take the time to check the facts. They just deny it.

From your standpoint, you may find it to your financial advantage to apply for a car loan or mortgage at multiple lenders when looking for the best rates and terms. Or you may find yourself in a situation where you are applying at a second source because the first lender, which had already pulled your credit report, changed the rates or terms at the last minute or decided not to issue the credit.

If for whatever reason the number of inquiries into your credit file during the year begins to mount up, here are your strategies:

First, if you applied to one lender who changed the terms, add a note to your credit file stating the facts. (See Strategy #65.)

Second, when applying for new credit or loans, state on your application or verbally that you have applied for other credit, the reason, and the results. That way, the creditor will not be surprised at the extra inquiry. You will appear to be an honest, up-front person.

Third, use a little-known authorization rule to get unauthorized inquiries removed from your credit file. To inquire into your credit file, a credit bureau member/subscriber must have your written authorization. When you complete an application for credit, an authorization is often included in the fine print, but not always. You will often find inquiries into your credit file for which you gave no authorization. You have the absolute right to have these unauthorized inquiries removed immediately, which makes your credit file appear "cleaner." To get the unauthorized inquiries removed, send one copy of the form letter below to the credit bureau and another to the unauthorized inquirer. Check three weeks later to be certain the inquiry has been removed from your credit file.

FORM LETTER TO REMOVE UNAUTHORIZED CREDIT INQUIRIES

TO: (Credit Reporting Agency)   FROM: _____

_____   _____

_____   _____

          SS #: _____

RE: Unauthorized credit file inquiry

The following inquiry, which was not authorized by me, appears on my credit report.
Please remove reference to this inquiry immediately from my file.

          Merchant name _____   Address _____
          Account # _____

Strategy #77
AFTER A SERIES OF ON-TIME PAYMENTS, REQUEST THAT A MERCHANT OF LENDER RERATE YOU TO R-1, OR I-1.

A credit bureau does not give you a credit rating, only your creditors do. The credit bureau simply records data exactly as it is presented to it by each of your creditors. Let's say you fell behind in your payments to a department store. After reviewing your credit file, you notice that the store still shows a rating of "R-3, pays 60–90 days late" even though your last four payments have been made on time.

Make a special trip to the department store and request to see the credit manager. After a friendly greeting, use the four magic words: "I need your help." Explain that although you were late in the past, you had a good reason then but the problem no longer exists, and your last few payments were, and all future payments will be, made on time. You go on to say that you have been a good customer of the store for some time and expect to continue a long relationship since this is one of your favorite stores. However, the store still rates you as an R-3 on your credit file, and the credit manager could sure help you and your family by upgrading you to an R-1. You may be surprised to know that if the credit manager likes you, 75% of the time he or she will do just as you requested.

Although it is not within your power to get the credit bureau to change any data that is technically correct, your creditors can upgrade your status anytime they choose. This strategy alone will give you tremendous control over your credit rating and credit profile. Once your credit rating is upgraded to R-1 or I-1, those inquiring into your file need never know that it was ever anything else.

Strategy #78
AVOID HIGH-INTEREST OR PAYMENT-LENGTHENING DEBT CONSOLIDATION LOANS.

A common temptation of those who feel they are drowning in debt is to opt for the temporary relief of a finance company or bank "bill paying" or debt consolidation loan. On the surface the move seems logical; the total monthly payments will come down and provide some cash flow relief. Long term, however, these loans are often a disaster because the payment relief comes by creating a greater amount of debt for a longer period of time.

A typical consolidation loan is made on the following basis. First, you add up the balances on all of your current bills including:

- department store charge accounts
- doctor and hospital bills
- credit cards
- payments on accounts that are delinquent
- personal loans from banks or credit unions
- loans used to finance appliances or electronic equipment
- miscellaneous bills

Normally, everything but a home mortgage and overfinanced automobiles is thrown into the refinancing pot. If an automobile is paid down or paid off, the lender will usually want to include the car and the balance of the car loan in the deal to increase both the lender's collateral and interest return.

You apply for a loan to cover the total amount of your debt, and the lending institution, upon approval of the loan, issues checks to your creditors to pay off the balances of your outstanding accounts. You have now consolidated 5 to 20 accounts into one account with just one monthly payment to the lending institution. Your new payment is less than the total of the individual payments you were making each month before the consolidation.

Sounds like a great idea until you begin to understand the mathematics of a consolidation loan. Lower payments come by extending payments over a longer period of time—two to three years longer. When the same amount of money is borrowed over a longer period, even at the same interest rate, there is far more interest to pay, meaning that additional hundreds or thousands of dollars in interest are added to the loan, actually putting the borrower deeper in debt. The short-term gain becomes long-term pain.

Financially illiterate Americans have learned to ask only two questions when borrowing: "What is my down payment?" and "What are my monthly payments?" If the answers to those questions are in the range the borrower can handle, the transaction is usually agreed to. In reality, there is a far more important question that should be asked: "What are my *total* payments?" It is the total payments, not the amount of a single payment, that will eat into your lifetime wealth and upset your long-term financial plan.

The second downside to a debt consolidation loan is the potentially higher interest rate. The fact that you need the loan in the first place is some evidence that you may not be the world's greatest money manager and may be somewhat of a greater financial risk to a lender. Remember, the goal of any lending institution is to loan money at reasonable rates only to those who can prove they don't need it.

If your debts are already out of control or you have a credit record of late payments, you will be turned down for the consolidation loan unless you have collateral, such as equity in your home, with which to underwrite the loan. That's sort of like refusing to loan the money to you but agreeing to loan it to your house, which is a better credit risk.

If your credit bureau file is still in good enough shape to warrant the loan, you can bet the interest rate will often border on the obscene. I have seen dozens of debt consolidation loans from finance companies that carry interest rates of 15 to 28% per year. With rates like that, it is improbable that the borrower will ever get out of debt. The irony lies in the fact that a high interest rate, when coupled with an extended payment term of two to three years, can still produce substantially lower monthly payments even though the total debt and total payments have been increased dramatically. Most borrowers never realize what hit them.

Here's how the consolidation system works:

Debts to Be Consolidated	Monthly Payments	Total Amount Due	Number of Pymts. Left	Interest Rates
5 credit cards	182	6,200	48	18%
3 doctor/hospital bills	200	2,300	12	12
4 department store accts.	90	1,800	24	18
1 furniture loan	151	1,700	12	12
Totals	$623	$12,000		

You owe $12,000 to 13 creditors, including 5 credit cards, 3 doctors and hospitals, 4 department stores, and a furniture retailer (see chart). Your payments are $623 per month, which with your other bills are stretching your income to the maximum. Wouldn't it be wonderful if you could cut those payments in half and feel some cash relief? You find a lender who will pay off your current bills, offer to cut your monthly payments in half, and allow you to write just 1 check a month instead of 13. How could you not be tempted? The problem is that to achieve these benefits you will increase your total debt by thousands in extra interest and increase the payoff terms on each of the accounts from one to four years.

Your new consolidation loan is for the same $12,000 you already owe, but the new interest rate on the loan is 19% plus $300 in up-front fees and equal monthly payments for five years. You hardly notice anything else when the loan officer tells you your new payments will drop to only $319 per month, a reduction of $304 per month. But $319 per month times 60 months is $19,140! You now owe close to $20,000 instead of $12,000 plus far less interest and are much deeper in debt for a much longer time. Should you take the loan for its short-term relief, you have dug the debt rut deeper and longer.

Now, go back and look at the chart again. If you continued paying the $623 per month, even though it would be a struggle, the medical bills and furniture loan would be completely paid in only 12 months, and your monthly payments at that moment would instantly drop $351 per month to only $272 per month, or $47 less than the payment created by the damaging consolidation loan. In addition, payments would drop another $90 after the next 12 months from the payoff of the department store accounts, leaving you with a payment of only $182 for 24 months on the credit cards instead of $319 per month for the 36 remaining months on the consolidation loan. Struggling in the short term can often ward off struggling over a longer term.

Now that it is obvious that a standard debt consolidation loan can be disastrous to your wealth, what can you do to get some instant relief?

Strategy #79
**USE THE GIVENS CASH-SAVING STRATEGIES TO
FREE UP MONEY REQUIRED FOR DEBT REDUCTION.**

Dozens of the strategies in this book will instantly increase your cash flow, freeing up at least $100 per week. Using a few strategies such as the ones on page 105 will do the trick.

Strategies	Chapter	Projected Savings
Auto insurance cost-cutting strategies	3	500
Life insurance cost-cutting strategies	6	700
Dropping life insurance on children	6	800
Creating tax deductions from a small business	25	1,500
Dropping gimmick insurance	5	900
Increasing allowances on W-4 form	21	800
		$5,200 per year
		or $100 per week

The $100 savings per week creates more than $400 per month in extra cash as the effects of your new strategies kick in, an amount far greater than the $304 reduction in monthly payments created by the consolidation loan. There's free money in knowledge.

Here's how to get the maximum out of the extra $400 you've freed up. Use half, or about $200, to give yourself some cash flow relief. You can apply it to your $623-per-month payments or use it for any other purpose you choose.

Apply the other $200 per month you've saved to debt reduction through extra principal payments. Pay more not less. Increase the total amount of your monthly payments from $623 to $823. Remember, the increase comes from found money, not from your paycheck. Since the $200 per month or $2,400 per year will be applied to the principal balances of your accounts, you will reduce your total debt almost 25% in the first 12 months alone, cutting further the total interest you will owe while paying off your entire debt. Sound like magic? Proper debt-reduction planning works like magic!

Strategy #80
APPLY EXTRA PRINCIPAL PAYMENTS FIRST TO ACCOUNTS WITH THE HIGHEST INTEREST RATES.

Now that you have the extra $200 per month to apply to debt reduction, the next question becomes, which accounts do you pay on or pay off first? The temptation will be to pay off those with the fewest payments and smallest balances left both to decrease the number of checks you are required to write each month and to give you a sense of success as you quickly pay off these small accounts. Although this approach may be emotionally logical, it is mathematically incorrect.

Your objective is to put your money where it will do the most good. Remember this principle—as the interest rate increases, more of the payment becomes the property of the lender and less of each payment is applied to your account balance. In our example (see chart, page 103), the credit cards and department store accounts with interest rates of 18% are those which you would derive the most financial benefit by paying off first. Pay off these accounts in full with your found money before you pay a dime extra on the medical bills or furniture loan, which have interest rates of only 12%.

Revolving charge accounts such as credit cards and department store accounts compute minimum monthly payments using a formula something like this. First the monthly interest is computed by applying $\frac{1}{12}$ of the yearly interest rate to the month's average balance on your account. An amount is then added to the monthly interest payment, which will be applied toward your principal balance and which will allow the account to be completely paid off in a specific number of months, usually 48 to 72. As your account balance goes up or down (depending on whether or not you continue charging while making payments), the same formula is applied to the balance at the end of each month until sometime, when you are much older, the account may actually become paid off. This number is referred to as the "minimum monthly payment."

Pay less than the minimum due and you quickly become subject to losing the credit card and your credit rating. On the other hand, nothing prevents you from paying more than the minimum. For instance, if your credit card account has a balance of $6,000 and an annual interest rate of 18% (1.5% per month), your minimum monthly payments might be computed as follows:

Minimum payment = 1.5% (balance) for interest + $\frac{1}{48}$ (balance) applied to principal
1.5% × $6,000 = $90, the interest portion of the payment
$\frac{1}{48}$ × $6,000 = $125, the amount to be applied toward principal
Total Minimum Payment = $90 + $125 = $215

A full 42% of your payment, or $90 of the $215, is interest kept by the company that has issued you credit. Think of it: in one month you paid 42% interest based on your payment amount. Only 58% or $125 went toward your $6,000 account balance. It's no wonder you don't seem to be able to make any headway. If the term of the debt is 72 months instead of 48 months, the situation is worse. Only $84 per month instead of $125 goes toward principal. Although your total payment of $174 is less ($84 principal plus the same $90 interest), you are in debt for two years longer while paying off the same amount of balance. You have heard me say this before: the minimum payment is calculated to guarantee that you will never get out of debt. There's your proof.

In general, your credit cards will have the highest interest rates of any of your debt and are the first target for any extra debt-reducing cash.

Strategy #81
REPAY STUDENT LOANS EARLY ONLY IF THE INTEREST IS OVER 9%.

Some of the deepest debt is incurred at the youngest ages through student loans. I talk constantly to graduates who upon leaving school have incurred a ten-year liability ranging from $20,000 to $120,000. What's worse is incurring half the debt and never graduating. What an education! That level of debt alone can create a paycheck-to-paycheck home environment for years to come. Although there are now companies that will consolidate student loans to lower the payments, you have already learned that lower payments come at the expense of even longer and deeper debt. No matter how you feel about the worth of your education after the fact, with the U.S. government chasing student loan dodgers through income tax returns, income tax refunds, and credit bureau reports, you will eventually have to pay up.

The question becomes, should you apply a debt reduction strategy such as extra principal payments to your student loans? The answer lies solely in the interest rate. Since one winning loan strategy is to stretch low-interest loans over as long a term as possible, but to prepay principal on high-interest loans, your plan is clear. Using 9% as the dividing line between high and low interest, prepay principal on student loans with interest rates above 9% but continue to make regular payments on any low-interest loans over the full term of the loan.

When you have extra money, don't apply it to your low-interest loans. Instead apply the money to any higher-interest loan (see Strategy #80) or invest it in a mutual fund family (see Chapters 31 and 32). These days school loans typically have interest rates as high as 12%, and these higher-interest loans become the target of your early payoffs. If at the same time you have even higher interest debt, such as credit card debt at 18%, pay off the credit cards even before you begin paying down your high-interest student loans.

Strategy #82
USE A COSIGNER TO HELP (RE)ESTABLISH YOUR CREDIT.

If you get parents or friends to cosign on mortgages, bank loans, or credit cards, creditors will extend credit to you they might otherwise refuse. A positive payment record will eventually qualify you for credit on your own. Although my advice to you is never, ever cosign a loan for someone else, don't hesitate to look for a willing cosigner when you need one.

Strategy #83
OVERCOME POOR CREDIT WITH A SECURED CREDIT CARD.

If credit troubles are reflected in your file, create enough new, good credit to offset the poor credit. Establish new credit sources as quickly as you can and keep *all* payments up to date. Bury the bad information among the good in your credit file.

The easiest way to establish or reestablish your credit is through a secured MasterCard or Visa card. Secured means that you have made a deposit, usually equal to the amount of credit you want, from $300 to $3,000. With some banks or agencies your deposit is put into an interest-earning CD. Avoid an agency fee or potential rip-offs by dealing directly with a card-issuing bank such as those listed below. After you have made regular, timely payments for six months or so, the security requirement is dropped and your deposit returned to you.

After you have made one or two payments, have your account reverified and your credit file updated by the credit bureau. Contact any of these financial institutions for a secured-credit-card application.

Charles J. Givens Organization/
American Pacific Bank
P.O. Box 19360A
Portland, OR 97280-9360
(800) 283-8441
(503) 245-5595
Card offered: Visa
Fee: $42

Spirit VISA
19590 East Main Street
Parker, CO 80134
(800) 779-8472
(303) 840-9945
Card offered: Visa
Fee: $49.95

Bank One Lafayette
P.O. Box 450
Lafayette, IN 47902
(800) 395-2555
Cards offered: Visa/MC
Fee: $35

Applied Card Services
P.O. Box 15414
Wilmington, DE 19850
(800) 262-3610
Cards offered: Visa/MC
Fee: $35

First Consumers
Lincoln Tower
10260 SW Greenberg Rd.
Portland, OR 97223
(800) 876-3262
(503) 293-6711
Card offered: MC
Fee: $48

Signet Bank
P.O. Box 85547
Richmond, VA 23285-5547
(800) 333-7116
Cards offered: Visa/MC
Fee: $20

INTEREST RATES:

American Pacific Bank/CJGO	17.00%
Applied Card Services	18.99
Bank One Lafayette	19.80
Signet Bank	19.80
First Consumers	20.50

As you can see, the interest rates are high, so high in fact you want to be certain to pay off your balance every month to avoid paying any interest at all. Remember your purpose is to use the secured card to reestablish your credit.

Strategy #84
TO REHABILITATE CREDIT, BORROW THE BANK'S MONEY AND USE IT AS SECURITY FOR A LOAN.

Banks love to make fully secured loans—to almost anyone. Here is how you get a bank to participate in your credit rebuilding plan. Look a loan officer straight in the face and say, "Mr. Banker, I need your help. I'd like to borrow $2,500. But wait, before you check my credit, let me tell you that you won't like what you see. I would like you to put the $2,500 in a savings account here in your bank and you can put a hold on the money. You will have no risk since you have the money, and by making monthly payments, I can (re)establish my credit."

The cost to you is minimal. Although you are paying interest on the loan, the bank is paying you interest on your savings account. Don't take "no" for an answer. Keep reaffirming that you need the banker's help and will eventually become an excellent customer. Persistence always overcomes barriers. Once you find a bank that will make the loan, make two payments within the first 30 days. Go to a second bank and repeat the entire process. You can show the loan officer at the second bank the one good credit reference you now have at the first bank. Make two payments at the second bank as well. Now you have two excellent credit references. After 90 days use the borrowed money in your savings accounts to pay off the balances of the loans. Have the credit bureau check your bank loan accounts, which now show that your payments were made on time and the loans were paid off early.

During one of the shakiest periods of my credit life, I used this credit rehabilitation strategy with great success. I had recently exited from the corporate world and bought a franchise for $5,000 to market motivational programs. Having been a typical medium-income, no-cash-on-hand corporate exec, I had to borrow the $5,000 and sell some stock to raise the start-up capital. I sold my home and boat and ventured off to Gainesville, Florida, where there was no competition for what I wanted to sell. The remaining money I had went out far faster than sales came in. After two months in Gainesville, and a week before Christmas, I was broke. MasterCard and Mobil had demanded their credit cards back. Indian givers! My burgundy Continental Mark III was suddenly repossessed because of only two late payments. A vacate notice from the apartment manager was stapled to the door—something about overdue rent.

No car, no credit cards, no credit, no rent money, no cash, no Christmas presents—no kidding! The next step was the one-stop source of instant credit in America no matter what your credit history—the pawn shop. With tears in her eyes, my wife, Bonnie, handed me our only pawnable asset—an $800 set of sterling silver flatware, a Christmas present from her parents the year before. The unconcerned pawnbroker and I played a tug-of-war between the measly $80 he originally offered and the $200 I thought I deserved. We finally called it quits at $125, of which $80 went for the kids' Christmas presents, and the other $45 for Christmas dinner.

The first "must" was a rental car—difficult to get without a credit card. I borrowed $40 from a friend and spent the afternoon talking about money with the operator of an independent car rental agency. After two hours I said, "By the way, my wife could use a car while I'm gone on business the next couple of days." When he asked for a credit card, I told him I didn't have one with me, but was prepared to put down a $40 cash deposit. I could hardly believe my eyes as he pulled out the rental contract with a smile on his face. That little car got me through the next three weeks, until I had the money to take it back and pay for it.

During the next month, I managed to stall the landlord, feed the family on cereal and fast-food hamburgers, and finally get some regular income from my new business venture. Still no credit, however. I went to a finance company and began: "Look, sir, give me some help. Loan me $300, but don't give me the money. Stick the check in your bottom desk drawer so you have no risk. I'll make payments, and you can give me a good credit report when anyone calls."

"Highly irregular," he said.

"Highly irregular situation," I responded.

After fifteen minutes of all the reasons why not, he finally said, "Why not?" And I was on my way to credit recovery. Later the same day, I went back to his office to sign the papers. Out of habit, I guess, they actually gave me the check. I did not pose a single objection. I used the $300 to open a checking account at a bank down the street and then promptly went over to the loan officer. I began with the "I need your help . . ." story and told him I was already a customer of the bank, handing him my checking account $300 deposit slip on which the ink was still wet. He loaned me $1,000 and held the money in a savings account as security. The next day, I wrote checks for two payments from the $300 I had originally put in the bank checking account and gave them to the teller with payment coupons. I wrote another $50 check to the finance company.

Still, I needed a car. A friend drove me to Orlando to a Cadillac leasing agency. Sol, the manager, explained that it was four o'clock and he couldn't run my application through the credit bureau until the next day. I pulled out my aces.

"Sol, I live in Gainesville," I said. "How about if I give you two excellent credit references—one bank and one finance company?" Sol called both and found that I was two payments ahead on each account. Neither bothered to tell him the loans were less than a week old. I drove off the lot with a beautiful new blue metal flake Sedan de Ville. Within another 30 days, I had $4,000 in the bank from my business, the rent paid, a new Cadillac, and much of my credit restored. The next month I was doing so well I went back to Sol and leased another brand-new Cadillac for my wife, Bonnie, to make up for the silverware. Nothing is impossible.

Chapter 9

BORROWING MONEY— MORTGAGE CONTROL STRATEGIES

Live within your income even if you have to borrow money to do it.

Josh Billings
Humorist
(1818–1885)

OBJECTIVE

SAVE TENS OF THOUSANDS ON ANY HOME MORTGAGE.

It has been said that you are worth what you owe. At least that's what you're worth to those you owe. Borrowing money has become an American way of life. In the next two chapters we'll look at powerful strategies for cutting the cost of borrowing money, new types of mortgages that can save you thousands, when it pays to refinance your home, and how to cut your interest 30% by choosing the right term for your automobile and personal loans. None of these strategies requires extra time or effort, only knowledge.

Strategy #85
LIVE FREE BY BUYING INSTEAD OF RENTING.

Before considering a mortgage, you must first decide if owning a home is better than renting. In all of my experience, I have found only two valid reasons for renting: (1) you live with your parents rent free, or (2) you live in a rent-controlled apartment in a city such as New York where you pay $300 a month for a place you would normally rent for $1,000.

Several years ago, I built a computer model to determine what happens financially to a person who buys instead of rents. The parameters included tax rates, interest rates, appreciation, closing costs, and the length of time lived in the home. The result? If you buy and live in a home for at least five years, you live free—your monthly payments, closing costs, insurance, and property taxes are returned to you through tax savings and your profit when you sell.

For example, let's say you buy a $100,000 home.

Price of House	$100,000
Down Payment	− 10,000
Mortgage Amount	$ 90,000
Mortgage Interest Rate	× 10%
One Year Interest Expense	$ 9,000
One Year Property Tax	+ 1,000
One Year Total Expenses	$ 10,000
Income Tax Bracket (state & federal)	× 35%
One Year Tax Savings	$ 3,500
Yearly Appreciation (6%)	+ 6,000
Total Tax Savings and Appreciation	$ 9,500

Your yearly interest expense is $9,000 and property taxes are $1,000 for a total of $10,000, but your investment return from tax deductions and appreciation is $9,500. Each year the interest portion of your payment decreases slightly until at the end of five years, if you sell, you get most or all of your money back. You have lived free. If instead you rent the same $100,000 home for $800 per month, you lose $9,600 per year or $48,000 during the five-year period. Why? There are no tax deductions and no appreciation.

Over the years rents go up, but buying locks in the size of your mortgage payment. If you don't own a home, buy one now. See *Financial Self-Defense*, Chapter 15, for where to find mortgages anyone can qualify for.

Strategy #86
IF YOU ARE SINGLE, LIVE FREE BY CREATING YOUR OWN LUXURY ROOMING HOUSE.

There is another strategy that allows singles or single parents to live free even while renting, and that is to sublet rooms to other singles.

Years ago, when I was single and on a limited budget, I used this strategy to live in comparative luxury in a magnificent home that was much more than I could have afforded by myself. The house was almost 5,000 square feet with five bedrooms in a posh suburb of Washington, D.C., and the rent was the equivalent of about $1,800 per month at today's prices. Because I was a single parent (my then-young son, Charles III, lived with me) sinking everything I had into the business empire I was building, that much rent money was more than I could handle alone.

The solution was simple and worked so well that I still recommend it to singles and single parents who want to live the good life before their ship comes in. I rented out three bedrooms to friends, and the income paid the rent. Although four single adults were living in the house, I divided the total rent by only three. My renters paid the entire rent. I was living free in a magnificent home. Two of the three worked the evening shift on their jobs so the house was virtually empty during the evening when Chuck and I were home. During the day when we were gone, the night-shift renters had the place to themselves. There was a house rule about no friends or parties in shared areas of the house when others were home, and everyone had assigned house-cleaning duties.

This strategy saved me the equivalent of over $21,000 in rent for that year, and since the rent money went directly to the landlord for a home I did not own, the entire amount was tax free! If you're single or a single parent looking for strategies that can help you overcome the lack of a second income, start with this one. If you don't like living with others, you can always go back to that closet-sized apartment you can afford by yourself. In addition, if you are a single parent and already own a home bigger than you need, you can use this strategy to provide much needed additional income.

Strategy #87
MAKE YOUR MORTGAGE DECISION YOURSELF, DON'T RELY ON THE MORTGAGE SALESMAN.

Borrowing mortgage money once was a simple matter of completing the paperwork and waiting to see if you qualified. Today, mortgage decisions include a dozen options. Whether you are buying or refinancing a home, the correct choice of a mortgage is as important as the right choice of the property itself. The last person who should make your decisions is the loan officer, whose motives and profit objectives may be in conflict with yours. Like all financial decisions, the best mortgage alternative can be chosen with formulas you have never before been shown. These formulas are the basis for the underlying wisdom of the strategies.

Strategy #88
IF THE FIXED RATE INTEREST YOU ARE QUOTED IS OVER 9¾%, TAKE THE ARM. IF THE FIXED RATE IS UNDER 9¾%, TAKE THE FRM.

If the interest rate remains the same for the term of your mortgage, you have an FRM, or fixed rate mortgage. Fixed rate mortgages have been the standard since the twenties. When interest rates began soaring in the early eighties, and mortgage companies became concerned about locking in low fixed interest rates, long-term adjustable rate mortgages were born. These mortgages are also called variable rate or flexible rate mortgages.

The interest rate of an adjustable rate mortgage (ARM) changes periodically, based on either a contractual agreement with your mortgage company or the changes of a published economic factor such as Treasury bill rates. Adjustable rate mortgages have a "cap" or maximum percent the interest rate may increase. A 9% ARM with a 4% cap would mean that the interest rate charged could never go over 13%. There are two types of ARMs, differentiated by the effects of interest rate changes on your monthly payments.

A. Adjustable payment ARM—Monthly payments are adjusted up or down to reflect changes in the mortgage interest rate. Adjustable payment is the most common form of ARM.

B. Adjustable term ARM—The total number of monthly payments is increased or decreased to reflect changes in the mortgage interest rates, but the amount of the monthly payment remains constant. If your original mortgage term was 30 years, over time it could be readjusted to 33 years or 28 years based on the interest rate changes that occur during your mortgage term. When interest rates go down, your mortgage term is shortened; when they go up, your mortgage term is lengthened.

You win with an adjustable rate mortgage when interest rates are low, and the mortgage company wins when the rates are high; 9¾% interest is the dividing line between high and low. Mortgage companies are now discovering that mortgage rates are low twice as often as they are high, giving the ARM advantage to the borrower. In addition, the interest rate on an ARM mortgage begins at an average of 2% less than the first year's fixed mortgage rate. When you can lock in a fixed rate of 9¾% or less, take the fixed-rate mortgage. Otherwise, if the fixed rate you are quoted is over 9¾%, take the ARM.

Strategy #89
CONVERT YOUR ADJUSTABLE RATE MORTGAGE TO A FIXED RATE MORTGAGE ONLY WHEN THE FIXED RATE IS LESS THAN 10%.

Most adjustable rate mortgages now come with a conversion option that goes something like this. Usually during the second to fifth year of your mortgage term you can choose to lock in a fixed interest rate and get rid of the adjustable, changing interest. When, if ever, is the conversion to your advantage? The correct answer is based on the formula in the previous strategy.

Anytime you have an ARM mortgage and your mortgage company will allow you to convert to a fixed rate at less than 10% and charge you no more than 1% of the mortgage balance as closing costs, convert to the fixed rate.

Otherwise, you will do better financially to hang on to your ARM. Because fixed interest rates are constantly changing over the term of your mortgage, you will want to check your mortgage company about every six months to find out the interest rate at which you could convert your ARM to an FRM.

Strategy #90
USE A GRADUATED PAYMENT MORTGAGE TO BUY MORE HOME WITH SMALLER MONTHLY PAYMENTS.

A graduated payment mortgage (GPM) is a feature of either a fixed rate or adjustable rate 30-year mortgage that has the advantage of lower than normal payments in the early years. The payments are then slightly higher than normal in the later years. Since the mortgage payments in the early years are often less than the interest due, the unpaid interest is added to your principal balance, a process called negative amortization. Payments are increased slightly each year on a predetermined basis, until your mortgage converts to positive amortization and becomes completely paid off at the end of the 30-year term.

The smaller payments in the early years of a GPM can help you qualify for or afford a home costing as much as 30% more. As your career flourishes and your income increases over the years, you will be able to afford the later increase in payments.

Strategy #91
USE A GROWING EQUITY MORTGAGE TO PAY OFF YOUR HOME IN HALF THE TIME WITH PAYMENTS YOU CAN AFFORD.

There is a second alternative for saving money on mortgages. Some mortgage lending institutions are now offering a little-known special 30-year mortgage called a growing equity mortgage (GEM). The first year's payments are about the same as with a 30-year mortgage. Payments then go up each year, but the extra amount of the payment is applied only to the principal balance so that your mortgage is actually paid off in 15 years, saving tens of thousands in potential interest payments. The GEM actually becomes a 15-year mortgage but with lower payments in the early years when money is normally the scarcest.

Strategy #92
THE BIGGER YOUR MORTGAGE, THE BETTER YOUR INVESTMENT.

Your home is more than a place to live, it can be one of the best investments you'll ever make. Even the size of your mortgage makes a difference.

There are four positive uses of a mortgage:

1. To increase the return on a real estate investment through the power of leverage
2. To buy a home without paying cash
3. To free up real estate equity for higher-return investments
4. To pay off nondeductible consumer loans with tax deductible equity loans

Leverage is the use of other people's money (OPM), and a home mortgage is an easy method of putting OPM to work. Earning $10,000 in a savings account at 10% would require an investment of $50,000 for two years. Thirty percent of your interest would be lost to taxes. Buy a $100,000 home with a $10,000 down payment, and if the home appreciates 5% per year, you have earned the same $10,000 in two years with no taxes. You only needed $10,000 of your own money instead of $50,000 to earn the same $10,000 over the two-year period. Based on your investment (down payment), your investment return on the home was 50% per year instead of just 10% in the savings account.

Strategy #93
GET A 15-YEAR INSTEAD OF A 30-YEAR MORTGAGE.

You can save tens of thousands in mortgage interest by putting the time value of money on your side. The mortgage company will automatically give you a 30-year term if you don't object. Why? Because 30-year mortgages make mortgage companies rich.

For every $50,000 you borrow at 12% interest for 30 years, your principal and interest will be $515 a month. At the end of five years (60 payments), you will have paid in $30,900, but reduced your principal balance by only $1,000. After 10 years (120 payments), you have paid the mortgage company $62,000—

more than the original mortgage amount—but have paid off only about $5,000 of the principal. You still owe $45,000!

Get a 15-year instead of a 30-year mortgage at the same interest rate and your monthly payments go up only about 22%. But for every $50,000 you borrow for just 15 years, you will save $80,000 in total interest payments. With the cost of homes today, the shorter-term mortgages can save you hundreds of thousands during your lifetime. After ten years of making monthly payments on a 15-year mortgage, you have paid off 45% of your original principal amount instead of only 10%.

No matter how big your mortgage payments are today, they will seem much smaller five years from now when your income will have increased, the value of the dollar has been reduced by inflation, but your mortgage payments have remained the same.

The shorter-term mortgage is an automatic method of building your wealth. If, however, you were to take the same amount each month without fail and invest in a no-load mutual fund family or other similar investment, you could earn even more. But the shorter-term mortgage is a guaranteed method of increasing your wealth that requires no discipline.

Strategy #94
CUT YOUR MORTGAGE TERM IN HALF WITH EXTRA PRINCIPAL PAYMENTS.

What if you have already locked yourself into a 30-year mortgage; are you stuck with it? Not at all. Although refinancing an existing 30-year mortgage to 15 years would result in thousands of dollars in new closing costs, you can pay off your 30-year mortgage in the same 15 years without refinancing by simply making extra principal payments.

On the first of the month when you write your regular mortgage check, write a second check for the "principal only" portion of the next month's payment. The principal is that tiny number on your amortization schedule next to the interest. If you didn't get an amortization schedule with your mortgage, your mortgage company, a real estate agent, or a friend with a home computer can print you one.

If you look at the early payments on a mortgage, you will be shocked at how much of the payment goes to interest and how little goes to principal. During the entire mortgage term the amount of the principal payment increases by a few cents and the interest paid decreases by the same amount even though your total monthly payment remains the same. There are five columns of importance on a mortgage amortization schedule: payment number, payment amount, principal, interest, and principal balance. The principal balance, the amount you still owe out of the original amount you borrowed, is reduced each month only by the principal amount you paid last month. Your mortgage company keeps all of the interest.

Here is a section of a typical amortization schedule showing the breakdown of payment numbers 60 through 63 of a 30-year (360-payment) mortgage.

Payment #	Payment Amount	Principal	Interest	Principal Balance	
60	$500	20.00	480.00	49,000.00	First Month
61	$500	20.30	479.70	48,979.70	
62	$500	20.70	479.30	48,959.00	Second Month
63	$500	21.20	478.80	48,937.80	

Notice how the principal increases slightly each month and the interest decreases by the same amount. On payment number 61 the principal portion of the payment increases $.30 from $20.00 to $20.30 while the interest drops $.30.

If this were your mortgage, when you write a $500 check for payment 60, you would write a second check for $20.30 representing the principal-only portion of payment number 61. The following month, you would write a check for payment 62, $500, and write a second check for $21.20, the principal portion of payment number 63. You are actually moving down your amortization schedule two months at a time instead of one. Your mortgage will be paid off in exactly half the time. How much will you save? You never pay interest on a payment whose principal is prepaid. When you make an extra principal payment, you save the entire amount of interest shown.

Paying the exact amount equal to the next month's principal is not a requirement but a convenient way of keeping track of your mortgage balance. Last year I received a letter from a lady who decided to use this strategy on a new 30-year mortgage, sent in an extra check for $200, and cut the term of her mortgage by 20 payments or 20 months, all with just $200 extra!

A few mortgage companies limit your minimum extra principal payment to the equivalent of one month's regular payment or allow you to pay off no more than $2,000 of your principal in one year without incurring an early-payment penalty. Read your mortgage contract to see if you must work with any special rules. These rules do not create a problem and still allow you to use the strategy as shown.

Some financial and real estate writers recommend the bi-monthly mortgage strategy. Instead of making a full payment on the first of the month, you pay half on the first and half on the fifteenth. Since you are making the equivalent of an extra half payment per year, a 30-year mortgage would be paid off in 22 years. However, this is an example of a concept that works only on paper since only one in twenty mortgage companies will allow you to split your payment once you have a mortgage. Using the extra principal payment strategy instead will pay off a 30-year mortgage in exactly 15 years. The only mortgages on which the mortgage company can refuse extra payments are county bond money mortgages and federal-government-subsidized mortgages. The government quite rightly feels that if you have extra money, what are you doing with a subsidized mortgage?

There are three conditions under which you would not make extra principal payments: if your mortgage interest rate is 9% or less; if you plan to live in the home less than three years; or if the house is a property you rent to others.

Never pay off low-interest mortgages—those under 9%. Instead, use the extra money in a better investment. If you don't plan to live in the home more than three years, extra principal payments will have little effect. Cutting the total interest paid on a rental property is not as important as cash flow. You make the payments on your home, the tenants make the payments on your rental properties.

Often I am asked if it wouldn't be better to keep a longer-term mortgage because the interest is tax deductible. The answer is no. To get $1 refunded from a home mortgage interest deduction, you must spend $3 in interest (31% bracket). Although the tax deduction is a bonus, interest is still an expense, costing you extra tens of thousands with or without the deduction.

Strategy #95
NEVER USE MORTGAGE GRACE PERIODS.

Using mortgage grace periods can damage your credit profile. Even though you are not charged a late penalty until the tenth or fifteenth of the month, a payment made after the first will be counted as late and could end up in your credit bureau file. Let me share with you my own experience.

After I bought my first 40 rental homes, I found I could create a tremendous float by mailing the mortgage checks so they would arrive at the mortgage company not by the first, but by the tenth of the month. The process also allowed me extra time to collect past-due rents to cover the mortgage payments. Using the grace period soon caught up with me. Even though all the mortgage companies gave me until the tenth or fifteenth of the month before a late charge was assessed, payments after the first were counted as 30 days late and that information began to show up in my credit file. My payments are now mailed to arrive by the first of the month.

Strategy #96
REFINANCE YOUR HOME ANYTIME AND EVERY TIME THE NEW INTEREST RATE IS AT LEAST 2% LESS THAN THE OLD RATE.

Knowing when to refinance is as important as choosing the right mortgage. Some believe you should never refinance; others will tell you to refinance anytime interest rates drop. Neither is correct.

You cannot save money by refinancing your home every time interest rates drop because of the additional closing costs you would be charged. The chart below will show you the approximate number of months it takes for low payments to make up for new average closing costs. A good rule of thumb is the 2% rule.

Difference in Interest Rate	Approximate Number of Months Required
2%	26 Months
3%	22 Months
4%	18 Months

If the difference between interest rates on your old and new mortgage is 2%, 26 months of lower payments will be required to offset the closing costs. It would take 22 months at a 3% difference and 18 months at a 4% difference to offset the closing costs! The lower payments from that point on will save you thousands.

To determine the actual number of months of reduced payments required to offset the new closing costs, divide the closing cost amount you are quoted by the amount you will save each month with your lower payment.

For example, it would not be wise to refinance a $40,000 mortgage at a 1% difference in interest rates. The amount saved each month would only be $30, and if the new closing costs were $2,000, it would take you 66 months, or 5½ years, to break even. You might sell your home before then, losing the difference. How long you intend to own your home, therefore, is also an important refinancing consideration.

Always ask if the closing costs of a loan or mortgage can be added to the loan amount. Use other people's money whenever possible.

Strategy #97
TURN YOUR HOME EQUITY INTO CASH WITH AN EQUITY LOAN.

If you have a low-interest first mortgage, the equity loan and not refinancing is the best alternative for freeing up your home equity. Unlike a regular mortgage, which gives you a fixed amount of money for a fixed term, the equity loan gives you a line of credit. You can borrow or pay back money at any time during the term of the loan, usually by writing a check against your loan account. You only pay interest on the money you borrowed, and you stop paying interest on any portion that you pay back. There is no prepayment penalty.

Equity loans are available from:

• Savings and loan institutions
• Banks (local and national)
• First- and second-mortgage companies
• Securities brokerage firms
• Mortgage brokers (independent mortgage sources)

The equity loan is usually an adjustable rate mortgage.

Shop around; the rates and terms vary from institution to institution. Expect to pay $80 to $140 for a required appraisal and the one to five points, which can usually be added to the mortgage amount. Eight points on a 15-year mortgage is the equivalent of about 1% interest. Therefore, when comparing equity loans, an 8½% interest rate with four points is the same as a 9% rate with no points. (See *Financial Self-Defense*, Chapter 15, for complete formulas and strategies for comparing loans.)

The maximum loan you can obtain is determined by a formula called the loan-to-value (LTV), usually 70 to 90% of the appraised value of your property, less any existing mortgage. If, for example, your home appraises for $110,000, the mortgage company's LTV ratio is 80%, and your first mortgage balance is $45,000, your maximum equity loan would be $43,000.

$$(LTV \times \text{Market Value}) - \text{Existing Mortgages}$$
$$= \text{Maximum Loan Amount}$$
$$(80\% \times \$110,000) - \$45,000 = \$43,000$$

Strategy #98
BORROW YOUR HOME EQUITY FREE BY COMBINING AN EQUITY LOAN WITH A GOOD INVESTMENT PLAN.

Home equity is like money in a shoe box gathering dust in your closet. It may make you feel good, but it is not working for you. There are a dozen good emotional reasons for accumulating a large amount of equity in your home, but not one good financial reason.

My Hungarian relatives lived on the south side of Chicago in an area known as Cottage Grove. Most worked for the Pullman Railroad Car Company until retirement. They lived in three-story row houses that they were somehow able to buy on their small salaries. To save money, they never took expensive vacations or spent much on themselves. One of life's biggest events after marriage and children was paying off the mortgage and celebrating the event with a mortgage-burning party. In this ethnic neighborhood where half the residents never learned English, a fire was built in the street in front of the now debt-free property. With great fanfare, the proud owners threw their canceled mortgage documents into the flames while the neighbors danced and sang in a joyous circle. Great party, but a losing financial strategy. They may have owned their homes, but that was *all* they owned.

BORROW YOUR HOME EQUITY FREE INVESTMENT PLAN

Equity Loan at 10% Interest for 15 Years

Amount Borrowed	Yearly Interest	Investment	Amount Invested	Expected Income	Cash Income	Deferred Income	Net Income	
$ 20,000	$ 2,000*	Mutual Funds[1]	10,000	15%	1,500	—	Total Income	4,500
		Discount. Mtg.[2]	10,000	30%	2,000	1,000	Interest Pymts.	−2,000
					$ 3,500	$1,000	Net Income	$ 2,500
$ 50,000	$ 5,000*	Mutual Funds[1]	25,000	15%	3,750	—	Total Income	11,250
		Discount. Mtg.[2]	25,000	30%	5,000	2,500	Interest Pymts.	−5,000
					$ 8,750	$2,500	Net Income	$ 6,250
$100,000	$10,000*	Mutual Funds[1]	50,000	15%	7,500	—	Total Income	22,500
		Discount. Mtg.[2]	50,000	30%	10,000	5,000	Interest Pymts.	−10,000
					$17,500	$5,000	Net Income	$12,500

* Only the interest portion of the monthly payments is shown since the principal portion of the mortgage payback is your money.

[1] Mutual Funds (see Chapter 31)
   No commissions using no-load funds
   Money Movement Strategy (Chapter 30) used to earn 15% per year average
   All earnings can be either withdrawn to make mortgage payments or reinvested

[2] Discounted Mortgages (see Chapter 35)
   Mortgages purchased at 40% discount from face value
   20% is current income from monthly interest received
   10% income is deferred until mortgage matures

Today millions of Americans are following the same dead-end path, living a financially austere life even though they have wealth that could be unlocked from the equity they have built up in their homes. Your home equity, if borrowed and re-invested, can be an excellent source of additional income. Using a combination of a low-interest home equity loan or mortgage and a good safe investment plan that pays an average of 20% per year, you can borrow your home equity free. You can have enough income from your reinvested home equity to both make your mortgage payments and improve your lifestyle. For every $50,000 of home equity, you can increase your income over $6,000 per year for the rest of your life without ever depleting your principal (see "Borrow Your Home Equity Free" chart).

The next step is to formulate your investment plan. Your investments must provide a return great enough to make the payments on your loan plus give you additional income. The three best investments for reinvested home equity are no-load mutual funds using the Money Movement Strategy, discounted mortgages, and tax lien certificates. All are completely described in the investment section of this book. Mutual funds and discounted mortgages have the advantage of making the money you are earning instantly available for use in making payments on your equity loan. The chart on the facing page will give you suggested investment plans based on the amount of equity you have available. Modify the suggested plans to fit your specific investment needs: maximum growth, maximum income, or maximum tax shelter. Make your plan before you withdraw the money from your equity loan account.

For 24 additional powerful mortgage strategies, see my book *Financial Self-Defense*, Chapter 15, "Harness the Power of a Home Mortgage."

If you need more information about borrowing your home equity, contact the Mortgage ClearingHouse at 1-800-668-5827.

Chapter 10

BORROWING MONEY—LOAN AND CREDIT CARD STRATEGIES

Having more credit than money, thus one goes through the world.

Johann Wolfgang von Goethe
(1749–1832)

OBJECTIVE

CUT THE COST OF BORROWING MONEY BY 30 TO 50%.

Automobiles, furniture, and other rapidly depreciating assets are certainly not investments, but when you buy them you face the same financing decisions as with mortgages. For instance, should you finance the automobile or other purchase or pay cash? Of course, the question only applies to those who have the cash.

Strategy #99
IF THE RETURN ON A POTENTIAL INVESTMENT IS LESS THAN THE INTEREST RATE ON A LOAN, PAY CASH. IF THE INVESTMENT RETURN IS MORE, BORROW TO BUY AND INVEST YOUR CASH.

To make cash or credit decisions you must first understand an important financial measuring stick called "opportunity cost," or what I call "opportunity lost." If you pay cash, you automatically lose the opportunity to spend or invest that cash somewhere else. If you could borrow at 12% to buy an automobile, but instead pay cash, your opportunity cost is what you could have earned by investing that same amount of money, minus the 12% interest. If you could have earned 15% in no-load mutual funds (you'll learn how later), your opportunity cost or opportunity lost would have been 3% (15% minus 12%). You would be losing an opportunity for earning an additional 3% on your money. In this case, the greater profit would come from borrowing to buy the automobile and investing your dollars in the mutual fund. However, if a 9% bank certificate of deposit is the best investment you know, you would be better off paying cash for the car. Paying cash instead of paying 12% interest is like investing your money at 12%. Every financial decision has an opportunity cost, and computing your opportunity cost will show you the correct decision.

Strategy #100
FINANCE AUTOMOBILES, FURNITURE, AND OTHER PERSONAL ASSETS NO LONGER THAN 24 TO 36 MONTHS.

In today's world of easy money, you become bombarded with opportunities to pay over time, rather than pay at this time. Choose a shorter term for your loans or credit cards and, as with a mortgage, over time you can put thousands in your pocket.

When it comes to borrowing, the only two questions Americans have learned to ask are "How much is my down payment?" and "What are my monthly payments?" The most important question should be "What are my total payments?" That's what eats into your lifetime wealth. "The longer the term, the lower the monthly payments" is a true statement, but the law of diminishing returns raises the total cost of borrowing for a longer term far beyond the benefit of lower payments. When you lengthen the term of a loan to reduce the payments, the total interest paid increases dramatically.

When you shorten the term, your monthly payments are slightly higher but two positive financial rewards are yours:

1. You pay less total interest; what you buy costs less.
2. A greater percentage of each payment is applied to the principal instead of interest. You are out of debt more quickly for only a few dollars more per month.

For example, let's say you buy a car on which you obtain a $10,000 loan at 14%. You have a choice of terms ranging from

24 months to 60 months. The choice you make can increase or decrease the amount of interest you pay by as much as 150%!

HOW THE TERM AFFECTS YOUR LOAN

				36-Month Loan Comparison	
Effect of Choice of Automobile Loan Terms					
A	B	C	D	E	F
	Monthly	Total	Total	Interest	Extra
Term	Payment	Paid	Interest	Saved	Payment
24 mos.	$480	$11,520	$1,520	—	—
36 mos.	341	12,300	2,300	—	—
48 mos.	273	13,100	3,100	$ 800	$ 68/mo.
60 mos.	233	13,960	3,960	1,660	108/mo.

Choose a 36-month loan instead of a 60-month loan and you save a total of $1,660 or about 17% of the cost of the car. Notice that by financing for 60 months instead of 24 months, you will pay $2,440 additional interest or 25% more for your car (column D, $3,960 − $1,520). The lender always wins with 48- and 60-month loans. You win with 24- or 36-month loans.

What do you do if you cannot afford the extra payment? Buy a car one to two years older and your payments will not be any more for the shorter term than if you had purchased a newer and pricier car for the longer term. Under no circumstances can you afford an automobile or other loan for a term longer than 36 months.

Strategy #101
MAKE EXTRA PRINCIPAL PAYMENTS TO CUT
PERSONAL LOAN TERMS AND INTEREST 30 TO 50%.

Not only can you make extra principal payments on a mortgage, you can do the same with any high-interest loan or to rid yourself quickly of 18% or greater credit card interest.

You can even pay off a 48-month automobile or furniture loan in 24 months by making extra principal payments along with your regular payments. If you just financed $10,000 at 14% interest for 48 months, start immediately including next month's principal payment along with this month's full payment. Look at the Automobile Loan Amortization Schedule below. Let's say you've made payment number one for $268.27, and you are ready to make payment number two.

AUTOMOBILE LOAN AMORTIZATION SCHEDULE

Month 1 through 5 of a $10,000, 14%, 48-month loan

Payment #	Amount	Principal	Interest	Balance
1	$268.27	$159.94	$108.33	$9,840.06
2	$268.27	$161.67	$106.60	$9,678.39
3	$268.27	$163.42	$104.85	$9,514.97
4	$268.27	$165.19	$103.08	$9,349.78
5	$268.27	$166.98	$101.29	$9,182.80

The first month of the loan you pay $268.27. The second month you pay:

> check #1—second month's regular payment of $268.27
> check #2—third month's principal of $163.42
> Total = $431.69

The third month you pay:

> check #3—fourth month's regular payment of $268.27
> check #4—fifth month's principal of $166.98
> Total = $435.25

The extra principal payments will pay off the loan in 24 months instead of 48 months. If your lender requires you to pay in increments of full payment amounts, in our example $268.27, make extra principal payments that equal a full payment every two or three months instead of a partial extra principal payment every month.

Strategy #102
TO ELIMINATE HIGH-INTEREST CREDIT CARD DEBT, PAY AN EXTRA $25 TO $100 EACH MONTH, PLUS THE MINIMUM PAYMENT, PLUS THE AMOUNT OF YOUR PURCHASES.

Using credit cards often feels like getting something for nothing, at least until the bill arrives. Credit card interest is often 18% or 1½% per month and should be a primary target for the "extra principal payment" strategy.

You'll be surprised how quickly you can eliminate your credit card debt with only a few extra dollars each month. Since your next month's interest payment is computed on this month's principal balance, making extra principal payments will rapidly decrease your monthly interest and balance.

Let's say, for example, your MasterCard balance is $1,100, your required monthly payment is $60, and you purchased $110 this month. To get rapidly out of debt you send in a check for $220 covering the following:

New purchases amount	110
Required monthly payment	+ 60
Additional principal payment	+ 50
TOTAL PAYMENT	$220

You can pay off your credit card balance in half the time with manageable extra principal payments. If you have to scrimp and save in some other area—do so. It's imperative that you come up with the extra money this month if your objective is to get out of debt. Otherwise, your credit card debt will never be paid off, exactly what the credit card companies love.

Strategy #103
REPLACE HIGH-INTEREST CREDIT CARDS WITH LOW-INTEREST CARDS.

Throw away your 18% MasterCards and Visas and replace them with low-interest credit cards. The state of Arkansas, for instance, has a usury law that limits the amount of interest that can be charged on any loan, including credit cards. There are banks in Arkansas that have issued MasterCards or Visas to out-of-state customers at as little as 10½ to 12% interest. A few (but only a few) other banks have also lowered their rates. Following is a list of the least expensive credit cards available as of this writing. Get your applications today and get rid of interest rates that keep you in debt forever.

Read *Financial Self-Defense*, Chapter 14, "High-Powered Credit Card Strategies."

Name of Bank	Interest Rate*	Type of Card	Yearly Fees	Out of State	Grace Period

Arkansas Federal
P.O. Box 8208
Little Rock, AR 72221-8208
(800) 285-4002
**Special Rate for Givens
  Organization Members
  Only**
	8.00	Visa/MC	$35	Yes	25

Wachovia Bank 2400 Piedmont Rd. Atlanta, GA 30324 (800) 241-7990	9.75	Visa/MC	$39	Yes	25
Oak Brook Bank P.O. Box 5033 Oak Brook, IL 60522 (800) 666-1011	10.15	MC	$39	Yes	25
Amalgamated Trust A3979 Chicago, IL 60690 (800) 365-6464	9.00	MC (Gold)	$37	Yes	25
People's Bank P.O. Box 637 Bridgeport, CT 06601 Application Requests: (800) 423-3273	11.50	Visa/Mc	$25	Yes	25
Bank of New York, DE 700 White Clay Center Newark, DE 19714 (800) 942-1977	12.15	Visa/MC	$0	Yes	none

*At the time of publication.

Chapter 11

SEND YOUR KIDS TO COLLEGE FREE!

Experience keeps a dear school, but fools will learn in no other.

Benjamin Franklin
Poor Richard's Almanac
1743

OBJECTIVE ————————————————————————

COMBINE A COLLEGE LOAN WITH AN INVESTMENT THAT WILL CUT THE REAL COST OF EDUCATING YOUR CHILDREN BY 50 TO 100%.

The traumas of raising children are no longer limited to diapers, grades, first dates, and first automobiles. The third-biggest expense you'll ever encounter, close behind income taxes and buying a home, is putting your kids through college. The cost of even the most modest four-year college education now exceeds $20,000 with room and board.

My parents began a college fund for me using U.S. Savings Bonds. By the time I was 13, there were several thousand dollars neatly tucked away for an education at MIT. Then, in 1953, my parents' business slipped past the point of no return. Their last attempt to save it was to withdraw the college funds and dump the money into the business. Less than a year later, they were bankrupt, and MIT became a faded dream.

Years later, my father did scrape together $300 to enroll me in Millikin University in Decatur, Illinois, but my $27-a-week shoe salesman's job didn't provide enough money to keep the education going. Second semester, it was over. I was still paying off the balance of the first semester's tuition, and the school would not let me enroll for another term without more money. Ironically, 25 years later, when the college found out that I had become financially successful, it had no shame in asking me for contributions.

My experience is certainly not unusual. Many parents have traditionally found themselves unable or unprepared to finance college educations for their children. Either they intended to save money while the children were growing, or they were sold a life insurance policy that eventually failed to create enough cash value to pay for college. Most educational investment plans are doomed to the same failure. Because of inflation over any 20-year period, parents end up using their lifetime savings or going deeply in debt to finance the education that an 18-year savings plan would not support.

Student loans are difficult to get if you are above the poverty level. Scholarships cannot be depended on, and if your child or grandchild is not able to dunk a basketball or scare off a 300-pound defensive lineman, the cost of college will usually put you in financial trouble.

There is a simple plan that will allow you to educate your child, grandchild, or even yourself in any college in America—free!

Strategy #104
BUY A HOME THAT WILL PAY OFF A COLLEGE LOAN.

About three months before your child begins college, buy a four-bedroom home, condo, or duplex with as big a mortgage as possible within a few miles of the college campus. Furnish your property in "early Salvation Army" and rent it to four students with leases cosigned by their parents. Then march yourself down to the college financial aid office and ask for a little-known type of college financing called the "PLUS loan" (Parent Loan for Undergraduate Students—see Chapter 12). Finance the entire education using a combination of the parent loan plus one or more of the commercial loans listed in the same chapter. Pay the loan off with profit from the sale of the property when your child graduates. During the four-year term, your property will appreciate dramatically because of the shortage of off-campus housing in almost every college campus area.

Choose a property within a couple of miles of the campus, so that transportation for your resident students is not a problem. The property should be four bedrooms for two reasons: maximum rent while you own the property, and maximum value when you sell. The house should be in good condition, requiring only cosmetic, not major, surgery. Now let's look at the details.

Strategy #105
TURN YOUR PROPERTY INTO A MINI STUDENT DORM.

Furnish your property with used, inexpensive furniture from a salvage store. You will want a bed, desk, chair, chest of drawers, lamps, and small bookcase for each bedroom, and basic furniture for the rest of the house. Let students supply their own linens and kitchen utensils. Don't be surprised if you can furnish the entire house for little more than $1,000. All the furnishings are tax deductible.

Strategy #106
RENT YOUR PROPERTY BY THE BEDROOM ON A YEARLY LEASE TO INDIVIDUAL STUDENTS, COSIGNED BY PARENTS.

Renting the property to students is the easiest part of the strategy. Since most students would rather live off campus, there is always a housing shortage. Place ads under the "share" column of the school and local newspapers, and post notices on the school bulletin boards. Most college admissions or student housing offices keep a registry of available housing, in which you will want to list your property.

Maximize your income by renting by the bedroom on separate leases. Check with others who own rental property in the area to determine the rent you should charge. You will find you can get $150 to $300 per student, per month, depending on the city, cost of properties in the area, and the shortage of housing. The total rent of $600 to $1,200 per month will be more than adequate to offset the mortgage, taxes, and maintenance costs and will give you extra money for college expenses.

Two caveats about renting to students. First, rent on a full year's lease, not a lease that covers only nine months of the school year, and give each student the option to sublease if he or she will not attend summer school. Secondly, make certain that parents cosign the lease. With a cosigner, you are protected from the problem of collecting for damage or unpaid rent.

Strategy #107
MAKE YOUR SON OR DAUGHTER THE PROPERTY MANAGER.

By making your child the property manager, you can reap tax and business benefits almost immediately. Pay your child a tax deductible salary of about $100 a month and let him or her handle the regular duties of a property manager including:

- Collecting rents
- Inspecting the property once a week for cleanliness and damage
- Renting the property when there is a vacancy
- Contracting any repair work that needs to be done
- Reporting to you on the financial and physical condition of your property

The $1,200 per year you pay your child is tax deductible, since the money is paid for property management. The deduction should save you $336 per year in taxes (28% bracket) or more than $1,300 over the four years. The tax deductible money you pay your student can be used for books, supplies, or food expenses.

Your student may make a couple of tax deductible trips home each year for property management training or business conferences. Of course, the IRS might look at the trip suspiciously, so be certain to document the training or conference. A trip is deductible if it has a legitimate primary business purpose.

You may also travel to inspect any out-of-town property twice per year and take a tax deduction for the cost of the trip. Be certain the primary purpose of the trip is the inspection or maintenance of the property, and the secondary purpose is to visit your child.

Strategy #108
USE THE REAL ESTATE TAX DEDUCTIONS TO GENERATE EXTRA CASH.

The depreciation deductions you claim each year for your mini student dorm give you immediate cash, which can be applied toward college expenses. Using 20% as an estimate of the value of the land, 80% as the estimated value of the house, and assuming you are in the 28% marginal tax bracket, the table below illustrates how much cash you will save in taxes for the four years of college.

Basis of Property	First-Year Depreciation	Four-Year Depreciation	Four-Year Tax Savings
$ 50,000	$1,800	$ 7,200	$2,016
$ 75,000	$2,700	$10,800	$3,024
$100,000	$3,600	$14,400	$4,032
$150,000	$5,400	$21,600	$6,048

The year you sell the property, be certain to use tax strategies to create enough additional deductions to offset the depreciation recapture you will add to your income. The financial relief of a graduated student will give you the extra money to pay any taxes due on the profits.

Strategy #109
USE THE PROFITS FROM YOUR INVESTMENT TO PAY OFF YOUR LOANS.

When your child graduates, the time has arrived to sell the property. At 8% per year appreciation, the property will be worth $15,000 to $40,000 more at the end of four years, depending on the original price. Because of the demand for housing in college areas, the increase in value of your property will be substantial. The best and simplest way of selling the property for top dollar is to run the following advertisement in the school and city newspapers:

"Send your child to college free—call me for details!"

You'll receive a dozen calls the first day alone. Since you have the proof you can send your child to college free, you will have no problem selling the property to the parents of an incoming freshman. In fact, you'll have several families bidding up the price.

During the past few years, several colleges have sent staff members to my workshops to learn the "free college" strategy, then built condominiums on or near the campus and sold them to parents who then resell them at a profit to other parents four years later. Everyone wants in on the act! Someday, most colleges will adopt the "free college" strategy. Until then, you can use it on your own to pay for one or more expensive college educations.

There are several other sources of college financial aid. In order to help you plan effectively, the following chapter will show you the financing options and sources for the best education loans. You may use the college loans with or without purchasing real estate. Awareness of your alternatives and proper planning will save you thousands of dollars when educating your children, your grandchildren, or yourself.

Chapter 12

FOUND MONEY FOR COLLEGE

Whether four years of strenuous attention to football and fraternities is the best preparation for professional work has never been seriously investigated.

Robert Maynard Hutchins

OBJECTIVE

TAKE THE MYSTERY AND FRUSTRATION OUT OF FINDING COLLEGE LOANS AND GRANTS.

In all of life, a college education is one of your biggest potential expenses. Most parents and students have little idea what's available for funding a college education, what to ask for, or where to look, and often fall victim to an uninformed financial aid office. In reality, there is money for everyone who knows where to look and how to apply for it. This chapter will show you the strategies for finding that money. If you have children who are now or may be attending college in the next few years, it will prove invaluable to you.

College money from sources other than parents or relatives can be divided into two basic categories: loans and grants. A student loan is money advanced by the government, a bank or financial institution, or the school itself that must be repaid at a set interest rate over a specific term of years. Payments on some loans for school begin immediately; on others, payments are deferred until after completion of college or when the student quits school. Loans are of two types—those that are made directly to students and those that are made to parents for use on

140

a student education but for which the parents must qualify and are responsible for repayment.

A grant is money given to a student to cover specific school expenses and need not be paid back. Scholarships are a form of grant. As you might suspect, loans are far easier to get than grants. Don't believe the ads and hype that there are thousands of grants going to waste. True, there are thousands of grants, but many are never used primarily because of the extreme requirements that must be met!

Just about anyone can finance a part or all of a college education if he knows the ropes—where to look, what to ask for, how to determine the best deals, and how to qualify. Let's begin with the grant and loan programs offered through the U.S. Department of Education. My objective is to help you simplify the search process.

Here are your basic government-sponsored options:

Loans	Grants
Stafford Loans	Pell Grants
Parent Loans for Undergraduate Students (PLUS)	Supplemental Educational Opportunity Grants (SEOG)
Supplemental Loans for Students (SLS)	College Work-Study (CWS)
Perkins Loans	

Although most federal government aid for students is made on the basis of need, the exceptions are the PLUS loans and the Supplemental Loans for Students (SLS).

Here are some of the requirements for qualifying for any of these programs. The student:

- must have a high school diploma or general equivalency diploma (GED)
- must be a U.S. citizen or eligible noncitizen
- must have a C average by the end of the second year to continue to qualify for the aid

Students must sign:

- an anti-drug-abuse act certificate
- a statement of registration status
- a statement of educational purpose that says the money will be used solely for education-related expenses
- an agreement to attend school at least 50% of the time.

Many college loans (but not grants) are made by banks or other commerical lending institutions, but the loans are secured by a government guarantee agency. The guarantor basically says to the lending bank that if the borrower doesn't repay the loan, the guaranteeing agency will repay. The bank has no risk, but the guaranteeing agency does. Therefore the qualifications you must meet in order to get the loan are determined by the government agency and not the bank or financial institution that is actually lending you the money. Using the lists and charts at the end of this chapter, you can locate local or national banks and other lenders from which you can obtain college money under the above programs.

Usually a greater percentage of a college education can be paid for or financed through a combination of government-sponsored loans and/or grants. As with any government programs, the paperwork is excessive and borders on abusive, but that's just part of playing the game.

Strategy #110
**BEGIN YOUR COLLEGE AID SEARCH BY APPLYING
FOR OR ELIMINATING THE POSSIBILITY OF
NEED-BASED AID.**

If you are applying for loans or grants that are based on need (see chart on page 149), you must first prove that need. If parents are above the poverty level in income, need is often difficult to establish. The fact that parents are living paycheck-to-paycheck is of little consequence. The higher the combined income, the more difficult the need-based aid is to get. However, for most students who have parents with even moderately substantial means, it is not impossible. Since grants represent free money and the loans with the lowest interest rates are made on the "need" basis, always start your search for opportunities in the need-based areas. Even a relatively small amount of money obtained from a grant or low-interest loan is usually worth the paperwork. Many who might have gotten no-cost or low-cost help never apply. Who knows, you may get lucky.

HOW TO APPLY FOR AID

You can use any one of a number of forms if you are applying for need-based federal student aid other than a Pell Grant; your school will indicate which ones. If you want to be considered for a Pell Grant, you must use one of the following forms:

- U.S. Department of Education's "Application for Federal Student Aid"
- United Student Aid Funds' "Singlefile Form"

Two other forms collect extra information used in applying for nonfederal aid, and organizations charge for processing that information:

- American College Testing Program's "Family Financial Statement"
- College Scholarship Service's "Financial Aid Form"

The Stafford, PLUS, and SLS programs require some additional steps. If you want to apply to more than one school and these schools use different student aid applications, you may be able to use a short form called a Request for Information Transfer and have the information from the federal portion of one application sent to another school of your choice. Check with the schools individually.

Send in your application as soon as possible after January 1 for the fall term of the year for which you want the aid. The initial processing time is four to six weeks before you will hear anything. Unless you are lucky, you will then be asked for confirmations, clarifications, and corrections before your application can be finalized. Don't be perturbed, be prepared.

If you have not had any response after six weeks, write or call the Federal Student Aid Information Center at the address and phone number listed at the end of this chapter.

THE STUDENT AID REPORT (SAR)

Four to six weeks after you apply for Federal Student Aid, you receive a Student Aid Report (SAR), which itemizes your eligibility for many government or school financial aid programs. Your SAR will contain three parts:

- Part 1—a summary of the information you initially gave with your application
- Part 2—the information review form on which you are requested and required to make any corrections to the information in Part 1
- Part 3—the Pell Grant Payment Voucher, which, if you qualified, is as good as money at the school you will attend

---

Strategy #111
ORDER THE FEDERAL GOVERNMENT FUNDING SOURCE AND FORMULA BOOKS AND INFORMATION.

In conjunction with the information contained in this chapter there are free government publications and information sources that will be a great help to you in locating and obtaining college funding.

Pell Grant Index Explanation	Federal Student Aid
Booklet	Information Center
Formula Book	The Student Guide
Dept. M-11	P.O. Box 84
Pueblo, CO 81009-0015	Washington, D.C. 20044
	800-433-3243

The Pell Grant and how to qualify are completely explained in the "Formula Book." The Federal Student Aid address or phone number can be used when you want to know the status of your application or if you need a duplicate SAR. The Information Center provides the following services at the toll-free number:

- helping you file an application or correct an SAR
- explaining the Request for Information Transfer (RIT) process
- checking on whether a school takes part in Federal Student Aid programs
- explaining student eligibility requirements
- mailing publications to you

FEDERAL GOVERNMENT GRANT AND LOAN PROGRAMS

PELL GRANT
The Pell Grant is a maximum of $2,300 per year awarded to qualified students and is given based on a formula that takes into consideration parents' discretionary income and assets and the student's discretionary income and assets. The calculation results in a Student Aid Index, which determines how much of the $2,300 a student gets.

CAMPUS-BASED AID PROGRAMS
Campus-based aid programs are federal grant and loan programs that are administered by the financial aid officer of each partici-

pating college or university. The student can go to school less than half time and still receive this kind of aid. The amount of aid depends on both proven financial need and the amount of available funds at your school. Unlike the Pell Grant, which provides funds to every eligible student, each school participating in campus-based programs receives a limited amount of funds each year for each program. When the money is gone, there are no more awards given for that year. Your strategy is to apply early and often—at least once per year while your student is in school. The campus-based college-funding opportunities are divided into three separate programs:

Supplemental Education Opportunity Grant (SEOG)

This grant is for undergraduates with exceptional financial need. Priority is given to those who have already qualified for Pell Grants. The maximum grant is $4,000 per year.

College Work-Study Program (CWS)

The College Work-Study Program provides jobs for undergraduate and graduate students who need financial aid and gives them a chance to earn money to help pay educational expenses. The grant guarantees the job. The pay is at least the current federal minimum wage but increases based on the type of work and skills required. Undergraduates are paid by the hour. Graduate students may either be paid by the hour or receive a fixed salary. The amount you earn is limited by the total CWS award.

Perkins Loan

A Perkins Loan is a low-interest (5%) educational loan for both undergraduate and graduate students. The school is actually the lender. The maximum allowable loan is $4,500 for those who are enrolled in a vocational program or have completed less than two years of a bachelor's degree program, $9,000 for undergraduates who have already completed two years of study, and $18,000 for graduate or professional study. A promissory note agreeing to repay the loan is required. You have a grace period of nine months after you graduate, quit school, or drop below half-time enrollment before you must begin repaying the loan. You can take up to ten years to repay.

FEDERALLY GUARANTEED COMMERCIAL LOAN PROGRAMS

STAFFORD LOANS

The Stafford Loan Program is the new name for the old Government Student Loan Program (GSL). Stafford loans are low-interest loans made by commercial lenders such as banks, credit unions, savings and loan associations, or even schools to students attending school at least half time. These loans are insured by a guarantee agency in each state and reinsured by the federal government. Depending on your financial need, you may borrow up to $2,625 a year if you are a freshman or sophomore; $4,000 if you are a junior or senior; and $7,500 a year if you are a graduate student. The total debt you can have outstanding as an undergraduate under the Stafford Loan Program is $17,250, including any amount that may have been borrowed under the old GSL Program. The total limit for graduate or professional study is $54,750, including any Stafford loans and GSLs made at the undergraduate level. Your state guarantee agency is the best source of information on the Stafford Loan Program. A list is provided at the end of this chapter.

There is an origination fee of about 5%, which will be deducted from each loan disbursement made to you. Your lender may also charge you an insurance premium of up to 3% of the loan principal, which will also be deducted from the money you receive. To qualify for a Stafford Loan the family must have an income of less than $30,000, which eliminates aid for most families with two wage earners.

PLUS AND SLS LOANS

The Parent Loan for Undergraduate Students (PLUS) and the Supplemental Loan for Students (SLS) are the easiest to obtain of all the government educational assistance programs, yet the least known. In fact many college financial aid offices won't even mention them unless you ask about them by name.

PLUS loans are for parents who want to borrow to help pay for their children's education. SLS loans work like PLUS loans but the money is lent to the student instead of the parents. Loans are made by a lender such as a bank, credit union, or savings and loan association and are based on the creditworthiness of the borrower and the ability to pay back the loan. For these loans in general, the higher the family income the easier the loans are to get.

PLUS enables parents to borrow up to $4,000 per year to a

total of $20,000 for each child who is enrolled at least half time and is a dependent student. A dependent student is one who derives more than half of his income from parents or a guardian and who is generally claimed as a dependency exemption on the parents' tax return. Under SLS, graduate students and financially independent undergraduates may borrow up to $4,000 per year to a total of $20,000. This amount can be in addition to money received from the Stafford Loan Program.

For a PLUS or SLS application, check your high school guidance counselor, the financial aid office of the school, or your state guarantee agency (see pages 153–58). After you fill out your part of the application, the school you plan to attend must complete its part, certifying your enrollment, the cost of your education, and your academic standing, and list any other financial aid you will be receiving. You or the school then submits the paperwork to the lender you've chosen. If a parent takes out a PLUS loan, the lender sends the full amount of the loan proceeds in the form of a check directly to the parent. If the student takes out an SLS, the lender sends the loan proceeds to the school.

PLUS and SLS loans have variable interest rates, adjusted each year. For 1991 the interest rate was 9.34%. There is no origination fee for PLUS and SLS loans, but the lender may deduct an insurance premium of up to 3% of the loan principal.

PLUS and SLS borrowers generally must begin repaying both principal and interest within 60 days after the last loan disbursement. However, if a deferment applies (including a deferment for being in school), borrowers do not begin repaying any principal until the deferment ends. You must continue to pay the interest during a deferment period unless the lender allows you or your parent(s) to wait until the deferment ends to repay it. For more specific information, contact your financial aid administrator, your lender, or the guarantee agency in your state.

NONGOVERNMENT COMMERCIAL LOAN PROGRAMS

While there has been much written about hard-to-get government funded or guaranteed student aid, the easiest way to get financing is from commercial college-loan sources on which far too little information has been dispensed. Commercial loans are made by banks or independent lenders set up specifically to loan money for college tuition and expenses. Instead of the government guaranteeing repayment, commercial lenders look to the financial stability and creditworthiness of the parents and students who will be responsible for making the payments.

Several commercial loan types are worth considering to cover college expenses, including: TERI, Nellie Mae, Sallie Mae, and PLATO.

TERI

The Education Resources Institute (TERI), a commercial lender, provides loans of as much as $20,000 annually per student with up to 20 years to repay. The guarantee fee is 4%. Think of these fees as points similar to those on a mortgage. The interest rate charged is equal to the prime rate plus 1 to 2% adjusted monthly. Recently, TERI loans were available at 11 to 12%. The plan is packaged under a variety of other names such as Value and Alliance, depending on the lender.

NELLIE MAE

The New England Marketing Corporation (Nellie Mae) offers similar loans called Excel and Share, which have the option of being secured as home-equity loans. Good idea? You bet. Securing with your home makes the interest tax deductible to you. Interest rate is prime plus 2 to 4 points. Mid-1991 rate: 12–13%.

SALLIE MAE

The Student Loan Marketing Association (Sallie Mae) guarantees a variety of undergraduate and graduate student loans. Its Family Education Financing program, offered through Bank of America and First American Bank, lets you borrow as much as $10,000 annually (or more if tuition is higher) at the Treasury-bill rate plus 4 points. In mid-1991 the interest totaled about 11.5%. The rate is adjusted monthly.

PLATO

The new PLATO loan lets parents or students borrow as much as $25,000 annually with as long as 15 years to repay at a rate of 3.85% above the commercial paper rate. The interest rate is adjusted monthly and was 11.8% in mid-1991. There is a one-time 4% loan origination fee for each amount borrowed. The guarantor is University Support Services.

BEST COLLEGE MONEY SOURCES

Government-Sponsored Programs

Name of Plan	Source	Type of Plan	Loan Made to	Amount	Interest Rate (1992)	Fees	Term of Loan	Other
Stafford Loan	Commercial lenders	Govt. loan	Qualified students	$2,625 in first 2 years $4,000 in second 2 years	8% for first 4 years of repayment 10% for last 6 years of repayment	5% origination fee	10 years	Family must have income under $30,000 and meet other tests
Perkins Loan	School	Govt. loan	Qualified students	$4,500 first two years $9,000 second two years $18,000 graduate study	5%	None	10 years	
Pell Grant	Federal government	Govt. grant	Qualified students	$2,300 maximum	None	(see Other)	Outright grant	Consult: Formula Book Dept. M-11 Pueblo, CO 81009-0015
Supplemental Educational Opportunity Grant (SEOG)	Federal government	Govt. grant	Qualified students	$4,000 annually	None	None	Outright grant	Undergraduates with exceptional financial need; preference to aid; preference to Pell Grant recipients
PLUS Loan (see Other)	Commercial lenders	Govt. guaranteed commercial loan	Parents of dependent students	$4,000 annually	Variable interest with a maximum of 12%. Principal can be deferred	3%	10 years	Obtained through local financial institutions
SLS Loan	Commercial lenders	Govt. guaranteed commercial loan	Qualified students	$4,000 annually	Variable interest with a maximum of 12%. Principal can be deferred	3%	10 years	Obtained through local financial institutions

BEST COLLEGE MONEY SOURCES (cont.)

Commercial College Loan Sources

Name of Plan	Loan Made to	Amount	Interest Rate (1991)	Fees	Term of Loan	Other
Knight Extended Repayment Knight Tuition Payment Plans	Parents/guardians	Borrow an annual amount for 4 years of college	10%	$50 onetime application fee	10 years	Credit check required; insurance benefits
Ten-Month Payment Plan (see Knight above)	Parents/guardians	10-month installment plan for annual tuition, fees, room and board, minus financial aid	None	$35 annual application fee	10 monthly payments beginning June 1	Insurance available; down payment required if plan participation occurs after June 1
Insured Tuition Plan (see Knight above)	Parents/guardians	Multiple-year installment plan for any number of years of education	None	$50 onetime application fee	Monthly payments typically beginning in April or May	Insured; payments may be increased or decreased without penalty
Monthly Budget Plan Academic Mgmt. Service 50 Vision Blvd. E. Prov., RI 02914 800-635-0120	Parents/student	10-month installment plan for annual tuition fees, room and board	None	$45 annual application fee	10 monthly payments beginning on June 1	Insurance is included in the fee; down payment occurs after June 1

Plan	Eligible	Amount	Rate	Fee	Repayment	Notes
Academic Line of Credit (see Monthly Budget above)	Parents/guardians	Up to $25,000 annually	Prime + 4%	No guarantee fee	Interest only option	Pay finance charge only on amount used
Interest-Free Monthly Payment Plan Tuition Mgmt. Systems	Parents/student	10-month installment plan for annual tuition, fees, room and board	None	$35 annual participation fee	10 monthly payments beginning June 1	Down payments required if plan participation occurs after June 1
No-Collateral Loan (see Tuition Mgmt. above)	Parents/guardians	$2,000–$20,000 annually	Prime + 1.5%	4% guarantee fee	Interest only for first 4 years; up to 20 years to repay	
No-Collateral Credit Line (see Tuition Mgmt. above)	Parents/guardians	Up to $20,000 per year	Prime + 1.5%	4% guarantee fee	Interest only for first 4 years; up to 20 years to repay	Interest charged only on the amount used
Tuition Plan Donovan St. Ext. Concord, NH 03301 603-228-1161	Parents/guardians	100% of college costs	15.95%		10 years	Available in 38 states

BEST COLLEGE MONEY SOURCES (cont.)

Commercial College Loan Sources

Name of Plan	Loan Made to	Amount	Interest Rate (1991)	Fees	Term of Loan	Other
TERI The Education Resources Institute 330 Stuart Street Boston, MA 02116 800-255-8374	Parents/ guardians/ students	Up to $20,000 annually	Prime + 1% to 2% adjusted monthly	4% guarantee fee	20 years	Also known as Value, Alliance
Nellie Mae New England Marketing Corp.	Parents/ guardians/ students	$2,000–$20,000 annually undergraduate $2,000–$7,500 annually graduate	Prime + 2% to 4%	4% guarantee fee	4–20 years depending on amount borrowed	Also known as Excel, Share; often secured by home-equity loans
Sallie Mae The Student Loan Marketing Assoc.	Parents/ guardians	Parent Plus Loan $4,000 annually	T-bill + 4 points		2–10 years	Meet other tests
		Family Educational Loan $10,000 annually		3–10 years	Minimum $22,500 annual income, meet other tests	
PLATO University Support Services	Parents/ guardians/ students	$25,000 maximum annually	3.85% above commercial paper	4% origination fee	15 years	

COLLEGE AID

Important Addresses and Phone Numbers

Federal Student Aid Information Center
P.O. Box 84
Washington, D.C. 20044

800-433-3243	General Information
301-722-9200	Use this number to find out if your application has been processed or if you want a duplicate Student Aid Report (SAR).
301-369-0518	Use this number if you are hearing impaired.
800-MIS-USED	Call this number if you have any reason to suspect fraud, waste, or abuse involving Federal Student Aid funds.

Pell Grant Index Explanation Booklet
Formula Book
Department M-11
Pueblo, CO 81009-0015

Nellie Mae
New England Marketing Corporation
50 Braintree Hill Park, Suite 300
Braintree, MA 02184
800-634-9308

PLATO
University Support Services
205 Van Buren Street, Suite 200
Herndon, VA 22070
800-767-5626

Monthly Budget Plan
Academic Management Service
50 Vision Blvd.
E. Providence, RI 02914
800-635-0120

Tuition Plan
Donovan St. Ext.
Concord, NH 03301
603-228-1161

TERI
The Education Resources Institute
330 Stuart Street
Boston, MA 02116
800-255-8374

Sallie Mae
The Student Loan Marketing Association
1050 Thomas Jefferson Street, N.W.
Washington, D.C. 20007
800-831-5626

Knight Extended Repayment
Knight Tuition Payment Plans
855 Boylston Street
Boston, MA 02116
800-225-6783

Interest-Free Monthly Payment Plan
Tuition Management Systems
226 Bellevue Ave.
Newport, RI 02840
800-722-4867

Additional College Funding Information Sources

The Scholarship Book: The Complete Guide to Private Scholarships, Grants and Loans for Undergraduates
Daniel J. Cassidy
Prentice Hall
Englewood Cliffs, New Jersey

Catalog of Federal Domestic Assistance
U.S. General Services Administration
Washington, D.C. 20405

College Financial Aid Annual
John Schwartz, editor
Arco Publications
New York

Government Assistance Almanac
J. Robert Dumouchel
Omnigraphics, Inc.
Detroit, Michigan

PLUS and SLS Loans

State Guarantee Agencies

The following is a list of the state guaranteeing agencies or nonprofit organizations that administer the PLUS and SLS loan programs. While the federal government sets the loan limits and interest rates for these programs, the states set their own limitations and conditions. You should contact these agencies for the latest information on loan availability, repayment and deferment conditions. The guarantee agency can also put you in touch with willing lenders.

Alabama
Alabama Commission on Higher Education
One Court Square, Suite 221
Montgomery, AL 36197

Alaska
Alaska Commission on Postsecondary Education
400 Willoughby Avenue
Box FP
Juneau, AK 99811

Arizona
Arizona Educational Loan Program
2600 North Central Avenue, Suite 621
Phoenix, AZ 85004

Arkansas
Student Loan Guarantee Foundation of Arkansas
219 South Victory
Little Rock, AR 72201

California
California Student Aid
  Commission
P.O. Box 945625
Sacramento, CA 94245

Colorado
Colorado Guaranteed Student
  Loan Program
11990 Grant, Suite 500
North Glen, CO 80233

Connecticut
Connecticut Student Loan
  Foundation
25 Pratt Street
Hartford, CT 06103

Delaware
Delaware Higher Education Loan
  Program
Carvel State Office Building
830 North French Street, 4th Floor
Wilmington, DE 19801

District of Columbia
Higher Education Loan Program
  of Washington, D.C.
1023 15th Street, NW
10th Floor, Suite 1000
Washington, D.C. 20005

Florida
Official of Student Financial
  Assistance
Department of Education
Knott Building
Tallahassee, FL 32399

Georgia
Georgia Student Finance
  Commission
2082 East Exchange Place, Suite
  200
Tucker, GA 30084

Hawaii
Hawaii Education Loan Program
P.O. Box 22187
Honolulu, HI 96822

Idaho
Student Loan Fund of Idaho, Inc.
Processing Center
P.O. Box 730
Fruitland, ID 83619

Illinois
Illinois State Scholarship
  Commission
106 Wilmot Road
Deerfield, IL 60015

Indiana
State Student Assistance
  Commission of Indiana
964 North Pennsylvania Street
Indianapolis, IN 46204

Iowa
Iowa College Aid Commission
201 Jewett Building
9th and Grand Avenue
Des Moines, IA 50309

Kansas
Higher Education Assistance
  Foundation
6800 College Boulevard, Suite 600
Overland Park, KS 66211

Kentucky
Kentucky Higher Education
  Assistance Authority
1050 U.S. 127 South
Frankfort, KY 40601

Louisiana
Governor's Special Commission
  on Education Services
P.O. Box 44127
Capitol Station
Baton Rouge, LA 70804

Maine
Maine Department of Educational
and Cultural Services
Division of Higher Education
Services
State House Station 119
Augusta, ME 04333

Maryland
Maryland Higher Education Loan
Corporation
2100 Guilford Avenue, Room 305
Baltimore, MD 21218

Massachusetts
Massachusetts Higher Education
Assistance Corporation
Berkeley Place
330 Stuart Street
Boston, MA 02116

Michigan
Michigan Department of
Education Guaranteed Student
Loan Program
P.O. Box 30047
Lansing, MI 48909

Minnesota
Higher Education Assistance
Foundation
85 East 7th Street, Suite 500
St. Paul, MN 55101

Mississippi
Mississippi Guaranteed Student
Loan Agency
P.O. Box 342
Jackson, MS 39205

Missouri
Coordinating Board for Higher
Education
P.O. Box 1438
Jefferson City, MO 65102

Montana
Montana University System
33 South Last Chance Gulch
Helena, MT 59620

Nebraska
Higher Education Assistance
Foundation
Cornhusker Bank Building
11th and Cornhusker Highway,
Suite 304
Lincoln, NE 68521

Nevada
Nevada Guaranteed Student Loan
Program
Nevada State Department of
Education
400 West King Street
Capitol Complex
Carson City, NV 89710

New Hampshire
New Hampshire Higher Education
Assistance Foundation
P.O. Box 877
Concord, NH 03302

New Jersey
New Jersey Higher Education
Assistance Authority
C.N. 543
Trenton, NJ 08625

New Mexico
New Mexico Educational
Assistance Foundation
P.O. Box 27020
Albuquerque, NM 87125

New York
New York State Higher Education
Services Corporation
99 Washington Avenue
Albany, NY 12255

North Carolina
North Carolina State Education
    Assistance Authority
P.O. Box 2688
Chapel Hill, NC 27515

North Dakota
Bank of North Dakota
Student Loan Department
P.O. Box 5509
Bismarck, ND 58502

Ohio
Ohio Student Loan Commission
P.O. Box 16610
Columbus, OH 43266

Oklahoma
Oklahoma State Regents for
    Higher Education
500 Education Building
State Capitol Complex
Oklahoma City, OK 73105

Oregon
Oregon State Scholarship
    Commission
1445 Willamette Street
Eugene, OR 97401

Pennsylvania
Pennsylvania Higher Education
    Assistance Agency
660 Boas Street
Harrisburg, PA 17102

Rhode Island
Rhode Island Higher Education
    Assistance Authority
560 Jefferson Boulevard
Warwick, RI 02886

South Carolina
South Carolina Student Loan
    Corporation
Interstate Center, Suite 210

P.O. Box 21487
Columbia, SC 29221

South Dakota
Education Assistance Corporation
115 First Avenue, SW
Aberdeen, SD 57401

Tennessee
Tennessee Student Assistance
    Corporation
400 James Robertson Parkway
Suite 1950, Parkway Tower
Nashville, TN 37219

Texas
Texas Guaranteed Student Loan
    Corporation
P.O. Box 15996
Austin, TX 78761

Utah
Loan Servicing Corporation of
    Utah
P.O. Box 30803
Salt Lake City, UT 84130

Vermont
Vermont Student Assistance
    Corporation
Champlain Mill
P.O. Box 2000
Winooski, VT 05404

Virginia
State Education Assistance
    Authority
Six North Sixth Street, Suite 300
Richmond, VA 23219

Washington
Washington Student Loan
    Guaranty Association
500 Colman Building
811 First Avenue
Seattle, WA 98104

West Virginia
Higher Education Assistance
  Foundation
Higher Education Loan Program
  of West Virginia, Inc.
P.O. Box 591
Charleston, WV 25322

Wisconsin
Wisconsin Higher Education
  Corporation
2401 International Lane
Madison, WI 53704

Wyoming
Higher Education Assistance
  Foundation
American National Bank Building
1912 Capitol Avenue, Suite 320
Cheyenne, WY 82001

Puerto Rico
Higher Education Assistance
  Corporation
P.O. Box 42001
Minillas Station
San Juan, PR 00940

Part II

TAX-REDUCING

STRATEGIES

Chapter 13

MAKING YOUR LIFE LESS TAXING

People who complain about the tax system fall into two categories—men and women.

Barry Steiner
Pay Less Tax Legally
1982

OBJECTIVE ————————————————————————

CUT YOUR INCOME TAXES BY 50%.

The biggest lifetime expense you'll ever encounter is neither a home nor a college education, but income taxes. What we were never taught is that the amount of income tax you are liable for has little to do with your total income, and everything to do with your knowledge of tax strategies.

The importance of an effective tax plan cannot be overstated. One-third to one-half of all the wealth you will accumulate in your lifetime is dependent on your tax-reducing plan and not your income, investments, or retirement program.

The new tax laws mean a tax increase for two out of three families with an income of over $20,000. All of the flag-waving by Congress proclaiming a great tax decrease is purely political, not practical reality. Over 50 once-automatic deductions have been eliminated or curtailed, and the elimination of income averaging and especially the favorable capital gains tax rates puts a bigger tax burden on investors, retired people, and the upwardly mobile. The best defense is still a good offense—a tax plan that uses the new tax laws to decrease instead of increase your taxes.

161

Where do we begin? By learning to turn the money you spend into legitimate tax deductions. Up to 60% of your income each year can become tax sheltered if you combine personal expenses with tax deduction strategies. Just about every strategy you can logically and legally use to cut your taxes is contained in this and the following chapters.

At 19, I dropped out of Millikin University after one semester, far short of the $300 tuition necessary to remain enrolled. Needing money to help support my mother and brother, I went to work in a foundry dumping slag—molten metal waste—from the furnaces. If you ever want a job that will motivate you to do something with your life, work in a foundry for a while. That same year I started a rock-and-roll band—Chuck Givens and the Quintones—and I was soon making more money playing music on weekends than I made working in the foundry all week. Then came my first shocking experience with the tax system. My record-keeping skills were almost nonexistent, but I put together what I had and headed for the tax preparer's office. After only five minutes, I left with an assurance I could pick up my completed tax return in a week. When I returned, I got the shock of my life.

"I've got some good news and some bad news," muttered the CPA. "The good news is your tax return is completed. The bad news is you owe the IRS an extra $2,000."

At the tender age of 19, I had never seen $2,000 in one place at one time and I knew that I had absolutely no chance of putting that much money together anytime in the foreseeable future. My mind played visions of police cars and prisons.

In self-defense, I drove to the Federal Building in Decatur, not to turn myself in, but to pick up every publication the IRS would give away free. I was determined to learn something about a tax system that was about to put me under. I didn't realize what I had asked for and carted two full armloads of IRS material to the car. During the next three months, I scoured the pages looking for tax relief. Constantly, it seemed, I came upon possible deductions the CPA had never mentioned. At the end of the three months, right before April 15, I completed another return myself. Based on my calculations, I did not owe the IRS the extra $2,000 and was entitled to a refund of some of the taxes that had been withheld from my paychecks at my full-time job. I was sure I'd made a mistake.

Returning to the CPA's office, I asked, "Where did I go wrong?"

"You're not wrong," he said, "you're absolutely right."

The shock must have registered on my face. "What do you mean?" I said. "You had me scared to death, owing the IRS $2,000 I don't have, and yet when I do my own return, I get money back."

With a look of disgust, he came halfway out of his chair. "Let me tell you something, son! I am a tax preparer, not your financial adviser. You are paying me to take your numbers and put them on the tax forms. If you don't know how to tell me about what you're doing, I have no reason or responsibility to take the deductions."

The light went on; I got it! If I ever wanted to protect myself from overpaying income taxes, I must learn everything possible about the tax system. No one, not even a tax preparer or CPA, was going to do it for me the way it needed to be done. That experience has probably saved me more in income taxes than most people will make in a lifetime.

I have spent the last 25 years learning everything possible about the tax system and how to maximize your spendable income by minimizing your taxes. The tax system is not your enemy, unless you don't understand it. Your objective is to work with the tax system from an ethical business perspective. In business, the objective is to increase profits by reducing expenses. In your personal life, your objective is to increase your spendable income by reducing your taxes.

I am not a tax protester, nor am I out to destroy the American tax system. I love this country and the opportunities it has given me. What I want for America is equality of tax opportunity. Why should only the superrich know how to make tax laws work in their favor? Equality of tax opportunity will never be achieved through so-called tax reform, but only through education in the form of tax-reducing strategies—the strategies you are about to learn.

Strategy #112
USE ONLY TAX STRATEGIES, NEVER LOOPHOLES OR TAX CHEATING.

In pursuing the dream of lower taxes, it is never necessary to resort to tax cheating or loopholes, or even to question the legality of the tax system. There is a big difference between cheating, loopholes, and strategies.

TAX CHEATING is understating your income or claiming tax deductions for assets you don't own or expenditures you never made. Tax cheating may bring you fame and fortune as in the case of Billie Sol Estes, who claimed tax deductions for nonexistent Texas grain bins, but jail and other legal penalties always outweigh the fame and can cost you your fortune.

LOOPHOLES are untested areas of the tax law that allow you to claim "default deductions" that Congress and the IRS might have rules against had they had the foresight to see the possibilities. Since a specific "no" does not exist, you create a loophole by saying "yes" to a shaky deduction. Loopholes are often sought after by desperate, high-income taxpayers who never took the time to plan. Some loopholes are used purely out of greed, others are taken because of the gambling instinct. There is only one "do" about loopholes, and that is "don't."

TAX STRATEGIES are positive, legal uses of the tax laws to reduce your income taxes. Tax strategies are actions you take that automatically and legally qualify you for additional deductions. These action strategies can include opening an IRA account, starting a small business, buying real estate, and 75 other possibilities. Some tax strategies, like those just mentioned, are straightforward and obvious. Other strategies, such as traveling on tax deductible dollars and a tax deductible college education for your children, are just as legal, just as easy to use, but less understood.

One question I am asked over and over again: "Is paying less taxes really legal, patriotic, and moral?" For some reason many people seem to confuse our tax system with the United Fund, whose slogan is "Pay your fair share." By following the tax laws and regulations when you use tax strategies, you automatically pay your fair share, even if your share amounts to zero. Two neighboring families, each with a $30,000 annual income and two children, could both be paying their fair share of income taxes, even if one family paid $5,000 and the other paid nothing at all. It's the way the American tax system was designed.

We have a system that imposes taxes, not on your total income, but on a far smaller number known as your taxable income; your residual income after you subtract your exemptions, adjustments, and deductions. Within the difference between total income and taxable income lie your opportunities for applying legal, powerful tax-reducing strategies.

Not long ago on the "Donahue" show, during one of the best national discussions on tax strategies in which I have ever participated, a lady caller said she thought reducing your taxes was cheating. She made $15,000 working, didn't have an IRA, and her husband was even a tax attorney! Her feeling was that she wanted to pay taxes to help the homeless. This may come as a surprise to you, as it did to her, but very few of your federal tax dollars go to the homeless, or many other places you might prefer the money to go. By learning legal strategies for reducing her taxes, she could have given her tax savings directly to the homeless herself.

Another woman in the studio audience felt that paying more taxes was patriotic. The courts say that paying taxes has nothing to do with patriotism whether you pay a lot or none at all. The money goes into the economy whether paid to the government or used by you for a deductible purpose.

The question of legality and morality of tax deductions was settled once and for all over 40 years ago by the United States Circuit Court of Appeals in an opinion written by Judge Learned Hand.

> Anyone may so arrange his affairs that his taxes shall be as low as possible; he is not bound to choose that pattern which will best pay the Treasury; there is not even a patriotic duty to increase one's taxes.

This decision should govern both your tax plan and your tax attitude. Rearranging your affairs to create deductions where you had none before is the secret to paying less in taxes. All of the tax strategies you will learn will legally and easily reduce your taxes by thousands each year. Your job is to pick those strategies that best suit you and your family. Tax strategies should form one-third of your written financial plan.

How much time is required? Reducing your taxes is basically a do-it-at-home, do-it-yourself, do-it-in-your-spare-time project, requiring no more than a few minutes a week. What you'll soon discover is that one hour spent learning and applying a legal tax strategy will save you $100 to $300 in taxes. That's like having a $100- to $300-per-hour tax-free job.

Strategy #113
DETERMINE YOUR TAX BRACKET TO TRACK YOUR TAX SAVINGS.

Our nation has a graduated tax system. That means the more you make, the more they take. Many taxpayers incorrectly believe that by earning more money they can end up with less money because they move into a higher tax bracket. Not so. The higher bracket percentage applies only to the additional income you earn and does not affect the amount of taxes you pay on the amount of money you were already earning. Never fall back on the excuse that you don't want to make more money because you will end up in a higher bracket. Instead, make all the money you can and reduce the taxes you pay by using "Tax Strategies."

The first step is to know your tax bracket. It's like assessing the damage—knowing the percentage of each dollar you earn that is lost forever. For example, if you are in the 28% bracket, you work from nine to eleven-thirty each day for the government, and the rest of an eight-hour day for yourself.

Your *effective tax bracket* is the percentage of your total income you pay in taxes. If your total income is $40,000 per year and you pay a total of $5,000 in federal, state, and local taxes, your effective tax bracket is 12.5% ($5,000 divided by $40,000 = 12.5%). In tax planning, knowing your effective tax bracket will motivate you to create a good tax plan.

Your *marginal tax bracket* is the percent in taxes you pay on your top dollar of taxable income. It is also the percent of tax you will pay on one additional dollar of income, or, conversely, the percentage you will save in taxes for each additional dollar of tax deductions you create.

The chart on page 167, "Tax Rate Schedules Under Tax Reform," will show you your marginal bracket and the amount of tax you will pay based on your taxable income in 1994 and beyond. Your marginal tax bracket is the percentage shown in the right-hand column of each schedule.

There are three types of personal income taxes: federal, state, and local. Everyone is subject to federal taxes, but ten states have no state income tax. Most people are not subject to local income taxes, except in large metropolitan areas such as New York City and Washington, D.C.

Most federal income tax deductions are allowed on most state tax returns. The average percentage for those who pay state taxes is 7% applied to taxable income. Add 7% to your federal marginal tax bracket, if you are subject to state income taxes, and you can see why you have so little money left.

TAX RATE SCHEDULES UNDER TAX REFORM
1994 and Beyond

Married Filing Jointly

Taxable Income	Marginal Bracket
$ 0	15%
38,000	28
91,850	31
140,000	36
250,000	39.6

Married Filing Separately

Taxable Income	Marginal Bracket
$ 0	15%
19,000	28
45,925	31
70.000	36
250,000	39.6

Single

Taxable Income	Marginal Bracket
$ 0	15%
22,750	28
55,100	31
115,000	36
250,000	39.6

Head of Household

Taxable Income	Marginal Bracket
$ 0	15%
30,500	28
78,700	31
127,500	36
250,000	39.6

Strategy #114
CUT YOUR ADJUSTED GROSS INCOME TO INCREASE ALLOWABLE DEDUCTIONS AND REDUCE TAXES.

Under the new tax laws the amount of medical and miscellaneous deductions you can claim is partially dependent on your adjusted gross income (AGI). Since medical expenses are deductible only in excess of 7.5% of AGI, and miscellaneous expenses such as job-related expenses are deductible only in excess of 2% of AGI, your goal is to reduce your adjusted gross income.

Use the chart below, "Computing Your Adjusted Gross and Taxable Income," to help you increase certain itemized deductions. Notice that a business loss, IRA contributions, and real estate deductions all reduce your adjusted gross income (AGI).

COMPUTING YOUR ADJUSTED GROSS AND TAXABLE INCOME

Using last year's tax return or an estimate of this year's income and expenses, complete this form to determine your adjusted gross income, taxable income, and marginal tax bracket.

Part 1   Income

A
Included

$ _____ Wages
_____ Profit from a small
business
_____ Annuity income
_____ Pension income
_____ Profit from sale of
investments
_____ Interest or dividend income
_____ Rental income
_____ Royalty payments
_____ Other
$ _____ TOTAL TAXABLE INCOME BEFORE DEDUCTIONS

B
Not Included

$ _____ Tax-free bond interest
_____ Tax-free insurance
proceeds
_____ Gifts
_____ Inheritances
_____ Social Security (tax-free
portion)
_____ Other
$ _____ TOTAL (TAX-FREE INCOME)

Part 2   Deductions That Reduce Your AGI (adjusted gross income)

$ _____ Loss from small business
   _____ Deductible contributions to an IRA or Keogh
   _____ Contribution to pension plan of an S corporation
   _____ Alimony payments
   _____ Premature withdrawal penalty from CDs
   _____ Deductions from real estate investments
   _____ Other
$ _____ TOTAL AGI DEDUCTIONS

Part 3   AGI & Taxable Income Calculation

Total Taxable Income from Part 1A	+ $	_____
Subtract: AGI Deductions from Part 2	−	_____
Adjusted Gross Income	$	_____
Subtract:		
Schedule A Deductions (total)*	−	_____
Deductions for Dependents ($2,450 each)	−	_____
TAXABLE INCOME	$	_____

Part 4   Computing Your Effective Tax Bracket

Your Federal Bracket (from tax rate schedule)	+	_____ %
Your State Tax Bracket (estimated)	+	_____ %
YOUR EFFECTIVE TAX RATE		_____ %

You can easily determine your adjusted gross income (AGI) by subtracting Part 2 deductions from Part 1A income. Other Schedule A deductions and deductions for dependents are then subtracted from your adjusted gross income to determine your taxable income.
*Schedule A deductions include interest, medical, charitable contributions, taxes, and miscellaneous deductions often referred to as itemized deductions.

As you use the tax strategies in this book, keep track of your deductions as you create them. You will notice that as your taxable income gets smaller, your taxes become less and your spendable income increases. The purpose of a good tax plan is having more money to spend.

Chapter 14

TAX RETURN FILING STRATEGIES

Take it off, take it all off!

Gypsy Rose Lee
Entertainer/Author
1936

OBJECTIVE

REDUCE YOUR TAXES AND CHANCES OF AN AUDIT AT THE SAME TIME.

The four-letter word that keeps most people from becoming better "tax strategists" is *fear*. Most fear in life comes from lack of knowledge, not from any real threat. In the case of the IRS, fear is usually founded in fantasy, not fact—fear of an audit, fear of embarrassment, fear of harassment, and worse yet, fear of jail. Unless you are an outright tax cheater, you have nothing to worry about. To succeed financially you must have the confidence to use tax strategies. Confidence and courage come from knowledge of how the tax system really works, and how to use the system in your favor while keeping both the IRS and Congress on your side.

Years ago, when I was designing computer systems for a major corporation, I was a member of an association of computer professionals that included current and former IRS computer systems designers and programmers. Often, late at night, over a beer or two, they would tell me little-known secrets of the IRS computer system. The tax strategies in this chapter are based partially on information obtained at those late-night social gatherings and from my experience over the years in working with thousands of taxpayers and tax professionals.

Strategy #115
USE THE LONG FORM—YOU CANNOT PAY MORE IN TAXES, ONLY LESS.

You may be one of the few who thinks you don't need a tax plan because you fill out the short form and can't take deductions. That's the first tax mistake. Those who fill out the short form are paying the absolute maximum tax that can be paid on that level of income.

Always complete the 1040 long form to identify potential tax deductions. If you don't have more than the standard deduction, the long form will point out where your tax plan is lacking. Completing the long form will also familiarize you with the process of turning deductions into dollars. Those who have never completed a long form are those who usually claim they understand little about taxes. Long forms are a necessary part of tax strategy training and are not at all difficult. Use tax publication 17 as your guide. Filing the long form can never cost you more, only the same or less.

Strategy #116
CHOOSE AN AGGRESIVE TAX PREPARER OR NONE AT ALL.

Whether or not you use a tax preparer is strictly a matter of choice. Almost 60% of taxpayers use a tax preparer, and with the complexity of the new tax laws, more will probably look for help.

A good tax preparer is an aggressive tax preparer, and like four-leaf clovers, they are hard to find. Many tax laws and rules are written to intimidate tax preparers into becoming unnecessarily meek, mild, and conservative, even though these same laws and rules don't apply to you as a taxpayer. If your tax preparer is full of warnings, such as "I wouldn't take that deduction, it might send up a red flag," and short on explanations, the money you are paying for so-called tax advice pales beside the money you are unnecessarily paying in taxes.

The most effective way to choose a tax preparer is to interview several with one key question: "How much in taxes did you pay last year?" If the answer is much more than zero, or a hedge like "None of your business!" you are dealing with a tax loser, not an effective tax preparer. If a tax expert can't help himself pay less tax, how can you expect that he will be able to help you? Another approach is to quiz your friends until you find one who is near the zero tax bracket. Use his or her tax preparer. But even if you use a tax preparer, you must still learn to communicate effectively about taxes.

Strategy #117
PREPARE YOUR OWN RETURN—AT LEAST ONCE.

One question I am often asked at my workshops is "Should I prepare my own return?" The answer is yes—completely once, and partially each year. Without understanding how adjustments, credits, and deductions affect your return, you will never feel confident about handling the tax system. You can save yourself both money and time at tax preparation time if you pencil in your income and deductions before you take your papers to a tax preparer. This process will discipline you into becoming a better record keeper as well as operate as a checklist to be certain you have everything organized. Your tax preparation will become much easier and the bill much smaller.

There are also hidden traps in the way that your tax preparer may take deductions. Tax preparers may, for instance, choose alternatives for automobile, interest, or investment deductions that save preparation time but give you far less in deductions. You must be in a position to tell your preparer what forms and formulas to use if you want to pay less in taxes.

Strategy #118
TIME YOUR REFUND TO EARN EXTRA INTEREST.

The IRS must send you any refund due within 45 days from the date you file or April 15, whichever is later. If your refund is late by even one day, you are entitled to interest from the filing date. To get your interest you may have to notify the IRS by sending in a claim. Always calculate the number of days between filing and refund.

Strategy #119
DON'T APPLY THIS YEAR'S REFUND TO NEXT YEAR'S TAXES.

Your 1040 form will give you an option: get your refund in cash or apply your refund to next year's taxes. Never give the IRS the use of your money free! If you end up owing more money because of understated income or interest income you forgot to claim, you will have to pay from your bank account. The IRS will not let you take the additional money owed out of your prepayment. Put your refund in your investment account and let it work for you instead of for the IRS.

Strategy #120
AVOID TAX PENALTIES; DON'T BE CONCERNED ABOUT INTEREST.

Refer to the following "Penalties and Interest on Tax Returns" chart and you will see what it costs to file late, make mistakes, or even cheat.

Mention the word *penalty* and most taxpayers cringe. The two biggest penalties, negligence and fraud, are also the easiest to avoid. These penalties are never assessed arbitrarily or used as a threat, but only to punish taxpayers who intentionally try to cheat or who don't report all income.

The biggest honest taxpayer's penalty is imposed for not having the extra money to pay extra taxes due when filing a return. The penalty is .5% per month plus interest of three points over the three-month T-bill rate. The total interest and penalties paid each month are, therefore, only slightly more than the 18% interest of credit cards you may carry in your wallet. Not pleasant, but not enough to break you either. Interest and penalties are assessed only on the extra taxes due, not on your taxable income.

You must file your tax return or request an extension by April 15 whether or not any taxes are due. The late filing penalty is 5% per month up to 25% maximum. There is no penalty unless you owe money. You have three years to file for a refund or two years after the tax was paid, whichever is later. If you file an amended tax return claiming additional deductions, you will receive interest on your additional refund from 45 days after your original return was filed up to the date your amended return was processed.

All penalties are easily avoided by proper planning and filing an honest return.

PENALTIES AND INTEREST ON TAX RETURNS

Interest (Paid and Received)

Underpayment of tax	3 mo. T-bill Rate + 3%
Overpayment of tax	3 mo. T-bill Rate + 2%

Penalties for Tax Law Violations

Civil Violations   *Penalty*

Unpaid taxes	.5% per month up to 25% + interest
Negligence	5% of underpayment + interest
Failure to file return when due (60-day grace period)	$100 or taxes due
Bad check charge	1% of check
Frivolous or incomplete return	$500
Frivolous lawsuit against the IRS	$5,000
Overvaluation of property	10% to 30% of underpayment
Intent to evade taxes	75% of underpayment + 50% of interest
False withholding information	$500
Failure to file partnership return	$50 ea. partner per month; max. 5 months

Criminal Violations

Willful failure to pay or file	Up to $25,000 + 1 year prison
Willfully falsifying return	Up to $100,000 + 3 years prison
Intent to evade taxes	Up to $100,000 + 5 years prison
False withholding information	Up to $100,000 + 1 year prison

> ### Strategy # 121
> ## WHEN IN DOUBT, DEDUCT IT.

Most taxpayers think they are doing themselves a favor by being ultraconservative in taking deductions. Nothing could be further from the truth. If you are tax deduction "shy," not only do you end up spending thousands of dollars in unnecessary taxes, you don't even reduce your chances for audit. Most audits are done at random and have little to do with whether you take all of your allowable deductions or only a few.

If you want to reach your financial goals, you must adopt the winning tax strategy: WHEN IN DOUBT, DEDUCT IT. Take everything the law allows. Follow the rules, but deduct all gray areas in your favor. Gray areas are not loopholes or an attempt to get around the tax laws, but areas of ambiguity and uncertainty about what Congress or the IRS really meant. You have just as much chance of winning your point as the IRS does. You'll be surprised, as you learn about taxes, at how much of the code is ambiguous. Simple record keeping and tax strategies will always have you prepared to win your point. When you hear a tax preparer say, "I wouldn't take that deduction even though it is legitimate, it might send up a red flag," fire him.

Strategy #122
SIGN YOUR RETURN YOURSELF.

Believe it or not, the IRS audits a greater percentage of returns signed by "experts" than by individual taxpayers. The reason? The IRS found that tax professionals make more mistakes than taxpayers. The statistics are as follows:

- 30% of returns prepared by taxpayers contain errors
- 40% of returns prepared by CPAs and accountants contain errors
- 60% of returns prepared by franchised tax preparers contain errors

If a tax preparer has prepared your return, he must, by law, sign it, but if you simply get tax advice or assistance in preparing your return, you may sign it yourself. Signing your own return cuts your chances of being audited by about 20%, but does not prevent you from taking a professional with you if you are audited.

There is an exception. If you earn over $50,000 per year in total income, your chances of being audited are less if a CPA or tax preparer signs your return. The IRS somehow believes that even though you are smart enough to earn that kind of money, you are not smart enough to prepare your own tax return.

Strategy #123
FILE YOUR RETURN LATER, NOT EARLIER.

The later you file, the less your chances for audit. If you file your tax return each year after April 1, you have automatically reduced your chances for audit by about 40% over those who file in January, February, and March. The reduced chance for audit is due to a quirk in the IRS's computer program and how it selects returns for possible audit. The IRS will tell you it's not true, but it is. Here's how it works.

The IRS brass meets each year to decide how many returns will be audited for each deduction category. The IRS has only 24,500 auditors and has suffered recent budget cuts like all governmental branches. The number of returns to be selected for each deduction category is programmed into the computer. Returns for possible audit are then selected on a "first come" basis, and when the total number of returns for a category has been chosen, the computer stops selecting. The later you file, the more categories will be full.

Strategy #124
FILE AN AUTOMATIC EXTENSION FORM 4868.

You can reduce your chances for audit even further by filing IRS Form 4868—Automatic Extension of Time to File. The automatic extension gives you an extra four months—until August 15—to file your tax return for the previous year. Interest is charged on unpaid taxes at less than 1% per month but there is no late-filing penalty. Another two-month extension can be requested in writing and is almost always granted, moving your required filing date to October 15.

For more information about tax preparers that utilize the Charles J. Givens tax strategies, call the Charles J. Givens Tax Connection Division at 1-800-333-4652.

Chapter 15

WINNING THE TAX AUDIT

You pays your money and you takes your chances.

Punch
1846

OBJECTIVE

GAIN THE UPPER HAND IN A TAX AUDIT.

Isn't it strange how the possibility of an audit makes you feel guilty even when you're not?

An audit is nothing more than your opportunity to prove to the IRS that you are a good record keeper. If you're not, your first audit can go a long way in motivating you to become one. Fear of being audited comes from a lack of knowledge, not from any real IRS threat. All of us will be audited once or twice in a lifetime no matter how carefully our returns are filled out. Be prepared rather than scared.

The first time I was audited was 1963. The item in question: a $35 education deduction for a night-school course in English literature. I felt it helped me improve my job skill, which was writing excuse letters to irate customers who had not received their orders. The auditor, a very pleasant lady indeed, said, "English composition, yes; English literature, no. No deduction." Since the rest of the return passed, I reluctantly acquiesced and paid the $1.17 in extra taxes. It must have cost the IRS $500 in time and correspondence to collect my money.

Strategy #125
DON'T REACT TO AN AUDIT AS MORE THAN IT REALLY IS.

According to the IRS, an audit is "an impartial review of a tax return to determine its accuracy and completeness." An audit is not an accusation that you have done something wrong, only a request for more information. Knowledge of audit objectives and proceedings give you the same level of power and clout that most taxpayers attribute to the IRS. Knowledge can reduce an audit to the impartial review it is supposed to be.

Of course an audit is a hassle. Anything you do that doesn't contribute to your wealth, health, family, relaxation, or goals is a hassle. Grin and bear it. Look at an audit as part of the game, just as painful exercise is part of building a strong body.

Most people try to avoid an audit by being conservative and maintaining a low profile. The thousands of extra dollars a person pays in federal income taxes over the course of a lifetime to avoid one or two audits is simply not worth the price. More importantly, being overconservative doesn't really help reduce your chances for audit.

What are your real chances for being audited in any one year? Out of 96 million individual tax returns, less than 2 million returns are audited—about 2%. Even so, it is important to know the rules of the game.

Based on past performance of the IRS, here are your percentage chances for being audited by income and profession.

Individuals:

Your Income/Profession	Chance for Audit
Under $50,000	2%
Over $50,000	8%
Professionals	25%
Known criminals	50%

Your Small Business:

Business Income	Chance for Audit
Under $10,000	3%
$10,000–$30,000	2%
Over $30,000	7%

If placed on a shelf, the tax code, regulations, and manuals would stretch 40 feet and fill close to 50,000 pages. It's no wonder the tax system is such a mess; even the IRS is confused. The General Accounting Office of the United States has said that IRS phone representatives give the wrong answer to at least one out of every ten questions asked. *USA Today* hired CPAs to call the IRS with a list of ten questions. The IRS gave the wrong answer 40% of the time.

I realize these facts aren't particularly comforting, but at least you can begin to see that IRS professionals are human and make mistakes. Understanding this situation will help you walk into any audit feeling a bit more confident.

Tax returns are chosen for audit using three entirely different parameters. The first parameter is referred to as "Random Selection—the TCMP Audit," which stands for "Taxpayer Compliance Measurement Program," and is based on random selection. It doesn't matter how much or how little you make, or what deductions you take, everyone who files a tax return has an equal chance for a TCMP audit.

Each year only about 40,000 out of the 96 million returns are selected for the TCMP audit. The purpose, according to the IRS, is to find out exactly where taxpayers make mistakes, and even where they tend to cheat. The audit is so thorough that if you have children, you may be asked to bring birth certificates to prove they are your dependents. Don't be too concerned. About one-third of TCMP-audited taxpayers walk out the door with a bigger refund check in hand.

The second technique used by the IRS for selecting audit candidates is called "Target Group Selection." IRS experience shows that certain professions have high cash incomes, which shouldn't come as any big surprise. Any profession from which the IRS feels it can collect the greatest amount of extra taxes for the number of man-hours spent has a higher audit profile. These groups include doctors, dentists, lawyers, airline pilots, and accountants—all the people you'd like your son or daughter to marry.

Last but certainly not least is the "Discriminant Function System" or DFS. DFS is a point system. The deductions on your return are compared to what the IRS considers the "norm " for a person in your profession, in your area, and with your income. The greater the difference between your tax return and the "norm," the higher number of points you are assigned. If your DFS score gets too high, you may be chosen for an audit.

If you are selected by computer, two IRS employees must agree that there is a good chance of collecting additional taxes before you are actually issued an audit notice.

Strategy #126
DELAY AN AUDIT AS LONG AS POSSIBLE.

Keep in mind that the world of the IRS is not a clandestine, behind-the-scenes ring of spies bugging your phone and watching you through infrared binoculars. The IRS is simply a big collection business run by the government, and your success with the system is assured when you take an honest, business-like approach.

If you are picked for an audit, the audit notice will usually be in the form of a computer-generated letter. Federal law states that the "time and place for an audit must be convenient to both parties." Your strategy is to delay the audit for as long as possible. You may send a registered letter to the IRS in answer to the audit notice stating, "The time is not convenient." Your response automatically postpones the audit. Eventually, after several postponements, you will receive a letter or call from a "real live person," instead of a computer, asking you to choose the time. By that time you will have all your records in order.

Strategy #127
NEVER GO TO AN AUDIT UNTIL YOU GET THE REASONS FOR THE AUDIT IN WRITING.

Before you agree to an audit time, get all the following information in writing. The IRS must give you written answers to the following questions, if you ask, before you are required to appear.

Why? Why is the IRS auditing your return? Why does the IRS think it may be able to collect more taxes? Is there an error that can be rectified easily without an office visit? Can you furnish copies of supporting documents by mail?

Which? Which parts of your return are being audited? Ask for a specific answer. The answer the IRS gives to this question limits the audit to these parts of your return. Some of the information you require may come with the audit notice, and some you may have to request yourself, in writing.

What? What papers does the IRS want to see? Take to the audit only the papers requested, not your shoe boxes full of old receipts, contracts, and checks. If the IRS says bring "everything," request that they be more specific by listing what "everything" includes.

There are some important ground rules you will want to follow during the audit.

Strategy #128
LET THE AUDITOR LOOK AT YOUR DOCUMENTS ONLY ONCE.

The auditor has the right to look at each of your documents only once. Under a recent ruling, if your auditor wants to look at your papers a second time, written permission must be obtained from the U.S. secretary of the treasury. It can be done, but the auditor usually won't go to all the trouble if you mention the rule.

Strategy #129
IN AN AUDIT, NEVER PART COMPANY WITH YOUR ORIGINAL DOCUMENTS.

Don't leave original copies of your documents with the IRS. A tax court has ruled that you are still responsible for your records, even if they are lost or misplaced by the IRS. Point the ruling out to the auditor if he or she wants to keep your papers to work on later.

Strategy #130
DON'T LET THE AUDITOR COPY YOUR TAX FILE.

Tax law does not give the IRS blanket permission to build a file from copies of your personal papers. You must produce supporting documents if requested, but not copies for the IRS's file.

Strategy #131
LEARN HOW TO BEHAVE IN AN AUDIT.

It's important to mind your manners when you're being audited. But contrary to what many people believe, you can be aggressive and well-mannered at the same time. Here are the rules to follow:

- Say little; smile a lot. Never volunteer information.
- If you feel strongly about your position, let the auditor know. Often the auditor will let the point go in your favor.
- Provide as much documentation as possible for each point in an audit.
- Don't give up, even if you don't have all the documentation.
- Don't make too many concessions.
- Don't be rushed unless you feel hurrying will work in your favor.
- Don't complain about the tax system; the auditor pays taxes, too.
- Don't take your crumpled-up receipts in a brown paper bag. That old strategy won't work anymore. Auditors are trained to believe that if you keep your records in a disorganized manner, there must be an error in there somewhere.
- Don't take the Fifth Amendment. Tax protesting is a disaster. The jails and courts are full of people who believed such nonsense would work.
- Don't try to tape-record the conversation. The IRS found from experience that recording tended to fluster auditors. Recording once was a great way to get control of an audit, but now, you will have to go to court to get permission to record. Even if you win, it's not worth the trouble.
- Act with confidence that you're right. You probably are.

Strategy #132
IF YOU DON'T GET WHAT YOU THINK YOU DESERVE, GO BEYOND THE AUDITOR.

If all else fails and you can't get the decision you want, you still have a few cards to play.

STEP 1: ASK FOR THE SUPERVISOR.
Auditors are taught to rule gray areas in the IRS's favor; supervisors are taught to rule gray areas in favor of the taxpayer. Supervisors also have a greater knowledge of the tax law and its application than do auditors. Supervisors are the first level of

the public relations effort at the IRS, so they try to please. I cannot tell you how many stories I hear in my workshops of those who have paid extra taxes for denied deductions when the auditor was 100% incorrect, because the individual being audited didn't know what to do next.

STEP 2: CALL THE PROBLEM RESOLUTION.

The PRO was set up to help keep the IRS out of court. The Problem Resolution Office has the power to compromise and resolve taxpayer disputes. You'll find the phone number for the PRO in the phone book under U.S. Government, Internal Revenue Service, Problem Resolution Office.

STEP 3: TAKE 'EM TO COURT.

You may use the small claims tax court to settle any dispute with the IRS once and for all. The taxes in question must be under $10,000. You are not required to take an attorney, and the regular courtroom rules of evidence are relaxed. You present your side of the argument; the IRS presents its side. The impartial judge listens, leaves the courtroom, eats a sandwich, returns, and tells you his decision. The decision is final—no appeals.

STEP 4: USE THE APPEALS AND REVIEW SYSTEM.

If the taxes in question are over $10,000, you must use the regular appeals and review system to appeal the auditor's decision. The cost involved will obviously be more, but good planning and understanding of the do's and don'ts of taxes will avoid any problem. IRS publications completely outline the appeals and review procedure.

Strategy #133
IF A TAX PREPARER PREPARED YOUR RETURN, TAKE HIM OR HER TO AN AUDIT.

If a tax preparer prepared the return, you should certainly take him or her to the audit. If you feel you are knowledgeable and confident about taxes and your return, you can handle it yourself. But you will want to take a professional if the taxes in question are significant, or if you tend to react emotionally. IRS auditors are not intimidated by tax professionals, but they do speak the same language. If you paid for the service, use it.

Strategy #134
APPLY THE STATUTE OF LIMITATIONS TO AN AUDIT.

Once you file, the IRS has a limited time to challenge your return. The statute of limitations is effective three years from the day your return was due, April 15 or the date the return was filed, if later. If you understate your total income by 25% or more, the statute of limitations is six years. If your return is fraudulent, there is no statutory limit to the IRS audit period. If the statutory period has expired, you cannot be audited no matter how badly the IRS might wish to audit you.

The pendulum swings both ways. You also have a limit of three years to amend your return and two years to claim any overpaid taxes, or forgotten deductions.

Strategy #135
AGREE ONLY TO A LIMITED EXTENSION OF AN AUDIT.

If you're being audited and are close to the statutory limit, you will be asked to sign an extension. Instead of signing the form the IRS will give you, which leaves your entire return open to examination past the statutory period, request and sign Form 872, "Limited Extension." This procedure leaves open to examination only the parts of your return in question, which are those specified in the "Limited Extension" form.

Strategy #136
PUT A STOP TO THE HASSLE AUDIT IF YOU'VE BEEN
AUDITED DURING THE PAST THREE YEARS.

If you are audited on any part of your return in one year and the audit produces no change, or only a small change, you should not be audited on the same part of your return for the next three years. The IRS often will not apply this rule unless you bring it up.

Several years ago, during one of my Money Strategies workshops, a young man stood up abruptly stating that he had been audited for the same deductions three years in a row and was to appear for an audit again on Monday. He decided to test the hassle audit rule based on what he had learned in the workshop.

When he pointed out to the auditor that he had been audited three years in a row, the auditor checked the files and said, "You're right; we didn't realize we had audited you last year." The audit was over as quickly as it began.

To sum it up, your best defense in an audit is a good offense. Be civil, knowledgeable, and assertive. Remember, knowledge eliminates both fear *and* bigger tax bills! The more you learn about how to report your income and deductions correctly, the less your chances for audit.

If you are currently being audited or have an audit or collection problem with the IRS, call the Charles J. Givens Organization Tax Defense at 1-800-333-4652.

Chapter 16

FAMILY TIES

*The only difference between death and taxes is that death
doesn't get worse every time Congress meets.*

Will Rogers
Author/Actor
(1879–1935)

OBJECTIVE ————————————————————————————

TURN FAMILY EXPENSES INTO TAX DEDUCTIONS.

A family is like a business, and great dividends accrue to all
family members when the business aspects of a family are
recognized. Both business and family rely on income. Business
income is derived primarily from the sale of products and
services; family income is derived from a lifetime of personal
services to your own or someone else's company. Both families
and businesses have expenses including housing, transportation, utilities, insurance, storage, payroll (including family allowances and spending money), vacations, negotiations,
purchase and sale of assets, communication, praise, discipline,
and, of course, taxes. By applying good business principles to
the daily operation of a family, money-making and tax-saving
strategies can put thousands of extra dollars into the family
coffers.

FAMILY REAL ESTATE STRATEGIES

Strategy #137
SELL YOUR HOME TO YOUR CHILDREN.

Those who reach retirement age usually have a large portion of their assets tied up in their home; they are house rich and often cash poor. One solution, without moving, is to sell your home to your children once you are over 55 years old.

Both parents and children generate tremendous financial and tax benefits. The parents are able to unlock the equity in their home tax free without having to move, while the children receive depreciation and other tax deductions as well as the future appreciation of the property. The home, because it is then owned by the children, is a protected part of the parent's estate. If Congress has its way, the maximum amount that will be allowed to pass through an estate, tax free, will be reduced from the current $600,000 to as little as $200,000. Getting your home, one of your most expensive assets, out of your estate is an important step in your estate plan. Here is how the strategy works:

Parents sell their home to their children at fair market value, determined by appraisal. The children purchase the property with a conventional 80% mortgage. The parents can hold a second mortgage note for all or part of the balance and cosign on the first mortgage if necessary to help the children qualify.

An alternative strategy is for the parents to get a new mortgage or equity loan before selling to the children and then let the children assume the mortgage. The cost of assumption is usually 1% unless the loan is a no-qualifying FHA or VA loan, which can be assumed for $45.

For example, if the home is paid for and worth $150,000, parents would receive $120,000 cash from an 80% mortgage.

Parents may elect, using IRS Form 2119, to take the once-per-lifetime $125,000 tax exemption to tax-protect the accumulated profits from the sale of the home.

Parents rent the home from the children. In order for the children to qualify for the depreciation and other tax deductions, parents must pay them at least 80% of fair market rental value. If the fair market rent is $600, parents must pay at least $480 per month or about $6,000 per year. The rent money is a portion of what parents earn from reinvesting their home equity.

With a combination of investments such as mutual funds and discounted mortgages (see Part III: "Powerful Investment Strategies") and an average after-tax net of 15%, parents' income from reinvested home equity would equal $18,000 per year. After paying the $6,000 in rent, parents have increased their tax-free income by $12,000 per year or $1,000 per month for the rest of their lives.

Parents may wish to increase their rental payments to the children in order to help equal the payments on the mortgage. The tax deductions the children receive will also help offset the mortgage payments. Here is how:

Basis for depreciation	= $120,000	($150,000 purchase price
	=	minus 20% land value)
Yearly depreciation deduction	$ 4,364	(Based on 27½-year
		depreciation schedule)
Taxes saved at 31% bracket	= $ 1,353	per year

The children now own an appreciation property throwing off generous tax deductions and have built-in property managers, their parents. Parents will want to lease the property back from the children with a lifetime lease, so if parents and children have a spat, parents won't end up in the street. Don't laugh, it has happened.

Strategy #138
BUY A HOME WITH YOUR CHILDREN OR GRANDCHILDREN.

Buying a home with and for your children or grandchildren can be a financially and personally rewarding experience. The children or grandchildren agree to live in and maintain the property as well as make the mortgage payments. Both parents and children get the tax and appreciation benefits of a sound real estate investment with no management headaches.

If you are the co-owner who lives in the property, you enjoy these financial and tax benefits:

• You qualify for a mortgage you might not be able to get on your own.
• Your down payment is reduced or eliminated altogether.
• You can stop renting and start building equity for the future.
• When you sell, you may use the tax deferral rules for rolling over your share of the profits to another home without paying taxes.

- You are allowed a tax deduction for your share of the mortgage interest and property taxes.

If you are the parent or grandparent who co-owns but does not live in the property, you enjoy these financial and tax benefits:

- You can help someone you care about own a home.
- You have a resident property manager.
- There is no vacancy problem.
- You are allowed a tax deduction for your share of the depreciation, interest, tax, and maintenance expenses.

Although the resident owner is not allowed to take depreciation, the nonresident owner can. This strategy can also be used by parties who are not related. Profits on the eventual sale of the property are divided based on the percentage ownership of each party.

Strategy #139
BUY A HOME AND RENT IT TO YOUR CHILDREN WITH AN "OPTION TO BUY."

Helping your children succeed in life is a noble and personally rewarding experience. One of the greatest opportunities to help your children after they get out of school is to assist them in participating in the American dream—the buying of a home. Owning a home is still a great source of pride, produces a feeling of accomplishment, and is certainly one of the best true tax shelters left after tax reform. (See Strategy #85, page 113.)

As in most money matters, parents make major financial errors when helping children buy a home because of lack of understanding of the tax laws. The "normal" method is for the parents to give or loan the down payment to the adult child. True, the house can be purchased using this method, that is, if the child qualifies for the mortgage, but parents gets only emotional, not financial, benefits.

By structuring the house-buying transaction in a slightly different way, not only can parents help their children, but they can also earn tremendous tax deductions in the process. Instead of giving or loaning the full amount of the down payment to the child, the parents buy the home themselves and then rent it back to the child. The parents actually have title to the home and therefore can take 100% of the tax deductions for depreciation, real estate taxes, and other expenses, saving hundreds each year in taxes.

Strategy #140
USE THE 80% FAIR MARKET RENT RULE TO QUALIFY YOURSELF FOR TAX DEDUCTIONS ON FAMILY-RENTED PROPERTIES.

IRS rules state that you can rent to a family member and still take all the allowable real estate rental-property deductions, including depreciation, provided you charge your renter/family member at least 80% of the fair market value rent each month. Fair market value rent is the amount for which a similar property in the same area of town would rent. If the rent in the area for a house or condo similar to yours is $700 per month and you charge your family member at least $560 (80% × $700), you will have complied with the rule and be entitled to all deductions.

To qualify, be certain that the money actually changes hands each month and that you and your family member complete a simple lease, which you can get at any office supply store.

Strategy #141
RENT TO YOUR PARENTS TO SUBSIDIZE THEIR INCOME AND QUALIFY FOR TAX DEDUCTIONS.

Here is an interesting situation that I get questions on constantly. Let's say that one or both of your parents are living but are getting up there in years. Because of poor planning, their income is small, too small to have a nice place to live. It would not be practical or desirable for your parent or parents to live with you or your family, but you do want to help and at the same time cut the amount you pay out to a minimum.

Maybe your parents' dream is a condo in Florida, still an inexpensive place to buy property. There is a way you can help them financially and at the same time derive all of the real estate tax benefits as a cash rebate to you. You help your parent or parents to buy the property by paying the minimum down payment. To qualify for a 5% to 10% down payment, put your parents' name on the original deed, which makes them the co-owner occupants, and you then qualify for a low-down-payment mortgage. Later they can sign over their interest to you as a gift to avoid eventual probate.

Here is the transaction:

Purchase price	$125,000
Down payment	− 10,000
Balance to finance	$115,000

You obtain a 10½%, 30-year mortgage for the balance of
$115,000. The principal and interest amount to $1,056 per
month plus another $100 to cover real estate taxes and insur-
ance, making the total monthly payment $1,156. Using the 80%
formula in Strategy #137, you rent to your parents for $640,
which is 80% of the fair market rental value of $800 per month
for the area.

Because your property qualifies as a rental, you can depreciate
the basis of the property equally each year over 27.5 years and
deduct it from your taxes. The basis is your total cost minus
about 20% for land, which is not depreciable.

Purchase price	$125,000
Subtract: value of land, 20%	− 25,000
Basis of property (for depreciation)	$100,000

$$\text{Depreciation deductions} = \frac{Basis}{27.5} = \frac{\$100,000}{27.5} = \$3,636 \text{ per year}$$

All expenses you pay out above what you take in are also
deductible to you except for approximately $50 of the mortgage
amount that is applied to the principal. You are paying out
$1,156 and taking in $640 for a net tax loss of $516 per month
minus the $50 principal payment.

Your deductible loss not including depreciation, therefore, is
$5,592 per year (12 months × $466).

Now it all adds up:

Depreciation deduction	$3,636
Deductible expenses over income	5,592
Total yearly deductions	$9,228

Cash rebate from tax savings:
35%* × $9,228 = $3,229

*35% is the combined federal and state tax bracket percentage.

By correctly setting up the purchase of a home for your parents as in our example, you will get a tax cash rebate of $3,229 per year or $32,290 over the next ten years, money that would have been lost had you simply bought your family members a home and made part or all of the payments. Your cash tax savings will pay three months of mortgage payments each year for your parents or other family members, saving you a full 25% of the cost of caring for your family financially.

Strategy #142
IF NECESSARY, SUBSIDIZE YOUR PARENTS OR OTHER FAMILY MEMBERS WITH A ONCE-A-YEAR, LUMP-SUM GIFT.

As is often the case, unfortunately, your parents may not have the money to make all of the rental payments necessary to meet the 80% fair market rental test. In our example, 80% is $640 per month. Let's say your parents can pay $340 per month and you would have to pay the additional $300. If you paid the difference yourself or gave the money directly to your parents in monthly installments, you would not be allowed any rental property deductions.

However, there is nothing to prevent you from accomplishing the same objective in transactions of nonrelated amounts of money. Here's your strategy. You give your parents, let's say, $5,000 per year in a lump sum as a Christmas gift. Your parents then have the option of doing anything they wish with the money, including paying the full amount of the $640 per month rental, thus allowing you to receive enough rent to qualify for all the tax deductions.

FAMILY INVESTMENT DEDUCTION STRATEGIES

Strategy #143
TURN YOUR INVESTMENT PLAN INTO A TAX SHELTER BY DEDUCTING INVESTMENT EXPENSES.

A family investment plan should generate more than current income or a brighter future; it should create hundreds in extra investment expense deductions.

Most taxpayers mistakenly think that expenses associated with their investment plan are no longer deductible. Even the simplest investment plan can generate $500 to $1,000 of yearly deductions.

IRS rules are very clear on the subject:

> Expenses incurred in the production and collection of investment income are deductible as part of Schedule A, Miscellaneous Deductions.

Use the Deductible Investment Expenses checklist (page 194) as a guide to investment expense deductions and investment expense planning. All other investment expenses you incur may be added to the list.

Strategy #144
DEDUCT THE COST OF A VCR OR HOME COMPUTER USED IN INVESTMENT OR TAX PLANNING.

Use your VCR, home computer, or cassette recorder 40% of the time for tax and investment planning and 40% of the cost or market value is deductible.

Keep records of your deductible and personal usage for 90 days each year to allocate the deductible percentage.

When determining the deduction for your home computer or VCR, use straight-line (alternate MACRS) depreciation over a six-year period unless the asset is *also* used in your small business.

You may first combine the investment and business use percentages in determining your allowable deduction. If used more than 50% of the time for business, you may use the asset expensing method. If used less than 50% of the time for business, use the six-year straight-line (alternate MACRS) method.

DEDUCTIBLE INVESTMENT EXPENSES

_____ Accounting fees $ _____

_____ Automobile expenses   _____

_____ Books and audio- and videotape courses on investing   _____

_____ Brokerage fees (deducted as part of the investment   _____
cost when you sell investments)

_____ Calculator, adding machine, cassette recorder,   _____
typewriter

_____ Costs of collecting interest and dividends   _____

_____ Cost of managing investments for a minor   _____

_____ Financial advice on audio- and videotapes (e.g., The   _____
Charles J. Givens Financial Library)

_____ Home computer used for investment planning and   _____
record keeping

_____ Investment advice (except for tax-exempt investments)   _____

_____ Investment interest (up to amount of investment   _____
income)

_____ IRA set-up costs, if billed separately   _____

_____ Legal costs   _____

_____ Proxy fight expenses   _____

_____ Safe deposit box rental   _____

_____ Salary of bookkeeper or others who keep your   _____
investment records

_____ Subscription to investment publications   _____

_____ Trips to look after investments such as improved real   _____
estate

_____ Videotape recorder used for investment education and   _____
advice

NONDEDUCTIBLE INVESTMENT EXPENSES

Costs of travel to stockholder meetings
Costs of trips to investigate prospective rental property
Cost of travel to investment seminars
Home office expenses

The percentage from the straight-line depreciation table is multiplied by the depreciable basis of the asset. The depreciable basis is the deductible percentage times the cost or market value, whichever is less. Use Form 4562 and the straight-line table below to calculate your deduction. Enter the investment and tax planning portion of the deduction on Schedule A under miscellaneous deductions. Enter the business deduction portion on Schedule C for a proprietorship or other appropriate business tax form. See Chapter 25, "Getting Down to Business," for a more in-depth explanation of depreciation methods.

STRAIGHT LINE

(Alternate MACRS)
Depreciation Table

Year	% Deductible
1	10
2	20
3	20
4	20
5	20
6	10

MISCELLANEOUS DEDUCTIONS STRATEGY

Strategy #145
**TAKE ADVANTAGE OF THE SCHEDULE A
MISCELLANEOUS DEDUCTION RULES BY COMBINING
OVER 50 POTENTIAL DEDUCTIONS.**

Even though there is a 2% floor on miscellaneous deductions based on your AGI (adjusted gross income), most taxpayers with a little planning can have between $1,000 and $2,000 of allowable deductions because of the wide range of potential deductions included in this category. On the next page is a partial list to use as your guide.

DEDUCTIBLE MISCELLANEOUS EXPENSES

Unreimbursed employee travel expenses
   Airline, auto $ _____
   Meals   _____
   Entertainment   _____
Tax advice   _____
Tax preparation   _____
Appraisal fees, casualty losses, and contributions   _____
Investment expenses*
   IRA custodial fees   _____
   Safety deposit box   _____
   Investment advice   _____
Employee business expenses (use Form 2106)**
   Automobile   _____
   Education   _____
   Legal fees   _____
   Association dues   _____
   Job hunting and interviews   _____
   Employment agency fees   _____
Office in the home
   Depreciation or rent   _____
   Utilities   _____
   Family salaries for job assistance   _____
Moving expenses   _____

*See Deductible Investment Expenses checklist for complete list (page 194)
**See Potential Deductions for Employees for a complete list (pages 282–84)

ALLOWABLE MISCELLANEOUS DEDUCTIONS
COMPUTATION CHART

A floor of 2% of adjusted gross income applies to your miscellaneous deductions. All of your expenses above the floor are deductible. Use this chart to estimate your allowable miscellaneous deductions.

Adjusted Gross Income $ _____
(from last year's return or estimated for this year)

Adjusted Gross Income	Nondeductible Amount of Miscellaneous Expenses
$ 2,000	$ 40
5,000	100
10,000	200
15,000	300
20,000	400
25,000	500
30,000	600
35,000	700
40,000	800
50,000	1,000
60,000	1,200
70,000	1,400
80,000	1,600
90,000	1,800
100,000	2,000
200,000	4,000

Total Miscellaneous Deductions $ _____
Nondeductible Amount   − $ _____
ALLOWABLE DEDUCTION $ _____

> *Strategy #146*
> ## USE THE CHILD-CARE CREDIT AS ONE OF YOUR MOST POWERFUL TAX REDUCERS.

If you are struggling to pay your child-care bills, there is one saving grace—the federal tax break. Taking your child to a day-care center is not the only way to get the child-care tax credit. According to the IRS, you can even pay a relative to provide daytime child care and receive a tax credit as long as the relative is not claimed as your dependent on your tax return. However, you cannot claim a credit for money paid to your own child under age 19 whether or not you claim the child as a dependent.

To calculate the credit, apply the tax credit percentage shown below to your family's adjusted gross income. For example, if a couple earns $45,000 a year and spends $3,600 on child care for their two children, their tax credit is 20% of $3,600, or $720. The child-care credit maximum is $2,400 for one child and $4,800 for two children. A credit, unlike a deduction, is a dollar-for-dollar tax rebate. If you have children, this strategy provides one of your most powerful tax shelters. To claim the credit, you must provide the IRS with the name, address, and Social Security number of the person providing the child care or the tax-payer identification number of a child-care facility. You claim your credit on Form 2441.

| | | Maximum Tax Rebate | |
Adjusted Gross Income	Child-Care Tax Credit	One Child	Two or More
$10,000 or less	30%	$720	$1,440
10,001–12,000	29	696	1,392
12,001–14,000	28	672	1,344
14,001–16,000	27	648	1,296
16,001–18,000	26	624	1,248
18,001–20,000	25	600	1,200
20,001–22,000	24	576	1,152
22,001–24,000	23	552	1,104
24,001–26,000	22	528	1,056
26,001–28,000	21	504	1,008
More than 28,000	20	480	960

Strategy #147
DEDUCT THE COST OF *MORE WEALTH WITHOUT RISK* AND *FINANCIAL SELF-DEFENSE.*

Because *More Wealth Without Risk* and *Financial Self-Defense* are primarily tax and investment planning books, a great way to start your new approach to maximizing family deductions is to deduct these books as tax preparation expenses on Schedule A. Even though the retail prices printed on the inside covers are $14.00 and $14.00, your deduction is limited to the amount you actually paid for each book. All of your other book purchases each year that can reasonably be considered tax, investment, and/or business advice books can also be deducted in the same way.

Chapter 17

WHOM DO YOU TRUST?

While you're alive, the IRS will attempt to take what you've made. When you're not, the IRS will attempt to take what it missed.

Charles J. Givens

OBJECTIVE

BEAT THE DREADED GIFT TAX AND ESTATE TAX PROBATE HOAX, AND PROTECT YOUR ASSETS THROUGH THE USE OF TRUSTS.

To achieve financial success you must consider one topic most people don't enjoy discussing. In fact, they do everything possible to avoid the subject—estate planning. Since estate planning can only be done while you are still living, you might more appropriately call it "life planning." By law your estate doesn't exist until the moment you are no longer living. Then whatever plan you have made or failed to make is locked in forever.

Why don't people do a better job of estate planning? Because it forces them to deal mentally with their own mortality. People who would knowingly choose to sacrifice themselves to save a loved one will leave that loved one the burdens and nightmares of dealing with a poorly planned estate simply because it is easy to avoid. No one makes you do it. The true value of what you leave behind, however, may well be determined by how well you plan your estate.

Almost everyone has heard of a will, but far fewer people than you may think have even gone that far in estate planning. If you have much more than the clothes on your back and a few thousand in assets, a will is woefully inadequate and can allow incredible things to happen to your assets that you never intended. If you don't have even a will, things can happen that you never even imagined!

Just the words *estate plan* make the process sound expensive, complicated, and final. But as you'll see, estate planning can be made relatively easy and inexpensive. Expensive and complicated is what eventually results from the lack of an effective estate plan. Your estate plan is simply your wealth distribution plan and is a must no matter how much or how little wealth you might end up with.

Let's first look at the problems a will can cause as your only estate planning tool.

Probate—the court action of proving that a will is valid. Probate in America is an expensive and antiquated rip-off process that allows attorneys and the court system to end up with a good chunk of your hard-earned money—8% to 15%, in fact. The probate system has long outlived its usefulness and is detrimental to your heirs and to your estate. Contrary to popular belief, a will does not eliminate probate.

Time—Depending on the complexity of an estate, the probate process can take months or even years, even in small cases. Generally, nothing can be distributed until the process is complete. Time delays can cause tremendous hardships, particularly when there are estate taxes to pay. The IRS won't wait for its share of an estate and will have no problem arbitrarily forcing the sale of any assets at fire-sale prices to pay the taxes. The IRS has no heart—only rules.

Disability—While some people do plan for their eventual demise, few people plan for possible disability, mental or physical. A will offers you no protection. Who would look after you if you were disabled? Who would run your personal and business affairs? If any of these questions are unresolved, a court will decide the answers for you and will appoint someone paid by you even though that someone might have been your last choice if you still had the right or ability to choose for yourself.

Children—If your children are minors at the time of your death, they cannot get your assets. If you have neglected to do so, a guardian will be appointed by a court to take total control of your children and those assets you've bequeathed to your children.

While you would like to think that the appointed individual would continue to look after the best interests of the children, the exceptions and horror stories are legendary.

Costs—Probate court costs, attorneys' fees, appraisal and accounting costs all become wasted, unnecessary expenses that diminish what you have worked so hard to build all your life. These costs do not even count the time and headaches that your loved ones will spend in going through the process. All of these usual problems can easily be eliminated, but not with a will alone.

Tax Planning—A will provides no tax plan. Taxes cannot be forgotten in estate planning. Although a will gives you no tax protection, there are other alternatives that do.

Most people have heard of trusts but have no idea whether or not they could benefit from establishing one. In this chapter we'll clear up the mystery of trusts and show you how at different times in your life, maybe now, you can use different forms of trusts as a powerful wealth-control and wealth-preservation tool. You will also learn how you can educate your parents or grandparents on how the establishment of a trust might better preserve and distribute assets while they are living or from their estate.

What is a trust? A trust is nothing more than a document giving specific instructions that by law must be followed by a trustee whom you appoint. Trusts have been declared legal in all 50 states, and the trust documents are becoming fairly standardized, making them easier and less expensive to put together and understand.

To help you understand trusts, let's begin with an understanding of gift taxes and gift tax exclusions.

Strategy #148
USE THE GIFT TAX EXEMPTION RULES TO MOVE ASSETS TO FAMILY MEMBERS WITH NO GIFT TAXES.

Although money or property you give to your child or anyone is not tax deductible, give too much in one year to one person and you trigger additional taxes—the dreaded gift tax, with tax rates of 18 to 55%. The gift tax is in addition to the up to 31% federal income taxes you have already paid on the same money!

Avoiding the gift tax is relatively easy. Don't give your child or anyone else more in cash or property in one year than is exempt from gift taxes. Over the years, Congress has continually changed the amount exempt from gift taxes. Currently the exemption is:

up to $10,000 per year from one individual to any number of others
up to $20,000 per year from a couple to any number of others

There is no limit on the total amount that can be given as gifts in one year without gift taxes as long as you don't give over the $10,000 or $20,000 exempt limit to one person.

For example, if you have two children, you and your spouse could give each of them up to $20,000 per year in cash, investments, real estate equity, or other property exempt from gift tax. If you have no spouse, you would be limited to an exempt amount of $10,000 per year per child. Similarly, if your aging grandmother wanted to begin divesting herself of assets to keep them out of probate and exempt them from potential estate taxes, as well as gift taxes, she could, if single, give up to $10,000 per year to each child and/or grandchild without triggering the gift tax.

The rules seem clear enough once you know them, but all gift transactions are not quite so simple. For instance, let's say a mother has a home worth $220,000 and wants to give it to her two children. If she deeds the home to the children, each child would technically be receiving $110,000 in one year. Since only $10,000 per child would be exempt from gift taxes, the gift tax on the $100,000 balance per child would be $18,200, even though the child received no cash. The mother just meant to lovingly give the house away to the children who would inherit it anyway. But because neither she nor the children understood gift taxes, she inadvertently made herself liable for $36,400 more in taxes. What was meant to be an asset for the children is now a major liability for her.

Remember, a bureaucracy such as the IRS has no feelings. It doesn't care what you meant to do or what you didn't know, it only cares about what you actually did and how much you owe. Although you can reverse a transaction such as this in the same tax year, once the following January 1 rolls around, it's too late. Your decisions are locked in.

There are two exclusions from gift tax limits, one for education and one for medical expenses. In addition to the $10,000 per recipient per year limit, you can give or receive any amount for education paid directly to an educational institution and/or for medical expenses paid to a health care provider.

Strategy #149
USE JOINT OWNERSHIP ONLY AS A TEMPORARY ESTATE PROTECTION STRATEGY—NOT A PERMANENT ESTATE PLAN.

Many couples who have become aware of the necessity of an estate plan feel that they are protected if assets such as homes, cars, investments, and bank accounts are simply titled jointly in both names. Joint ownership with the right of survivorship means that upon the death of the first spouse (or owner) the second spouse (or owner) automatically inherits the interest of the first spouse.

Joint ownership does have the advantage of avoiding probate. For instance, a jointly held bank checking or savings account would not be frozen until probate was complete, while a bank account not held jointly would be. But joint ownership as a single strategy can create big tax problems. Although the surviving spouse can get any amount of assets with no estate tax levied, upon the death of the second spouse all but $600,000 is taxed. Joint ownership without additional planning will lose the tax exemption protection possible on a total of $1,200,000 in assets (see Strategy #155).

Strategy #150
INVEST FOR YOUR CHILDREN OR AGING FAMILY MEMBERS USING A CUSTODIAL ACCOUNT, NEVER A JOINT ACCOUNT.

Almost every family or parent opens savings or investment accounts for children. Some accounts remain small, containing only Christmas or birthday-present money; other children's accounts grow quite large as parents accumulate money for a college education or attempt to move cash or investments to their children for their future.

There is a right way and a wrong way to open and list the names on an investment account for your children. The right way is called the custodial account; the wrong way is to do what all too many parents and grandparents do—open a joint account.

A custodial account is a form of trust in which an adult acts as trustee and the child is the beneficiary. The child cannot touch the money without permission of the trustee until the child reaches the age of majority. The major difference is who pays the taxes and whose tax bracket applies, the adult's or the child's. Open a joint account (an account with two names) or buy stocks or other investments in both your and the child's names and half of the interest or profits will be taxed to you— automatically, no matter how you fill out your tax return. Normally you will not discover your mistake until an audit, when the IRS will go back three years, assess you the taxes you didn't think you owed, and then just about double the tax amount with compounded interest plus penalties. What you meant to do for your child or grandchild is irrelevant at that point, and both you and the child have lost money.

Your strategy? Open a custodial account and the tax problem is totally circumvented.

How is a child's interest and investment income taxed? Interest and investment income are known in tax lingo as unearned income, which sounds like money you didn't deserve. Salary, commissions, and earnings from a business are earned income. For a child, earned and unearned income are taxed differently. With a custodial account, the interest or investment income is totally taxed to the child.

Here's how your child's interest and investment income (unearned income) is taxed:

Amount of Interest or Income	Amount of Tax
First $600	no tax
Second $600	15% tax
Above $1,200	child under 14—parents' top tax rate up to 39.6%
	child 14 or older—15% up to $22,750 of total income

Why is a young child's income above $1,000 now taxed at the parents' rate? Because prior to tax reform the Givens Organization and others had developed fantastic tax strategies that legally allowed parents to invest tens of thousands of dollars for their children with the earnings being taxed at incredibly low rates. When too many Americans learn and use legal tax strategies, Congress often changes the tax laws so no one can benefit. Our tax system is based on the fact that it is acceptable for a few smart taxpayers to use legal but unusual strategies to save taxes, but not everyone.

Most states have now adopted the Uniform Gift to Minors Act, which allows you to open a savings or investment account solely for the benefit of your child, parent, or someone else, registered in the name of a custodian or trustee. The custodian can be you, your spouse, another family member, or, in some states, anyone. The child has legal title to the funds or investments, but the custodian makes the decisions on how the money is to be invested or reinvested.

There are, however, some strange and potentially damaging rules for custodial accounts that you must be aware of in order to eliminate any potential problems. If, for example, before your child reaches age 21 you die while acting as custodian of an account you set up and funded with your money, the value of your child's account will be taxed as part of your estate. Not a problem if your estate is small, but your child could lose 18 to 55% of his or her own money to your estate taxes if your estate is over $600,000. It is better, therefore, to name someone other than yourself as custodian if these conditions apply.

Strategy #151
APPOINT YOUR SPOUSE INSTEAD OF YOURSELF AS CUSTODIAN OF CHILDREN'S ACCOUNTS FUNDED BY YOU.

Even though it may be better for tax purposes to appoint someone else to be custodian, it is usually preferable to keep the management of your children's funds within the immediate family and out of the hands of in-laws or other relatives. But then how do you prevent your child's money from being taxed to your estate should something happen to you before your child is grown?

You give the money to your child or children as an individual (not as a couple), and since your spouse is not the donor, your spouse can be named custodian without the assets in the child's account being included in either your or your spouse's estate. If you want to give more than $10,000 in a year to a child, you can reverse the process, setting up a second account for each child to which your spouse contributes and on which you act as custodian.

Strategy #152
SET UP AN AGE 21 TRUST FOR EACH CHILD TO CUT INCOME AND ESTATE TAXES, AND AVOID PROBATE.

There is little-known special trust that can be set up by parents under Internal Revenue Code 2503(c) called an age 21 trust. One purpose of the trust is to cut the potential taxes in half on money that is meant eventually for a child at age 21. Here's how it works. Up to $20,000 of cash or property can be deposited into the trust each year by the two parents without triggering any gift taxes. Unlike a custodial account, you can even put real estate into an age 21 trust.

The income from the trust is not taxable to either the parents or the children, but to the trust itself. In 1991, trusts paid a low tax rate of only 15% of the first $1,500 of income. Contrast that rate to the up to 39.6% the parents might pay on the same income each year if they just kept the money in their own investment account until the child was 21, or if they paid taxes of up to 31% on investment income of over $1,000 for their children under 14 because of the kiddie tax (see Strategy #150). You will want to give considerable thought to the age 21 trust since the funds or property, once placed by you in the trust, technically belong to your child, and your child will receive total control of the principal or assets at age 21.

The other major benefit of an age 21 trust is an estate-planning benefit. If anything happens to the parents, the trust income can be given directly to the child or to the child's guardian without the guardian's having access to the assets in the trust. We have all heard the horror stories of guardians who have squandered assets left by parents to their children. At age 21 the child gets control of the assets. The age 21 trust totally avoids probate and never becomes part of the parents' estate for evaluating estate taxes since the money is actually in trust for the child.

You can choose to set up an age 21 trust for one or each of your children as long as they are under 21 years old. You may contribute any amount you choose to the trust each year, up to the gift tax limits, or stop contributing to the trust at any time.

Strategy #153
USE TRUSTS EVEN WITH SMALL ESTATES TO SAVE HUGE PROBATE AND ADMINISTRATIVE COSTS.

The most common misunderstanding about trusts is a belief that they are just for the wealthy. The confusion comes from the popular concept that the primary reason for having a trust is to save taxes, and if you don't have a big estate, there will be no estate taxes to pay anyway. What a mistake. Remember the other problems from which your will doesn't protect you: probate costs, time delays, disability, and financial protection for your children. Circumventing these problems is an equally important reason to have a trust.

Trusts are often avoided because of the fear of the cost of setting one up. Even if you go to an expensive attorney and have a trust set up for you and your spouse including the writing of or changes to your wills, don't agree to pay more than $1,500 for an estate under $600,000. Now I realize that this is money you are having to pay now and the cost of probate is money your heirs will have to pay later, but if you feel strongly about the expense, don't hesitate to ask your heirs to put up the money for you. They are the ones whom the trust is going to protect. You may find that this is the fastest money you ever raised.

Using an expensive attorney is the most costly method of setting up a trust. You can pay as little as $25 for a do-it-yourself kit, or $900 to $1,000 to have a trust company establish the trust for you. However, if you use the do-it-yourself method, it is important to have an attorney familiar with trusts review what you have done.

Another estate planning or trust avoidance excuse frequently heard is that because a couple jointly owns all their assets, they don't need a trust. At best, joint ownership will only defer probate until the last of the two individuals dies. Joint ownership does not provide disability protection or protection for minor children. In fact, it can cause more problems. If one of the couple becomes disabled or incapacitated, property cannot be sold without the incapacitated spouse's signature.

Joint ownership does not eliminate or save one dime of estate taxes. Taxes are simply deferred in the case of a married couple, and all taxes become due upon the death of the last spouse. Without estate planning, and depending upon the size of the estate, little may be left after probate and taxes. If money or property is held jointly by partners or relatives other than spouses, even greater problems are created.

Strategy #154
SET UP A REVOCABLE LIVING TRUST TO PROVIDE TRUST PROTECTION WHILE YOU ARE STILL ALIVE.

A living trust or inter vivos trust, unlike a will or other types of trusts, takes effect while you are alive. Wills and many other types of trusts become effective only upon your death. Once written and funded, the living trust holds your assets and will eventually avoid all of the costs and delays associated with the probate system. That's right, the living trust completely circumvents the probate nightmare. The living trust also allows disability protection, guardian appointment for minor children, and reduction or even elimination of estate taxes.

Perhaps the biggest reason that people don't set up a trust is that they fear losing control. That fear is unfounded if you use a revocable living trust. Even the name tells you that it is revocable or cancelable at your discretion. You are in control. In fact, you can even be all of the parties in the trust—the grantor (the person who sets up the trust), the beneficiary (the person who gets the benefits of the trust), and the trustee (the person who runs the trust). You may be wondering how you are going to be the beneficiary and get the benefits of the trust if you die. That would be a great trick. But you can be the beneficiary of the trust while you are living, and at the same time choose other beneficiaries and trustees to take over after you are not. While you are alive, you do have control and you can change your mind at any time.

All assets owned by a couple or an individual should be transferred to the living trust. The trustee, who can be you or you and your spouse, has the management power over all these assets or investments. It can save you time, money, and legal hassles. A good example of the benefits of a living trust is seen in real estate transactions. Often in anticipation of potential disability or becoming incapacitated, a person will give a durable power of attorney to another to conduct his or her affairs. With a durable power of attorney, if the principal becomes incapacitated, the agent or person who has been empowered to act for the benefit of the principal must convince every financial institution and title examiner that he or she actually has the authority. The process is often time consuming and frustrating. With a trust, the trustee controls the title, and there are no problems in effecting real estate transactions.

Trust real estate transactions, dozens of which I have done myself, are easily accomplished with no hassle whether the trustee is buying or selling. A living trust also provides for a continuity of management, much like the retiring of the president of a corporation and assumption of his duties by the vice president. Upon the death of the creator of the trust, the new trustee takes over and is directed by the trust documents to distribute the assets directly to the heirs, with language similar to that used in a will. The trust entirely avoids the probate process. The trust can even include marital bypass provisions, which would allow a couple to give away an estate of up to $1.2 million instead of only $600,000 without the payment of any estate taxes.

For free information on setting up an RLT, call the estate planning administrator for the members of the Charles J. Givens Organization at 1-800-333-4652.

Strategy #155
USE YOUR REVOCABLE LIVING TRUST TO SHELTER $1.2 MILLION FROM ESTATE TAXES INSTEAD OF THE NORMAL $600,000.

By now, you know the primary benefits of setting up a trust:

- no probate
- disability protection
- asset protection for children
- cost saving
- time saving

Let's add the saving of potential estate taxes. The amount you save in estate taxes will depend upon the size of your estate. Although saving estate taxes isn't the only reason to create a trust, the tax savings can be a tremendous additional benefit.

Estate taxes aren't complicated, they are just expensive. If you don't have a big estate, you don't have to concern yourself with finding lots of deductions for estate taxes as you must with income taxes. Estate taxes are fixed—there are few exemptions or deductions. Estate taxes, however, must be paid quickly. They are due within nine months of death and must be paid in cash. The government will not care that the estate is tied up in probate because of a will or lack of one. It will not care that there is a soft real estate market, or that stock prices are temporarily down. The government will simply want its money, in cash. If the IRS must sell everything of yours at a forced auction to raise that cash, it has that power and will use it. Therefore, one major objective in estate planning is to use a trust to reduce estate taxes to the absolute minimum.

The U.S. estate tax system is a graduated tax system based on the total value of the assets in the estate. The first $600,000 for an individual or couple is exempt. Additionally, there is an unlimited marital deduction, meaning you can give or leave an unlimited amount of money and property to a spouse, estate tax free. But the positives end there. Estate taxes are due on the entire estate upon the death of the last spouse. As shown in the following table, estate taxes can turn a fortune into a small fortune. For estate tax computations the value of everything you own, including a life insurance policy meant to pay estate taxes, is thrown into the pot.

ESTATE TAX TABLE

Size of Taxable Estate	Amount of Tax	Plus % of Excess
$ 600,000	$ 192,800	37%
750,000	248,300	39
1,000,000	345,800	41
2,000,000	780,800	49
3,000,000	1,290,800	55
5,000,000	2,390,800	55
10,000,000	5,140,800	55

Even though the tax code says that each individual is entitled to a $600,000 exemption from estate taxes, a married couple is, believe it or not, counted as one individual. That's right, there is only one $600,000 exemption granted to a couple.

A revocable living trust can be used to separate the assets of the married couple so that the couple can be counted as two separate individuals for estate tax purposes. When complete, this process creates what is called an "A/B trust" or "His and Her trust." Based on what is written in the living trust documents, upon the death of the first spouse the money and property in the estate are separated into two parts. Part A is exactly $600,000 of cash or property, representing the amount exempt from estate taxes. There are two choices for what you can do with Part A assets.

- This $600,000 can be directly given to your children or grandchildren upon the death of the first spouse with the balance of the estate going to the surviving spouse, or
- The $600,000 can be put into another living trust so that your children and/or grandchildren have title to the assets but cannot touch them while your spouse is still living. That way your spouse can receive the income or other benefits from the $600,000 or investments. Your home could also be included in this $600,000 so that your spouse could continue to live in it.

Part B is the balance of the estate, whether $100,000 or $1 million or more. Part B is given directly to the surviving spouse, and because the marital bypass rule is used there are no estate taxes due regardless of the size of Part B. The unlimited marital-deduction rule simply means that the government will defer tax on a couple's estate until the death of the last spouse. Then, the government collects on what are now the combined remaining assets of the couple before anything goes to children, grandchildren, charity, or others. However, $600,000, Part A, has already been removed from the combined assets estate tax free.

Upon the later death of the second spouse, an additional $600,000 becomes estate tax exempt. Because the assets were originally separated, both spouses were able to claim a $600,000 exemption at different times so the total amount exempted from estate taxes equals $1.2 million instead of just $600,000. This simple, perfectly legal, but often overlooked strategy can save you up to $193,000 in unnecessary estate taxes. Compare that money with the maximum $1,500 cost to set up the trust.

Even though from a federal estate tax standpoint no federal estate taxes are due if the value of an estate is below $600,000, estate taxes or inheritance taxes can be due in some states. In states such as California the amount is so significant you may want to change your permanent residence in later years. Every year a bill is introduced in Congress to lower this $600,000 federal estate tax exemption. The last bill suggested $225,000, but so far none has passed. Estate taxes are calculated on everything you owned including the current value of your home and property, retirement plans, and any life insurance you may have that is not separated into an insurance trust.

Strategy #156
TRANSFER OR RETITLE YOUR ASSETS TO YOUR TRUST NOW AND WITH EVERY ACQUISITION.

The next important step in insuring that your trust works the way you intended is to fund the trust. For your trust to be able to protect your assets, you must legally retitle your assets, all of them, in the name of the trust. That process is called funding the trust. Once your trust is written and established, placing your assets under control of your trust is done once for the assets you currently own and then on a lifelong, ongoing basis for every asset you buy or acquire as time goes on.

These assets include your:

- homes
- vehicles
- boats, planes
- safe deposit box contents
- securities investments (stocks, bonds, mutual funds)
- real estate
- interest in a business you own
- bank accounts
- company stock
- anything else of value

Retitling is no big deal and can be done by a combination of your:

- attorney
- bank
- brokerage company
- mortgage company
- title company
- self

Financial firms retitle assets and investments into trusts every day, so they will have no problem handling your request. After retitling, check on your next account statement to be sure the retitling was actually done. You can transfer real estate to your trust yourself by getting blank copies of a quitclaim deed at an office supply store. You retitle property into the name of the trust, have it notarized, and record the deed at the courthouse. That's all there is to it. Each property requires a separate deed.

Your stockbroker or financial planner can retitle your investments, and you can drop by your bank to retitle your bank accounts. If your vehicles are financed at the bank, you can handle the titles while you're there. If your car or other vehicle is paid off, you will already have the title and can send it in to the state with the new owner being listed as your trust. Before retitling your vehicles or any other asset on which you carry insurance, be certain to check with your insurance company for the proper insurance procedure.

If you own a nonincorporated business, there is no title document. To transfer your interest to the trust, you simply list the business on a trust schedule attached to your trust documents. If your business is a corporation, you reregister your stock shares in the name of the trust. If you own shares in a partnership, change the partnership agreement if necessary to provide for transfer of ownership to a living trust.

It doesn't matter what you name your trust. Often retitling ends up looking something like this:

Givens Family Trust   or   Bill and Martha Von Horn
Charles J. Givens, Trustee   Trust

When it comes to transferring your assets and accounts to your trust, there is no margin for error. If something slips by without being legally placed into your trust, and you have no pour-over will, that asset has no trust protection no matter what you actually intended.

Strategy #157
SAVE ESTATE TAXES WITH AN IRREVOCABLE LIFE INSURANCE TRUST.

One of the sales pitches used to sell life insurance is that the life insurance proceeds your heirs collect are not subject to income taxes. That is true for two reasons, one of which can cost your estate big unexpected dollars. The first reason is that the premiums you paid were paid with money on which you had already paid income taxes, so you are considered to have already been taxed on the death benefit received by your heirs. The second reason is that no one is subject to paying income taxes after death. Instead, your estate pays estate taxes. If the beneficiary of your insurance policy is your estate, the entire amount of the insurance proceeds is subject to 18% to 55% estate taxes, even though the actual money was meant to pay estate taxes.

If your estate value including the amount of your life insurance is over $600,000, estate taxes must be paid unless your estate is going to your spouse. In that case the taxes are only deferred until the evaluation of your spouse's estate later on.

Many people are sold life insurance to pay estate taxes only to discover too late that the insurance itself is subject to estate taxes. The salesperson's answer? Buy more life insurance. Remember the incredible size of the estate tax bite—18% to 55%! You could buy a policy for $500,000 to pay estate taxes out of which up to an additional $250,000 in estate taxes would have to be paid.

You can easily circumvent the estate taxes on the life insurance that is meant for your heirs by setting up a life insurance trust. The trust becomes the beneficiary of the money from your insurance so your estate is not subject to paying taxes on the money received. Your family members are the beneficiaries of your insurance trust, through which they receive the insurance proceeds, or the money can be invested through the trust with your family receiving the income while preserving the investment capital.

To circumvent estate taxes your life insurance trust is set up as an irrevocable trust. What can you do then if you change your mind about the person to whom you want the money to go? You buy only term insurance for the trust, and if you change your mind, you stop paying the premiums. The policy lapses and your irrevocable trust has no assets so in effect you have revoked an irrevocable trust.

In *Financial Self-Defense*, Defense #51 and the Resource section, you will find the strategies and documents for setting up your own insurance trust.

For free information on setting up an RLT, call the estate planning administrator for the members of the Charles J. Givens Organization at 1-800-333-4652.

Strategy #158
USE THE SPECIAL ROLLOVER PROVISION TO ENABLE THE MONEY FROM YOUR RETIREMENT PLAN TO ESCAPE ESTATE TAXES.

Chances are you already have a trust. Surprised? If you contribute to a retirement plan such as an IRA, Keogh, 401(k), 403(b), or other similar plan, you have one form of trust. Your retirement program, unlike most trusts, is set up primarily to benefit you, not your heirs. A retirement plan cannot be retitled into your trust, nor can it be held jointly with another individual. When you established your plan, you named a beneficiary, probably

your spouse. The money in your retirement plan will escape
probate unless you have named your estate as beneficiary, or
failed to name anyone. Surprisingly, this mistake often happens,
particularly with single people.

Under normal rules, when an individual dies, the retirement
plan's assets are paid out and all income taxes are due. The one
exception is if a spouse is named beneficiary and the spouse
elects to exercise a special rollover provision. This option allows
your spouse to roll over the retirement plan assets into his or
her own IRA. Even if the deceased spouse didn't have an IRA,
the law allows the remaining spouse to set one up for this
specific purpose. If the rollover strategy is used, taxes will
continue to be deferred in the spouse's IRA and thousands of tax
dollars are saved.

Because of this special rollover provision, the spouse should
be named primary beneficiary under any retirement plan. Who
should be the contingent beneficiary and who should be the
beneficiary if you have no spouse? Your revocable living trust.

Strategy #159
USE SOME TYPES OF TRUSTS TO INSULATE AGAINST THE COST OF LAWSUITS AND JUDGMENTS.

There were 100 million lawsuits filed in the world last year; 95
million of them were in the United States. Last year, 40,000
attorneys were practicing law in Japan. Law schools in America
graduated that many last year alone. No wonder people are
concerned about lawsuits. The entire legal system is out of
control. While the real criminals are let out of prisons by the
court system to prevent overcrowding—heaven forbid they
should become uncomfortable—millions of Americans are sued
every year for what amounts to nonsense. The problem is, even
if you prove you are right, by that time you could have spent
thousands, even tens of thousands, defending yourself. If you
lose, the consequences can be financially staggering.

The more assets you acquire, the bigger a target you become.
Malpractice suits, contract disputes, errors and omissions, negligence, and accidents are all concepts that could rob your family
of everything you have worked to build. Fortunately, some
types of trusts can protect you and your family from these
financial hazards.

Since a trust is a separate entity from you, it can give you protection. A few courts have held that if your assets are in a revocable trust, you technically have control of the assets and therefore the court has the right to order you to turn them over. A family limited partnership provides the asset protection and control you want over your assets. Conversely, if you are in a high-profile, high-liability position, you may want to consider a nonrevocable trust, which would give you total protection. The downside, of course, is that you must surrender control of a nonrevocable trust to someone else. But that could be a close family member. Once opposing attorneys find you own no assets on which they can collect, the suits and attorneys often just go away.

Strategy #160
PROTECT YOUR ESTATE FROM A LIABILITY CLAIM BY INCREASING CONTRIBUTIONS TO YOUR IRA, 401(K), KEOGH, OR SIMILAR RETIREMENT ACCOUNTS.

An overlooked advantage of socking money away in employment-related retirement plans is that most courts have held that your money in these plans is untouchable by your creditors—even from a court-awarded liability claim and sometimes the IRS. In other words, the amount you have in your retirement plan becomes your own personal insurance policy. See Chapter 18, "Doubling the Profits in Your Employer's Retirement Plan," for how to maximize these protected contributions and earnings. Although this liability protection is not written into law, it has been created by the decisions of several courts.

Strategy #161
BE CERTAIN TO HAVE AN UPDATED WILL IN ADDITION TO YOUR TRUSTS.

After all of this talk about trusts, you might assume that you don't need a will. Even though you have a trust, you will still need a will to handle loose ends. The type of will you need with a trust is called a pour-over will. The term pour-over means that anything else that you have remaining outside your trust pours over into your trust at death. The amount may be nothing, it may be a lot, or it may even be something special.

The pour-over will is simply added protection in case you forgot to title something in the name of your trust or you bought something that wasn't billed correctly. You may have even inherited assets you forgot to title to your trust.

If you would like the estate planning administrators for members of the Givens Organization to help you set up your own trust, call 800-333-4652 and our estate planning division trust consultants will help you determine which trust is necessary and most beneficial.

Strategy #162
USE TAX-DEFERRED ANNUITIES TO AVOID PROBATE.

A tax-deferred annuity is an investment tax shelter set up through an insurance company. Although the money you invest in an annuity is money on which you have already paid taxes, the earnings compound tax free until you make a withdrawal. You will find a complete discussion of tax-deferred annuities as investments along with my annuity strategies and recommended annuities in Chapter 34. Here we want to cover the advantages of using annuities as part of your estate plan.

First and foremost, annuities have by law certain benefits usually associated with life insurance. You name one or more beneficiaries, and upon your death the annuity investment automatically passes to your heirs without going through probate. In essence, the annuity has the same probate bypassing power as a trust. If for instance you had $100,000 in an annuity investment in mutual funds and something happened to you, the money, including the principal you invested plus all the compounded earnings, would go to your heirs hassle free. You would save $8,000 to $15,000 in unnecessary probate fees and up to a year or more of unnecessary waiting.

In the eighties the tax rules for early withdrawals from annuities were changed to resemble those for such retirement plans as IRAs and 401(k)s (see Chapter 18). Let's review these rules.

- You pay taxes only when you withdraw money from your annuity and only on the money withdrawn. Taxes are computed by adding the gains withdrawn to your taxable income for that year.
- If you withdraw any of your annuity money before age 59½, you will be assessed an additional 10% tax penalty on any gain.

If you earn 15% or more using the Money Movement Strategy in Chapter 30, you should never have to touch your principal. You get the income, and your heirs get the principal with no probate problems.

What money do you invest in a tax-deferred self-directed annuity? As you get older, let's say over 50, you can choose to put into the annuity extra cash from which you don't need the income. As explained in Chapter 34, your money is not stuck there; you can withdraw it at any time for any purpose. The selected annuities become no-load or noncommissioned after about six or seven years, so there is no deferred sales charge.

One word of caution. Although you can normally put unlimited sums of money into annuities in lump sums or through periodic payments, the insurance company will attempt to get you to "annuitize" or agree to a monthly guaranteed payout plan with a guaranteed income for you and your spouse over a period of years. As inviting as it sounds, the plans benefit the insurance company more than they will you. Don't do it. As you get older, be sure to place your money in an insurance company that will allow you to treat the lump sum just like any other investment, taking money out when you choose so that the principal stays intact and does not become the property of the insurance company.

If you want help determining which annuities may be best for you, call The Insurance ClearingHouse at 1-800-522-2827.

Here is a chart that will help you visualize the different uses of the trusts we have discussed.

TRUST COMPARISON CHART

Type of Trust	Revocable or Irrevocable	Purpose	Who Should Consider
Life Insurance Trust	Irrevocable	Keep life insurance proceeds from being subject to estate taxes	Everyone with life insurance
Living or Inter Vivos Trust	Revocable	Keep assets and your estate out of probate	Everyone
A/B or Dual Trust	Revocable	Turn a $600,000 tax exemption into $1.2 million while giving lifetime income to spouse	Married couples who have or will have over $600,000 in assets
Retirement Trust (includes 401(k)s, IRAs, TSAs, etc.)	Revocable	Accumulate investment assets that compound tax free; avoid probate	Everyone
Age 21 Trust	Irrevocable	Save taxes on money invested for children	Parents with minor children
Annuities	Revocable	Accumulate invested assets for future income that compounds tax free; avoid probate	Anyone who has a fully funded retirement plan or does not qualify for a retirement plan (retirement trust)
Irrevocable Trust	Irrevocable	Give estate-tax free assets to your heirs at your death that you want to accumulate now	Anyone with children and assets over $600,000 who doesn't want the assets distributed until a future time

Chapter 18

DOUBLING THE PROFITS IN YOUR EMPLOYER'S RETIREMENT PLAN

Don't look back. Something may be gaining on you.

Satchel Paige
How to Keep Young
1953

OBJECTIVE ────────────────────────────────

CREATE A MILLION-DOLLAR RETIREMENT PLAN WHERE YOU WORK.

The last easy-to-use million-dollar tax shelter may be your retirement plan. Retirement plans don't come with instructions for maximizing either tax benefits or profits; and as a result, most participants lose at least 75% of the potential riches. You can have total financial freedom when you retire, without sacrificing your current lifestyle, if you learn to use your retirement plan options effectively.

A retirement plan can be described by three distinct sets of options: contribution options, investment options, and withdrawal options. You must know the answers to the following questions in order to maximize the profits from your plan. Go through the list entering the answers you know. Find out the answers you don't know from your plan descriptions and documents or from your employer's payroll or benefits office.

In this chapter you will learn the most powerful strategies ever developed for maximizing the profits and tax benefits from any employment-related retirement plan. In Chapter 33, "IRA and Keogh Investment Superstrategies," you will learn similar strategies for maximizing profits from retirement plans you create yourself.

UNDERSTANDING YOUR RETIREMENT PLAN OPTIONS

Fill in answers to all questions based on what you know about your retirement plan or will learn in this chapter. Find the missing answers by contacting your payroll or benefits office and by reading your plan description. In this chapter you will learn to use the answers for your benefit.

Contribution Options

What kind of plan does my employer offer—401(k), 403(b), 457, or SEP?   _____

What is the maximum I can deposit each year into all plans based on my current salary? (Strategy #165) $ _____

How much of my contribution is deductible from my taxable income? $ _____

Does my employer give me any matching funds? What percent?   _____%

What is the commission or load on my contributions?   _____

Investment Options

What are my choices for investments, i.e., the three to five different types of funds?   _____

How often can I change investments?   _____

Do I have a choice of sponsors offering different investments?   _____

Should I move my existing retirement plan money now to a better investment? (See Chapters 30 and 34.)   _____

How can I earn 15% or more per year instead of less than 10%? (See Chapter 33.)   _____

Can I get my employer to put in a better plan if the one I have is weak?   _____

Withdrawals

At what age can I withdraw my money with no penalty?   59½

What is the penalty if I withdraw before then?   10%

What is the withdrawal method that minimizes the taxes?   _____

Under what conditions, such as disability or financial hardship, can I withdraw my money with no penalty?   _____

Can I borrow from my plan? How much right now? $ _____

Should I withdraw my money in a lump sum, annuity payments, or use the IRA rollover rules when I retire?   _____

COMPARISON OF EMPLOYER SALARY DEDUCTION PLANS (1994)

Tax Code Section or Technical Name	Popular Name	Designed for	Maximum Employee Contribution 1994	Maximum Optional Employer Contributions	Salary Required to Contribute Maximum	Borrowing Option (Strategy #171)	Rollover Option (Strategy #176)	Averaging Option (Strategy #175)	Catch-up Provision (Strategy #195)
401(k)	deferred comp.[1] plan	corporate employees	20% of salary up to $9,240	25% of salary up to $30,000 minus employee's contributions	$48,200 gross	Yes	Yes	Yes	No
403(b) TSA	tax-sheltered annuity	teachers and tax-exempt-org. employees	16.67% of salary up to $9,500 minus employee's deductible contribution[3]	up to $30,000 minus employee's contributions	$56,700	Yes	Yes	Yes	last 3 years up to $12,500
408(k) SEP	simplified employee pension plan	small corporation plan—less than 25 employees	15% of salary up to $8,475	up to $22,500	$61,600	No	Yes	Yes	No
457	deferred comp.[1] plan	state and local government employees	25% of salary up to $7,500	None[2]	$30,000	No	No	No	last 3 years up to $15,000
TSP	Federal Thrift Savings Plan	federal and civil service employees	10% of salary up to $9,240	None	$92,400	Yes	Yes	Yes	No

1. comp. = compensation
2. 457 covered employees are usually also covered by additional state plan with no options.
3. Approximately equal to 20% of compensation.

Strategy #163
LEARN THE COMMON FEATURES TO UNSCRAMBLE THE MYSTERY OF RETIREMENT PLANS.

All of the employment-related retirement plans have the following rules and procedures in common. Refer to the Comparison of Employer Salary Deduction Plans chart on the previous page for the amounts and percentages that apply to your plan.

CONTRIBUTIONS

- Contributions to your plan are made through payroll deductions—that is, money is withheld from your paycheck and deposited in your investment account. Your employer has chosen an administrator and investment vehicle such as a mutual fund family or insurance company. You usually set up your plan and choose your investments by talking to a salesperson from the company that administers your plan.
- Each year the money you contribute is deducted from your income before federal and state income taxes are applied, which has the same mathematical effect as if the money were tax deductible. Thus, 100% of your money goes into the investment before taxes up to your maximum pretax limit.
- Maximum contributions each year are limited by Congress to a percentage of your income, up to a maximum dollar amount. The maximum dollar amounts on some types of plans, such as the 401(k) and SEP, are adjusted each year for inflation. Typically, the maximum contribution is increased by about $200 per year.
- If you work for two employers and contribute to more than one plan, for example a 401(k) and a 403(b), you are generally limited to a maximum combined contribution of the maximum amount for the plan with the higher contribution limits. You and your spouse can both contribute to different plans up to the maximum of your contribution limits.

INVESTMENTS

- Investment earnings from your plan are not subject to income taxes and are automatically reinvested. The mathematical effect is tax-free compounding, one of the best ways to build wealth ever devised.
- Most plans now give three to five different investment choices within the plan, such as stock and bond mutual funds coupled with an interest-bearing investment and often company stock.

Knowing how and when to choose these different investments is the secret to doubling your profits with no additional investments.

WITHDRAWALS

- Federal and state income taxes are due only when you withdraw (not borrow) the money and only on the amount of money withdrawn. You compute the taxes owed using IRS guidelines when you file your tax return for the year.
- If you withdraw or take any money out of the plan before age 59½, you can incur a 10% federal government penalty in addition to the taxes owed. The penalty is paid to the IRS and is not deductible. The taxes you owe are combined with your total taxes for the year by adding the amount of any withdrawal to your taxable income on your 1040 form.
- Some types of plans allow no-penalty withdrawals for emergencies or severe financial hardships. Your employer makes the qualification determination. There are exceptions to the rule you will learn, which can work in your favor.
- Tax laws permit borrowing on corporate and tax-sheltered annuity plans (401(k), 403(b)) if your employer sets up the option, but not on federal, state, and local government plans such as the 457s and SEPs. Borrowing is not considered a withdrawal and therefore is not subject to taxes and penalties, unless defaulted, according to new regulations, after one year.

Strategy #164
CONTRIBUTE TO YOUR RETIREMENT PLAN NOW—DON'T WAIT UNTIL LATER.

You can't be too young to start contributing to a retirement plan. Waiting until your bills are paid or until you have enough extra money could be one of the top five biggest opportunities lost during your lifetime! Read the following statement carefully. It will amaze you.

If you invest $2,000 in a tax-deferred retirement account each year between the ages of 20 and 25, and never invest another dime, you will have more money when you reach age 65 than if you wait until you are 25 and invest $2,000 every year for the next 40 years in the same account at the same rate of return.

To develop success habits you must begin by applying success principles, one of which is "DO IT NOW!"

Hard to believe? Here are the facts. Invest $2,000 at the end of each year into a retirement plan at 15% between the ages of 20 and 25 and you will have $3,612,000 waiting for you at age 65. Remember you contribute nothing more after age 25. However, if you wait to begin your contributions until age 25 and then contribute $2,000 at the end of each year for the next 40 years, you will have $3,558,000 in your account at age 65. Start maximizing your contributions now no matter what it takes.

Strategy #165
CONTRIBUTE THE DEDUCTIBLE MAXIMUM TO YOUR EMPLOYER'S RETIREMENT PLAN.

There are four major types of qualified retirement plans offered by employers and funded through payroll deductions. A qualified plan is one that is put together under IRS guidelines. Many union plans, for instance, are nonqualified, and these rules will not apply. Determine which kind of plan you have and calculate your deductible (nontaxable) maximum contribution for this year.

401(K)—DEFERRED COMPENSATION PLAN FOR CORPORATE EMPLOYEES

Employees may contribute up to 15% of their gross compensation or a maximum of $9,240 per year, tax deferred. The employer can also contribute money to the plan that is not currently taxable. The more your employer contributes, the better the plan. The $9,240 limit may be increased for inflation in future years. The best 401(k) plans are those that offer mutual funds as investment options.

408(K) SEP—SIMPLIFIED EMPLOYEE PENSION PLAN FOR EMPLOYEES OF SMALL COMPANIES—LESS THAN 25 EMPLOYEES

Employees may contribute up to 15% of gross compensation or a maximum of $9,240 per year, tax deferred. The employer may contribute up to $22,500 or even $30,000, in some instances, per year minus the employee's contribution, also tax deferred. The more your employer contributes, the better the plan. The best SEP plans are those that offer mutual funds as investment options. Money in SEPs, like money in IRAs, can be contributed until April 15 of the year following the tax year.

403(B)—DEFERRED COMPENSATION PLAN (TAX-SHELTERED ANNUITY) FOR PUBLIC SCHOOL AND NONPROFIT ORGANIZATION EMPLOYEES

Employees may contribute approximately 20% of gross compensation up to $9,500 per year, tax deferred. The employer has the option of contributing up to the difference between the employee contribution and $30,000, also tax deferred, although few, if any, employers use this option. Most public school employees are also covered by a separate pension plan over which the employee has no control. The best 403(b) plans offer mutual funds as investment options.

457—DEFERRED COMPENSATION PLAN FOR STATE, COUNTY, AND CITY EMPLOYEES

Employees may contribute 25% of gross compensation up to $7,500 per year tax deferred. Employers may not contribute. Most municipal employees are also covered by a separate pension plan over which the employee has no control. The best 457 plans offer mutual funds as investment options.

FEDERAL THRIFT SAVINGS PLAN/FEDERAL EMPLOYEE RETIREMENT SYSTEM (FERS)

Civil employees can contribute up to 5% of salary. The federal government does not contribute. FERS workers can contribute up to 10%, and the government will match 50 cents on the dollar. The maximum FERS contribution, therefore, is 15%.

To make it easy to plan your payroll withholding amount per paycheck, refer to the chart on the following page. You can use the chart to determine how much a specific amount deducted from each of your checks will total each year. You can also use it to determine how much you would have to contribute every paycheck to reach a specific goal amount per year.

RETIREMENT PLAN EMPLOYEE CONTRIBUTIONS PLANNING CHART
Frequency of Paycheck/Number of Pay Periods per Year

A Total Yearly Contribution	B Monthly 12	C Twice Monthly 24	D Bi- weekly 26	E Weekly 52
$1,000	$ 83	$ 42	$ 38	$ 19
2,000	167	83	77	39
3,000	250	125	115	58
4,000	333	167	154	77
5,000	417	208	192	96
6,000	500	250	231	115
7,000	583	292	269	135
7,500[1]	625	312	288	144
8,000[2]	667	333	308	154
9,000[2]	750	375	346	173
9,500[3]	791	396	365	183

1. $7,500 is the maximum for a 457 plan.
2. $9,240 is the maximum for 401(k) and SEP plans.
3. $9,500 is the maximum for a 403(b) plan.

To determine how much you must have deducted from each paycheck per pay period to contribute a specific yearly amount or the maximum you can contribute, find the total you want to contribute in column A, then read across to the column that represents how often you receive your paychecks. For example, if your objective or maximum-contribution limit based on your salary is $5,000, read across the $5,000 row until you locate your paycheck frequency. If you receive biweekly paychecks (a paycheck every 14 days), you would use column D, which shows that $192 deducted per paycheck will put $5,000 tax free into your plan each year.

To determine how much per year will be contributed to your plan if you choose a specific deduction amount per paycheck, first locate the approximate amount you intend to have deducted from each paycheck under the column heading that represents your paycheck frequency. Then follow the row to column A and you will find the approximate total amount you will be contributing each year. For example, you or you and your spouse determine that you will contribute $130 per paycheck to your plan and you receive a paycheck twice monthly, on the first and fifteenth. Using column C on the chart, locate the number closest to $130, which in this example is $125. Follow the row to the left and you will see that your yearly contribution will be approximately $3,000.

After determining your yearly contribution and adding any amount contributed by your employer, you can then use the total, along with your expected earnings per year, to determine how much money will be in your account at any time in the future.

Once you have made your determination of the amount to be withheld from each paycheck, contact your company payroll or benefits person or department and make the change by signing the appropriate form. Some plans allow changes at any time, others only at specific times of the year. The more often you can make changes, the better the plan.

Strategy #166
USE THE DOUBLE-DEDUCTION BENEFITS OF ANY QUALIFIED RETIREMENT PLAN TO BUILD YOUR WEALTH.

From what you have already learned in this book, you have strategies that will make or save you hundreds or thousands every year for the rest of your life. Some of these savings can be put into your tax-sheltered retirement plan, and over time you can transform them into millions.

Yearly taxes are the biggest detriment to your wealth-building plan, and Congress, through the establishment of a double-deduction retirement plan, has created your best taxless opportunity. In all retirement plans, there are two tax shelters: your contribution is made without taxes taken out, and the money your contribution earns year after year compounds tax free. This double tax-free compounding effect is what will eventually and automatically make you wealthy.

Within your contribution limits, the money you invest in your plan is deducted from your taxable income for the year. If you are in the 28% federal tax bracket, your tax saving is 28% of your contribution. If your tax bracket is 31%, the tax saving is 31% of your contribution. If you live in a state with a 7% additional state tax, you are saving 38 cents out of every taxless dollar you invest right from the start. Here's an example:

$7,000	Your contribution this year
× 38%	Your tax bracket (state and federal)
$2,660	Tax savings—in cash!

Your yearly earnings compound tax free as long as your money remains invested. That means each year you earn the equivalent of interest on interest with no depletion or deduction for taxes. The concept of "earn now, deal with the taxes later" is known as a tax deferral.

Many supposedly knowledgeable CPAs and accountants have incorrectly advised clients not to contribute much to retirement tax shelters since the taxes will be due someday anyway. What nonsense! You pay no current taxes on both the amount invested and the income earned from the account. If you were, instead, to invest your money after taxes were deducted and then pay taxes again on your investment earnings each year, you would lose twice. As much as 38% is lost to taxes from your initial investment capital, and then up to another 38% of what you earn is lost to taxes before your money is reinvested. Tax-free compounding can increase your account balance hundreds of percentage points by the time you retire or withdraw the money because you are using the tax money as additional investment capital. So what if you eventually pay the original tax money. By then it has multiplied itself two to ten times in earnings, most of which you get to keep.

Let's look at $7,000 of your income invested in one year with and without retirement-plan protection.

INVESTMENT ACCOUNT PROFILE AFTER ONE YEAR WITH AND WITHOUT TAX PROTECTION

	With Tax Protection	Without Tax Protection
Amount Contributed to Plan	$7,000	$7,000
Taxes on Income at 35%	− 0	−2,450
Net Investment After Taxes	$7,000	$4,550
Earnings 1st Year at 15%	+1,050	+ 682
Account Balance Before Tax on Earnings	$8,050	$5,232
Tax on 1st-Year Earnings at 35%	− 0	− 239
Account Balance After One Year	$8,050	$4,993

In just one year there is a $3,000 difference in the two accounts even though you began with the same $7,000. The second year you begin earning interest on $8,050 in the tax-protected account, but on only $4,993 in the taxed account. You can imagine what effect this mathematical process has on your future.

You can now see how small investments in tax-deferred retirement accounts make millionaires out of smart money managers. Think of it this way. You're going to get older anyway, you might as well be getting older and richer at the same time. Look over the Power of Tax-Free Investing and Compounding chart below to see how your retirement plan will build your fortune over the next 5 to 30 years. Using the strategies in Chapters 30 and 31, you will be able to average as much as 15% per year in your retirement plan.

POWER OF TAX-FREE INVESTING AND COMPOUNDING

15% Compounded Annually
Tax Rate 35% (State and Federal)

$2,000 per Year Available to Invest Before Taxes

End of Year	With Tax Protection	Without Tax Protection
5	$ 15,000	$ 8,000
10	46,000	22,000
15	113,000	45,000
20	253,000	83,000
25	547,000	145,000
30	1,168,000	247,000

$4,000 per Year Available to Invest Before Taxes

End of Year	With Tax Protection	Without Tax Protection
5	$ 30,000	$ 17,000
10	93,000	44,000
15	226,000	91,000
20	505,000	166,000
25	1,095,000	290,000
30	2,337,000	494,000

$7,000 per Year Available to Invest Before Taxes

End of Year	With Tax Protection	Without Tax Protection
5	$ 52,000	$ 30,000
10	163,000	78,000
15	395,000	158,000
20	884,000	290,000
25	1,916,000	507,000
30	4,089,000	864,000

What a difference! That should clear up any doubts raised by financial folks who don't know what they are talking about.

Strategy #167
USE THE SWITCHING OPTION AND MONEY MOVEMENT STRATEGY™ TO EARN 15% IN YOUR EMPLOYER'S RETIREMENT PLAN.

Ninety percent of all employment-related retirement plans now give you options for investing. You are no longer required to stick your money in a low-paying, fixed-interest, 7% or 8% guaranteed-return investment. If you were your money, you wouldn't even consider working that cheaply!

Most retirement plan investment alternatives are actually mutual funds offered through mutual fund families or insurance companies that have been chosen by your employer or the administrators of your retirement plan. Your choices for investments are usually three or more of those shown in the following chart. Notice that the name shown in the retirement plan documents and the salesperson's description are often different from the names normally associated with the investment itself. The first column shows the actual name of the investment, usually identified by the type of security, such as stock, bond, or money market (see Chapter 30). The word *fund* means that you are investing in an already established portfolio or group of stocks, bonds, or money market instruments as opposed to the one investment you own if you put your retirement plan money in your company's stock purchase plan.

Which investment option should you choose? You are often told that your choice should depend on the difference in risk. But using the words *high risk* and *low risk* when describing the difference in the real chance you are taking with your money is like saying that if you cross the street in front of your house twice today instead of once, you have doubled your risk of getting hit by a car, therefore crossing a street twice is high risk. The real difference in risk is negligible and should have little bearing on your decision of which investment to choose regardless of your age or desire for security. Using the Money Movement Strategy you will learn later in Chapter 30, you will move your money from one type of fund to another based on changes in the prime interest rate and not because of opinions about the direction of the economy or outdated ideas about risk. Money Movement has proven to be the best easy-to-use strategy for retirement plan investing for more than ten years. It is a strategy you can depend on to safely double the earnings you could get from bank CDs or fixed-rate, low-interest retirement plans.

Most company plans allow you to switch investments from one to four times per year. Since your money is tax sheltered, there are no capital gains taxes to pay when you switch investments.

YOUR RETIREMENT PLAN INVESTMENT OPTIONS

Investment	Retirement Plan Name	Salesman's Description
Stock fund	Equity or variable	High risk
Bond fund	Bond fund	Medium risk
Stock/bond fund	Balanced fund	Medium risk
Money market fund	Variable interest	Low risk
Fixed or variable interest rate investment	Guaranteed or variable interest	Low risk
Company stock	Company stock	Company stock

The fixed or variable interest rate and company stock investments are the only options in most plans that are technically not mutual funds. The interest-rate investments pay a guaranteed or sometimes variable interest rate without the potential for capital appreciation inherent in stock and bond funds or company stock.

Company stock is usually offered to employees at a discount, usually 15%, and often must be held until termination or retirement. The 15% discount is attractive as long as there is an option for selling the stock within a couple of years and moving to another investment. Company stock can drop in value or become worthless based on the fortunes of your company, over which you probably have little personal control.

Although corporations usually offer only one investment plan, some school systems, such as Orange County, Florida, offer over 50 plans and sponsors. If you are employed by an organization that offers more than one plan, you may transfer your money to a new plan if you wish based on the transfer rules of the plans. In many plans, if you change sponsors or withdraw your money during the first five years, you will be charged an extra back-end load or surrender charge.

RETIREMENT PLAN WITHDRAWAL OPTIONS

Sooner or later you will stop contributing and start withdrawing and enjoying the money you have accumulated for so many years. That's why you set up the plan in the first place. The money you withdraw can be used to replace income that disappears when you retire, can be spent rewarding yourself with dream trips and vacations, can be used to help you retire to a warm climate, or for any other meaningful purpose. If you have followed the strategies as I have outlined them, your retirement accounts will provide you with luxurious living for the balance of your life instead of only an income supplement.

How you make your withdrawals is important to preserving your wealth. There are little-known rules you can turn into strategies for getting more flexibility and control over the money in your plan.

Strategy #168
USE THE WITHDRAWAL EXCEPTION RULES TO GET MONEY OUT OF YOUR RETIREMENT ACCOUNT BEFORE AGE 59½.

Most employees contribute far too little to retirement plans because they are afraid their money will be tied up until retirement and not available for personal or emergency financial situations. Not true. Here are some little-known options for getting money out of your account before retirement.

- Most company-sponsored retirement plans allow you to withdraw money penalty free to offset a financial hardship or because of death or disability. If you are strapped financially, a committee set up by your employer, using IRS guidelines, can allow you to take money out of your employer's 401(k), 403(b), or 457 penalty free. Check with your employer to find out how the rules are applied in your company and see Strategy #169.
- Most employer plans now have a loan provision, allowing you to borrow up to $50,000 at any time with no taxes or penalties. Even though all 401(k) and 403(b) plans qualify under the tax rules, your employer and plan sponsor must offer the borrowing option. See Strategy #170.
- If you retire before age 59½ but after you are 55, you're allowed to withdraw your money with no penalty.

- If a court orders you to pay money to a spouse or child from your retirement account, the withdrawal is not subject to the penalty.
- There is no penalty for the withdrawal of dividends earned in an Employee Stock Option Plan (ESOP).

Strategy #169
USE THE SPECIAL PENALTY-FREE 401(k) HARDSHIP RULE TO FUND YOUR HOME PURCHASE, FOR COLLEGE EXPENSES, OR TO STOP A FORECLOSURE.

There are some methods included under the hardship rule that make your retirement money relatively easy to get at. Some of these areas you and I might think of as costly, but not necessarily as a hardship or financial emergency. They include:

- the down payment for a home
- college expenses for yourself, your child, or your spouse
- paying off big medical bills

Your employer decides if you qualify for the penalty-free withdrawal. You don't have to create a detailed analysis of your financial situation or submit a financial statement. You must, however, state to your employer that you cannot pay the expenses with your income or insurance by liquidating assets, or by borrowing without causing more hardship. Keep in mind that you will have mandatory withholding and a 10% surtax if withdrawn before age 59½. Plan ahead for your net hardship needs.

In the unlikely and undesirable event of a threatened mortgage foreclosure, often caused by being out of work for an extended period, the little-known hardship rule also allows you to withdraw money to bring your house payments current. If you have extraordinary medical expenses, withdrawals from an employer's plan used to pay medical expenses that exceed 7.5% of your adjusted gross income (regardless of whether or not you itemize your deductions) are not subject to penalties. Of course, if you have assets such as money in other investments, you would not want to take the money out of your 401(k) plan to fund these expenses anyway. Use this rule and your 401(k) money only as a last resort, but don't pass up the home or the college education for lack of ready funds. Your contribution to your 401(k) is limited for one year after the year of a hardship distribution. Plans other than the 401(k) have similar hardship rules.

Strategy #170
GET YOUR RETIREMENT PLAN MONEY TAX AND PENALTY FREE BEFORE AGE 59½ BY BORROWING INSTEAD OF WITHDRAWING.

Yes, it's true that if you withdraw your 401(k), 403(b), or other retirement plan money before age 59½, you could pay about 30% federal tax and 10% penalties, for a total as high as 40%, plus any state and local income taxes. The fear of having too much money stuck where you can't reasonably get your hands on it without big losses is what causes most younger people to pass up the retirement plan wealth-building opportunity.

But what if I told you that your money can be taken out of your plan anytime you wish for any purpose and you would pay no tax or penalties, no matter what your age?

How? Don't withdraw it, borrow it.

Congress included a little-known but powerful option in retirement plan tax rules that allows you to borrow up to $50,000 from your 401(k) or 403(b) both tax free and penalty free. Here are the rules:

- If the vested amount in your account is $20,000 or less, you can borrow up to a total of $10,000 including any previous loans. Your contributions are always considered vested (belonging to you). Your employer's share of the contributions becomes yours (vested) over five to seven years.
- If the vested amount in your plan is more than $20,000, you can borrow up to 50% of the money vested. The maximum you can have borrowed at one time is $50,000.
- You must repay the loan within five years in equal quarterly payments (or ¹⁄₂₀ of the loan amount every three months). You can pay back the money earlier if you choose with no penalties.
- You can choose to pay back the loan with regular deductions from your paycheck so that you don't need to concern yourself with lump-sum payments every quarter.
- You are actually using your account balance and your continuing salary as security for the loan repayment. Technically this is a non-sense rule because the money you are borrowing is your own.
- The interest you pay is normally paid to yourself and can be deductible if used for business or investments, or if secured by a mortgage on your home.

If you have been married for more than one year, there is a new rule that if your account is set up subject to "joint and survivorship rules," as most are, your spouse must sign a consent form allowing you to borrow against your account.

About 75% of employers with qualified retirement plans now allow borrowing. It is up to your employer, but your employer has no reason not to allow borrowing, except maybe a little extra paperwork. Convince your employer that the borrowing option is one of the best no-cost benefits that can be offered to employees. Your employer will then set up the borrowing option with whoever administers the plan. Unfortunately, Congress left out the borrowing option for state and local government employees who contribute to a 457 deferred compensation plan.

Strategy #171
MAKE A TAX-FREE DOWN PAYMENT ON A HOME USING THE RETIREMENT PLAN BORROWING STRATEGY.

There is one more little-known, major opportunity Congress threw into the qualified retirement plan rules. If you borrow from your retirement plan to make a down payment on a home, you don't ever have to pay the borrowed money back, there is no stipulated prepayment period.

Think of it. This rule actually allows you to make a tax deductible down payment on a home by funneling the money first through your 401(k) or 403(b). You put money into your plan and take a deduction from your income for the money you contributed. When you buy your home, you borrow the money from the plan (see Strategy #170) for the down payment, tax and penalty free. Since your home is also a tax shelter, you have doubled the tax-saving power of the transaction. Your retirement money has not been spent nor has it disappeared. You have simply shifted it to a new investment, the equity in your home.

If your plan assesses interest on the loan, even the interest you pay (generally to yourself) is tax deductible provided you give your plan a second mortgage note for the loan. That note makes any interest you pay fully deductible because it is mortgage interest. (See Strategy #183.)

Strategy #172
GET YOUR NEXT RAISE TOTALLY TAX FREE BY FUNNELING IT TO YOUR RETIREMENT PLAN.

A few years ago when there were a dozen tax brackets instead of the current five, a comment often heard from employees everywhere was, "I'm concerned about getting a raise since it might put me in a higher tax bracket." The concern was always unfounded, since only a portion of a raise, not your entire salary, could be taxed at a new higher rate. (See marginal tax brackets, page 167.)

But wouldn't it be great if you could get your entire next raise totally tax free? You can—even without anyone's permission. Your strategy is to have the entire amount of your raise deducted from your paycheck and put into your retirement plan account. Since the money you put into your plan is not taxable that year, you have at that point received the entire amount of your raise in cash, tax free! You then put the cash into your investment plan. You just never saw the money so you won't miss it. Yet your raise will now help in the creation of your million-dollar retirement plan.

Any amount of matching funds your employer contributes and every dime in interest, dividends, or appreciation you earn that year are also deposited into your account with no taxes. The exciting part of this strategy is that there is no financial sacrifice required on your part. You are not taking a cut in your paycheck or lifestyle to fund the plan since the money is new money from your raise.

Here is an example: You are earning $35,000 per year but contributing little to your 401(k). You receive a raise of 5% or $1,750. You tell your employer to deduct the entire amount from your paychecks and deposit the money into your retirement plan. Your employer contributes 50% of what you put in or an additional $875. The total currently tax-free addition to your investment plan is $2,625, saving you approximately $900 in state and federal income taxes. Instead of receiving $1,750 in your paycheck minus $600 for taxes or a net of $1,150 for the year, you have parlayed your raise into $2,625 plus investment earnings for the year. Using this simple strategy, you have more than doubled your raise in one year.

Strategy #173
AVOID THE 10% PENALTY BY WITHDRAWING FROM YOUR RETIREMENT PLAN AFTER AGE 59½.

There is no 10% penalty applied to a retirement plan withdrawal after age 59½ no matter what the reason or method of withdrawal. The amount you withdraw, if part of your or your employer's tax-free contribution, is added to your taxable income for the year. The withdrawal method you choose, however, will determine the amount of taxes you pay. As your job income decreases when you retire, one purpose of the penalty-free withdrawals will be to replace that lost job income.

Strategy #174
USE THE LUMP-SUM AVERAGING METHOD ONLY IF YOU NEED THE CASH FROM YOUR RETIREMENT PROGRAM.

If money is withdrawn in a lump sum from an employer's retirement plan, the averaging-method option reduces your taxes to a minimum. The averaging method mathematically allows you to treat your lump-sum distribution as if you received an equal portion of the money each year for five or ten years. Those who were over 50 years old on January 1, 1986, may elect ten-year averaging at any age. Those under 50 on that date may use only five-year averaging after they reach 59½. Lump-sum averaging may now be used only once per lifetime. The old tax law allowed averaging every time a person changed jobs or retired, no matter what age.

The purpose of lump-sum averaging is to prevent your withdrawals from putting you in a higher tax bracket. Because of the five-bracket system under the new tax laws, the averaging method does not cut your taxes nearly as much as before tax reform and makes the IRA rollover option far more attractive and the averaging option less attractive.

If your employer's retirement plan withdrawal qualifies for lump-sum averaging, it also qualifies for the tax-free rollover to an IRA. If you needed to take the entire amount of cash out of your plan, something you won't ever want to do, the averaging method would at least minimize your taxes.

Strategy #175
USE THE IRA ROLLOVER RULES TO CIRCUMVENT THE TAXES ON A RETIREMENT PLAN LUMP-SUM DISTRIBUTION.

When you change jobs or retire, your objective is to get control of your 401(k), 403(b), or SEP money without paying taxes. The rollover rules allow you to move your entire company retirement plan to any IRA without the $2,000 one-year IRA contribution restriction and without paying taxes or penalties. You request a check from your former employer for the amount in your account, and you have 60 days from the date you receive the money to deposit it in the IRA. The only exception is the 457 plan, which cannot be rolled over. Since the rollover allows you to move your money without tax consequences, it is your best alternative for:

• getting control of your retirement money
• keeping your money totally tax sheltered
• achieving greater earnings through self-directed investments.

Your employer is required to withhold 20% of your retirement plan distribution for estimated income taxes. If you do not have sufficient personal funds to replace the 20% withholding within the 60-day rollover period, the amount withheld for estimated taxes would be considered a premature distribution and is subject to income taxes and the 10% penalty. If you cannot replace the 20% that was withheld by your former employee when you open your new plan, use instead the employer-to-employer transfer in the next strategy.

Strategy #176
OPEN YOUR ROLLOVER IRA IN A NO-LOAD MUTUAL FUND FAMILY.

By using the Money Movement Strategy (Chapter 30) with your rollover account, you may average up to 15% per year, tax sheltered. If your rollover account is $200,000 you will average $30,000 per year at 15% and double your money in under five years. If you are withdrawing 10% each year, but earning 15%, not only does your principal remain intact, it is actually growing even while you are withdrawing money as income.

Strategy #177
AVOID THE EMPLOYER-TO-EMPLOYER TRANSFER OF YOUR RETIREMENT ACCOUNT.

When you change jobs, you have the option of moving your retirement plan from one employer to another with no tax consequences, which preserves your right to lump-sum averaging. The downside to this employer-to-employer transfer is that your options for investing are limited to those in your new employer's plan. Better to do the IRA rollover! You can usually continue to use your current employer's plan for one year or more even after you leave, but your strategy is to get control of the money, which means moving it to an IRA.

Strategy #178
NEVER ANNUITIZE YOUR COMPANY RETIREMENT PLAN.

Instead of receiving a lump sum, many plans and companies allow you to use your retirement money to buy a lifetime annuity contract from an insurance company. Based on life expectancy tables published by the insurance company, you receive monthly checks for from ten years to the rest of your life. Another option allows you to take less initially in your monthly annuity check and guarantees your spouse will receive partial annuity payments only if you go first.

The annuity option makes only the insurance companies wealthy and is mathematically your worst withdrawal option even though it sounds appealing. There are three drawbacks to the annuity option:

- The insurance company annuity tables give you monthly checks that are far smaller than you should receive for an account that size. There is nothing you can do about it once you have given your money to the insurance company.
- Your remaining principal in most contracts becomes the property of the insurance company if you die—your heirs don't get a dime. Your only way to fight back is to live a long time.
- The monthly check amounts are based on an extremely low investment return on your principal, which is now not actually yours, but is owned by the insurance company. You get only the monthly payments.

All retirement accounts now have a required uniform starting date for mandatory withdrawals. This withdrawal is not optional, but a few strategies will enable you to minimize or eliminate the taxes on mandatory withdrawals.

You must start making withdrawals from all your retirement plans by April 1 of the year following the year you become 70½ years old. The minimum yearly withdrawal amount is based on an IRS life expectancy table for you or you and your spouse. The rule of thumb is that your yearly withdrawal will be about 10 to 15% of the money in your account each year. Your goal is to control the amount of the withdrawal to create the maximum benefit for yourself. In *Financial Self-Defense*, Chapter 19, are the strategies I've developed for changing the amount of money you are required to withdraw for your own benefit.

Strategy #179
CREATE A TAX WASH WITH TAX DEDUCTIONS THAT OFFSET THE TAX CONSEQUENCES OF ANY RETIREMENT ACCOUNT WITHDRAWAL.

By using the tax strategies in the tax section of this book, you can create enough additional tax deductions each year to make a retirement account withdrawal effectively tax free. Your withdrawal is not directly taxed. Instead, the amount of the withdrawal is added to your income for the year and taxed at your highest marginal bracket amount (e.g., 31%).

Every $1,000 of new deductions you create through a small business, family tax strategies, travel deduction strategies, real estate rental properties, etc., has the effect of tax-sheltering $1,000 of your taxable withdrawal, and once you have an equal amount of new deductions and withdrawals, you are effectively making all your withdrawals totally and permanently tax free!

ENJOY YOUR RETIREMENT MONEY

It is all right to spend the money from your retirement account for pleasure. Withdraw all you want. That's what it is for. Too many successful retired people spend too much time trying to preserve capital instead of spending and enjoying it. You can't take it with you. So far no one has yet discovered a way to attach a U-Haul to a hearse.

Chapter 19

TRAVEL THE WORLD ON DEDUCTIBLE DOLLARS

Money is a guarantee that we may have what we want in the future. Though we need nothing at the moment, it insures the possibility of satisfying a new desire when it arises.

Aristotle
Nicomachean Ethics
(384–322 B.C.)

OBJECTIVE

MAKE YOUR VACATIONS AND TRIPS TAX DEDUCTIBLE.

Imagine visiting Honolulu, New York, or even Hong Kong, and having Uncle Sam pick up one-third of your travel expenses. You can enjoy the privilege by making your vacations and trips tax deductible.

Strategy #180
USE JOB INTERVIEWS TO MAKE VACATIONS DEDUCTIBLE.

If you work for someone else, the easiest way to make your vacations deductible is with job interviews. The tax code says that if, while you are traveling, you go on a job interview for the same type of job you now have, you are entitled to take a tax deduction for up to the entire amount you spend traveling. Who "entitles" you? Congress. It just never got around to telling us.

Keeping tax records is easy. Have the personnel department where you apply make a copy of the job application. When you get home, drop it in your tax file with your airline, hotel, food, and rental car receipts and your trip is deductible. Whether your job is executive, truck driver, nurse, or secretary, the only requirement is that the job you apply for must be the same or similar to the one you have now. If you are between jobs, you may qualify for the deduction by applying for the same type of job as the last one you had.

You may qualify to make all of your travel expenses deductible by following a few simple IRS rules.

To deduct 100% of expenses, the purpose of the trip must be primarily related to job search activities. For instance, you could spend a minimum of two hours per day or four hours every other day, not including weekends, working on your deductible purpose. Keep the records of the time spent in your daily planner. You may set up multiple interviews, contact a personnel agency, or conduct research at the local library on the companies and the area—all of which counts toward your time requirement.

There is only one outside risk when using the job interview strategy. You might get the job! But that's career advancement, certainly one of your more important goals.

You have created a win-win strategy. You either get the tax deduction or a better job, big promotion, and even palm trees in the wintertime. Your objective is to set up your entire financial life with win-win strategies. No matter what the outcome—you profit. Your spouse may also use the "job interview strategy" to make his or her expenses deductible.

What if you are offered the job and turn it down? Can you still take the tax deduction? That depends. If you were not offered your salary requirements or job terms, you have every right to turn down the position and claim the deduction. If you are offered your terms, it would not be right to take the deduction since the IRS could correctly claim that your job hunting was not a serious endeavor. You are not trying to kid the IRS—it doesn't fool easily—but only to take deductions for which you actually qualify.

Write ahead to line up interviews. Your public library has telephone books for most major cities. Use the form letter on page 245 to set up interviews, and to establish the job search purpose of your trip.

There are unlimited ways to apply the job interview strategy.

A young woman named Lisa, who worked for the governor of the state of Virginia and sang in nightclubs around Richmond as a part-time job, had always dreamed of singing on a cruise ship as part of the band. Lisa called Carnival Cruise Lines and was finally able to talk to a cruise director while he was in port. The cruise director told her she was welcome to try out with the band, but they were always at sea. That was just what she had hoped to hear!

Magnificent Widgets
101 Lite-My-Way Lane
Phoenix, Arizona

Attn: W. W. Hirem
Personnel Director

Dear Mr. Hirem:

I have been interested in your company for some time and am considering relocating to Phoenix.

During March, I will be in the area and would appreciate the opportunity to stop by your company to complete an application and possibly discuss the opportunities available with Magnificent Widgets. If there is any problem, please let me know. Otherwise, I will phone for an appointment while I am in the area. Thank you.

Sincerely,

She booked passage on a cruise to Bermuda, during which the band leader let her entertain the passengers for a few nights as an audition. Lisa loved it, the band leader thought she was great, but there just wasn't enough money available to hire another person. Lisa asked the band leader to put it in writing so she could place the refusal in her tax file.

That year, Lisa took a tax deduction for her cruise to Bermuda as a job interview and the IRS allowed the deduction. The reason is clear; she did go on a legitimate job interview, which she adequately documented. How fortunate that the job interview was on the cruise, and the minimum time she could spend on the cruise was one week!

Strategy #181
START A SMALL IMPORTING COMPANY.

You can even make your international travel deductible by starting a small importing company. Your total investment? Two empty suitcases. Take them with you to Mexico, South America, the Far East, and even Europe. While you are at your destination, your tax strategy is to go shopping. While visiting the market-places and bazaars, you buy the beautiful handicrafts and hand-made items that are so inexpensive overseas and so incredibly expensive when you see them in the gift shops and department stores back home. These are your imports and that's what goes in the suitcases. Pick the things you know your friends would love to own.

When you get home, have a party and invite all your friends right down to your distant acquaintances. They are your custom-ers. After you serve the "tax deductible refreshments" bring out all your beautiful imports—with a price tag on them. You will find, like so many who use this strategy, that you'll sell out the first night and make more than enough profit to pay for your next trip. At tax time you may take a deduction on Schedule C for all of your international travel expenses. After all, Tupper-ware made a billion dollars selling plastic bowls at friendly home parties. Think what you can do with the beautiful items you bring back. Happy bargain hunting!

My first experience at importing came during my first trip to Mexico. I was 26, and two friends and I scraped together enough gas and hotel money to get us from Nashville to Monterrey, Mexico. With the couple of hundred extra expense dollars, I bought leather coats for $8 each and beautiful colored ceramic plates that sold in gift shops for $30. They cost me just $2. Everything I brought back was gone instantly as my friends grabbed for their favorites as if they were at a bargain basement sale.

The government will help you. There is no customs duty on artwork or handicrafts, no matter how much you bring into the country. In any case, you can bring back $400 per person of dutiable items free and pay only 10% of cost on the next $1,000.

Strategy #182
BECOME AN "OUTSIDE AGENT" FOR A TRAVEL AGENCY.

You can have the benefits of a travel agent or agency without changing careers or starting your own agency. By acting as an "outside agent" for any travel agency, you qualify to receive part of the travel agency's commission—up to 50%. The travel agency normally receives 10% of the cost of the airline tickets, and 15% commission on the ground arrangements such as hotels and tours. Choose a destination you would like to visit, and one that your friends and associates might also enjoy. Print simple brochures or fliers that explain your adventure and distribute them to fellow employees, club members, or even neighbors. The travel agency can furnish you with "shells"—partially printed brochures with color pictures and blank areas for insertion of time, date, and specific information about your trip.

As an outside agent you will have the chance to travel free. You'll usually get one complimentary trip for every 15 people who pay the regular price. The commission income from your trip will show your intent to make a profit and allow you to take a tax deduction for any of your money spent.

After your first successful trip, whether you take 3 or 50 people, begin planning other trips. You now have the right to travel anywhere to familiarize yourself with possible locations and hotels for group trips. Your travel costs are, of course, deductible.

If your part-time travel enterprise earns you about $6,000 in commissions in any one year, you qualify for free and discounted airline tickets, as well as "familiarization" trips around the world with discounts of as much as 75%. I enjoy travel so much I finally bought a travel agency. While in Amsterdam recently, I pulled out my travel agent's business card at the beautiful Amstel Hotel and was promptly given a 50% discount on my entire stay—from $200 per night to $100 per night. The previous month, I flew on American Airlines round-trip, first class from Orlando, Florida, to Sacramento, California, for only $300, far less than the regular first-class fare of $1,200. On a recent safari to Africa, the regular cost of the land arrangements was cut in half, from $3,400 per person to $1,700, and the first-class airfare was 75% off, all tax deductible, of course, since I own the travel agency.

During the seventies, I personally took hundreds of people to Hawaii, Mexico, England, Ireland, France, and South America. As an outside agent putting the trips together, I knew I would enjoy myself. My share of the commissions amounted to about $5,000 per week plus free airfare and hotels. Not a bad way to travel.

You can get the same bargains by becoming a successful "outside agent."

Chapter 20

IN YOUR BEST INTEREST

Everything should be made as simple as possible, but not simpler.

Albert Einstein
Physicist
(1879–1955)

OBJECTIVE

MAKE CONSUMER INTEREST DEDUCTIBLE.

The Tax Reform Act of 1986 changed or eliminated over 50 favorite tax deductions. One of the most devastating to taxpayers is the nondeductibility of consumer interest. Consumer interest includes interest paid on credit cards and installment, personal, college, insurance policy, and automobile loans. But the new consumer interest rules do not limit the interest deduction for mortgage, investment, and business loans. By converting consumer loans to legitimate mortgage, investment, and business loans, you can preserve your interest deductions.

The consumer interest deduction did not disappear completely with the onset of tax reform, but was phased out over a five-year period beginning in 1987. Here are the percentages of consumer interest that were still deductible.

Year	% Deductible
1988	40
1989	20
1990	10
1991	0

249

Since $3 of tax deductions under tax reform gets you a cash refund of about $1, interest deductions dramatically cut the cost of borrowing money. Losing the interest deduction has the same effect as a tax increase.

FEWER INTEREST DEDUCTIONS MEANS GREATER TAXES

For a typical family that owns a home, interest deductions before tax reform averaged $12,000 or more per year. Here is an example of how you or others are hurt by the new nondeductible interest rules.

				Deductible	
	Interest Rate	Principal	One-Year Interest	Before Tax Reform	After Tax Reform
Home mortgage	11%	$ 80,000	$ 8,800	$ 8,800	$8,800
Car loans	13	12,000	1,560	1,560	0
Credit cards	18	4,000	720	720	0
Personal loans	12	5,000	600	600	0
Margin accounts	10	4,000	400	400	400
College loans	8	11,000	880	880	0
TOTALS		$116,000	$12,960	$12,960	$9,200

The amount of deduction lost in the example under the new law is $3,760 ($12,960−9,200). Under the old law, a $12,960 tax deduction for someone in the 40% tax bracket saved $5,184 in taxes, but under tax reform, with a deduction of $9,200, and a 28% bracket, the tax savings is only $2,576. The family in our example will pay $2,608 more in taxes from the loss of interest deductions alone.

Using the following strategies, you can significantly cut your taxes by making "consumer" interest deductible.

Strategy #183
USE AN EQUITY LOAN OR NEW MORTGAGE TO CREATE DEDUCTIBLE INTEREST.

Mortgages are treated differently from consumer loans in computing deductible interest. Beginning in 1988, the interest is deductible on your first and second home mortgages up to $1 million of total acquisition cost—the price you originally paid for the homes. You may also deduct the interest on up to $100,000 obtained from an equity loan on your homes no matter

what the money is used for. For most Americans all interest on refinancing will be deductible. Using the new rules, you can get an equity loan on your first or second home to pay off your nondeductible debt and increase your tax refund in the process.
Example:

Car loan 1	$10,000
Car loan 2	6,000
Credit cards	4,000
Personal loan	5,000
Total borrowed	**$25,000**

If the average interest rate on these loans is 12%, one year's interest is $3,000, but the interest is not deductible. If you use a qualified home equity loan for $25,000 to pay off the loans, the interest becomes deductible, and if you are in the 33% bracket, you get $1,000 additional cash back in your next refund check from the $3,000 interest deduction.

Strategy #184
QUALIFY YOUR BOAT OR RV LOAN FOR DEDUCTIBLE INTEREST.

If you own or buy a boat or recreational vehicle that has sleeping and toilet facilities, you may treat the asset as your second home. All of the interest is then deductible up to the acquisition cost limits. As long as the cost of your primary residence plus your boat or RV does not exceed $1,000,000, the interest is fully deductible.

Strategy #185
USE YOUR VACATION HOME AS A SECOND HOME INSTEAD OF A RENTAL PROPERTY.

To qualify your resort or vacation home as a rental property, you cannot use it yourself more than 14 days per year. If you do, you may deduct the mortgage interest expense only up to the amount of rental income. If the property is rented only occasionally, you may get a greater deduction by treating the property as a second home and deducting 100% of the interest.

If your income is too high for you to benefit from the $25,000 real estate expense deduction, deducting 100% of the mortgage interest on your vacation home is always your best tax alternative.

Strategy #186
BORROW THE MONEY FOR YOUR IRA.

The IRS ruled in 1987 that interest you pay on money borrowed to fund your IRA is deductible even though your IRA is a tax shelter. You take the full deduction for interest you pay, but are not taxed on the current IRA income. Use your money to pay off nondeductible debt and borrow the money for your IRA.

Example:

Bob and Eunice qualify for a $4,000 combined contribution to an IRA. This year they borrow the money from the credit union at 10% for their IRA and use their savings to pay off their Visa bill of $3,000 at 18%. Here is how they benefit:

$4,000	Borrowed for IRA
× .10	Interest—one year
$ 400	Interest paid on borrowed IRA money
× .31	Tax bracket
$ 124	*Refund from deductible interest*
$3,000	Visa bill
× .18	Interest rate on Visa card
$ 540	*Interest saved by paying off Visa bill*
$4,000	IRA money invested in mutual fund
× .15	Return on investment
$ 600	*Tax-sheltered earnings from mutual fund*
$4,000	Amount tax sheltered by IRA
× .31	Tax bracket
$1,240	*Refund from IRA deduction*

$ 124	Refund for deductible IRA interest
540	Interest saved by paying off credit cards
600	Tax-sheltered IRA earnings
1,240	Refund from IRA deduction
$2,504	*Total savings and earnings from plan*
−400	Interest paid on IRA loan
$2,104	**Cash saved or earned**

On an investment of $4,000 of borrowed money and using their $3,000 cash to pay off the Visa, Bob and Eunice have earned or saved $2,104, representing an over 50% return the first year on the $4,000 borrowed IRA money.

Borrow the money for your IRA or Keogh account if you don't have it. If you do, borrow the money anyway.

Strategy #187
PAY OFF HIGH NONDEDUCTIBLE INTEREST DEBT WITH LOW NONDEDUCTIBLE INTEREST DEBT.

If you have an insurance policy with an accumulated cash value, borrow on that policy at the 5% guaranteed interest rate and use the low-interest money to pay off your high-interest personal loans and credit cards. Even though the interest paid on the insurance loan will not be deductible, you may be saving as much as 14% per year interest by substituting low-interest insurance dollars for the high-interest dollars. You can often save more from an interest reduction than from an interest tax deduction.

Strategy #188
PAY CASH FOR CONSUMER GOODS, BORROW TO INVEST.

Since interest on investment loans is deductible, but interest on consumer loans is not, use borrowed money for investments and pay cash for items you would normally charge or finance.

To reorganize your debt for greater deductions, take money out of your mutual funds, CDs, and stocks and use the proceeds to pay off credit cards, car loans, or other nondeductible debt. Sell investments showing current losses first to take advantage of the investment loss deduction.

In a separate transaction, borrow money using an automobile loan, mutual fund margin account, or personal loan to replace your investment capital. The interest on the borrowed money is now deductible as investment interest and you still have about the same amount of money invested. When you borrow to invest, first put the lump sum of borrowed money in a separate bank account and buy your investments from that account. You can then trace the borrowed money directly to your investments to insure the tax deduction.

Strategy #189
SELL APPRECIATED INVESTMENTS TO QUALIFY YOUR INVESTMENT INTEREST EXPENSE AS A DEDUCTION.

Interest on investment loans is fully deductible, but only up to the amount of your investment income for the year. Investment income includes interest from CDs or savings accounts, dividends, and capital gains distributions shown on your mutual fund statement. Any capital gains elected to be used as investment income will be taxed at your highest marginal tax rate, which could be slightly higher than the regular 28% capital gains rate.

Each December, check to be certain your investment income will top your investment interest expense. If not, consider selling some appreciated mutual fund shares, stocks, or bonds, since the profits count toward your investment income. The appreciated value of an investment you still hold does not count as investment income until you sell.

Strategy #190
CONVERT CONSUMER INTEREST TO BUSINESS INTEREST.

Interest paid on business loans or personal loans to finance assets used full- or part-time in a business is deductible. The interest deduction is taken on tax Schedule C or other business tax forms, so the deduction is not limited by the standard deduction amount on tax Schedule A.

For instance, if you use your personal car financed with a personal loan in your small business and allocate 60% of its use as business, 60% of the interest you pay each year is tax deductible.

Example:

Jenny started a small business at home and used her car 60% of the time for business and 40% for personal purposes. Her car loan is $12,000 at 10% interest. Her total interest cost this year will be about $1,200, of which 60% will be deductible.

$1,200	Total interest paid
× .60	Deductible as business interest
$ 720	Tax deduction
× .31	Tax bracket
$ 223	Taxes saved

Interest you pay on a home computer or VCR loan is also deductible if the asset is used full- or part-time in your business.

Chapter 21

GIVE YOURSELF A
TAX-FREE RAISE

Making money is a slow process, losing it is done quickly.

Ihara Saikaku
(1642–1699)

**INCREASE YOUR TAKE-HOME PAY $50 TO $350 PER
MONTH.**

How many times have you said, "If I just didn't have so much
withheld from my paycheck, I could . . ." Three out of four
employees, including you, can legally give themselves a tax-free
raise of $50 to $350 per month in take-home pay by reducing the
amount withheld from their paycheck for federal and state
income taxes.

Strategy #191
**TO REDUCE THE AMOUNT WITHHELD FROM YOUR
PAYCHECK, ADD WITHHOLDING ALLOWANCES.**

The amount withheld from your paycheck for income taxes each
payday is controlled by an artificial, little-understood unit called
the withholding allowance. The number of allowances is chosen
by you and entered on tax form W-4. By federal law, you must
complete a W-4 form for your employer when you are first

256

employed and whenever your tax situation changes. You, not your employer, are responsible for determining how much is withheld from your paycheck.

On the W-4 form, called the Employee's Withholding Allowance Certificate (see pages 274–75), you enter or claim a number of allowances, usually ranging from 0 to 15. Theoretically, if you claim zero allowances, an amount is withheld from your paycheck that by year's end would equal the tax you would owe if you had no exemptions or dependents, including yourself, and no tax deductions. The mathematical purpose of the W-4 and your allowances is to make sure you have about as much withheld from your paychecks during the year as you will owe in federal income taxes at the end of the year. The amount you have withheld has nothing to do with determining how much tax you will actually owe.

Each allowance you claim on your W-4 form will reduce your withholding each year by about the same number of dollars you would save in taxes if you had an additional $2,450 tax deduction. The actual amount of money withheld per "allowance" varies slightly according to your income because your federal tax bracket could be 15%, 28%, 31%, 36%, or 39.6%. If you add allowances to your W-4 form, your paycheck gets bigger because less is withheld. If you reduce the number of allowances on your W-4 form, your paycheck gets smaller because more is withheld.

Don't confuse personal exemptions with allowances. Claiming allowances is done on the W-4 form. An exemption is a tax deduction of $2,450 (1994) for yourself and each dependent and is claimed on your 1040 tax return. Many people incorrectly believe that you are allowed to claim only one allowance for each dependent in your family. Yes, each dependent is worth one allowance, but you may also claim extra allowances for any other tax deductions you already have or can create using the tax strategies in this book. Your objective is to get the maximum number of dollars legally possible in every paycheck. By adjusting the number of allowances on your W-4 form based on the formulas that follow, you may be able to significantly increase your take-home pay, get some of your bills paid more quickly, or make some long overdue investments. First, let's take a look at the rules.

THE W-4 ALLOWANCE RULES

- You may legally add any number of allowances to your W-4 form that will enable you to break even with the IRS when you file your tax return. You won't owe the IRS, the IRS won't owe you.
- The number of allowances you may claim has little to do with the number of dependents you have and everything to do with the amount of tax deductions you can expect to claim by the end of the year.
- You and/or your working spouse may increase or decrease the number of withholding allowances you claim by completing a new W-4 form in the payroll department or personnel department at work. Your employer has the form, or you may obtain a copy from the IRS. Your current W-4 form always remains in effect until you make a change.
- If you claim more than nine allowances, your employer is required to send a copy of your form to the IRS. If the IRS can't understand why your taxes will be lower, and therefore why you are taking additional allowances, it may send you a form letter asking you to explain within 30 days. If you do not answer the letter, the IRS will ask your employer to reduce your withholding allowances to one until you do explain. You are always allowed, however, to claim more than nine allowances if you deserve them.
- If the number of allowances to which you are entitled decreases, you are required to file a new W-4 form within ten days. If the number of withholding allowances to which you are entitled increases, no one is required to notify you.
- If you get a refund each year, you are having too much withheld and need to increase your allowances. If you have to cough up additional cash each year at tax time, you are having too little withheld and should either decrease your allowances or, better still, increase your tax deductions through the implementation of my tax strategies.

Strategy #192
GET NEXT YEAR'S TAX REFUND THIS YEAR.

Ever get a refund? Most American taxpayers do and somehow feel they have put one over on the IRS. They have not. A refund is nothing more than a return of your own money, which you never owed to the IRS in the first place. You receive no interest and not so much as a thank-you letter! You wouldn't loan your money to your bank without interest; why would you loan it interest free to the IRS? This misunderstanding concerning refunds is so universal that 80 million out of a total of about 100 million taxpayers receive over $70 billion in refunds each year. The average refund check is $900. Imagine 80 million Americans each year making one of the biggest possible tax mistakes.

By adding allowances to your W-4 form, you can get next year's refund in this year's paychecks. That's correct. Instead of waiting until next year in June when those who file their tax returns on April 15 normally get their lump-sum refund checks, you can get your next year's refund in monthly installments this year!

How many allowances do you have to claim? The next strategy will help you determine the approximate number.

Strategy #193
ADD ONE ALLOWANCE TO YOUR W-4 FORM FOR EVERY $690 IN REFUNDS YOU GOT LAST YEAR.

Your employer uses tax publication Circular E to determine how much money to withhold from your paycheck for federal income taxes. You will find a page from Circular E on page 276.

Originally the table was worked out by the government so that claiming one additional allowance would add to your paycheck exactly the amount of money over a full year that claiming one additional child or dependent would save you in taxes when you filed your 1040 tax return. That's why so many people are confused and incorrectly believe that you can only claim one allowance for each dependent.

In 1994, each dependent you claim on your 1040 is worth an automatic $2,450 tax deduction. Not enough certainly to cause you to consider having more children, but a tax break on those you already have. The IRS calls these dependent deductions tax exemptions. Same difference.

How much tax does that dependent exemption save you? To determine the tax saved, multiply your deduction times your marginal or highest tax bracket. For instance, for couples who file jointly, 28% is the tax bracket on taxable incomes of $38,000 to $91,850 ($22,750 to $55,100 for singles). If total taxable income for a couple is under $38,000 ($22,750 for singles) the tax bracket is 15%.

If the dependent deduction for a couple is $2,450 and their marginal or highest tax bracket is 28%, the federal tax savings is about $690 per year (28% × 2,450) or over $50 per month. Therein lies the key to getting next year's refund this year. If your tax bracket is 28%, for every $690 in refund you got last year, add one allowance to your W-4 form and you will automatically add about $50 a month or $600 per year to your take-home pay. You receive the money without additional taxes. The money is tax free since taxes have already been deducted whether the money is withheld or paid to you.

Here is your paycheck-enlarging planning chart:

28% TAX BRACKET

Amount of Refund Check	Number of Allowances to Add to W-4 Form	Increase in Monthly Take-Home Pay	
$ 690	1	$ 58	
1,380	2	115	Use this chart if your taxable income is:
2,070	3	580	Single: $22,750–$55,100
2,760	4	773	Couple: $38,000–$91,850
3,450	5	966	Your tax bracket is 28%.
4,140	6	1,160	

Each additional allowance adds $50 to your monthly take-home pay.

Add the new number of allowances you are claiming from the chart above to the number you claimed last year and enter the total on line 5 of the W-4 Employee's Withholding Allowance Certificate, "Total number of allowances you are claiming" (see page 274).

Although it is not necessary to complete the worksheet on page 2 of the W-4 form to claim extra allowances, the worksheet is there to help you calculate your allowances if you don't have these simple formulas and charts (see page 275).

Refunds, of course, are not always divisible by $690. What if your refund is $500 or $1,398? A good rule of thumb is to add one additional allowance if you are halfway to the next allowance level, but don't add one more allowance if you are less than halfway. For example, if you refund was $850, it would fall between $690 and $1,380 shown in the chart. The halfway point is $1,035, and since your refund is less than $1,035, you would add only one allowance. But if your refund was $1,050, you would add two allowances since your refund is now greater than the halfway point of $1,035.

Since the tax-saving and paycheck-increasing value of one allowance is different for each of the five tax brackets, 15%, 28%, 31%, 36%, and 39.6%, let's create tables you can use if you are in the 15% or 31% tax bracket. (See Strategy #113 for a complete explanation of tax brackets.)

15% TAX BRACKET

Amount of Refund Check	Number of Allowances to Add to W-4 Form	Increase in Monthly Take-Home Pay	
$ 300	1	$ 25	
600	2	50	
900	3	75	Use this chart if your taxable income is:
1,200	4	100	Single: Up to $22,750
1,500	5	125	Couple: Up to $38,000.
1,800	6	150	Your tax bracket is 15%.
2,100	7	175	

Each additional allowance adds $25 to your monthly take-home pay.

31% TAX BRACKET

Amount of Refund Check	Number of Allowances to Add to W-4 Form	Increase in Monthly Take-Home Pay	
$ 650	1	$ 50	
1,300	2	100	Use this chart if your taxable income is:
1,950	3	150	Single: $55,000 to $115,000
2,600	4	200	Couple: $91,850 to $140,000
3,250	5	250	Your tax bracket is 31%.
3,900	6	300	
4,550	7	350	

Each additional allowance adds $50 to your monthly take-home pay.

Strategy #194
ADD MAKE-UP ALLOWANCES IF YOU BEGIN THE REFUND-RECOVERING PROCESS AFTER THE BEGINNING OF THE YEAR.

The strategy just discussed for getting next year's refund this year applies if you start at the beginning of the year, but when you go into your employer's payroll office to complete a new W-4 form, it may not be in January. The later in the year you complete your new W-4 form, the more allowances you will want to add since you have fewer paychecks in which to get the same amount of extra money. But how many? Follow the suggestions in the next chart for the balance of the year in which you begin using the strategy.

ADJUSTMENTS TO W-4 REFUND STRATEGY BASED ON MONTH YOU BEGIN (ROUNDED DOWN)

Allowances for Full Year	Jan–Mar	Apr–Jun	Jul–Sep	Oct–Dec
1	1	1	2	2
2	2	3	4	5
3	3	4	6	7
4	4	6	8	10
5	5	7	10	12
6	6	9	12	15
7	7	10	14	17

Here's how to use this chart. Let's say you are in the 28% tax bracket so you use the chart on page 260 to compute your extra allowances. If your refund was approximately $2,400 and you anticipate that it will be about the same next year, the chart shows that four allowances would increase your take-home pay $200 per month. Over the 12 months beginning in January, you would get the $2,400 this year instead of in a lump sum next year after you filed your return and waited for your refund. But let's say it is now July. There are only six months left this year to get back the $2,400. Therefore, you must adjust your W-4 to the number of allowances that will add $400 per month to your paychecks for the six remaining months. Using the adjustments chart above, read down the left-hand column and find the four allowances you determined you would need if you had a full

year (shaded area). Reading across that row to the July–
September column, you will see that you have to add eight
allowances to get the same amount of money over the balance of
this year. Don't forget, at the beginning of the following year,
you must adjust your allowances back to a level that would
allow your withholding adjustment to be spaced out over the
entire year. So next January you will complete a new W-4 form
to reduce your allowances from eight back to four.

Increasing your take-home pay begins with getting next year's
refund this year, but that's not all. You also have the right to
reduce this year's withholding for any new tax-reducing strategies you will employ this year. Strategies such as putting money
in an IRA or increasing your 401(k) contributions, buying a
rental property, or starting your own small business will reduce
the total taxes you will owe for the year. We will discuss later
how to build a powerful tax plan with these kinds of strategies.
In the next strategy, I'll show you how to use your W-4 form to
get these tax savings now as an increase in this year's take-
home pay.

Strategy #195
ADD ONE ADDITIONAL ALLOWANCE TO YOUR W-4
FORM FOR EACH $2,450 TAX DEDUCTION
YOU CREATE.

As you create new tax deductions using my tax strategies, don't
wait until next year to receive the resulting refund. You can add
extra allowances to your employment W-4 form anytime as you
create the additional deductions. Here is a typical example of a
couple who converted new tax deductions to immediate cash
using their W-4 form.

Sally and Bert Adams, who have two children, calculate that
during the current tax year they have or will create a total of
$12,500 in new tax deductions with their new tax-reducing plan.
To create new tax deductions, Sally and Bert do the following:

- Set up their payroll withholding to contribute an additional $2,500 to
  Bert's 401(k) plan.
- Buy two rental properties, which will give them a net tax deduction
  through depreciation and other expenses of $6,000 for the year.
- Start a small business, making some of their personal assets deductible, including their automobile, home computer, VCR, and a part of
  their home. Total estimated small-business paper loss is $4,000.

Their total new deductions for the year are estimated at $12,500. Dividing $12,500 by $2,000, Bert adds six allowances to his W-4, which in turn adds $300 per month or $3,600 per year to his take-home pay. The $300 extra per month will pay all of the contributions to Bert's 401(k) and help with the expenses of operating their new rental properties. Look at the W-4 form on pages 274–75, and you will see how the allowances are calculated.

Strategy #196
WORK TOWARD THE ZERO TAX BRACKET AND LEGALLY ELIMINATE MORE OR LESS ALL INCOME TAX WITHHOLDING.

Even with the radical changes in the tax code in 1986, it is still possible to get into the zero tax bracket if your income is less than $60,000 per year. The zero tax bracket means you legally owe no taxes for the year. What you own, you keep.

For instance, these three deductions have the potential for sheltering up to $45,000 of income.

Strategy	Deduction
Rental real estate	$25,000
Small-business losses	12,000
401(k) plan contribution	8,000
Total deductions	$45,000

Add to the above deductions $8,600 of personal exemptions for a family of four and another $4,400 of guaranteed Schedule A zero bracket amount deductions, and this couple could earn up to $58,000 per year and pay zero federal and state income taxes. That's correct. None. In addition to saving thousands in taxes, they have created three major assets that will grow in value: real estate, a small business, and a 401(k) retirement account.

When your tax plan gets you into the zero bracket, you can stop tax withholding altogether. Turn to the front of the W-4 form on page 274. Notice line 7 says:

> I claim exemption from withholding and I certify that I meet **BOTH** of the following conditions for exemption:
>
> • Last year I had a right to a refund of **ALL** Federal income tax withheld because I had **NO** tax liability; **AND**
> • This year I expect a refund of **ALL** Federal income tax withheld because I expect to have **NO** tax liability.
>
> If you meet both conditions, enter "EXEMPT" here . . .

When you are in this enviable position, you can declare yourself legally tax exempt and the IRS has even provided you the form with which to do it! Use your tax-reducing plan and your W-4 as your ticket to an instant increase in your monthly spendable income and recover part or all of your income tax withholding.

> *Strategy #197*
> ## TURN A $1,200-A-YEAR TAX REFUND INTO OVER $250,000 BY INVESTING YOUR REFUND IN A TAX SHELTER.

Now that you know how you can add $50 to $350 to your take-home pay each month with no sacrifice, what can you do with the money? Well, you could spend it, apply it to your debt reduction plan (see Strategy #79), or, as an optimum strategy, you can turn your yearly refund into $250,000 to $500,000 to be used later in life in any way you choose.

A little money goes a long way if given enough time. Invest $100 of your refund each month in any tax shelter that gives you tax-free compounding and you will transform hundreds into a small fortune. Look at the table below and you will see what you can build in 15, 20, or 25 years with only a $100 or $200 investment every month in a tax-sheltered retirement plan such as a 401(k), 403(b), or a self-directed IRA. If the plan uses a mutual fund family as the investment vehicle, 15% is a reasonable estimate of your compounded yearly return (see Chapters 18 and 30).

INVESTING YOUR REFUND				
Yearly Refund	Monthly Investment at 15%	15 Years	20 Years	25 Years
$1,200	$100 per month	$ 67,000	$150,000	$325,000
$2,400	$200 per month	$134,000	$300,000	$650,000

Amazing? You bet, when you consider the above can be accomplished without pain, budgeting, or sacrifice.

If you have a 401(k) or 403(b) or similar retirement plan at work, first increase your allowances as shown in Strategy #191, which will increase the amount in your monthly paychecks by $100 to $200. Then have the same amount deducted from your paycheck and put into your retirement plan. You'll never miss the money from your monthly spendable income since you never had it to begin with. You just created it. If you have no retirement plan at work and the prospects for getting one anytime soon appear remote, use an IRA or any of the self-directed, tax-sheltered annuities listed in Chapter 34 as your tax-free compounding investment vehicle.

Strategy #198
USE YOUR REFUND AS AN INVESTMENT IN YOUR RETIREMENT PLAN AND GET UP TO A 35% CASH REBATE.

The person who said you can't have your cake and eat it, too, obviously never heard of perpetually rising flour or qualified retirement plans. You can use your yearly refund to create your mini-fortune, plus get the government to rebate to you 35% of the money you invest—both at the same time. To get this extra benefit requires only that you invest through any plan that triggers an automatic tax reduction for the money you invest. Your 401(k) or 403(b) retirement plan at work and an IRA or Keogh are examples. Your first choice would be your employer's retirement plan since you can have the money deducted from your paycheck, but an IRA will produce the same mathematical results.

Because you are able to deduct the full amount of your contribution from your taxable income, the same effect as taking a tax deduction for your contributions, the federal government will refund to you the equivalent of the money you invest multiplied by your tax bracket of 39.6%, 36%, 31%, 28%, or 15%. In addition, most states allow the same deductions, saving you another 7 to 10%. Your total rebate can be 35% or even more.

For example, using the W-4 strategy, let's say you receive in your paychecks an additional $2,400 yearly refund in equal monthly installments of $200, which you then have deducted from your check and invested in your 401(k). At the end of the year, since you do not have to claim the $2,400 as income, you don't have to pay state or federal taxes of about 35%, or $840. The net effect is that you have invested the full $2,400 in your mini-fortune-building account, plus received $840 in cash in a tax refund to add to the $2,400 you invest.

The tax laws can be incredible wealth builders and wealth preservers when you know how to use them correctly.

Strategy #199
USE YOUR W-4 FORM TO INCREASE YOUR TAKE-HOME PAY WHEN YOU HAVE SMALL-BUSINESS LOSSES.

As discussed in Chapter 25, "Getting Down to Business," during the first couple of years of starting a part-time small business, you may generate and deduct significant "paper losses" created by tax deductions for items and assets that you already owned or bought. The business-use percentage becomes an immediate tax deduction as an expense or through depreciation.

You can use your W-4 form to turn these deductions into an immediate increase in your monthly cash flow. "Losses" from any unincorporated business are transferred from line 31 on Schedule C to line 12 of your 1040 form and become a dollar-for-dollar tax deduction with no limitations. You will automatically owe less in total taxes because of your business loss. Each $2,450 in net business loss equates to one extra allowance on your W-4 form (see Strategy #195), which at the 28% tax bracket will put an extra $57 per month or $680 per year in your take-home pay.

If you already started or plan to start a small business on the basis of my recommendations in Chapter 25, pencil in your estimated income and deductions on tax Schedule C. Divide any estimated losses from the business and any new deduction strategies by $2,450 and add that number of allowances to your W-4 form at work. Get those tax savings now!

Strategy #200
AVOID PENALTIES AND INTEREST BY ADJUSTING
YOUR WITHHOLDING ACCOUNT EACH DECEMBER TO
AT LEAST THE 90% LEVEL.

You cannot escape interest and penalties by paying late in the year for taxes due on quarterly estimated tax returns. The IRS will reallocate the taxes due by quarters and charge interest and penalties, but you can pay last-minute catch-up through payroll withholding and avoid all penalties and interest.

As long as you have 90% of the federal income taxes you owe withheld by December 31, it doesn't matter when you paid them. This tax rule can allow you to accomplish two objectives. First, if you have had too little withheld during the year, you can figure the appropriate total federal income taxes you will owe, multiply by 90%, and have that additional amount taken out of your paychecks during December. Use the box provided on the front of the W-4 form for extra amounts you want withheld (see W-4 form on page 274). Be certain to tell your payroll department that the amount must be taken out in December. If the payroll department doesn't deduct the extra money until January, you will be assessed the underwithholding penalty and interest.

Second, if you had extra income during the year for which you did not file a quarterly return and which would not put you over the total taxes you paid the previous year, you could have the extra taxes due withheld from your and/or your spouse's paychecks in December and you would avoid even the "reallocation of quarterly payments not paid" rule. Amazing, but true.

Therefore, around Thanksgiving every year make it a habit to compute your income for the year and the taxes due, and check your last paycheck stub for the total federal income taxes that have been withheld from your checks so far. Don't forget to combine the taxes withheld from your spouse's checks with your own if you file jointly.

Strategy #201
NEVER USE EXTRA ALLOWANCES AS A PERMANENT CASH FLOW INCREASE OR TO PROTEST TAXES.

Although the government will gladly accept and hold your excess withholding money with no interest, you are not allowed to do the same thing with money that belongs to the IRS.

Now that you know how to increase your take-home pay dramatically, here is a thought that may be running through your mind. "Why don't I increase my allowances so that nothing is taken out of my check, and then at tax time I'll come up with all the money I owe the IRS. In the meantime, I'll use the money to invest, pay bills, or just to have a great time." Nice thought, but it won't fly.

By the end of the year, you are required to have had withheld at least 90% of the total federal taxes you will owe, or you will be assessed interest and penalties on the difference. Although these extra charges won't break you, it would be money down the drain.

In other words, if you will owe $7,000 in total taxes for the year based on your job income, you must have had at least $6,300 withheld ($7,000 × 90%) to avoid automatically assessed interest and penalties. The IRS computer does the calculations from your return, and if you are under 90%, it sends you a notice for the extra assessment, so don't think yours will just slip by in all the paperwork. If you had $8,500 withheld during the year but only owed $7,000, you would get the difference, $1,500, back as a refund with no interest.

The amount you actually end up owing in taxes has nothing to do with how much you have withheld during the year. When you get a refund, you have not beaten the IRS, you have been beaten by the IRS, since it is your own money being returned.

During the seventies and early eighties a lot of so-called tax protesters were around—those who claimed that income taxes were illegal or against the Constitution, or that, since American currency was no longer on the gold standard, the money was worthless and couldn't be used to pay taxes. Some even made considerable money writing books on the subject. Evidently tax court judges never read the books because many of these protesters were given jail sentences for tax evasion and thousands of others were assessed big penalties.

One reason your employer is required to notify the IRS if you claim over nine allowances is that some protesters used to claim one hundred allowances, which would stop withholding altogether. Take every allowance to which you are entitled, even ten or more, but take only those allowances to which you are legally entitled. Otherwise, you will be assessed penalties and interest.

Strategy #202
USE YOUR W-4 FORM AND PAYROLL WITHHOLDING FROM A JOB TO AVOID FILING QUARTERLY ESTIMATED TAX RETURNS.

To avoid extra interest and penalties, remember you must have paid into the IRS 90% of what you will owe in taxes by the end of the year. If that money is not paid to the IRS through your employer's payroll withholding, you are required to file a quarterly return of your estimated taxes and pay the estimated taxes due each quarter—every three months.

To put it mildly, filing quarterly is a pain, but one that normally must be endured if you owe more than $500 in taxes at the end of the year. Every 90 days you have to fill out another estimated tax return and write a check to the IRS. Don't think you can put it off until the end of the year and then pay the taxes due all at one time. Up until a few years ago, you could get away with it, but now the IRS computer system has been programmed to split an end-of-year, lump-sum payment into quarterly payments and to send you a delinquency notice for all interest and penalties due. The delinquency penalty is 5% of the additional tax you owe for every month you are late, up to five months or 25%. That means for every $1,000 in taxes you could be assessed as much as $250 in penalties, plus you will pay interest at about 1% per month on the unpaid taxes.

No, you won't go to jail, but you will owe more to the IRS than just the taxes, and you know what that would do to your attitude—not to mention your bank account.

For all those who have a small business plus a full-time job, or those who file jointly while one spouse works for an employer and the other owns a business, or retired couples in which one works and one has other nonjob income, there is a painless way to avoid the necessity of filing quarterly *and* all the potential penalties and interest. If you have a job plus a small business or

HOW TO AVOID FILING QUARTERLY ESTIMATED TAX RETURNS

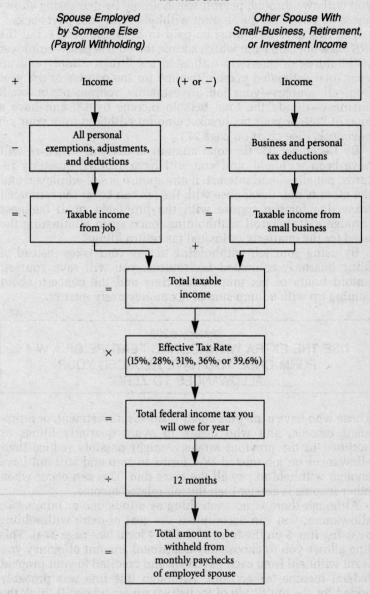

Spouse Employed by Someone Else (Payroll Withholding)		Other Spouse With Small-Business, Retirement, or Investment Income
+ Income	(+ or −)	Income
− All personal exemptions, adjustments, and deductions	−	Business and personal tax deductions
= Taxable income from job	=	Taxable income from small business

+

= Total taxable income

× Effective Tax Rate (15%, 28%, 31%, 36%, or 39.6%)

= Total federal income tax you will owe for year

÷ 12 months

= Total amount to be withheld from monthly paychecks of employed spouse investment income, *decrease* the allowances on your W-4 form and/or your spouse's form until you have covered all the taxes you will owe through payroll withholding. By decreasing allowances you *increase* the amount withheld from your paychecks.

The rule says 90% must be paid in by December 31, but the IRS does not care from which source the 90% is paid—employer withholding or quarterly estimated tax filings. Simply add up your total estimated taxable income for the quarter or the year from all sources—your job, investments, retirement, or small business—divide the total taxable income by 12, and have a total of 28% or your tax-bracket amount withheld from your job paycheck. (See chart on page 271.)

By December 31, the total amount of tax you will owe will have been withheld, and you will have avoided quarterly returns, penalties, and interest. If one spouse is self-employed and the other is not, the spouse with the job can cover the estimated taxes due for the spouse with the profitable small business through extra payroll withholding, once again eliminating the need for the quarterly estimated tax return filings.

By using your job withholding to pay your taxes instead of filing quarterly estimated tax returns, you will save yourself untold hours of tax preparation time and the concern about coming up with a lump sum of tax money every quarter.

Strategy #203
USE THE EXTRA WITHHOLDING FEATURE OF A W-4 FORM ONCE YOU HAVE REDUCED YOUR ALLOWANCES TO ZERO.

Those who have a job plus small-business, investment, or retirement income, and who desire to avoid quarterly filings as outlined in the previous strategy, might possibly reduce their allowances on job-related W-4 forms to zero and still not have enough withheld to pay all the taxes due. This can occur when other income is greater than the job-related income.

Although there is no such thing as minus one or minus two allowances, you can accomplish the goal of extra withholding by using line 5 on the front of the W-4 form (see page 274). This line allows you to choose any additional amount of money you want withheld from each paycheck and credited to your prepaid federal income tax account. Although this line was probably added for the multitude of foolish taxpayers who still think the size of a refund determines how badly they beat the IRS, it will do nicely for your purposes.

First determine the total extra taxes you will owe for the year *after* you have reduced your and your spouse's W-4 allowances at work to zero. You can look up the amount in IRS Circular E. Your employer has one. Then divide the balance you will owe by the number of paychecks you will receive for the remainder of the year. That's the number to include on line 5 of your W-4 form, "Additional amount, if any, you want deducted from each pay." By the end of the year you will have had all the necessary taxes withheld for both your job and your other income, and you have still avoided the dreaded quarterly estimated tax return filing. Don't forget to include any small-business self-employment taxes you will owe when calculating the extra taxes due.

Form W-4 (1994)

Want More Money In Your Paycheck?
If you expect to be able to take the earned income credit for 1994, you can have part of it added to your take-home pay. For details, get Form W-5 from your employer.

Purpose. Complete Form W-4 so that your employer can withhold the correct amount of Federal income tax from your pay.

Exemption From Withholding. Read line 7 of the certificate below to see if you can claim exempt status. *If exempt, complete line 7; but do not complete lines 5 and 6.* No Federal income tax will be withheld from your pay. Your exemption is good for 1 year only. It expires February 15, 1995.

Note: *You cannot claim exemption from withholding if (1) your income exceeds $600 and includes unearned income (e.g., interest and dividends), and (2) another person can* claim you as a dependent on their tax return.

Basic Instructions. Employees who are not exempt should complete the Personal Allowances Worksheet. Additional worksheets are provided on page 2 for employees who adjust their withholding allowances based on itemized deductions, adjustments to income, or two-earner/two-job situations. Complete all worksheets that apply to your situation. The worksheets will help you figure the number of withholding allowances you are entitled to claim. However, you may claim fewer allowances than this.

Head of Household. Generally, you may claim head of household filing status on your tax return only if you are unmarried and pay more than 50% of the costs of keeping up a home for yourself and your dependent(s) or other qualifying individuals.

Nonwage Income. If you have a large amount of nonwage income, such as interest or dividends, you should consider making estimated tax payments using Form 1040-ES.

Otherwise, you may find that you owe additional tax at the end of the year.

Two Earners/Two Jobs. If you have a working spouse or more than one job, figure the total number of allowances you are entitled to claim on all jobs using worksheets from only one Form W-4. This total should be divided among all jobs. Your withholding will usually be most accurate when all allowances are claimed on the W-4 filed for the highest paying job and zero allowances are claimed for the others.

Check Your Withholding. After your W-4 takes effect, you can use Pub. 919, Is My Withholding Correct for 1994?, to see how the dollar amount you are having withheld compares to your estimated total annual tax. We recommend you get Pub. 919 especially if you used the Two Earner/Two Job Worksheet and your earnings exceed $150,000 (Single) or $200,000 (Married). Call 1-800-829-3676 to order Pub. 919. Check your telephone directory for the IRS assistance number for further help.

Personal Allowances Worksheet

A	Enter "1" for **yourself** if no one else can claim you as a dependent	**A** 1
B	Enter "1" if: { • You are single and have only one job; or • You are married, have only one job, and your spouse does not work; or • Your wages from a second job or your spouse's wages (or the total of both) are $1,000 or less. }	**B** 1
C	Enter "1" for your **spouse.** But, you may choose to enter -0- if you are married and have either a working spouse or more than one job (this may help you avoid having too little tax withheld)	**C** 2
D	Enter number of **dependents** (other than your spouse or yourself) whom you will claim on your tax return .	**D** ____
E	Enter "1" if you will file as **head of household** on your tax return (see conditions under **Head of Household** above) .	**E** ____
F	Enter "1" if you have at least $1,500 of **child or dependent care expenses** for which you plan to claim a credit . .	**F** ____
G	Add lines A through F and enter total here. **Note:** This amount may be different from the number of exemptions you claim on your return ▶	**G** 4

For accuracy, do all worksheets that apply.	• If you plan to **itemize or claim adjustments to income** and want to reduce your withholding, see the Deductions and Adjustments Worksheet on page 2. • If you are **single** and have **more than one job** and your combined earnings from all jobs exceed $30,000 **OR** if you are **married** and have a **working spouse or more than one job,** and the combined earnings from all jobs exceed $50,000, see the Two-Earner/Two-Job Worksheet on page 2 if you want to avoid having too little tax withheld. • If **neither** of the above situations applies, **stop here** and enter the number from line G on line 5 of Form W-4 below.

·········· Cut here and give the certificate to your employer. Keep the top portion for your records. ··········

Form **W-4** Department of the Treasury Internal Revenue Service	**Employee's Withholding Allowance Certificate** ▶ For Privacy Act and Paperwork Reduction Act Notice, see reverse.	OMB No. 1545-0010 **1994**

1 Type or print your first name and middle initial Bert J.	Last name Adams	**2** Your social security number 339 : 84 : 2164

Home address (number and street or rural route) 991 Tempeco	**3** ☐ Single ☒ Married ☐ Married, but withhold at higher Single rate. **Note:** *If married, but legally separated, or spouse is a nonresident alien, check the Single box.*
City or town, state, and ZIP code Altamonte Springs, FL 32714	**4** If your last name differs from that on your social security card, check here and call 1-800-772-1213 for more information · · · · ▶ ☐

5	Total number of allowances you are claiming (from line G above or from the worksheets on page 2 if they apply) .	**5** 9
6	Additional amount, if any, you want withheld from each paycheck	**6** $
7	I claim exemption from withholding for 1994 and I certify that I meet **BOTH** of the following conditions for exemption: • Last year I had a right to a refund of **ALL** Federal income tax withheld because I had **NO** tax liability; **AND** • This year I expect a refund of **ALL** Federal income tax withheld because I expect to have **NO** tax liability. If you meet both conditions, enter "EXEMPT" here . . . . ▶	**7**

Under penalties of perjury, I certify that I am entitled to the number of withholding allowances claimed on this certificate or entitled to claim exempt status.

Employee's signature ▶	**Date ▶** 1-15 , 19 94
8 Employer's name and address (Employer: Complete 8 and 10 only if sending to the IRS)	**9** Office code (optional)	**10** Employer identification number

Cat. No. 10220Q

Form W-4 (1994)   Page **2**

Deductions and Adjustments Worksheet

Note: *Use this worksheet only if you plan to itemize deductions or claim adjustments to income on your 1994 tax return.*

1	Enter an estimate of your 1994 itemized deductions. These include: qualifying home mortgage interest, charitable contributions, state and local taxes (but not sales taxes), medical expenses in excess of 7.5% of your income, and miscellaneous deductions. (For 1994, you may have to reduce your itemized deductions if your income is over $111,800 ($55,900 if married filing separately). Get Pub. 919 for details.)	1	$ 8,100
2	Enter: { $6,350 if married filing jointly or qualifying widow(er) $5,600 if head of household $3,800 if single $3,175 if married filing separately }	2	$ 6,350
3	**Subtract** line 2 from line 1. If line 2 is greater than line 1, enter -0-	3	$ 1,750
4	Enter an estimate of your 1994 adjustments to income. These include alimony paid and deductible IRA contributions	4	$ 12,500
5	**Add** lines 3 and 4 and enter the total	5	$ 14,250
6	Enter an estimate of your 1994 nonwage income (such as dividends or interest)	6	$ 0
7	**Subtract** line 6 from line 5. Enter the result, but not less than -0-	7	$ 14,250
8	**Divide** the amount on line 7 by $2,500 and enter the result here. Drop any fraction	8	5
9	Enter the number from Personal Allowances Worksheet, line G, on page 1	9	4
10	**Add** lines 8 and 9 and enter the total here. If you plan to use the Two-Earner/Two-Job Worksheet, also enter this total on line 1, below. Otherwise, **stop here** and enter this total on Form W-4, line 5, on page 1.	10	9

Two-Earner/Two-Job Worksheet

Note: *Use this worksheet only if the instructions for line G on page 1 direct you here.*

1	Enter the number from line G on page 1 (or from line 10 above if you used the Deductions and Adjustments Worksheet)	1	
2	Find the number in **Table 1** below that applies to the **LOWEST** paying job and enter it here	2	
3	If line 1 is **GREATER THAN OR EQUAL TO** line 2, subtract line 2 from line 1. Enter the result here (if zero, enter -0-) and on Form W-4, line 5, on page 1. **DO NOT** use the rest of this worksheet	3	

Note: *If line 1 is **LESS THAN** line 2, enter -0- on Form W-4, line 5, on page 1. Complete lines 4–9 to calculate the additional withholding amount necessary to avoid a year-end tax bill.*

4	Enter the number from line 2 of this worksheet	4	
5	Enter the number from line 1 of this worksheet	5	
6	Subtract line 5 from line 4	6	
7	Find the amount in **Table 2** below that applies to the **HIGHEST** paying job and enter it here	7	$
8	**Multiply** line 7 by line 6 and enter the result here. This is the additional annual withholding amount needed	8	$
9	Divide line 8 by the number of pay periods remaining in 1994. (For example, divide by 26 if you are paid every other week and you complete this form in December 1993.) Enter the result here and on Form W-4, line 6, page 1. This is the additional amount to be withheld from each paycheck	9	$

Table 1: Two-Earner/Two-Job Worksheet

Married Filing Jointly				All Others	
If wages from **LOWEST** paying job are—	Enter on line 2 above	If wages from **LOWEST** paying job are—	Enter on line 2 above	If wages from **LOWEST** paying job are—	Enter on line 2 above
0 - 3,000	0	39,001 - 50,000	9	0 - 4,000	0
3,001 - 6,000	1	50,001 - 55,000	10	4,001 - 10,000	1
6,001 - 11,000	2	55,001 - 60,000	11	10,001 - 14,000	2
11,001 - 16,000	3	60,001 - 70,000	12	14,001 - 19,000	3
16,001 - 21,000	4	70,001 - 80,000	13	19,001 - 23,000	4
21,001 - 27,000	5	80,001 - 90,000	14	23,001 - 45,000	5
27,001 - 31,000	6	90,001 and over	15	45,001 - 60,000	6
31,001 - 34,000	7			60,001 - 70,000	7
34,001 - 39,000	8			70,001 and over	8

Table 2: Two-Earner/Two-Job Worksheet

Married Filing Jointly		All Others	
If wages from **HIGHEST** paying job are—	Enter on line 7 above	If wages from **HIGHEST** paying job are—	Enter on line 7 above
0 - $ 50,000	$370	0 - $ 30,000	$370
50,001 - 100,000	690	30,001 - 60,000	690
100,001 - 130,000	760	60,001 - 110,000	760
130,001 - 220,000	880	110,001 - 220,000	880
220,001 and over	970	220,001 and over	970

Privacy Act and Paperwork Reduction Act Notice.—We ask for the information on this form to carry out the Internal Revenue laws of the United States. The Internal Revenue Code requires this information under sections 3402(f)(2)(A) and 6109 and their regulations. Failure to provide a completed form will result in your being treated as a single person who claims no withholding allowances. Routine uses of this information include giving it to the Department of Justice for civil and criminal litigation and to cities, states, and the District of Columbia for use in administering their tax laws.

The time needed to complete this form will vary depending on individual circumstances. The estimated average time is: **Recordkeeping** 46 min., **Learning about the law or the form** 10 min., **Preparing the form** 69 min. If you have comments concerning the accuracy of these time estimates or suggestions for making this form more simple, we would be happy to hear from you. You can write to both the **Internal Revenue Service,** Attention: Reports Clearance Officer, PC:FP, Washington, DC 20224; and the **Office of Management and Budget,** Paperwork Reduction Project (1545-0010), Washington, DC 20503. **DO NOT** send the tax form to either of these offices. Instead, give it to your employer.

☆ U.S. GOVERNMENT PRINTING OFFICE:1993-345-119   *Printed on recycled paper*

MARRIED Persons—BIWEEKLY Payroll Period
(For Wages Paid in 1994)

If the wages are—		And the number of withholding allowances claimed is—										
At least	But less than	0	1	2	3	4	5	6	7	8	9	10
		The amount of income tax to be withheld is—										
$0	$250	$0	$0	$0	$0	$0	$0	$0	$0	$0	$0	$0
250	260	2	0	0	0	0	0	0	0	0	0	0
260	270	3	0	0	0	0	0	0	0	0	0	0
270	280	5	0	0	0	0	0	0	0	0	0	0
280	290	6	0	0	0	0	0	0	0	0	0	0
290	300	8	0	0	0	0	0	0	0	0	0	0
300	310	9	0	0	0	0	0	0	0	0	0	0
310	320	11	0	0	0	0	0	0	0	0	0	0
320	330	12	0	0	0	0	0	0	0	0	0	0
330	340	14	0	0	0	0	0	0	0	0	0	0
340	350	15	1	0	0	0	0	0	0	0	0	0
350	360	17	2	0	0	0	0	0	0	0	0	0
360	370	18	4	0	0	0	0	0	0	0	0	0
370	380	20	5	0	0	0	0	0	0	0	0	0
380	390	21	7	0	0	0	0	0	0	0	0	0
390	400	23	8	0	0	0	0	0	0	0	0	0
400	410	24	10	0	0	0	0	0	0	0	0	0
410	420	26	11	0	0	0	0	0	0	0	0	0
420	430	27	13	0	0	0	0	0	0	0	0	0
430	440	29	14	0	0	0	0	0	0	0	0	0
440	450	30	16	2	0	0	0	0	0	0	0	0
450	460	32	17	3	0	0	0	0	0	0	0	0
460	470	33	19	5	0	0	0	0	0	0	0	0
470	480	35	20	6	0	0	0	0	0	0	0	0
480	490	36	22	8	0	0	0	0	0	0	0	0
490	500	38	23	9	0	0	0	0	0	0	0	0
500	520	40	26	12	0	0	0	0	0	0	0	0
520	540	43	29	15	0	0	0	0	0	0	0	0
540	560	46	32	18	3	0	0	0	0	0	0	0
560	580	49	35	21	6	0	0	0	0	0	0	0
580	600	52	38	24	9	0	0	0	0	0	0	0
600	620	55	41	27	12	0	0	0	0	0	0	0
620	640	58	44	30	15	1	0	0	0	0	0	0
640	660	61	47	33	18	4	0	0	0	0	0	0
660	680	64	50	36	21	7	0	0	0	0	0	0
680	700	67	53	39	24	10	0	0	0	0	0	0
700	720	70	56	42	27	13	0	0	0	0	0	0
720	740	73	59	45	30	16	2	0	0	0	0	0
740	760	76	62	48	33	19	5	0	0	0	0	0
760	780	79	65	51	36	22	8	0	0	0	0	0
780	800	82	68	54	39	25	11	0	0	0	0	0
800	820	85	71	57	42	28	14	0	0	0	0	0
820	840	88	74	60	45	31	17	3	0	0	0	0
840	860	91	77	63	48	34	20	6	0	0	0	0
860	880	94	80	66	51	37	23	9	0	0	0	0
880	900	97	83	69	54	40	26	12	0	0	0	0
900	920	100	86	72	57	43	29	15	1	0	0	0
920	940	103	89	75	60	46	32	18	4	0	0	0
940	960	106	92	78	63	49	35	21	7	0	0	0
960	980	109	95	81	66	52	38	24	10	0	0	0
980	1,000	112	98	84	69	55	41	27	13	0	0	0
1,000	1,020	115	101	87	72	58	44	30	16	2	0	0
1,020	1,040	118	104	90	75	61	47	33	19	5	0	0
1,040	1,060	121	107	93	78	64	50	36	22	8	0	0
1,060	1,080	124	110	96	81	67	53	39	25	11	0	0
1,080	1,100	127	113	99	84	70	56	42	28	14	0	0
1,100	1,120	130	116	102	87	73	59	45	31	17	3	0
1,120	1,140	133	119	105	90	76	62	48	34	20	6	0
1,140	1,160	136	122	108	93	79	65	51	37	23	9	0
1,160	1,180	139	125	111	96	82	68	54	40	26	12	0
1,180	1,200	142	128	114	99	85	71	57	43	29	15	1
1,200	1,220	145	131	117	102	88	74	60	46	32	18	4
1,220	1,240	148	134	120	105	91	77	63	49	35	21	7
1,240	1,260	151	137	123	108	94	80	66	52	38	24	10
1,260	1,280	154	140	126	111	97	83	69	55	41	27	13
1,280	1,300	157	143	129	114	100	86	72	58	44	30	16
1,300	1,320	160	146	132	117	103	89	75	61	47	33	19
1,320	1,340	163	149	135	120	106	92	78	64	50	36	22
1,340	1,360	166	152	138	123	109	95	81	67	53	39	25
1,360	1,380	169	155	141	126	112	98	84	70	56	42	28

Chapter 22

WORKING FOR TAX DEDUCTIONS

The objective of the employee is to work just hard enough so as not to be fired and the objective of the company is to pay just enough so the employee won't quit.

Unknown

OBJECTIVE

USE YOUR JOB TO CREATE BIG TAX DEDUCTIONS.

When I was an employee back in the sixties, I was always told that employees get no tax breaks, and most employees still believe that. While exorbitant sums are withheld from their paychecks, most act blessed if they get a refund, no matter how small. Employees may "get" no tax breaks, but there are many ways to use your job to "create" sizable tax deductions and significantly reduce your withholding taxes. You can also insure that you will eventually get maximum Social Security benefits by setting up your own Social Security monitoring system.

> ### Strategy #204
> ### CHECK YOUR SOCIAL SECURITY RECORD EVERY
> ### FIVE YEARS TO PREVENT AND CORRECT ERRORS.

Although you may already feel "socially secure," Uncle Sam's Social Security system is going to dip into your lifetime earnings anyway. In 1994, your contribution equaled 6.2% for old age, survivor, and disability insurance (OASDI) and 1.45% for Medicare hospital insurance (HI) or a total of 7.65% of your income up to $60,600—you continue to pay the 1.45% for Medicare hospital insurance. Moreover, Social Security payouts are small and even, in some cases, taxable. The overall failure of the Social Security system is that it was designed as a modest old-age insurance plan and not as a lifetime personal-investment retirement account.

Although a few politicians in Washington in early 1991 were making overtures about reducing the maximum wage base, it just won't happen. Here's why. Your money does not go into an individual account in your name, then get invested in government treasury bills, which would at least double your money every eight to ten years. Instead, your money is deposited into a general fund from which Congress determines the amount of money doled out to you in monthly payments at the time you retire. That would be like your banker determining the interest to pay you on your CDs, not when you invest, but when you withdraw your money.

The first person ever to collect from the Social Security system was Ida M. Fuller of Ludlow, Vermont. Soon after the establishment of the system, she paid in a total of $70 before retirement, then took out over $20,000 in benefits over the rest of her life. What a system! Sounds like the kind of financial wizardry they use in Washington to get the country deeper into debt. Social Security is actually an additional 15.30% tax. That's right—15.30%, not 7.65%. The hidden portion of the tax is the amount paid by your employer that matches the amount you pay, money that could instead have been added to your salary.

Once you have created some financial success in your life and your retirement years are not dependent on Social Security, the price to be paid for getting that few hundred extra dollars a month in a Social Security check seems like such a waste. For 10 years I was able to escape the Social Security system by receiving my income through my nonprofit foundation, but even the nonprofit Social Security loophole was eventually closed.

So what do you do about it? First and foremost, do what almost no one does. Make sure that you are credited with every dime coming to you.

The Social Security Administration works solely from records that find their way to the administration from your employer through the banking system. Errors occur every year—millions of errors—and you can be assured that some will crop up in your account.

You must create your own audit trail by checking your account credits and balance once every five years. Not to do so can cost you thousands of lost dollars during your lifetime. There is little chance you will ever be paid more from the system than you are due, but there is a good chance you could be paid less.

Here's all it takes:

- Call your local Social Security office and ask for form SSA-7004-PC, "Request for Earnings and Benefit Estimate Statement."
- Complete the form and mail to Social Security Administration, Box 20, Wilkes-Barre, PA 19711 (a copy of the form is on page 280).
- When you get your statement, review it carefully. It is up to you, not the Social Security Administration, to find any mistakes.
- If you find an error or if there is something you don't understand, contact your local Social Security office.
- Repeat the process every five years.

Assuming that the Social Security system never makes an error and that therefore you don't have to check your accounts is a sure way to lose money!

Strategy #205
IF YOU WORK AS AN INDEPENDENT CONTRACTOR, TREAT YOURSELF AS A SMALL BUSINESS AND NOT AS AN EMPLOYEE.

Tens of thousands of salespeople, computer people, and others who work on a per-product basis are employed by companies as "independent contractors." How can you tell if you are one? The test is simple. If your company withholds federal income taxes and Social Security from your paychecks, it is treating you as an employee. If, on the other hand, you are paid the full amount of your commissions or earnings and you are expected to pay the IRS yourself, you are being treated by your company as an independent contractor.

Although the IRS has stringent guidelines about whom a company can and cannot designate as an independent contractor, with stiff potential penalties for not following the guidelines, these penalties apply only to the employer and not to you as the employee. If it were up to the IRS, there would be no "independent contractor" status, since employees automatically have taxes withheld while independent contractors do not. Because independent contractors are responsible for their own

SOCIAL SECURITY ADMINISTRATION

Request for Earnings and Benefit Estimate Statement

To receive a free statement of your earnings covered by Social Security and your estimated future benefits, all you need to do is fill out this form. Please print or type your answers. When you have completed the form, fold it and mail it to us.

1. Name shown on your Social Security card:

First   Middle Initial   Last

2. Your Social Security number as shown on your card:

☐☐☐ - ☐☐ - ☐☐☐☐

3. Your date of birth: Month   Day   Year

4. Other Social Security numbers you have used:

☐☐☐ - ☐☐ - ☐☐☐☐
☐☐☐ - ☐☐ - ☐☐☐☐

5. Your Sex: ☐ Male   ☐ Female

6. Other names you have used (including a maiden name):

7. Show your actual earnings for last year and your estimated earnings for this year. Include only wages and/or net self-employment income covered by Social Security.

   A. Last year's actual earnings:

     $ ☐☐☐,☐☐☐.☐☐
     Dollars only

   B. This year's estimated earnings:

     $ ☐☐☐,☐☐☐.☐☐
     Dollars only

8. Show the age at which you plan to retire: ☐☐

                (Show only one age)

9. Below, show the average yearly amount that you think you will earn between now and when you plan to retire. Your estimate of future earnings will be added to those earnings already on our records to give you the best possible estimate.

Enter a yearly average, not your total future lifetime earnings. Only show earnings covered by Social Security. Do not add cost-of-living, performance or scheduled pay increases or bonuses. The reason for this is that we estimate retirement benefits in today's dollars, but adjust them to account for average wage growth in the national economy.

However, if you expect to earn significantly more or less in the future due to promotions, job changes, part-time work, or an absence from the work force, enter the amount in today's dollars that most closely reflects your future average yearly earnings.

Most people should enter the same amount that they are earning now (the amount shown in 7B).

Your future average yearly earnings:

$ ☐☐☐,☐☐☐.☐☐
Dollars only

10. Address where you want us to send the statement:

Name

Street Address (Include Apt. No., P.O. Box, or Rural Route)

City   State   Zip Code

I am asking for information about my own Social Security record or the record of a person I am authorized to represent. I understand that if I deliberately request information under false pretenses I may be guilty of a federal crime and could be fined and/or imprisoned. I authorize you to send the statement of earnings and benefit estimates to the person named in item 10 through a contractor.

Please sign your name (Do not print)

▲

Date   (Area Code)   Daytime Telephone No.

ABOUT THE PRIVACY ACT
Social Security is allowed to collect the facts on this form under Section 205 of the Social Security Act. We need them to quickly identify your record and prepare the earnings statement you asked us for. Giving us these facts is voluntary. However, without them we may not be able to give you an earnings and benefit estimate statement. Neither the Social Security Administration nor its contractor will use the information for any other purpose.

payment of income taxes and Social Security, thousands sometimes delay until the last minute and then don't have the money left to pay, giving the IRS more work and headaches.

You, however, can turn your independent-contractor status into big tax savings. Independent contractors are technically in business for themselves and therefore are allowed to take all regular and necessary expenses as business deductions, which can create hundreds or even thousands in extra tax deductions. Many independent contractors, however, treat themselves as employees on their tax returns and either miss the available deductions or take the deductions on tax form 2106, "Employee Business Expenses," which becomes part of Miscellaneous Deductions Schedule A and is subject to deduction limitations.

Miscellaneous deductions are subject to a 2% floor, meaning that only those deductions that exceed 2% of adjusted gross income (AGI) are deductible. The combined deductions on Schedule A are then subject to another limit called the 0% bracket, which for 1994 is $6,350 for couples filing jointly and $3,800 for singles. Only Schedule A deductions above that amount are deductible. In other words, use Form 2106 and you have two chances to lose all or part of your deductions.

However, when you fill out "Schedule C—Profits or Loss from Business," your deductible expenses are not subject to any limitations. You preserve 100% of the allowable deductions. Always enter your income and expenses on Schedule C instead of Form 2106 when you qualify for both.

Strategy #206
DEDUCT EVERY DOLLAR YOU SPEND THAT IS RELATED TO YOUR JOB.

Did you know that when you spend money on items and events related to your job and you are not fully reimbursed by your employer, all or part of those expenses is deductible on your personal tax return? Most employees do spend their own money on job-related items and lose hundreds or thousands per year in potential tax deductions because they don't keep track or know how to take the deductions.

The deductions you may take as an employee of someone else's company are almost identical to the deductions you could take if the business were yours. An important part of your tax reducing plan involves keeping track of every potentially deductible dime of your employee business deductions.

You do not need your employer's permission to take these deductions. You simply itemize your job-related expenditures on Form 2106 (see pages 296–97) and enter the total on Schedule A. In the tax code these tax deductions are referred to as "employee business expenses," which is also the IRS's name for Form 2106. Also deductible are expenses you incur when you are on a job search, as well as moving and relocation expenses when you've found a job.

Let's begin with an extensive checklist of all your potential employee business deductions, and then I'll show you the strategies for maximizing each. In some cases you will be referred to other strategies in the book such as those in Chapter 25, "Getting Down to Business," when the deduction rules are the same as shown in another strategy.

POTENTIAL DEDUCTIONS FOR EMPLOYEES

Deduction	Strategy #
Assistants	208
Salaries paid to family members or others	
Auto Expenses	209
Auto club membership	
Insurance	
Interest on auto loan	
Nonreimbursed business mileage	
Parking and tolls	
Sales tax	
Child Care Tax Credits	146
Baby-sitters	
Day-care center	
Nondependent relatives	
Dues and Subscriptions	213
Association dues	
Subscriptions to business-related magazines	
Union dues	
Education	210
Business-related books	
Convention costs including travel	
Correspondence courses	
Job- or personal-development-related books	
Job-related education	
Night school classes	
Seminars and tape courses	

Deduction	Strategy #
Travel Expenses	217
Airfares	
Car rentals	
Hotels	
Laundry and dry cleaning	
Meals (50%)	
Parking fees	
Passport fees	
Taxi fares	
Telephone, fax, and express mail	
Tips	
Tolls	

> ### Strategy #207
> ### SET UP AN "ACCOUNTABLE" REIMBURSEMENT PLAN
> ### WITH YOUR EMPLOYER TO CIRCUMVENT
> ### THE 2% FLOOR.

When you spend money on a regular basis for travel and/or entertainment that is related to your job, even if you are reimbursed, the money can add up to big amounts. The IRS requires your employer to report your reimbursements as income on Form W-2, and you are then required to deduct your expenses on Schedule A as "miscellaneous expenses." That means along with any other miscellaneous deductions, you will be able to deduct only the amount that is over 2% of your adjusted gross income (AGI). If your AGI was $40,000, you could lose up to $800 of the deductions (2% × 40,000). This loss is happening to thousands of employees who are not even aware that there is an alternative. In addition, you may end up paying Social Security taxes on reimbursed company expenses.

The alternative: set up an accountable reimbursement plan with your employer to circumvent the 2% floor. If your plan meets the following IRS rules, there is a tax wash and no possible loss. In other words, using these rules, you are allowed to deduct the full amount of your expenses from the amount you are reimbursed by your employer, and you do not even have to show your reimbursed expenses or account for them on your tax return! Here are the rules to qualify:

- You must turn in to your employer an accurate accounting of all your actual expenses including credit card charges.

• You must pay back to your employer any advances above your actual business-related expenses.

Don't miss this opportunity to plug a hole that may be costing you hundreds per year in extra hidden taxes.

Strategy #208
PAY YOUR SPOUSE OR KIDS TO ASSIST YOU WITH YOUR JOB.

If your spouse or kids can help you with the work you do on behalf of your employer, the money you pay them is tax deductible. For instance, your spouse or children could do typing, research, make phone calls, or prepare reports. Your children could be paid a tax deductible salary for stuffing envelopes, filing or sorting papers, or answering the business-related phone. The rules for hiring and paying deductible salaries to family members are completely outlined in Chapter 25, "Getting Down to Business," Strategy #240.

You also have the right to pay someone outside the family a tax deductible fee for helping you perform any duties required by your job. For instance, if you are a salesperson, you can personally pay someone else to do the paperwork and reports so you can concentrate on selling. The money you pay is deductible to you. At the end of the year, you give your assistants a 1099 or W-2 form, whichever is appropriate, showing the amount you paid them and take the deduction for the same amount on Form 2106.

Strategy #209
DEDUCT YOUR JOB-RELATED AUTO EXPENSES.

When you use your automobile at your employer's request to run errands, drop off the mail, or pick someone up at the airport, and your employer does not reimburse you, you may deduct 29 cents per mile. Many employees are required to use their own car for their employer on a regular basis and are not reimbursed or are reimbursed less than the IRS standard mileage rate. If you are reimbursed less than 29 cents per mile, the difference is deductible. If you are an employee, the mileage between your full-time job and a second job, if you have one, is also deductible.

Two uses of your automobile are not deductible under any circumstances—personal use and commuting. "Personal use" includes mileage for vacations, shopping, taking the kids to school, or visiting friends. "Commuting" is the driving between your home and your job. Commuting is not deductible, even if you drive to a different company office each day, make business-related stops on the way to work, or carry tools or samples in your car, unless the tools or samples require a special vehicle.

There are, however, special rules for salespeople, inspectors, real estate agents, and construction workers. If you are in one of these occupations, your mileage from home to the first location and from the last location to home is not deductible. But the rest of the mileage between other stops you make during the day is deductible at 29 cents per mile.

You may choose either the actual-expense method of deducting your automobile expenses or the standard mileage rate of 29 cents per mile. See Chapter 25, "Getting Down to Business," for which method is likely to give you the biggest deduction.

You deduct your employee-related automobile expenses on Form 2106. You may also deduct the business-related portion of your car loan interest, insurance, and other expenses on the same form. The personal use portion of the interest on your car loan is no longer deductible, but the business use percentage is. The business percentage of your sales tax can be added to the cost of the car and depreciated if you choose the actual-expense method for your deduction.

Don't overlook any of these important automobile deductions available to you as an employee. They can add up to big dollars.

Strategy #210
DEDUCT YOUR JOB-RELATED EDUCATION EXPENSES.

You may take tax deductions for any education, books, tapes, seminars, or adult classes that help you perform your present job more effectively. The deductions include tuition, lab fees, and mileage or other travel expenses. You must be employed when you take the education for which you claim the deduction.

No deductions are allowed if the education is required to meet the minimum education standards for your job, for example, state licenses for hairdressers, teachers, or CPAs. Although, logically, you would think that required education would be the most deductible, the deduction applies only to optional job-related education.

If your employer requires you to take specific courses or training for your present job and you pay for part or all of the tuition, take the deduction. Doctors and nurses can deduct the cost of courses and programs that keep their knowledge current.

As an employee you cannot deduct education expenses that have the primary purpose of qualifying you for a better job. For instance, an airline navigator was not allowed deductions for the money spent getting his pilot's license even though he already worked for an airline and flew in the cockpit. The IRS ruled that a pilot has a different job or career than a navigator.

Don't forget to deduct the costs of night school classes, job-related conventions you attend for which you are not fully reimbursed, the tuition for correspondence courses, audio- or videotape programs you acquire, and seminars you attend. Keep a yearly record of all such expenses.

Strategy #211
DEDUCT LUNCHES, DINNERS, AND ENTERTAINMENT FOR PROSPECTS, CLIENTS, OR SUPPLIERS.

Entertainment means spending money on people associated with your job or company at:

- restaurants
- sporting events
- nightclubs
- your yacht or boat
- your home
- other social environments

The secret to claiming this deduction is complete records. Pay by credit card. List the names of the people you entertained and the specific business purpose or discussion on your credit card receipt. You do not have to include a report about the business purpose. A few key words will do. If you are asked to substantiate the expense, here's what the IRS will be looking for. Be sure to note both on your receipts.

- You must show a business purpose, or
- You must discuss business during or directly before or after the entertainment.

If you have only a business relationship, not a personal relationship, with those you entertain and keep good records, the IRS seldom questions the business purpose of the entertainment. The IRS looks more closely, however, when you are deducting entertainment expenses for occasions involving friends and family. Nonetheless, if your spouse is present because someone you are entertaining for business purposes has his or her spouse there as well, entertainment expenses relating to your spouse are deductible.

Do not be afraid that entertainment deductions will "red flag" your return. Just keep good records. Not taking legitimate deductions for fear of so-called red flags would be like telling your bank not to pay you interest because the IRS might question it.

You may deduct only 50% of your entertainment expenses that are not reimbursed by your employer. This is the same 50% rule that applies to your business-related meals.

Strategy #212
DEDUCT THE COST OF EQUIPMENT, ELECTRONICS, EVEN PERSONAL ITEMS YOU USE IN CONNECTION WITH YOUR JOB.

First let's look at the deduction of a cellular phone or personal computer, fax machine, copier, or items that more and more employees are acquiring. These items, as well as almost all equipment and electronic items, can be deducted over a period of one to five years using either the asset expensing rules, also known as section 179, or the MACRS depreciation methods.

Don't let the technical jargon scare you. These are important and potentially huge deductions whether you are an employee or own your own small business. Refer to Strategies 247 to 255 for an explanation of how these deductions are taken. The following discussion assumes that you are now familiar with asset expensing, MACRS, and straight-line depreciation.

If you are required to use your own cellular phone, computer, or other equipment on the job, and use it more than 50% of the time for business, you may use the asset expensing rules to write off up to $17,500 of the business portion of the cost in a single year. This method gives you the greatest deduction and can allow you to write off up to 100% of the cost even before you've paid for the item.

If the item is used less than 50% of the time for business purposes, you must use the slower straight-line method of depreciation. Begin by getting a letter from your employer stating that you are required to have and use the equipment. A disagreeable IRS auditor might also require you to show that you really need the equipment to do your job or that you would be "disadvantaged" if you didn't have it.

If you lease a computer, cellular phone, copier, fax machine, or other equipment, the business-use percentage of the lease payments is deductible by you as an employee. If you use the item both personally and for business, keep records using the strategies in *Financial Self-Defense*, Chapter 17, "How to Keep Records for Maximum Tax Deductions."

If your business-related purchases, such as a calculator or microcassette recorder, are under $200, you can normally write off the total amount in the year you buy the item. Supplies for equipment used by you as an employee are also deductible as an employee expense.

Strategy #213
DEDUCT MAGAZINE SUBSCRIPTIONS, AND ASSOCIATION OR UNION DUES.

If you personally pay for subscriptions to magazines with articles related to your job, take the deduction. Professional journals, trade publications, and publications from associations to which you belong are clearly deductible.

Other regular business, management, or sales publications that help you with ideas for performing your job better are deductible even if you also derive personal enjoyment from them. If, for example, your job requires you to stay on top of the news, news magazines or cable news services bought by you would be deductible. Your hometown newspaper, however, has been deemed by the IRS not to be business, career, or job related.

Make a list of everything to which you subscribe. Don't forget to include newsletters in both printed and audio form. Check off and add up the cost of those that relate to your job or career and take the deductions on Form 2106.

Dues you pay to an association, business group, civic group, or union are also deductible. Make a list of what you pay out to belong to trade and career-related associations. Your dues to the Chamber of Commerce, Junior Chamber of Commerce, or similar organizations can be deducted. If you belong to a union, both dues and initiation fees can be taken off your taxable income.

However, no deductions are allowed for the money you must contribute to a union pension fund that will be used to fund an annuity.

Strategy #214
DEDUCT A HOME-BASED OFFICE WHEN USED FOR YOUR EMPLOYER.

You may take tax deductions for an office in your home where you do job-related work, provided:

- the office is your principal office, meaning you don't have a desk or work area at your employer's regular place of business
- the office is used to meet with customers, suppliers, or patients
- you have an area set aside that you use "regularly and exclusively" for your employer's benefit

Even supplies, equipment, and furniture you use in your home office become deductible. If you own your home, you may use the depreciation rules to deduct some of your home office expenses. If you rent, you may deduct a portion of your rent. In both cases you may deduct a portion of your utilities, maintenance, improvements, and telephone. Under new rules, you can no longer take a deduction for renting your home to your employer.

You take all employee business expense deductions as miscellaneous itemized deductions on Schedule A. Outside salespeople often qualify under these office-at-home rules, as do employees whose main or branch office is not located in the same area or city as their home. Based on recent court rulings, however, if an employee does administrative paperwork in addition to regular job duties that require a non-office environment, the expenses for an office in the home can be deducted.

Strategy #215
DEDUCT YOUR JOB-SEARCH EXPENSES AND END UP WITH A BETTER JOB.

If you are career motivated, you are constantly exploring new horizons, maybe even traveling to look at companies and new job opportunities. Travel and other job-search expenses such as employment agency fees and résumé preparation expenses are deductible. Read Strategy #180 to learn the rules for planning your out-of-town job interviews as tax deductible trips.

Now, let's look at some other important job-search deductions and rules.

Your deductions are limited to the money you spend looking for the same kind of job you have now. Looking for a different kind of job or career doesn't qualify.

Employment agency or "headhunter" fees are deductible if you pay them. Of course, if you are later reimbursed, you must include that amount as income on your tax return.

The cost of preparing a professional-looking résumé, long-distance calls, and mailing costs related to a job search are also deductible. Don't forget to keep the records. You may take job-search-related deductions whether you get a job or not.

If you want to move ahead quickly in your career, when should you begin your job search? The day after you got your last job. In America, you move up the business success ladder fastest by changing companies, not waiting for your boss to retire. However, if you love where you are even though your salary is growing at a snail's pace, be certain to use every strategy in this book that could apply to you so you can afford to stay at your current job.

Strategy #216
PLAN YOUR JOB MOVES AROUND DEDUCTIBLE RELOCATION EXPENSES.

The U.S. Labor Department says that workers change jobs an average of seven times during their working career. Some of those jobs may require moves to other cities. With a little planning and knowledge of the applicable tax rules, all those moves can be tax deductible. Your moving expenses are deducted on Form 3903 and cannot be reduced or affected by the 2% miscellaneous deduction floor (see Strategy #145). That means you can deduct the full amount.

Your moving expenses are deductible if the distance between your new job location and your old personal residence is 50 miles or more. At this moment Congress is thinking about increasing the minimum moving distance to 200 miles. The 50-mile deductible rule applies whether you are an employee or self-employed. If you are in the armed services, you may deduct the cost of moving your family to a new base, even overseas.

To qualify for the moving-expense deduction, you must use what is called the 39-week test, but normally that's not difficult. The rule says you must continue to be a full-time employee in the new area for 39 weeks following the start of your new job. You can change jobs, but you must continue to work in the same area. If you lose your job other than for willful misconduct after you begin work, the rule does not apply. If your employer transfers you to a new area, you do not have to meet the test. Interestingly, if you are married, either spouse can qualify by working the required 39 weeks. If you are self-employed, the required time in the new area in order for you to take the relocation deduction is 78 weeks. Here is another important point. You can take the deduction for the year you move even though you have not yet completed all 39 weeks.

These are the expenses you can deduct:

- cost of professional movers, including packing and 30 days of storage
- travel costs for you and your family

You may deduct the full amount of your direct expenses. The moving deduction can effectively get the government to reimburse you for one-third or more of your total moving expenses.

If you are reimbursed for some or all of your moving expenses, you do not report the money received as income on your 1040 tax return unless you actually deducted the expenses in an earlier year. Moving expenses that are not paid for by your employer are deductible in computing adjusted gross income. If you are on active military service and move under an order, you do not have to report any reimbursement up to the actual cost of your move.

The deduction for moving expenses and its benefits are overlooked by thousands of relocating employees every year.

Strategy #217
DEDUCT YOUR JOB-RELATED TRAVEL EXPENSES EVEN WHEN THE TRAVEL HAS A PARTIAL PERSONAL PURPOSE.

Almost any money you spend on travel that relates to your job on behalf of your employer is deductible, even if it is not a purely business trip. Just keep careful records. If you are reimbursed by your employer, your deduction is the amount of job-related travel expenses in excess of what your employer pays you back.

If you prefer not to have to keep receipts and records for meals while on job-related travel, there is an alternative. You can deduct, when you are away from home and in the United States, a daily allowance of $26. If you are in a major city or more expensive area, your deduction is $34. The IRS publishes a list of the $34-per-day cities in Publication 1542, "Per Diem Rates."

To take travel expenses as deductions, you must be outside the area of your tax home. Your home for tax purposes is considered your place of business, not your residence. Outside the area means outside the metropolitan area of your business location.

In general, job-related travel expenses that you may deduct include transportation, lodging, or meals (50% deductible). See the list on page 284. Your deduction includes tips, telephone, and laundry costs.

Strategy #218
DEDUCT THE EXPENSES OF A COMBINATION BUSINESS-VACATION TRIP.

You can have fun and get the deduction, too—that is, by keeping records for a combination business-pleasure trip that show business was your primary motive. The amount of time you spend on business activities is the key in determining your primary purpose. Keep time records of your business-related activities in your daily planner.

Although not written in stone, a good rule of thumb is that your trip was primarily for business if you spent at least four hours every other day on business, or you can show that your business purpose involved one or more specific meetings that required you to be in that city or place at that time.

The number-of-business-hours rule applies if you intend to do business over an extended period of time. If you attend specifically scheduled meetings or job interviews and then extend your time in the area to include only vacation or personal activities, you can still deduct your airline or car expenses to and from, plus the hotels, meals, and other related expenses while conducting business, but your expenses for your purely personal days are not deductible.

For more information on how to deduct cruises, conventions, and trips outside the United States, see Strategy #259 in Chapter 25, "Getting Down to Business."

Strategy #219
USE FORM 2106 TO CALCULATE YOUR EMPLOYEE BUSINESS EXPENSES.

Whether you travel to make sales, sit behind a desk, or run equipment, Form 2106 is your ticket to computing all of your nonreimbursed, job-related expenses. First list your employee business expenses on Form 2106 and then transfer the total to Schedule A—Miscellaneous Itemized Deductions. To illustrate how to put these deductions together, let's look at a typical example.

Rob Walters is an assistant manager for a small parts company. He seems to be constantly spending his own money on behalf of his company, but never gets totally reimbursed. He drives his car every day to deposit the company mail at the post office. Deduction: 4 miles a day × 250 days a year = 1,000 miles. Incidental mileage for errands for his boss adds another 400 miles per year. For six months he supplemented his income with a second job at 15 miles a day for 100 days for a total of 1,500 miles.

The company purchased a new computer system during the year, and Rob took two night school courses to learn how to operate the system better. Rob's boss said they were necessary courses, but didn't feel the company could afford the tuition. Rob spent $275 of his own money on tuition, books, and supplies, and added on another 300 driving miles for a total of 3,200 employee business miles. Rob spent $84 of his own money on job-related books and magazines, and $60 on a portable calculator, and paid his kids $400 during the year to sort and file items related to his job.

What are Rob's total deductions?

Automobile (3,200 × .29)*	$ 928
Education, books, calculator	419
Kids' salaries	400
TOTAL DEDUCTIONS	**$1,747**

*The mileage rate method is used for the automobile deduction. For an example of the actual-expense method deduction, see Chapter 25.

Look at Form 2106 (pages 296–97) to see how Rob calculated and claimed his employee business deductions.

Under the tax rules, the employee business expenses shown on Form 2106 are lumped together with other miscellaneous itemized deductions on Schedule A.

If Rob's employee business expenses are $1,747 (refer to the previous example) and his other miscellaneous itemized deductions are $1,500, his total miscellaneous itemized deductions equal $3,247. Let's say Rob's total income is $42,000, and his adjusted gross income is $21,000. His total deductions of $3,247 are reduced by $420 because 2% of adjusted gross income must be subtracted from the total miscellaneous itemized deductions (2% × $21,000 = $420). The balance is 100% deductible. In our case, Rob is allowed a deduction of $2,827, which saves him about $792 in taxes based on his 28% bracket.

As you can see, employees do get significant deductions, but most never know enough to take them.

Form **2106**	**Employee Business Expenses**	OMB No. 1545-0139
Department of the Treasury Internal Revenue Service (O)	▶ See separate instructions. ▶ Attach to Form 1040.	**19**93 Attachment Sequence No. **54**

Your name	Social security number	Occupation in which expenses were incurred
Robert Walters	377 00 2946	Asst. Mgr.

Part I Employee Business Expenses and Reimbursements

STEP 1 Enter Your Expenses		Column A Other Than Meals and Entertainment		Column B Meals and Entertainment	
1	Vehicle expense from line 22 or line 29	1	928 00		
2	Parking fees, tolls, and transportation, including train, bus, etc., that **did not** involve overnight travel	2	0 00		
3	Travel expense while away from home overnight, including lodging, airplane, car rental, etc. **Do not** include meals and entertainment	3	0 00		
4	Business expenses not included on lines 1 through 3. **Do not** include meals and entertainment	4	819 00		
5	Meals and entertainment expenses (see instructions)	5			0 00
6	**Total expenses.** In Column A, add lines 1 through 4 and enter the result. In Column B, enter the amount from line 5	6	1,747 00		0 00

Note: *If you were not reimbursed for any expenses in Step 1, skip line 7 and enter the amount from line 6 on line 8.*

STEP 2 Enter Amounts Your Employer Gave You for Expenses Listed in STEP 1

7	Enter amounts your employer gave you that were **not** reported to you in box 1 of Form W-2. Include any amount reported under code "L" in box 13 of your Form W-2 (see instructions) . . .	7	0 00		0 00

STEP 3 Figure Expenses To Deduct on Schedule A (Form 1040)

8	Subtract line 7 from line 6	8	1,747 00		0 00
	Note: *If both columns of line 8 are zero, stop here. If Column A is less than zero, report the amount as income on Form 1040, line 7, and enter -0- on line 10, Column A.*				
9	Enter 20% (.20) of line 8, Column B	9			0 00
10	In Column A, enter the amount from line 8. In Column B, subtract line 9 from line 8	10	1,747 00		0 00
11	Add the amounts on line 10 of both columns and enter the total here. **Also, enter the total on Schedule A (Form 1040), line 19.** (Qualified performing artists and individuals with disabilities, see the instructions for special rules on where to enter the total.) . . . . ▶	11			1,747 00

For Paperwork Reduction Act Notice, see instructions.   Cat. No. 11700N   Form **2106** (1993)

Form 2106 (1993)

Part II — Vehicle Expenses (See instructions to find out which sections to complete.)

Section A.—General Information

			(a) Vehicle 1		(b) Vehicle 2	
12	Enter the date vehicle was placed in service	12	1 / 1 /92		/ /	
13	Total miles vehicle was driven during 1993	13	10,500	miles		miles
14	Business miles included on line 13	14	3,200	miles		miles
15	Percent of business use. Divide line 14 by line 13	15	30	%		%
16	Average daily round trip commuting distance	16	12	miles		miles
17	Commuting miles included on line 13	17	3,000	miles		miles
18	Other personal miles. Add lines 14 and 17 and subtract the total from line 13.	18	4,300	miles		miles

19 Do you (or your spouse) have another vehicle available for personal purposes? ☐ Yes ☐ No

20 If your employer provided you with a vehicle, is personal use during off duty hours permitted? ☐ Yes ☐ No ☐ Not applicable

21a Do you have evidence to support your deduction? ☐ Yes ☐ No

21b If "Yes," is the evidence written? ☐ Yes ☐ No

Section B.—Standard Mileage Rate (Use this section only if you own the vehicle.)

22	Multiply line 14 by 28¢ (.28). Enter the result here and on line 1. (Rural mail carriers, see instructions.) 29¢ for 1994.	22	928	00

Section C.—Actual Expenses

			(a) Vehicle 1	(b) Vehicle 2
23	Gasoline, oil, repairs, vehicle insurance, etc.	23		
24a	Vehicle rentals	24a		
b	Inclusion amount (see instructions)	24b		
c	Subtract line 24b from line 24a	24c		
25	Value of employer-provided vehicle (applies only if 100% of annual lease value was included on Form W-2—see instructions)	25		
26	Add lines 23, 24c, and 25	26		
27	Multiply line 26 by the percentage on line 15	27		
28	Depreciation. Enter amount from line 38 below	28		
29	Add lines 27 and 28. Enter total here and on line 1.	29		

Section D.—Depreciation of Vehicles (Use this section only if you own the vehicle.)

			(a) Vehicle 1	(b) Vehicle 2
30	Enter cost or other basis (see instructions)	30		
31	Enter amount of section 179 deduction (see instructions)	31		
32	Multiply line 30 by line 15 (see instructions if you elected the section 179 deduction)	32		
33	Enter depreciation method and percentage (see instructions)	33		
34	Multiply line 32 by the percentage on line 33 (see instructions)	34		
35	Add lines 31 and 34	35		
36	Enter the limitation amount from the table in the line 36 instructions	36		
37	Multiply line 36 by the percentage on line 15	37		
38	Enter the **smaller** of line 35 or line 37. Also, enter this amount on line 28 above	38		

Chapter 23

TURN YOUR HOME INTO
A TAX HAVEN

*He worked like hell in the country so he could live in the city,
where he worked like hell so he could live in the country.*

Don Marquis
Journalist
(1878–1937)

OBJECTIVE

GENERATE THOUSANDS IN EXTRA TAX DEDUCTIONS FROM YOUR PRINCIPAL RESIDENCE.

You don't have to look far to find tax deductions; thousands of dollars of deductions can be found right under your roof. In this chapter, you'll learn several tax-saving strategies available to you simply because you are a homeowner. If you are not a homeowner, your first priority is to become one, and these strategies should help motivate you.

> **Strategy #220**
> **TURN YOUR HOME IMPROVEMENTS INTO TAX DEDUCTIONS.**

Your home improvements become a tax shelter when you sell your home. If you own a home, you already realize how easy it is to pour thousands of dollars into your property to make your home environment just the way you want it to be. Improvements are any expenses that add to the value of your home and are differentiated in the tax law from repairs. Improvements make your home more valuable; repairs only help maintain the current value. Following are examples of home improvements and home repairs to assist you in understanding the difference.

Home Improvement (Deductible when home is sold)	Home Repair (Nondeductible)
paneling a room	replacing a scratched or broken panel
new shrubbery	replacing dead shrubbery
installing a fence	painting a fence
carpeting a room	replacing or cleaning your carpet
paving a driveway	repairing cracks in your driveway
adding a room	painting a room

"Upgrading" can also turn nondeductible "repairs" into deductible "improvements." If you upgrade something that needs repairing, such as a hot-water heater, roofing, or carpet, the difference between the repair cost and the upgrade cost is considered an improvement and is deductible. Examples of upgrades include the following:

• replacing a 30-gallon hot-water heater with a 60-gallon, energy-efficient hot-water heater
• replacing asphalt-shingle roofing with expensive Spanish-tile or cedar-shake roofing
• replacing $4-per-yard standard carpeting with $16-per-yard plush Antron IV carpeting

Remember, the difference is deductible.

If you upgrade a part of your home that does not need repairing, the entire cost may be considered an improvement. Improvement expenses include all labor that is not your own or your spouse's. Making a home improvement provides you with a great opportunity to use the family tax strategy—"Hire Your Children and Grandchildren." You may not be able to deduct the work you personally do on your home, but you can hire your children and grandchildren to help with the work and deduct amounts paid to them.

Take the deduction for improvements on Form 2119 when you sell your home. Keep receipts for all home improvements.

Strategy #221
DEDUCT LAST-MINUTE PRESALE FIX-UP EXPENSES.

Before you sell a home, there are usually repairs and fix-up expenses ranging from a few hundred to several thousand dollars—all necessary to get your home in salable condition. Any normal nondeductible repairs you make within a 90-day period before you sell your home are tax deductible on Form 2119, line 11.

Strategy #222
USE THE TAX DEFERRAL OPTION TO AVOID TAXES WHEN YOU SELL YOUR HOME.

Congress has passed special rules for homeowners that make it possible to enjoy huge cash profits from the sale of a personal residence without becoming liable for immediate taxes. In order to qualify for the homeowner's tax deferral, you must buy or build another personal residence of equal or greater value within 24 months of the sale of your first home. The 24-month purchase period of the new home can begin before or after the sale of your current home, so you actually enjoy a 48-month qualifying period.

Using the "homeowner's tax deferral" rules means you pay no taxes now, but you must report your profit by using Form 2119. The cost basis of the new home you purchased is reduced by the amount of the profit from the sale of your first home. Should you sell a home sometime in the future and not buy another home that qualifies for the homeowner's tax deferral, you would be liable for taxes on all of the accumulated profits. Your strategy, therefore, is to always own a home and buy a more expensive home each time you sell. All of the equity you accumulate from home to home is tax sheltered as long as you use this strategy.

If the purchase price of the new home you buy is less than the sale price of your old home, you must claim the difference as profit. The difference is taxable in the year your new home is purchased. Let's say you sell your home, which cost $70,000 for $90,000 and decide to buy a condo for $85,000. Your profit on the sale is $20,000. How much can you defer using the homeowner's deferral rules? Since the purchase price of the new residence is $5,000 less than the sale price of your previous home, you must claim the $5,000 as taxable profit this year. Therefore, $15,000 ($20,000 profit − $5,000 taxable) is the amount you can defer from taxes.

If, because of separation or divorce, you sell your home and split the profits with your ex-spouse, you are only required to buy a home costing half as much as the one you sold.

If you don't buy another home within 24 months, you will be liable for taxes on the profits of the home you sold plus any deferred profits from the sale of previous homes you have owned.

Strategy #223
DON'T INVEST THE PROFITS FROM THE SALE OF YOUR OLD HOME IN YOUR NEW HOME.

To qualify for the homeowner's tax deferral, you are not required to reinvest any of your profit from the sale of your old home in the new home, only to buy a home of equal or greater value.

Therefore, when you sell your home, use the profits in a powerful investment program that will earn more than the interest you would pay on a home mortgage. Buy your new home using as big a mortgage as possible.

Let's look at the home sale of Martin and Marie Jones of Kansas City to see how the tax deferral process actually works.

The Joneses sell their home for $110,000. They originally purchased the home eight years ago for $65,000. The presale fix-up expenses were $1,000, and they paid Jacob Realty $7,000 in commissions for selling the home. Their new home costs $120,000, so, using the homeowner's tax deferral rules, there is no taxable gain on the sale of their old home. They are able to defer or postpone the taxes on their profit of $38,000 ($110,000 sale price − $7,000 commission − $65,000 cost = $38,000 cash profit).

The Joneses report the transactions involving the sale of the old residence and purchase of their new residence on Form 2119 in order to qualify for the homeowner's tax deferral. See the sample form on page 302.

On their new $120,000 home the Joneses can either make a down payment using the $38,000 profit from the first home or make a minimum down payment of $12,000. In either case the fixed interest rate is 10%. What should they do?

The correct strategy in real estate is to maximize your cash available for more liquid investments. Real estate ties up your money long term. The Joneses should take the $26,000 difference in the down payments and invest the money in mutual funds or discounted mortgages that will return 20% or more. The difference in mortgage payments can be made using part of the investment income. At a 20% investment return, the $26,000 will generate $5,200 while the $26,000 extra mortgage amount will cost only $2,600 per year in tax deductible interest.

Form **2119**		**Sale of Your Home**	OMB No. 1545-0072
Department of the Treasury Internal Revenue Service		▶ Attach to Form 1040 for year of sale. ▶ See separate instructions. ▶ Please print or type.	**1993** Attachment Sequence No. **20**

Your first name and initial. If a joint return, also give spouse's name and initial. Last name	Your social security number
Martin and Marie Jones	776 24 3394

Fill in Your Address Only If You Are Filing This Form by Itself and Not With Your Tax Return	Present address (no., street, and apt. no., rural route, or P.O. box no. if mail is not delivered to street address)	Spouse's social security number
	City, town or post office, state, and ZIP code	

Part I General Information

1	Date your former main home was sold (month, day, year) . . . . ▶ **1**	3 / 24 / 93
2	Have you bought or built a new main home?	☐ Yes ☐ No
3	Is or was any part of either main home rented out or used for business? If "Yes," see instructions . .	☐ Yes ☐ No

Part II Gain on Sale—Do not include amounts you deduct as moving expenses.

4	Selling price of home. Do not include personal property items you sold with your home . . .	**4**	110,000 00
5	Expense of sale (see instructions)	**5**	7,000 00
6	Amount realized. Subtract line 5 from line 4	**6**	103,000 00
7	Adjusted basis of home sold (see instructions)	**7**	65,000 00
8	**Gain on sale.** Subtract line 7 from line 6	**8**	38,000 00

Is line 8 more than zero?

— Yes ▶ If line 2 is "Yes," you **must** go to Part III or Part IV, whichever applies. If line 2 is "No," go to line 9.

— No ▶ **Stop** and attach this form to your return.

9   If you haven't replaced your home, do you plan to do so within the **replacement period** (see instructions)? ☐ Yes ☐ No
    ● If line 9 is "Yes," stop here, attach this form to your return, and see **Additional Filing Requirements** in the instructions.
    ● If line 9 is "No," you **must** go to Part III or Part IV, whichever applies.

Part III One-Time Exclusion of Gain for People Age 55 or Older—By completing this part, you are electing to take the one-time exclusion (see instructions). If you are not electing to take the exclusion, go to Part IV now.

10	Who was age 55 or older on the date of sale?	☐ You ☐ Your spouse ☐ Both of you
11	Did the person who was age 55 or older own and use the property as his or her main home for a total of at least 3 years (except for short absences) of the 5-year period before the sale? If "No," go to Part IV now . .	☐ Yes ☐ No
12	At the time of sale, who owned the home?	☐ You ☐ Your spouse ☐ Both of you
13	Social security number of spouse at the time of sale if you had a different spouse from the one above. If you were not married at the time of sale, enter "None" . . . . ▶ **13**	
14	**Exclusion.** Enter the **smaller** of line 8 or $125,000 ($62,500 if married filing separate return). Then, go to line 15 . . . . **14**	

Part IV Adjusted Sales Price, Taxable Gain, and Adjusted Basis of New Home

15	If line 14 is blank, enter the amount from line 8. Otherwise, subtract line 14 from line 8 . .	**15**	38,000 00
	● If line 15 is zero, stop and attach this form to your return.		
	● If line 15 is more than zero and line 2 is "Yes," go to line 16 now.		
	● If you are reporting this sale on the installment method, stop and see the instructions.		
	● All others, stop and **enter the amount from line 15 on Schedule D, col. (g), line 4 or line 12.**		
16	Fixing-up expenses (see instructions for time limits)	**16**	1,000 00
17	If line 14 is blank, enter amount from line 16. Otherwise, add lines 14 and 16	**17**	1,000 00
18	**Adjusted sales price.** Subtract line 17 from line 6	**18**	102,000 00
19a	Date you moved into new home ▶ / / **b** Cost of new home (see instructions)	**19b**	120,000 00
20	Subtract line 19b from line 18. If zero or less, enter -0-	**20**	0 00
21	**Taxable gain.** Enter the **smaller** of line 15 or line 20	**21**	0 00
	● If line 21 is zero, go to line 22 and attach this form to your return.		
	● If you are reporting this sale on the installment method, see the line 15 instructions and go to line 22.		
	● All others, **enter the amount from line 21 on Schedule D, col. (g), line 4 or line 12,** and go to line 22.		
22	Postponed gain. Subtract line 21 from line 15	**22**	38,000 00
23	**Adjusted basis of new home.** Subtract line 22 from line 19b	**23**	82,000 00

Sign Here Only If You Are Filing This Form by Itself and Not With Your Tax Return	Under penalties of perjury, I declare that I have examined this form, including attachments, and to the best of my knowledge and belief, it is true, correct, and complete.
	Your signature Date Spouse's signature Date
	▶ ▶
	If a joint return, both must sign.

For Paperwork Reduction Act Notice, see separate instructions.   Cat. No. 11710J   Form **2119** (1993)

Printed on recycled paper

*U.S. Government Printing Office: 1993 — 345-329

Strategy #224
TAKE THE ONCE-PER-LIFETIME $125,000 TAX EXCLUSION TO SAVE AS MUCH AS $35,000 IN TAXES.

You can create your own tax-free retirement program using your home and a special tax exemption created by Congress.

Once you, or your spouse, reaches age 55 and sell your home, you may elect to exclude from taxes up to $125,000 of the accumulated profits. The full exclusion can save you over $35,000 cash in taxes. Your strategy is to apply the homeowner's tax deferral rules from home to home until you or your spouse is over age 55. When you sell after 55, use Form 2119 to permanently tax exempt up to $125,000 of the accumulated profits. To qualify, you must have lived in the home for any three out of the five previous years before selling. You may use the exclusion as an individual or as a couple only once per lifetime.

If you and the person you are planning to marry are over age 55 and both own homes, you would be smart to both take the exclusion by selling your homes and making your profits tax exempt before you marry. Use tax form 2119, part three, to claim your exclusion.

An unusual court case involved a divorced couple who jointly owned a property on which the accumulated profit totaled $250,000. After their divorce, their home was sold and they each claimed the full $125,000 exclusion. The IRS said no. In an appeal, the tax court ruled in favor of the couple and allowed the full $250,000 exclusion based on the court's interpretation of the tax laws.

Since the exemption can be used only once per lifetime, continue to use the homeowner's deferral rules from home to home until you have accumulated close to the $125,000 exemption limit even if you are over age 55.

Strategy #225
CREATE A DEDUCTIBLE OFFICE AT HOME.

There is a myth perpetrated by unknowledgeable tax preparers that establishing a business office in your home will either flag you for an audit or cause you to be taxed on the home office deductions when you sell your home. Both premises are absolutely false. In his first term of office, President Reagan stressed

the importance of the free enterprise system and encouraged
regulations that would make it easier to begin a small business
with little or no red tape. At the same time he pressured the
IRS to reverse its position on home businesses and allow tax
deductions without hassle for the expenses involved. Since
1982, the IRS has reversed many of its positions relative to a tax
deductible office in the home, but most people, including many
tax professionals, are not aware of the positive changes that have
taken place. Here are the current rules for deducting an office in
your home.

RULE 1: Items you may deduct for an office in your home include
utilities, repairs, maintenance, improvements, decorating, insurance, and depreciation if you own the property, or a portion of
the rent, utilities, and improvements if you are a tenant.

RULE 2: To take the deduction for an office in the home you must
meet any one of the following conditions:

- Your home office is the primary office for your business and you do
  not have another office in the same city or area. You may not claim a
  deduction for an office in the home if you are a realtor, or a professional with another office, or if you have office space in a retail shop,
  warehouse, or plant. Teachers may not claim a deduction for an office
  in the home even if they grade papers or talk to students at home.
- You regularly see clients or patients in your home.
- You take care of children in your home or conduct home parties or
  sales meetings for your multilevel marketing business.
- You have an office in your home which is the primary and only office
  you use on behalf of your employer.

RULE 3: You may also take tax deductions if you rent out a room
or rooms in your home to college students or tenants.

RULE 4: You must use the area you call your office "regularly and
exclusively" for business, although the area does not have to be
a separate room. You may also deduct an area you use exclusively for a workshop or storage.

   The IRS has denied the deduction to those who use their
office area for other purposes, such as watching television or
storage of personal items. The IRS will normally not ask to visit
your home for inspection, but you will want to follow the
correct procedures.

RULE 5: You may compute the deductible percentage of your
expenses in one of two ways. Choose the method that gives you
the greatest tax deduction.

Method #1—Divide the number of rooms you use for tax deductible purposes by the total number of rooms in your home or apartment, not counting bathrooms. One out of five rooms used for deductible purposes would give you a 20% deduction.

Method #2—Divide the square footage of the area you use for tax deductible purposes by the total number of square feet in your home or apartment. A 2,000-square-foot home with a 400-square-foot area set aside for a deductible purpose would give you the same 20%.

RULE 6: Since you have already deducted interest on your home mortgage and property taxes as personal tax deductions, you must reduce your total home office deductions by the amount of personal deductions you have already taken for the deductible areas. See IRS publication 334 for the formula.

RULE 7: Your tax deduction is limited to the total amount of income your business earned during the year.

RULE 8: You are not penalized for home office deductions when you sell your home, provided you do not have an office or business area in your home the year you sell. Get rid of your home office the year before you intend to sell your home. Up to 1982, if you took the depreciation deduction, you would not be able to defer the entire profit from the sale of your home if you bought another home. You may, under current tax law, defer the entire profit.

GETTING THE MOST FROM THE HOME YOU OWN

1. Always own a home; don't rent.
2. Turn your home improvements into tax deductions when you sell.
3. Deduct all fix-up expenses you incur within 90 days of the date you sell your home.
4. When you sell, always buy another home of equal or greater value to defer taxes on the profits.
5. After age 55, use the $125,000 exclusion rule to make your accumulated profits tax exempt.
6. Don't invest the profits from the sale of your old home in the new home. Make the minimum down payment and put your cash in better investments.
7. Use a part of your home as the main office for your small business.
8. Use Form 2119 to claim all deferrals, improvements, and exclusions when you sell a home.

Chapter 24

MAKE YOUR BOAT, PLANE, OR RV TAX DEDUCTIBLE

True, you can't take it with you, but then, that's not the place where it comes in handy.

Unknown

OBJECTIVE

FIND BIG TAX DEDUCTIONS FOR YOUR RECREATIONAL ASSETS.

The great outdoors! Who can resist it? Exploring rivers, lakes, and cruising ocean waters for the big catch, while waiting for the camera crew of "American Sportsman" to arrive; donning the wings of eagles and flying three-dimensionally free in a personal and private plane; getting close to nature at the seashore, or high in the mountains in your own plush home on wheels. These are the dreams that inspire us to work harder. Vacations and leisure-time activities cost money. But from my own experience, I can assure you that you can easily reduce the cost of owning and operating recreational assets up to 30% by making your boat, plane, or motor home legally tax deductible.

There are two uses of recreational vehicles that qualify them for tax deductions. The first is direct use in a small business; the second is third-party leasing.

Strategy #226
USE YOUR BOAT, PLANE, OR MOTOR HOME IN YOUR SMALL BUSINESS TO CREATE TAX DEDUCTIONS.

You can turn what is now a hobby—flying, fishing, or sailing—into a tax deductible small business enterprise simply by showing the intent to make a profit. The tax code stipulates that assets used in a business that contribute directly to the production of income are tax deductible, even if you own them personally. Entertainment expenses, such as food, cleanup, and fuel, are deductible as business expenses. Depreciation, however, is not deductible unless you find a business use other than entertainment. Here is a good example.

My friend Tom lives and breathes fishing. He would rather fish than eat, except for eating fish. Year after year, weekend after weekend, he trailers his 23-foot Sea Craft behind his Ford van from his home in Richmond, Virginia, to the fertile fishing grounds of the Chesapeake Bay over a hundred miles away. Continually pouring money into gas, maintenance, fishing tackle, and motel expenses left Tom feeling as if he were working for his boat, instead of the other way around.

One day, while bobbing about in two-foot swells, Tom and I began to discuss what he could legally do to be able to take tax deductions for some of his expenses. Tom was already selling his catch of sea bass and bluefish to local restaurants, often at a handsome profit, which meant that he was in a tax deductible business. He had never thought of taking the deductions.

Tom also wrote to manufacturers of fishing rods, reels, and lures, to see if he could become a distributor, and received several enthusiastic replies, especially from the smaller companies. He was excited and well on his way. He bought several samples at wholesale (50% off) and began to show them to fellow fishermen. He used his boat to house, display, and demonstrate his new line of fishing equipment. Not only has Tom picked up some unexpected income from his venture, his expensive hobby has now become a personally and financially rewarding, tax deductible small business. Look how Tom benefited the first year alone from his small fishing-related business (table, page 308).

Item	Cost	Cash Spent	Annual Tax Deduction	% Business Use
Boat	$26,000	$ 4,000	$ 6,500	50%
Boat fuel	1,800	1,800	900	50
Van fuel	900	900	450	50
Sample costs	750	750	750	100
Cost of van	12,000	2,000	3,000	50
Motels, food	2,800	2,800	1,400	50
TOTALS		$12,250	$13,000	

Because Tom is in the 38% tax bracket (31% federal and 7% state), he received an additional refund of $4,940 (38% of his $13,000 deduction), significantly reducing the cost of his former hobby.

Here's another creative example of how to make your recreational assets deductible. Bart, a member of my organization, always loved flying, but didn't feel he could afford to own a plane. He estimated that he could buy a used, four-seater Cessna for about $22,000. Even though the cost of fuel and maintenance was slightly out of his budget at the time, Bart reasoned that if he could make a good part of his expenses tax deductible, he could afford the plane immediately.

Bart combined his interest in flying with another interest, photography, and started a small business he calls "Aerial Photos by Bart." He printed brochures and business cards and contacted realtors, the Chamber of Commerce, and the city planning commission about his new venture. He also ran ads in the classified section of the newspaper offering to give guided air tours for new families moving into the area. (For this he was required to get an additional license.) His weekend, part-time business is thriving, and he was able to convert two hobbies into a fun and profitable business. Most of all, he was able to afford his dream of owning his own plane.

There are countless ways to use recreational assets in a small business and take advantage of the tax deductions and profit potential. Here are a few ideas:

- using your plane for flying lessons
- sailing lessons on your sailboat
- chartered fishing trips on your fishing boat
- water-skiing lessons using your boat and tax deductible skis

* using your motor home as the principal office for your small business or to display your products or services
* using your motor home as a traveling billboard with your ad painted on the side

You may also deduct the business-use percentage of the interest you pay on the loan to purchase recreational assets, since business but not personal interest is deductible.

Strategy #227
USE THIRD-PARTY LEASING TO MAKE RECREATIONAL ASSETS DEDUCTIBLE.

A second method of making your recreational assets deductible and depreciable is "third-party leasing," which means offering your boat, motor home, or airplane for rent at "fair market rental value," using someone other than yourself as the leasing agent.

Why not just rent it yourself? The IRS has ruled that if you attempt to rent your recreational assets yourself, your deductions are limited to twice the amount of time the asset is actually rented. If you rented the asset four weeks per year, even though it was available for rent all year, your deduction for depreciation and other expenses would be limited to 8 weeks, instead of 52.

When you are renting through a third party—another company normally in the business of leasing—your recreational asset is considered to be used for business purposes the entire time the asset is available for rent, whether rented or not. If you use the asset for two weeks per year and it is available for rent the balance of 50 weeks, you would be allowed 11½ months or ²³⁄₂₄ of the total available tax deductions, including asset expensing and depreciation.

Leasing agents can be found for boats at most marinas; for planes at flight services or the FBO at any airport; and for motor homes in the yellow pages under Motor Homes—Renting and Leasing.

If you operate your leasing activity as an investor, your current deductions will be limited by the passive-investment rules. You can claim deductions each year only up to the amount of your passive income.

If you are active in the leasing activity, approving all leases, formulating a business plan, contracting for maintenance, doing regular inspections, and keeping the business records yourself, you will qualify to take all the deductions, including depreciation, against current income.

Even with the passive loss rules you may use the current tax deduction to shelter up to 100% of the leasing income.

Take the deductions and show your income on tax schedule C.

Of course, if your boat or motor home means so much to you that you don't want anyone else to use it, you'll just have to pay the bills yourself!

Strategy #228
DEDUCT THE INTEREST ON YOUR BOAT OR MOTOR HOME AS A SECOND HOME.

The new tax rules allow you to deduct the mortgage interest on both a first and second personal home up to $1,000,000 of acquisition cost. Normally, we think of a home as bricks and wood on a stationary concrete foundation. However, the writers of tax reform chose to define a home as almost anything with living quarters. Why then wouldn't the definition include a sailboat, yacht, or motor home with living quarters? It does, at least, until someone decides to change the law. Living quarters include a galley or kitchen, bathroom facilities, and sleeping quarters. If a boat or motor home you own or buy fits this definition, deduct the loan interest on tax schedule A.

Chapter 25

GETTING DOWN TO BUSINESS

*By working hard eight hours a day, you may eventually get to
be boss and work hard twelve hours a day.*

Robert Frost
Poet
(1874–1963)

OBJECTIVE

**START A SMALL BUSINESS FOR FUN, PROFIT, AND
HUGE TAX DEDUCTIONS.**

America was firmly established in the 1700s as the country
of independent small-business people, the country for turning
dreams into reality and wealth. For 200 years the American
business principle has survived and prospered, and today small
business falls under Congress's favored tax status. During the
past ten years, while 2 million smoke-stack industry jobs were
lost or eliminated, small business accounted for all of the 10
million new jobs that absorbed men and women into the work
force. Whether you start small and stay small or eventually
become a corporate giant, for the tax benefits alone it's worth
starting a small business.

While I was in the Soviet Union for the first time in 1985, I
had a lengthy conversation with one of the Soviet tourist guides.
"What do you do," I asked, "if you want to start your own
business in the Soviet Union?"

"Defect to the West," she answered matter-of-factly.

How fortunate, I thought, that we live in a country where small-business opportunities are so easy to come by. And now in the 1990s with the failure of communism, people in countries all over the world will share the opportunity Americans have always taken for granted.

My father started his first business when he was 10, sitting in the limbs of oak trees in La Grange, Illinois, waiting for rattle-snakes to slither along so he could trap them with a forked stick around the base of the head. He would then stuff them into a burlap bag and cart the snakes off to a local laboratory where they were sold for 17¢ a piece. My father, when he was younger, was always positive, aggressive, and incredibly calm under pressure—three winning characteristics for all successful entre-preneurs.

My first crack at the wonderful world of self-employment was a carry-out food service founded by me and my neighbor J. Allen Furguson. I was 11. Al had a gas hot plate and a refrigerator in his basement. So during the summer months we fixed lunch for all the neighborhood housewives who hated to cook three meals a day. Day after day we cooked a batch of hot dogs and hamburg-ers and delivered them semihot throughout the neighborhood for a quarter apiece. After gutsy negotiations with the grocer on the corner, we could buy three pounds of hamburger for a dollar, instead of the normal 38¢ a pound, and a loaf of bread for 14¢. Soon I was hooked. I liked the independence, freedom of choice, and unlimited opportunities that owning your own business brings. Unfortunately, I didn't stick with it. Why, I thought then, should I work the restaurant business for pennies when I could live in luxury off my 50¢-a-week allowance? Besides, there was baseball.

My own entrepreneurial experience has taught me that suc-cess in business is 80% marketing and only 20% dependent on your product or service, no matter how good your product or service. You have to work at it. But there are many great returns from starting your own business. Here are just a few. Check off those that are important to you.

- sense of accomplishment
- desire for wealth or greater income
- a sense of freedom and independence
- an opportunity to be creative
- a chance to meet people
- a chance to turn work into fun
- a chance to be your own boss and stop working for others

- an opportunity to transform personal expenses into legitimate tax deductions

---

Strategy #229
TURN ANY SMALL BUSINESS INTO A TREMENDOUS TAX SHELTER.

A business can be part-time or full-time, can require a large capital investment or no investment, can have no employees or many employees, and can be run out of a home, apartment, retail store, or office. Starting a small business, even part-time, should be considered by everyone who already works for someone else or who is retired. The possibilities are endless and so are the financial and tax opportunities and benefits—if you understand the rules. A small business, even run part-time from home, can create $6,000 to $10,000 of tax shelter every year, no matter how profitable the business is or isn't.

How small is a small business? Well, the U.S. government says that a small business is any business that grosses under $4 million per year!

In a small business, the personal things you own and do become fully or partially tax deductible when you declare that the items or activities are connected to your small business. To emphasize the importance of a small business as part of your tax strategy, here is a list of what can become deductible through your small business that is not normally deductible to you as an individual.

THINGS YOU OWN AND DO THAT CAN BECOME DEDUCTIBLE IN A SMALL BUSINESS

	Deductions I Have Now	Deductions I Would Like to Have
• Your automobile or van		
• Your automobile expenses—gas, insurance, parking, and tolls		
• Your interest on loans for cars and other assets		
• Your home		
• Your employees' wages, even if your employees are your children or spouse		

	Deductions I Have Now	Deductions I Would Like to Have
• Your boat, motor home, or airplane		
• Your home computer		
• Your domestic and foreign travel		
• Your entertainment and restaurant expenses		
• Your videotape recorder		
• Your income from your job or investments		
• Your books and subscriptions		
• Your educational audio- and videotape courses		
• Your calculator, typewriter, and cassette recorder		
• Your repairs to your automobile or other equipment		
• Your utilities and telephone		
• Your investment in a small-business retirement plan		

These deductions are just a sampling of the tax power of creating and operating your own small business; there are many more potential deductions. If you are not getting tax deductions for these expenses, plan to start a small business immediately, even part-time. If you already have a small business or if you are a self-employed professional, there are strategies and tax techniques we will cover in this chapter that your tax advisers never told you about.

Any business idea creates the potential to succeed financially. Small businesses started with little capital and winning ideas have resulted in the creation of thousands of new millionaires and multimillion-dollar corporations; McDonald's, Apple Computer, and Texas Instruments are well-known examples. As the old Coca-Cola bottles stated so clearly—"No deposit, no return." If you don't experiment with your ideas, you have no chance of success at all.

For those who are beginners, let's first concentrate on starting a part-time business. You'll discover how to make all of the expenses of your small business legally tax deductible through the small-business tax umbrella. If you own your own business already, use the strategies in this chapter as your business tax strategy checklist, putting into place those you have missed.

When you have a small business, almost every related business activity becomes legally tax deductible, even if you derive pleasure or fun in the pursuit of profits. If the business initially generates little income, it may still generate hundreds or thousands of dollars of tax deductions, which can be used to tax-shelter income from other areas of your life such as your job, your investments, or your retirement plan (see Strategy #231).

Let's get started.

Strategy #230
BEGIN YOUR BUSINESS AS A "SOLE PROPRIETORSHIP" INSTEAD OF AS A CORPORATION.

The easiest form of business to create is a "sole proprietorship." A sole proprietorship is you or you and your spouse operating a business. You use your Social Security number as the business ID for tax purposes, and you don't even report to the IRS that you are a business until you file Schedule C the following year. Most at-home, part-time businesses should start as sole proprietorships. The cost of incorporating and the paperwork involved are not worth the expense at this point. As your business grows and becomes highly profitable, you can consider incorporation. An inexpensive comprehensive small-business liability insurance policy will protect you from personal liability without the need to incorporate.

Strategy #231
USE YOUR BUSINESS "PAPER" LOSSES TO TAX-SHELTER JOB AND INVESTMENT INCOME.

With a sole proprietorship, or even an "S" corporation, you *are* your business; all of your tax deductions in excess of your business income can be used to reduce your personal federal and state income tax bill. In fact, small business is one of the few true tax shelters left after the 1986 tax law revision that still allows the use of tax deductions from one source, your business, to offset taxable income from other sources such as your job, your investments, or your retirement plan. Look at line 12 on the front of Form 1040, "U.S. Individual Income Tax Return" on page 317 and you'll notice that "Business income or loss" is included with all your other sources of income. A business becomes a personal tax shelter when it shows a "paper" loss.

Your personal taxable income is actually reduced by the total amount of your business deductions in excess of income, and your personal income taxes are reduced accordingly. If your first-year business income is $2,000 but your deductible expenses are $10,000, the $8,000 difference or loss is computed on tax schedule C, "Profit or Loss from Business," and entered on line 12 on the front of your 1040 individual tax return. The amount of the loss is subtracted from your job or other income and therefore becomes a dollar-for-dollar tax deduction.

The same thing happens if you own an "S" corporation, in which the business operates as a corporation, but all income or losses flow with certain limitations directly through to your personal tax return. Business losses for an "S" corporation are taken from Schedule K-1 and entered on 1040 Schedule E.

Look at the sample 1040 form that follows. Notice that Jim and Laura Franklin earned $40,000 from their regular full-time jobs as shown on line 7. This year they started a small business, and by taking advantage of the potential deductions that I will show you in this chapter, their "paper loss" was $8,000. Their small business loss reduced their taxable income from $40,000 to $32,000. Since their tax brackets (state and federal) total 35%, they save $2,800 in taxes. That cash they will keep in their checking account for other purposes.

Paper losses occur when you are able to take more in deductions in one year than the amount of additional cash you actually spend on business-related items that same year. For instance, strategies such as using your personal automobile, computer, and other assets in your business or hiring your children to work in your business for salaries instead of allowances create tax deductions for money you have already spent or would have spent even if you didn't have the small business. These are the types of deductions that can create "paper losses" without the expenditure of additional cash.

Because of these huge allowable deductions, paper losses are common in a new small business for the first couple of start-up years. In addition, these same types of personal expenses that now become legitimate business deductions shelter from taxes the income you earned from the sales of your product or service.

Form **1040**	Department of the Treasury—Internal Revenue Service **U.S. Individual Income Tax Return** (O) **1993**		IRS Use Only—Do not write or staple in this space.

For the year Jan. 1–Dec. 31, 1993, or other tax year beginning _____ , 1993, ending _____ , 19 ___ | OMB No. 1545-0074

Label		Your first name and initial Last name	Your social security number
(See instructions on page 12.) **Use the IRS label.** Otherwise, please print or type.	L A B E L H E R E	Jim and Laura Franklin	347:80:5995
		If a joint return, spouse's first name and initial Last name	Spouse's social security number 322:63:8106
		Home address (number and street). If you have a P.O. box, see page 12. Apt. no.	**For Privacy Act and Paperwork Reduction Act Notice, see page 4.**
		City, town or post office, state, and ZIP code. If you have a foreign address, see page 12.	

Presidential Election Campaign (See page 12.)	▶	Do you want $3 to go to this fund? . . . . If a joint return, does your spouse want $3 to go to this fund?	**Yes**	**No**	Note: Checking "Yes" will not change your tax or reduce your refund.

Filing Status

(See page 12.)

Check only
one box.

1 ☐ Single
2 ☒ Married filing joint return (even if only one had income)
3 ☐ Married filing separate return. Enter spouse's social security no. above and full name here. ▶
4 ☐ Head of household (with qualifying person). (See page 13.) If the qualifying person is a child but not your dependent, enter this child's name here. ▶
5 ☐ Qualifying widow(er) with dependent child (year spouse died ▶ 19 ___). (See page 13.)

Exemptions

(See page 13.)

If more than six
dependents,
see page 14.

6a ☐ **Yourself.** If your parent (or someone else) can claim you as a dependent on his or her tax return, do not check box 6a. But be sure to check the box on line 33b on page 2 . . . .

b ☐ **Spouse** . . . .

c	**Dependents:** (1) Name (first, initial, and last name)	(2) Check if under age 1	(3) If age 1 or older, dependent's social security number	(4) Dependent's relationship to you	(5) No. of months lived in your home in 1993

No. of boxes
checked on 6a
and 6b ☐

No. of your
children on 6c
who:
• lived with you ☐
• didn't live with
you due to
divorce or
separation (see
page 15) ☐

Dependents on 6c
not entered above ☐

d If your child didn't live with you but is claimed as your dependent under a pre-1985 agreement, check here ▶ ☐

e Total number of exemptions claimed . . . .

Add numbers
entered on
lines above ▶ ☐

Income

Attach
Copy B of your
Forms W-2,
W-2G, and
1099-R here.

If you did not
get a W-2, see
page 10.

If you are
attaching a
check or money
order, put it on
top of any
Forms W-2,
W-2G, or
1099-R.

7	Wages, salaries, tips, etc. Attach Form(s) W-2	7	40,000	00
8a	Taxable interest income (see page 16). Attach Schedule B if over $400 . . .	8a		
b	Tax-exempt interest (see page 17). DON'T include on line 8a	8b		
9	Dividend income. Attach Schedule B if over $400	9		
10	Taxable refunds, credits, or offsets of state and local income taxes (see page 17) .	10		
11	Alimony received	11		
12	Business income or (loss). Attach Schedule C or C-EZ	12	(8,000	00)
13	Capital gain or (loss). Attach Schedule D	13		
14	Capital gain distributions not reported on line 13 (see page 17) . . .	14		
15	Other gains or (losses). Attach Form 4797	15		
16a	Total IRA distributions . 16a	b Taxable amount (see page 18)	16b		
17a	Total pensions and annuities 17a	b Taxable amount (see page 18)	17b		
18	Rental real estate, royalties, partnerships, S corporations, trusts, etc. Attach Schedule E	18		
19	Farm income or (loss). Attach Schedule F	19		
20	Unemployment compensation (see page 19)	20		
21a	Social security benefits 21a	b Taxable amount (see page 19)	21b		
22	Other income. List type and amount—see page 20	22		
23	Add the amounts in the far right column for lines 7 through 22. This is your **total income** ▶	23	32,000	00

**Adjustments
to Income**

(See page 20.)

24a	Your IRA deduction (see page 20)	24a		
b	Spouse's IRA deduction (see page 20)	24b		
25	One-half of self-employment tax (see page 21) . . .	25		
26	Self-employed health insurance deduction (see page 22)	26		
27	Keogh retirement plan and self-employed SEP deduction	27		
28	Penalty on early withdrawal of savings	28		
29	Alimony paid. Recipient's SSN ▶	29		
30	Add lines 24a through 29. These are your **total adjustments** . . . . ▶	30		

**Adjusted
Gross Income**

31	Subtract line 30 from line 23. This is your **adjusted gross income.** If this amount is less than $23,050 and a child lived with you, see page EIC-1 to find out if you can claim the "Earned Income Credit" on line 56 . . . . ▶	31		

Cat. No. 11320B   Form **1040** (1993)

Strategy #232
OPERATE YOUR ACTIVITY AS A BUSINESS, NOT AS A HOBBY.

A business, according to the IRS, is any activity conducted on a regular basis with the intent to make a profit. But you are not required to make a profit in order to claim tax deductions. In order to be a business you must have a product or service that you offer regularly to the public. For tax purposes, you are a business if you sell or attempt to sell a product or service whether you actually call yourself a business or not. Your business is born the day you first offer your product or service for sale.

Intent to make a profit is what differentiates a "business" from a "hobby." A hobby is an activity that may produce income, but is operated primarily for pleasure without the intent of making a profit.

As a small business, you may deduct all of your ordinary and necessary operating expenses, no matter how great or small your income from that business. If you have more income during the year than expenses, the difference is your taxable profit. If you have more expenses than income, the difference is your excess tax loss and can be used to reduce the taxes due on your other income.

If you are running your activity as a hobby, you may still deduct your expenses, but only up to the amount of your income. Therefore, with a hobby there can be no "loss" for tax purposes, but you can still take all of the same tax deductions as in a business as long as those deductions don't exceed the income. Don't believe those who tell you that you get no deductions if your activity is a hobby.

You can show your intent to operate a business instead of a hobby by:

- Talking regularly to potential or actual customers and keeping a list
- Opening a separate bank account in your business name
- Having a telephone, even at home, in your business name
- Keeping good records of income and expenses
- Printing business cards, fliers, or brochures about your business
- Showing that your business, if successful, has the potential to generate more income than expenses. That means putting together a business plan.

Strategy #233
SHOW A PROFIT THREE OUT OF FIVE YEARS TO QUALIFY FOR CONTINUING EXCESS TAX DEDUCTIONS.

You are presumed to be engaged in a profit-making business if you show a profit in three out of five consecutive years. That means that the first two years you automatically qualify to take deductions in excess of your business income. Many taxpayers, as well as some tax professionals, incorrectly believe that the three-out-of-five rule means that if your business is still showing an operating loss after two years, you automatically lose all future tax deductions as well as those you have already taken. Not true. The first two years are considered the "ruling period" in determining whether your activity is a business or a hobby and are used by the IRS as a guideline only.

At the end of two years, if you are still showing a loss, you can use one of these many strategies:

1. Show a profit during the next three years and you will continue to be presumed to be a business. All your business-related expenses continue to be deductible.
2. Continue your activity, but as a hobby, taking deductions only up to your level of income. In other words, 100% of your business income is still deductible each year.
3. File IRS Form 5213 called "Election to Postpone Determination as to Whether the Presumption That an Activity Is Engaged In for Profit Applies," which postpones the determination of whether you are a profit-making business until after the fifth year.
4. Start another business; after all, this is America. Your ruling period starts over. You cannot, however, simply change the name of your current business in order to start a new ruling period.
5. Continue to run your business at a loss but be prepared to show the IRS that you have the intent to make a profit and have a reasonable chance of eventually doing so by putting together a written business plan. I have seen businesses continue losses and be allowed the deductions for four to eight years because the owners could show they expected to make a profit eventually.
6. Choose a business activity such as timber or animal breeding, showing, training, or racing, which requries that you show a profit in only two out of seven consecutive years.
7. Close the business. You will still keep your past years' tax deductions.

Strategy #234
ELIMINATE BUSINESS MYTHS AND OPERATE WITH
BUSINESS KNOWLEDGE.

There are so many myths and misunderstandings about how to start and run a business that the confusion prevents many people from ever getting started.

Here are the real facts no matter what you've heard from misinformed folks:

- You don't need to operate your business full-time or incorporate to take tax deductions.
- There are no requirements regarding how much money you must invest or that you must invest any money at all in order to take the deductions.
- If you are a "sole proprietorship," you do not need a tax ID number; your Social Security number will suffice, as long as you have no more than three employees who are not family members.
- You are allowed to take tax deductions on assets you buy and use in your small business, even if you buy the assets on credit.
- If you use assets part-time in your business and part-time personally, you may deduct the business portion of the cost.
- Investments such as real estate do not fall under the three-out-of-five year profit rule, but real estate should be treated as an investment, not a small business. You will still get investment deductions (see Strategy #143).
- Managing your own investments or collectibles is not considered a business, but does qualify you for investment tax deductions (see Strategy #143).
- Having a small business does not "flag" your return for audit. Only 1% of individual returns and 2% of small-business returns are audited.
- You may claim more tax deductions than income.
- Your automobile or other asset does not have to be in a business name to qualify for tax deductions.
- Record keeping and tax forms for a small business are relatively easy to complete.
- You don't need any special licenses or permits from local or national government agencies before you can take tax deductions.

> *Strategy #235*
> **CHOOSE A SMALL BUSINESS IDEA THAT IS EXCITING,
> FUN, AND IN ALIGNMENT WITH YOUR INTERESTS
> AND ABILITIES.**

There are no limits to the number of ideas for creating a small business, even one that requires little or no capital. If you need ideas for your small business venture, use the Small Business Ideas chart to get your mind moving.

The important thing is to pick something you love to do or make and turn it into a small business. Instead of looking for the most profitable idea or the ideal business, pick something you enjoy doing and your business will stand a far greater chance of success.

SMALL BUSINESS IDEAS

Services:

- Automobile tune-up
- Automobile washing, waxing
- Care for ill or elderly
- Carpet cleaning
- Catering
- Clown for children's parties
- Consulting (in anything)
- Dance instruction
- Day care for children
- Doing anything for anyone
- Flower arranging
- Foreign-language teaching
- Interior decorating
- Lawn maintenance
- Maintenance for real estate investors
- Manager for musical groups
- Office janitorial service
- Painting/wall papering
- Party organizer for adults or children
- Pet boarding
- Photography—portraits, weddings
- Real estate property management
- Real estate sales
- Roommate locating
- Teaching—golf, tennis, music
- Tool, saw, and scissor sharpening
- Tutoring
- Typing
- Videotaping—parties, weddings

Products:

- Cake baking and decorating
- Candle making
- Catering
- Christmas tree ornament making
- Dressmaking
- Jewelry making
- Making and delivering office lunches
- Quilt making
- Used books or records—buying and selling
- Woodworking from your woodworking shop

Direct Marketing:

- Amway
- Prepaid legal services
- Shaklee products

Use the Business Start-Up Checklist on page 323 to assist you in getting your small business up and running in the shortest possible time.

Strategy #236
BUY BUSINESS EQUIPMENT, FURNITURE,
COMPUTERS, AND TOOLS AT BANKRUPTCY SALES
AND AUCTIONS AT LESS THAN HALF PRICE.

As you begin your small business and as it grows, you will need office furniture, business equipment, computers, telephone systems, and other expensive assets, even for a business run out of your home. You can buy them all at less than half price. Because so many big businesses file bankruptcy these days, there are sales and auctions of business furniture, assets, and equipment going on continually in almost every area of the country. Instead of shopping at the office supply or office furniture store and paying top retail dollar, shop the auctions and buy the same or even better furniture and equipment at a fraction of the cost.

Few business owners use this strategy, so sales and auctions often have surprisingly few bidders. Advertising for bankruptcy sales is severely limited and often written in difficult-to-decipher legal jargon, so few people are aware that the auctions are being held.

Begin your search by continually checking the legal notices in the classifieds of your daily newspaper. Most cities of any size also have a legal-notices paper, published weekly or daily. Check your phone book under Newspapers and visit the publishing office for a copy. Some magazine stands also sell the legal-notice paper. On page 324 you will find a typical ad for a bankruptcy sale of office equipment. Some U.S. district bankruptcy courts will put you on a mailing list. Give your district court a call.

Auctions are either oral bid or sealed bid. With an oral bid, each item or group of items is auctioned off with all bidders bidding out loud and against each other. The high bidder wins. Don't get carried away with your bid—there is always another sale another day.

Sealed-bid auctions require that you place your bid in a "sealed" envelope, often with a check for 10 to 50% of your bid, which is returnable if you lose. All bids are open at one time, often publicly. High bid wins.

BUSINESS START-UP CHECKLIST

___ Choose a business idea based on your interests, abilities, and the amount of time you want to spend.

Your Small Business Ideas
(see page 321 for additional ideas)

_____

_____

_____

_____

_____

___ Obtain Publication 334, "Tax Guide for Small Business," from the IRS and read Part I, "The Business Organization," and Part II, "Business Assets."

___ Choose a business form—sole proprietorship, partnership, or corporation. Sole proprietorship is the simplest.

___ Set up your business record-keeping system. Simple record-keeping books are available at any office supply store. Get IRS Publication 583. Read *Financial Self-Defense,* Chapter 2, "Creating a Records Management System."

___ Read *Financial Self-Defense,* Chapter 17, "How to Keep Records for Maximum Tax Deductions."

___ Choose a business name. If your last name is included in the business name, most states do not require you to file under the fictitious-name statute.

Business Name Ideas

_____

_____

_____

___ Set up a business checking account. When you are asked for your business ID number, give your Social Security number.

___ Print business cards and fliers.

___ Begin offering your product or services for sale to friends and others. Remember, any business is 80% marketing and only 20% dependent upon your product or service.

___ Learn everything you can about business from books, magazines, tape courses, seminars, and trade publications.

___ Get business educational materials form the Small Business Administration and the Charles J. Givens Organization.

Have fun. It's work only if you don't like what you are doing.

Make sure you inspect before you buy. Often there is a preauction time and date to inspect items.

IN THE UNITED STATES BANKRUPTCY COURT
FOR THE NORTHERN DISTRICT OF ILLINOIS
EASTERN DIVISION

IN RE:)   Case No. 91 B 10487
CABLE   )   Chapter 11
CORPORATION   )   Hon. Erwin I. Katz
    DEBTOR   )   Sale Date: June 10, 1991, 2:00 p.m.

DEBTOR'S NOTICE OF INTENT TO SELL ASSETS OUT OF THE ORDINARY COURSE OF BUSINESS, FREE AND CLEAR OF LIENS AND OTHER INTERESTS

TO: CREDITORS AND OTHER PARTIES IN INTEREST YOU ARE HEREBY ADVISED AS FOLLOWS:

1. The above-entitled case was commenced on May 15, 1991, by the filing of an involuntary petition for relief under chapter 7 of the Bankruptcy Code, 11 U.S.C. Section 101, et seq. (the "Code"), in the United States Bankruptcy Court (the "Court") against Cable Corporation (the "Debtor").

2. The Debtor has determined to sell certain of its assets. The Court has set a sale date of June 10, 1991, at 2:00 p.m. in Courtroom 1644 of the Everett McKinley Dirksen Building, 219 South Dearborn Street, Chicago, Illinois 60604, at which time and place you may bid to purchase these assets.   ← Date, time, and location of sale

3. Parties interested in acquiring all or any part of the Assets may submit bids in open court on June 10, 1991, at 2:00 p.m.   ← When and how

a. Bids will be accepted either for all of the assets in bulk, or on one or more individual lots. A listing of the individual lots will be available upon inquiry to Debtor's counsel, Robert D. Nachman, Schwartz, Cooper, Lolb & Gaynor, 20 S. Clark St., suite 1100, Chicago, IL 60603; by telephone (312) 845-3027; or fax (312) 726-0886, during regular business hours.

b. Bids for individual lots will be received in any amount.   ← The minimum bid

c. All bids must be accompanied by a nonrefundable deposit in the form of cash, irrevocable letter of credit or certified funds, in a minimum amount of fifty percent (50%) of the bid.   ← Deposit requirement

d. The balance of each successful bid is payable in cash within seven (7) calendar days of court approval of sale.   ← When the balance must be paid

4. FOR BOTH THE MACHINERY AND EQUIPMENT AND THE INVENTORY, THE DEBTOR WILL EXTEND A WARRANTY OF TITLE FOR THE ASSETS, BUT WILL EXTEND NO OTHER WARRANTIES. THEY WILL THUS BE SOLD "AS IS, WHERE IS," AND ANY WARRANTIES OF FITNESS FOR A PARTICULAR PURPOSE OR MERCHANTABILITY ARE EXCLUDED.   ← Are the items guaranteed?

5. All proceeds from the sale shall be paid to the American National Bank and Trust Company of Chicago ("ANB") in partial satisfaction of its first priority lien on the assets sold, up to the amount of ANB's secured claim. It is not anticipated that proceeds of the sale will be available for distribution to holders of unsecured claims. Pending the sale, ANB will advance to Debtor $23,000 for payroll, insurance, and advertising. To secure the advance, Debtor will grant to ANB a first lien and security interest in all property of the estate.   ← What is to be done with the money raised?

6. Inspection of the Assets will be permitted on May 31, June 3, 4, 6, or 7, 1991, at the Debtor's place of business, 1811 West Bryn Mawr, Chicago, Illinois, 60660 between the hours of 10:00 a.m. and 5:00 p.m. All persons wishing to inspect the Assets must give Debtor notice of intent to inspect the Assets on or before 3:00 p.m. of the prior business day. Notice may be given by telephone (312) 969-5900; or fax (312) 969-5933. An itemized list of Assets to be sold will also be available on-site during inspection times.   ← Preinspection times and dates

Greater success and profits in your small business are created in part by your ability to cut unnecessary costs. Auctions and bankruptcy sales give you that opportunity.

MAXIMIZING BUSINESS DEDUCTIONS

Big tax deductions are not something that happens to you but something you create through smart tax planning and the use of the following strategies. Your small business gives you lots of great opportunities for creating thousands each year in new tax deductions.

Strategy #237
BEGIN MARKETING IMMEDIATELY TO MAKE BUSINESS START-UP COSTS DEDUCTIBLE THE FIRST YEAR.

Business start-up costs that you incur prior to marketing a product or service must be deducted or amortized over a five-year period at 20% per year. Expenses you incur after your business begins are fully deductible in the year you spend the money. Begin marketing your product or service immediately to establish the starting date of your business. All start-up expenses will then be deductible in the current year.

Strategy #238
HIRE YOUR SPOUSE AND CREATE A DEDUCTIBLE IRA.

You can create up to a $1,750 tax deduction each year by hiring your nonworking spouse to work in your small business, and using the salary you pay your spouse to open a fully deductible IRA.

George owns a small sportswear company. He and his wife, Sally, contribute $2,250 to IRAs each year using the spousal IRA provision. He would like to be able to contribute $2,000 to an IRA for Sally, who hasn't worked for several years. George hires Sally to do his paperwork and filing and help him with correspondence, paying her by check $300 per month. George pays no additional taxes, nor does Sally, since they file jointly. What is income to Sally is a deduction for George. Sally puts the first $2,000 she earns into an IRA, saving the family more than

$500 in taxes. That won't, of course, prevent Sally from asking for a raise.

You can also hire parents or other adult family members to work in your small business. Ted's father, Ben, resides in a nursing home. Ben's only disability involves physical limitations of his legs. In addition to the money from Ben's Social Security check, Ted pays the nursing home $500 per month ($6,000 per year), none of which is tax deductible. Ted started a small mail order business in his home and hired his father to stuff, hand-address, and sort 500 envelopes per week. Ted pays Ben $500 each month for the work, and Ben uses the money to pay his own $500 monthly nursing home expense. Ted now takes a $6,000 yearly tax deduction, and Ben derives a sense of real worth by actively participating in his son's business venture. Ben is within the Social Security earnings limitation and therefore loses no Social Security payments due to the income.

Strategy #239
QUALIFY YOUR SPOUSE FOR SOCIAL SECURITY BENEFITS.

A recent tax law now requires the payment of FICA Social Security taxes when one spouse hires another. You can turn the new rule into greater retirement income.

Herb worked all his life at General Electric, while his wife, Ethel, managed the home and raised the kids. Although Ethel worked hard for the family, she doesn't qualify for maximum Social Security benefits. Herb started a small part-time sports equipment business and hired Ethel to manage the business and correspond with the customers. Herb pays Ethel a salary of $10,000 a year, from which she contributes to the family expenses. By paying Social Security taxes for ten years, Ethel is now qualified to receive Social Security income when she reaches age 65 for the rest of her life.

Strategy #240
HIRE YOUR CHILDREN AND GRANDCHILDREN AND MAKE KIDS' ALLOWANCES AND GIFTS DEDUCTIBLE.

As a teenager, I arose at 4:00 A.M. every morning to deliver the *Chicago Tribune* to west-end subscribers in my hometown of Decatur, Illinois. When everyone paid, my net profit was $7.40 a week for a daily four-mile bike ride. Eventually, my father offered me an evening job with his home improvement business. I was moving up the corporate ladder. Instead of riding four miles in the morning, I began riding four miles every afternoon to the C. J. Givens company, where my after-office-hours responsibilities included sweeping floors and taking phone messages. Boy, did that make me feel important! I felt more like a business executive than a part-time janitor. My father also felt great, taking a tax deduction for each of the five dollars he paid me once a week.

If you have or start a small business, even part-time, you can hire your children or grandchildren and turn nondeductible allowances, gifts, and expensive handouts into tax deductible salaries. Depending on their ages, the kids can perform any number of tasks including:

- cleaning the business office
- washing the business automobile
- answering the phone when you are away
- stuffing and addressing envelopes
- keeping track of inventory
- delivering products
- running business errands
- entering data on the computer

You can pay deductible salaries to children to perform jobs either for your small business or to help you in your regular employment. Give your family employee a W-2 form at the end of the year showing the salary paid.

Pay two children or grandchildren salaries of $20 per week each for a few hours of work instead of giving them nondeductible allowances, gifts, and handouts, and you have created a $2,000-per-year legal tax deduction. The money the kids earn can be used for school lunches, clothes, entertainment, investments, or even an IRA.

An example, hire your two children to work in your small business and pay them each $20 per week: $10 is used for entertainment and allowances, $10 each goes into an investment account in their names. Your tax deduction is the amount you pay the children. You save $645 per year if you are in the 31% bracket (2 children × $20 per week each × 52 weeks = $2,080; 31% bracket × $2,080 deduction = $645 cash tax saving). The kids are involved, having fun, learning responsibility, and you are pocketing over $600 a year from the tax savings.

Bob Vorse, a member of my organization, hired his 11-year-old son, who had a knack for computer programming. He started a small business and paid his son, Jeff, $10 per hour to write simple business programs. Jeff works three hours a week. Can Bob legally take a tax deduction for the $30 per week he pays his son? Yes, as long as Jeff actually does the work. Bob would have to pay a programmer from outside the family as much as $25 to $50 an hour for programming services, so he is within the rules. It doesn't matter that Jeff is only 11.

By using this strategy, Bob created a $1,500-per-year tax deduction (50 weeks × $30 per week). His home computer is now tax deductible because he is using it in his small business, and he is enjoying the benefit of working on an important project with his son. Since the $1,500 is Jeff's only income, Jeff pays no income tax.

Does the IRS frown on the hiring of family members? Not at all. The procedures and rules for hiring family members are well established in tax law and make hiring family members less troublesome than hiring other employees.

Here are the rules that qualify you for family-salary tax deductions:

1. The family members must do the work for which they are paid. It would not be honest or deductible to pay a family member for work not performed simply to claim a tax deduction.
2. You pay a family member a deductible salary of up to the amount you would have to pay a nonfamily member to do the same job. The pay cannot be excessive for the work performed. Squelch any tendency to overpay a family member in order to claim a greater tax deduction. However, someone from outside the family must be paid the minimum wage, so no matter how menial the job, the minimum wage is not unreasonable and is fully deductible.
3. Salaries paid to children under 18 are not subject to Social Security tax.

4. No federal income tax withholding is required if the child is paid under $3,800 per year.

5. You are not required to pay Federal Unemployment Insurance on children under 21 or spouses.

6. Salaries are treated as tax deductible wages by you as the employer, and as taxable income by your family member employees. You lose the tax advantages if you pay wages to a family member who is in a higher tax bracket than you.

7. The pay must be periodic. Pay family members by check at least once a month, as you would any employee. If you were to pay a year's worth of wages in the last month of the year, it would not appear that the intent was for wages. If you pay by cash, have someone else keep a written record of the payments to family members.

Strategy #241
WHEN YOU HIRE YOUR CHILDREN, KEEP THE $2,450 DEPENDENCY EXEMPTION YOURSELF.

You may at first think hiring your child or children may not be worth it because you might lose the dependency exemption. Not so. Each person in a family entitles the family to a $2,450 automatic exemption on its tax return just for being alive. Husband and wife each provide an exemption and neither is considered a dependent. Children or others you support are considered dependents. In general, you are entitled to take the $2,450 dependency deduction as long as you provide more than 50% of the dependent's income for the year and the dependent's income is under $2,450.

When you hire your child as shown in the previous strategy, you keep the tax exemption of $2,450 even though you are taking the tax deductions for salaries paid. You have effectively doubled the tax deductions you get for each child, allowing you to raise your children on tax deductible dollars.

There is an exception for your children who are full-time students or living at home and who are under the age of 19. You may claim the dependency exemption for your children in this category regardless of their income. No formulas, no tests, no limits.

Strategy #242
PAY YOUR CHILD UP TO $3,800 WITHOUT YOUR CHILD HAVING TO PAY TAXES OR FILE A RETURN.

Current tax rules require that a dependent child file a tax return and pay taxes only if his or her gross (total) income is over $3,800. That means you can pay each of your dependent children up to $3,800 as a salary and take the deduction for the same amount yourself without having to file a tax return for the child or children. The only exception is if your child has unearned (investment) income of $600 or more. Then you must file a return for your child whether or not you pay him or her a salary.

Strategy #243
BEAT THE KIDDIE TAX WITH A KIDDIE IRA.

Under tax reform, the first $600 per year of investment income for a child is not taxed, the next $600 is taxed at 15%, and any investment income above $1,200 is taxed at the parent's higher tax rate. These new rules make it difficult to build a college fund or to transfer investments and assets to your children and grandchildren without incurring extra taxes.

Salaries you pay your children can help circumvent this so-called kiddie tax if you put the money in an IRA. Even though a child does not pay taxes on a salary unless the salary is over $3,800, any earnings of over $1,200 per year from the investment of the salary will be taxed at the parent's rate. That's the so-called kiddie tax.

You can beat the kiddie tax rule by opening an IRA for your child. There is no age limit on an IRA, but the money deposited must come from employment. Since IRAs are tax deferrals whose income is not subject to taxes, the child may earn over $1,000 from IRA investments and pay absolutely no taxes. The money compounds completely tax free until it is withdrawn.

You can build a $50,000 college education fund by depositing only $2,000 for each of eleven years in the child's IRA and using any of the 15 to 20% per year investment opportunities you will learn in the investment section of this book. Using this strategy, you create a double tax deduction. Parents get the salary deduction and the child gets the IRA deduction and beats the kiddie tax on investment income.

Over the years I've seen families become incredibly creative with this strategy. A few years ago, a couple approached me after a workshop I was conducting, wanting to start their own small business and hire their child. "What can we do with our son?" they asked. "He is only seven months old." Barely old enough to walk and talk, let alone work. At the time I didn't have the answer, but that didn't stop them. A few months later I saw the couple again and they were beaming: "Well, we've done it; we now employ our son in our small business and take all the tax deductions."

My curiosity was piqued. "What can a toddler that age possibly do as a job?" I asked.

"After your workshop, we went to a baby-furniture store and got the owner to agree to let us sell his baby furniture for a commission at home parties. That's our small business. We pay our son $40 a week to model the cribs and bassinets. His $2,000-per-year salary is tax deductible, and we are putting the money away in an IRA just like you suggested for his tax deductible college education."

This couple achieved two objectives: funding their child's education, and creating a $2,000-per-year tax deduction in the process. Because they are in the 28% tax bracket, they save $560 each year in taxes, money that can be used on other things. The child pays no taxes on either the salary or the earnings in the IRA.

Yes, there is a 10% penalty when the money is taken out and used for college or other purposes, but after several years of tax-free compounding the penalty is virtually meaningless. At age 18 that 10% is the equivalent of only the last nine months of interest if invested using any of my 15% investment strategies you'll learn later.

Strategy #244
CIRCUMVENT THE SCHEDULE A MEDICAL EXPENSE LIMITATION THROUGH YOUR SMALL BUSINESS.

In the past few years Congress decided that too much tax money was being lost by allowing individuals and families to deduct their doctor, hospital, health insurance, and medicine costs on Schedule A. A new tax law was passed that limited the medical deduction that can be claimed on Schedule A to the amount over 7.5% of your adjusted gross income, which in turn is limited as part of the total itemized deductions that must exceed $5,700 for couples and $3,400 for singles. In other words, a great majority of families no longer get any medical expense deductions at all! If adjusted gross family income is $30,000, only the medical expenses over $2,250 paid out-of-pocket can be deducted, and then only to the extent the itemized deduction limit is exceeded.

If you have a small business, however, the deduction prospects for medical expenses are brighter. You may, as a small business owner, deduct 25% of all health insurance premiums you pay during the year on line 26 on the front of your 1040 form as an adjustment to income. No limits apply, just a straight deduction. If you are an active partner in a partnership or a shareholder of more than 2% of an "S" corporation, you also qualify for the deduction.

If you have a family of four and you are paying $300 a month or $3,600 per year for insurance, $900 become deductible on line 26, saving you about $300 cash in taxes. It's sort of like getting a little less than a 10% cash rebate for the premiums you pay. However, there is a limitation as to which small business owners qualify. If you or your spouse is qualified to participate in an employer's subsidized health insurance plan, you do not qualify for the deduction. But then so what? If your employer pays 50% of your total health insurance premiums of $3,600, you are getting the equivalent of $1,800 tax free—a better health insurance deal than even the $300 tax savings from the small business deduction.

Strategy #245
INSURE YOUR PERSONAL CAR USED PART-TIME IN YOUR SMALL BUSINESS AS A PERSONAL CAR, NOT A COMPANY CAR.

If you insure a car used part-time in your business as a company car instead of a personal car, your premiums can as much as double. The question then becomes: "If I buy a personal policy on my car, have an accident, and then the company discovers that I use the car part-time in my business, will it pay?" The answer is yes, and your insurance company normally won't cancel your policy for that reason. It may require you in the future to insure your car as a business car; that is, if it doesn't drop you for just having the accident.

Many insurance agents will tell you that it is O.K. with their insurance company for you to insure your car as a personal vehicle if all you do is use it occasionally for your small business. This approach, however, would not apply if the vehicle is a truck or van that is primarily a business vehicle or if your personal car is regularly driven by an employee other than you or your spouse. If you have any doubts or concerns, call your auto insurance agent. If you don't like the answers, check around for other companies that may treat the use of a personal car in business more favorably.

Strategy #246
CONSIDER BUYING AN AUTOMOBILE INSTEAD OF LEASING FOR GREATER DEDUCTIONS AND FLEXIBILITY.

To buy or lease, that is the question. Listen to a salesman pushing a lease and you will wonder why you even considered buying and borrowing the money for your automobile. But what is the mathematical truth when comparing the two options?

Since you are going to use the automobile in your small business, one important question is which financing method will give you the greatest deduction. Here are the rules for deducting a leased car that few know and salesmen often neglect to tell you about.

"DEDUCTIBLE PERCENTAGE." Car salesmen everywhere are still saying that if you lease, your payments are 100% deductible. Never get your tax advice from a car salesman. The tax law says that you may deduct only the business use percentage of the cost and operating expenses whether you buy or lease. If you use your car 60% for business and 40% personally, then only 60% of your lease payments are deductible.

"DEDUCTION LIMIT." Many who have leased their cars have done so thinking that they have beaten the maximum yearly depreciation deduction limit on luxury cars. When you buy a car, your maximum deduction each year is limited to the depreciation on a car costing $13,400 (see the chart on page 349). This rule was dreamed up by Congress to prevent smart businesspeople from quickly writing off the cost of Jaguars, Mercedes, BMWs, and other expensive cars. The part of the cost that is not deducted in the first five years because of the "luxury car" limits can, however, be deducted in subsequent years, so the deductions are not totally lost.

What if you are told by the leasing salesman that your lease payments have no such limitations. Is it true? Not on your life. Although you are not limited by the amount of the deduction you can take, if the car you leased has a fair market value of over $13,400, you must add a fixed-dollar amount each year to your taxable income as determined by Congress, creating the same effect as the luxury-car deduction limit! The added income applies to any car you rent or lease for more than 30 days. The amount that you must claim as income each year is reduced by any portion of the year you did not lease the car.

ADDITIONAL TAXABLE INCOME CREATED WITH AN AUTOMOBILE LEASE

Fair Market Value When Leased	Add to Your Taxable Income During the First Year of the Lease
$15,000	$ 4
16,000	9
17,000	17
18,000	22
19,000	28
20,000	34
25,000	64
30,000	92
35,000	115
40,000	149
50,000	206

See IRS Publication 917, Business Use of a Car.

Here are some other claimed but untrue benefits of a lease:

"NO DOWN PAYMENT." Cash is cash. When you lease a car, even though you are told there is no down payment, you normally put up the first and last one or two months' payments in advance. If your lease payment is $400 per month on a $20,000 car, you might have to come up with $1,200, and $1,200 is $1,200, whether you call it a deposit or a down payment. Either way, you don't get the money back.

If the down payment you would be required to make exceeds the required deposit on a lease for the same car, you are about to pay too much money for the car anyway and should shop elsewhere. If the same $1,200 is used as a down payment on a loan, you finance and pay interest only on the balance, in this case $18,800 ($20,000 − $1,200). When you lease and your money is held as a deposit, it is often not counted as a deduction from the total purchase price. Therefore, you continue to pay interest for the term of the lease on money you have already paid! Nice gimmick.

"PAYMENTS ARE LESS." The lower-payments feature of a lease is attractive, but like everything else, it occurs at your expense. How is it possible that if you lease a car, your payments are lower than if you finance the same car at your bank? Simple. During the lease term you are paying toward the principal or cost of the car only an amount equal to the expected depreciation of the car over the lease term. If you lease a $20,000 car and the leasing agent's book shows that the anticipated value after five years will be $7,000, the principal portion of your payments is enough to pay off only the $13,000 difference. At the end of the lease term, if you wanted the car, you would have to pay the $7,000 in a lump sum of cash, or by financing the car again. Otherwise, you would lose the car to the leasing company.

If you bought the car instead of leasing, your payments would be higher because the $7,000 residual would be included in your payments. In other words, at the end of the same period, you would not owe the $7,000 or lose the car; you would owe nothing and the car would be yours. Here there is no right answer. Yes, your payments are less with the lease, but your payments are not buying you a car.

The real downside to the lease is that to create lower payments, leases are usually four to five years. Once you have locked into a long-term lease, you cannot break it without paying huge amounts of cash. If you have a five-year lease on which you have made 18 months of payments and you want out, you might have to come up with $5,000 or more in cash to cancel. In effect, you would be restructuring your lease to an 18-month term, and you would have to come up with a lump sum representing the total difference in payments plus the costs of canceling.

In addition, most leases now limit the number of free miles you can drive during the period of the lease. Typically you are limited to 15,000 miles per year, over which you might be charged an extra 15¢ per mile. Drive 10,000 miles more than the limit shown in the contract and it will cost you an additional

$1,500 to get rid of the car if you decide to give it back at the end of the lease.

"A LEASE DOESN'T HAVE AN INTEREST RATE." A normal question to ask when leasing is, What is the interest rate? "Oh," you're told as if you were an idiot, "leases don't have interest rates, only a lease factor." A lease factor is the decimal fraction that when multiplied times the total lease basis or cost of the vehicle gives you the monthly payment. The lease factor actually is derived by determining the interest rate to be charged, but the interest rate never appears anywhere. There's the catch. How do you know you aren't paying 14%, 18%, or 22% interest? You may be and never know it.

See *Financial Self-Defense*, Defense #101: Never sign a car or equipment lease without knowing the annual percentage rate. You learn how to use your calculator to compute the real interest rate from any lease terms.

In addition to what you are told by the salesperson, your lease contract will require you to carry high-limit liability insurance and low-deductible comprehensive and collision limits. Although these insurance requirements are sometimes negotiable, they increase the real cost of driving the car the same as higher payments would. If these are not the limits you need (see Chapter 3), you lose both money and flexibility. Don't forget to watch out for the credit life and disability insurance gimmicks that will easily find their way onto your contract. Decline them (see Strategy #44).

Now that you understand car leasing, you are in a position to negotiate a better lease, but you can also see that leasing is no better (and in reality no different) from buying. Both are just methods of financing a car for which you don't intend to pay cash.

I am not fond of leasing because it is so easy for you to get jerked around and never know it. Here are the important rules to follow to assure yourself of the best deal when buying or leasing a car:

- Never buy or lease a car for over 36 months. If you do, you'll never be out of debt.
- Never buy a new car. Buy the car you want only after it is two years old. You'll save 50%. Generally leases are available only on new cars.
- Never sign a lease agreement without computing the APR.
- Never sign a lease agreement with an APR over 12%.
- Renegotiate the insurance required on a lease to the limits you want or turn down the lease.

- Realize that when you lease, you are stuck with the car for the term of the lease. You cannot sell it for enough to pay off the cost of a revised shorter-term lease.
- Never let emotion or desire creep into your car acquisition plan. Walk away if it isn't exactly the deal you want.
- Read *Financial Self-Defense*, Chapter 3, "Save up to 60 Percent on Every Car You Buy."

Strategy #247
USE YOUR PERSONAL ASSETS IN YOUR SMALL BUSINESS AND DEDUCT THE BUSINESS USE PERCENTAGE.

Using your personal equipment, such as home computers, videotape recorders, cassette recorders, calculators, tools, or furniture, in your business makes these assets deductible. The percentage of time you use an item for business versus personal use determines how much of the cost you can deduct. You may deduct the business use percentage of an item but not the personal use percentage.

It is important to understand the difference between personal and business use. Here are some examples. Your computer is used for business when used for record keeping, business projections, or computing your business tax deductions. Your videotape recorder is used for business when you buy or rent videotapes that relate to any phase of your business. Your video camera is deductible if you use it at conventions or lectures, for practicing sales presentations, or in any other way that relates to your business. Computer and video supplies are fully deductible when used for business purposes. The furniture in your business office, whether at home or at a separate location, is deductible. Your typewriter, filing cabinet, calculator, and cassette recorder are also deductible if used in your small business.

Any tools and equipment are deductible when used even part-time for a business purpose, such as:

- Musical instruments used in a band.
- A lathe and drill press in a home woodworking shop.
- A sewing machine used for making quilts or other items to sell.
- A steam-cleaning machine used in a part-time carpet cleaning business.
- Cameras and darkroom equipment used in a photography business.

Your tax deduction is computed based on the percentage of time you use the equipment for business, and the business percentage multiplied by the cost becomes your basis for depreciation or asset expensing. For instance:

Item Used in Small Business	Cost		Business Use		Tax Deduction Basis
Videotape recorder	$ 800	×	60%	=	$ 480
Video camera	700	×	60	=	420
Home computer	2,500	×	80	=	2,000
Office furniture	1,500	×	100	=	1,500
Tools & equipment	600	×	100	=	600
Typewriter	250	×	100	=	250
TOTAL	$6,350				$5,250

Since these assets are used over 50% of the time for business, they qualify for "asset expensing," which allows you to deduct as a onetime expense up to $17,500 each year. If you bought all of these items in the current tax year you could deduct 100% of the basis or $5,250, even if you still have payments left on your credit card (see Strategy #249).

If you already owned some of these items when you began your business and you use them over 50% of the time for business, you would deduct the cost using the MACRS depreciation method (see Strategy #250). If any of the items you own are used less than 50% of the time for business, you use the straight-line depreciation method (see Strategy #250). If your state and federal income tax brackets totaled 35%, a $5,250 deduction would save you $1,837 in taxes, a nice rebate on the electronics and equipment you own.

Strategy #248
USE THE SIMPLIFIED 90-DAY RECORD-KEEPING METHOD TO ALLOCATE THE BUSINESS AND PERSONAL USE PERCENTAGE OF ASSETS.

When you use assets both personally and for business, you must keep specific records to determine the percentage of time you use the assets for business. Remember, only the business use percentage is deductible.

IRS record-keeping requirements are not as complicated as they were a few years ago. For home computers and video recorders/cameras, the simplest, most effective system is to keep a sheet of paper taped to the equipment. You need only three columns.

Column 1: Date
Column 2: Amount of time used—personal
Column 3: Amount of time used—business

The IRS now allows you to keep the log for only three months out of the tax year, and if the percentage of business usage has been and remains consistent, you may use the three-month business percentage for the entire year, without further record keeping. Before tax reform, Congress created a mandatory "Adequate Contemporaneous" record-keeping rule that required you to keep detailed records of personal and business use for the entire year. Since no one in Congress could spell it, let alone wanted to use it, the record-keeping rules were changed and simplified. At the end of the year when doing your taxes, simply calculate the business use percentage by dividing the business use hours by the total hours used during your 90-day record-keeping period.

You can determine the business use percentage of your automobile by dividing the number of business miles driven by the total miles driven during the year. It's easy. Keep an automobile expense and mileage logbook either above your visor or on the dashboard where you can see it. Although you can use just a sheet of paper or small notebook, inexpensive auto-expense logs are available at office supply stores.

Each year on January 1, write down the mileage that is your beginning odometer reading for the current tax year and the end reading for last year. The difference between the reading on January 1 of this year and January 1 of last year is your total mileage for the year. If you are in the middle of a year when you begin using your car for business purposes, start with the mileage reading on that date.

Now all you need to do is keep a list in your logbook of the mileage of each business-related use of the car. When the car use is personal, no entry is required. At the end of the year, total the business miles driven, divide the total business miles by the total overall miles driven, and you have computed your business use percentage.

For example:

$$\frac{\text{Business miles} = 9{,}000}{\text{Total miles} = 17{,}000} = 53\% \text{ business use}$$

If you do not have the records, you are not prevented from taking the deduction, but in an audit you would have to convince the auditor verbally that your deduction was correct.

One of the best big tax deduction opportunities that comes with any business, even a part-time business, is depreciation. Depreciation is simply the deduction each year of a percentage of the cost of an expensive item that you use full- or part-time in your small business. When you buy any high-priced asset such as a car, computer, furniture, or equipment and use it in your small business, 100% of the money you paid reduced by the percent of time you use the asset personally becomes a tax deduction over a five- or seven-year period. These deductions can amount to hundreds, usually thousands, of dollars per year.

In essence, when you apply the depreciation formulas to the cost of your automobile, computer, VCR, cameras, or any other assets used full- or part-time in your business, the IRS is refunding you about one-third of the money you spent to buy the asset. To maximize your potential deductions, it is important that you learn how to use the rules and formulas for asset expensing, MACRS depreciation, and straight-line depreciation. We'll make them easy.

Strategy #249
USE THE ASSET-EXPENSING RULES FOR IMMEDIATE DEDUCTIONS ON BUSINESS ASSETS YOU BUY.

Asset expensing is the absolute best way to get maximum tax deductions quickly for the expensive assets or property you buy and use even part-time in your business. Section 179 of the Internal Revenue Code allows you to treat the first $17,500 of assets you buy each year and use in your small business as a currently deductible expense instead of a capital expenditure, which would be subject to long-term depreciation. This process is called "asset expensing." You may use asset expensing even on items such as a car or computer that you also use personally as long as the business use percentage is 50% or greater.

Here are the asset expensing rules. They are not at all complicated! Remember, you must use the property more than 50% of the time for business purposes to qualify for asset expensing. You then multiply the actual business use percentage times the cost of the property to determine how much you may deduct using the asset expensing rules. In most part-time businesses, the $17,500 limit covers everything bought for the year. You take the deduction for asset expensing on Form 4562, "Depreciation and Amortization." Asset expensing is used in lieu of depreciation, which is the process of deducting the cost over a period of several years. Once you have begun depreciating an asset, you cannot change your mind and amend your previous years' tax returns from depreciation to expensing.

The maximum amount you can deduct for asset expensing is limited to the taxable income of the business. In other words, you can use expensing to get you down to zero taxable income but cannot use expensing to show a loss. Once you have reached the zero taxable income level, any excess can be depreciated, creating a "paper" loss.

The asset expensing limit on an automobile is $2,860, which is the same as the maximum amount of depreciation that could be taken the first year on a car costing $13,400. The balance of the cost is deducted or depreciated over a five-year period.

You can take the full asset expensing tax deduction no matter when you bought the asset during the year. If you bought a second car costing $14,000 to be designated a business car, you could still claim the full $2,860 under asset expensing for the year even though you had only owned the car one day during the year and not even made a payment.

Asset expensing rules cannot be used on real estate or investment property. However, partners in a business or stockholders in an "S" corporation can *each* claim up to the $10,000 asset expensing limit for items used in the business.

Once you use asset expensing, be certain that your business use percentage does not drop below 50%. If it did, you would have to add to your income all the asset expensing deductions you took that were above the amount you would have received up to that year using the straight-line depreciation method.

Strategy #250
USE THE DEPRECIATION FORMULAS TO GENERATE BIG TAX DEDUCTIONS ON ITEMS THAT DON'T QUALIFY FOR ASSET EXPENSING.

The number of years over which you are required to deduct the cost of an asset is determined by Congress and is called the "life" of the asset. Most or all of the assets you will depreciate in your business will fall into the five- or seven-year class as shown in the chart on page 343. The methods or formulas for depreciating your assets over this period of years are also determined by Congress. Your two choices are the straight-line depreciation method and the MACRS depreciation method.

Straight-Line Depreciation Method—You take the same amount of depreciation each year over the life of the asset. An asset with a five-year life costing $1,000 would be depreciated at 20% or $200 per year for five years, at which time you would have deducted 100% of the cost. If you use an asset both personally and for business and the business use percentage is less than 50%, you must use the straight-line method. Otherwise straight-line is the least desirable because it gives you tax deductions less quickly than asset expensing or the MACRS depreciation method.

MACRS (Modified Accelerated Cost Recovery System) Depreciation Method—The MACRS depreciation method gives you greater tax deductions in the early years with the deduction amount decreasing each year. When the decreased deduction amount becomes less than the amount you would deduct using the straight-line formula, you are allowed to switch to straight-line depreciation until your asset is fully depreciated. The MACRS method is what is called a double-declining-balance formula. Don't let the term throw you. It just means you would get about double the depreciation the first year with the MACRS method as you would with the straight-line method. In your business you will normally choose the MACRS method for depreciating any items on which you can't use asset expensing but that you do use over 50% of the time for business.

ASSET LIFE
To calculate depreciation, you must first know the number of years over which you will be required to depreciate or to deduct

the cost of the asset. This period is called the asset life, and the asset lives for various types of property are shown below. The number of years for depreciation or asset life for property other than real estate is the same whether you use the straight-line or MACRS depreciation method. Commercial real estate must be depreciated over a 39-year period using the straight-line method only. The less the number of years in the asset life, the greater the tax deduction each year.

THREE YEARS (you won't use this category much):
- Breeding hogs
- Tools used in the manufacture of rubber products
- Race horses
- Tools used in the manufacture of fabricated metal and automobiles

Notice that the only items in the three-year class probably required strong lobbyists in Washington to get there.

FIVE YEARS:
- Automobiles
- Computers
- Copying machines
- Trucks
- Typewriters, word processors

SEVEN YEARS:
- Furniture and fixtures
- Cellular phones
- Video and still cameras
- Musical instruments
- Kitchen equipment
- Desks and filing cabinets
- Fax machines
- Videotape recorders
- Darkroom equipment

THIRTY-NINE YEARS:
- Office or commercial buildings
- Office in your home

THE HALF-YEAR RULE OR CONVENTION
To complete your understanding of depreciation, here are two other rules that limit the depreciation deductions you can take on an asset the first year. They are called the half-year convention and the last- (or mid-) quarter convention. No, these conventions are not opportunities for business travel but instead formulas for determining the maximum amount of your first-year depreciation.

The half-year convention requires you to treat all assets you will begin depreciating that year as if you bought and started using them on July 1. The effect is that you get exactly one-half of a regular full year's depreciation. For instance, depreciating your computer used 100% in your business over five years means that the first year your depreciation would normally be 20% of the cost if you used the straight-line method. Because of the half-year rule, you would instead be able to deduct only 10% because you would treat the computer as if you began using it on July 1.

What happens to the other 10%? You don't lose it, you simply take the other half year's deduction the sixth tax year. Therefore, the cost of an asset with a life of five years is really deducted over the course of six tax years, and items with a life of seven years are deducted over eight years. That's why the depreciation percentage charts that follow all seem to have an extra year. The half-year rule applies whether you are using MACRS or straight-line depreciation, but not if you are using the asset expensing method (see Strategy #249).

THE LAST-QUARTER RULE OR CONVENTION

Congress threw one other monkey wrench into the depreciation formula to thwart those who purchase lots of assets late in the year expecting to get a full half year's worth of depreciation. The concept was great—buy a car and equipment in December and take a full six months of depreciation and tax deductions before you even make a payment. This strategy is no longer possible because of the creation of the last-quarter convention. Here's the rule. If you buy 40% or more of the total business assets you purchase during the year in the last three months of the year, you must treat every asset as if you bought it in the middle of the quarter (three-month period) in which it was actually purchased.

Not only could this rule reduce your depreciation deductions the first year, but applying the formula to every item you bought and intend to depreciate is tedious, time-consuming, and fortunately unnecessary. Here are your easy-to-apply alternatives.

- Use the asset expensing rules to deduct most or all of the items you purchase. The last-quarter rule doesn't apply to asset expensing. Even if you start using them for business in December, you still get 100% of the full year's asset expensing deduction (see Strategy #249).
- Plan your purchases or start dates for the business use of your assets so that the 40% last-quarter limit is not exceeded.

One item that could easily cause you to exceed the 40% limit is the purchase of a car in the last three months of the year. Buy before October 1 and you get a full half year's depreciation up to

$2,860. Buy October 1 or after and the last-quarter rule is triggered, cutting your depreciation percentage from 20 to 5%. But if you use the car more than 50% of the time for business, you can use the asset expensing rules and get up to the maximum $2,860 deduction no matter when you buy the car.

Strategy #251
CONVERT TO STRAIGHT-LINE DEPRECIATION WHEN MORE DEDUCTIONS WILL BE GENERATED THAN BY MACRS.

The amount of depreciation taken using the MACRS method drops each year. (See the second chart on page 346.) When the amount of straight-line depreciation finally exceeds the amount of depreciation you can take using the MACRS double-declining-balance method, you can choose to switch to the straight-line method for the remaining years. Straight line means that the same amount of depreciation is taken each year for the life of the asset. Straight line is computed by dividing the basis by the number of years in the recovery period. The following chart will show you the year in which it is best to switch from the MACRS to the straight-line method. The second chart on page 346 already includes the switch to the straight-line method for the appropriate year.

DETERMINING WHEN TO SWITCH TO THE STRAIGHT-LINE METHOD

Recovery Period	Year to Switch from MACRS to Straight-Line
3-year	3rd
5-year	4th
7-year	5th

Strategy #252
USE DEPRECIATION TABLES TO SIMPLIFY YOUR DEPRECIATION CALCULATIONS.

The complicated-sounding formulas combining MACRS or straight-line depreciation with the half-year convention and the best year to switch to straight-line depreciation can be put into a simple table that you can use when completing your tax return. The percentages shown in the table below are those you apply each year to the original basis or business percentage of the cost of an item.

DEPRECIATION TABLES INCLUDING HALF-YEAR CONVENTION AND SWITCH TO STRAIGHT-LINE METHOD

	MACRS		Straight Line	
Year	5-Year Property	7-Year Property	5-Year Property	7-Year Property
1	20.00%	14.29%	10%	7.14%
2	32.00	24.49	20	14.29
3	19.20	17.49	20	14.29
4	11.52	12.49	20	14.28
5	11.52	8.93	20	14.29
6	5.76	8.92	10	14.28
7		8.93		14.29
8		4.46		7.14

For example, you start using your computer this year in your business. You bought it personally last year so it doesn't qualify for asset expensing. The cost was $4,400 and you use it 75% of the time for business based on the records you are keeping. Your basis is 75% of the cost or $3,300 (75% × $4,400). Using the table below, here is how you deduct your computer over the next five years.

Year	From MACRS/Straight-Line Depreciation Table		Basis		Depreciation Deduction for Form 4562
1	20.00%	×	$3,300	=	$ 660
2	32.00	×	3,300	=	1,056
3	19.20	×	3,300	=	634
4	11.52	×	3,300	=	380
5	11.52	×	3,300	=	380
6	5.76	×	3,300	=	190
	100%				$3,300

At the end of six years, the business portion of the cost has been completely deducted.

Strategy #253
INCREASE THE BUSINESS USE PERCENTAGE OF YOUR ASSETS TO OVER 50%.

If you use such personal assets as your car, VCR, furniture, or home computer part-time in your business, it is important that you get the business use percentage above 50%. If business use is less than 50%, you lose two important options.

First, you cannot use the extremely beneficial asset expensing formula on assets you use less than 50% of the time for business. This rule allows you to deduct up to $17,500 in one year for assets you purchase that might otherwise have to be deducted over a five- or seven-year period.

Second, you cannot even use the favorable MACRS depreciation method on assets used less than 50% of the time for business or already owned before you used them for business. You must use the straight-line method, which give you approximately half the tax deduction the first year of the MACRS method.

There are two ways to insure that you can take advantage of the benefits of using your assets over 50% for business.

- Increase the number of hours you use the asset for business. Simply find more business uses for the asset more often.
- Decrease the number of hours you use the asset personally.

Since you are the one required to keep the records, you are in a position to plan and control the number of hours and therefore the percentage of time you use assets for each purpose, business and personal. You must keep good records.

Strategy #254
CHOOSE THE AUTOMOBILE DEDUCTION METHOD THAT GIVES YOU THE GREATEST TAX DEDUCTION.

Because your automobile represents one of your largest personal expenses, it is also one of your greatest potential tax deductions. One method of making your automobile deductible is to use it in your small business. If you use your automobile 100% of the time for business, 100% of the mileage or expenses are deductible. The 100% deductible rule also applies to a two-car family that allocates one car for personal use and chooses the second, obviously more expensive car for deductible business use. If you use one automobile for both personal and business purposes, you must allocate by percentage the amount of deductible business use and nondeductible personal use, for example, 55% business use, 45% personal use.

Once you have determined the business use percentage, you then choose the overall automobile deduction method you wish to use. There are two options—the standard mileage rate and the actual cost method. Your choice? Obviously you will choose the one that gives you the biggest tax deduction.

Here is a rule of thumb even though you will still want to compute the deduction both ways. If you drive your car lots of deductible business miles, such as 15,000 or more each year, the standard mileage rate becomes more attractive. Plus, you don't have to keep as many receipts and records. If, however, you have a part-time business and your business mileage is low, let's say only 6,000 miles, but that is over 50% of your total mileage, the actual cost method will normally give you more in tax deductions.

Here are the two methods for deducting an automobile used in your business:

METHOD #1—Actual Cost Method
You may deduct the *cost* of the automobile through either:
    Asset expensing (See Strategy #249)
    Depreciation—MACRS or straight line (see Strategy #250)
You may deduct in addition *operating expenses*, including:

Gas	Cleaning
Insurance	Parking
Licenses	Sales Taxes
Maintenance	Taxes
Tires	Tolls
Loan Interest	

METHOD #2—Standard Mileage Rate
    29 cents per mile for all business miles (1994)
You may deduct in addition:

Loan Interest	Parking Fees
Property Taxes	Tolls

Compute your tax deduction using both methods. Use IRS Form 2106 as a worksheet. It has a section for using both formulas. You don't need to file Form 2106, but you choose the larger deduction you computed and enter the amount on

Schedule C. Once you have chosen the deduction method you wish to use, you may not change methods for the life of the car.

Tax preparers often automatically choose the standard mileage rate method because it is easier for them to compute. That can cost you big dollars. Always compute the deduction both ways yourself or you could lose important tax deductions.

To compute your automobile deduction using the actual cost method, you will have to determine the amount you can deduct each year based on the cost of the car. As a shortcut in determining the maximum amount of your automobile depreciation deduction, use the following table and IRS Form 4562. To take the deduction you multiply the percentages shown in the table by the depreciation basis of the automobile. The depreciation basis begins with the business use percentage times the cost of your car and is reduced each year by the amount of depreciation you claimed the previous years.

This table assumes you use your car more than 50% for business. Otherwise the straight-line method must be used.

AUTOMOBILE DEPRECIATION SIMPLIFIED CALCULATION TABLE
(MACRS METHOD)

Year	%	Your Deduction Maximum
1	20.00	$2,860
2	32.00	$4,600
3	19.20	$2,750
4	11.52	$1,675
5	11.52	$1,675
6	5.76	$1,675

The column on the right represents the maximum annual depreciation you may take on any car. This limit is meant to keep business owners from buying and depreciating luxury cars over the standard five-year period.

If only a percentage of your car is used for business, for example 60%, your first year limit would be 60% of $2,860 or $1,716. In addition, you may add to your deduction the actual operating costs and business portion of the interest on your car loan.

Strategy #255
**USE IRS FORM 4562 TO COMPUTE AND CLAIM ALL
ASSET EXPENSING AND DEPRECIATION
DEDUCTIONS.**

Your key to both asset expensing and depreciation deductions is IRS Form 4562. All of your deductions are entered on this form, and the total is then transferred to your business tax form, such as Schedule C for sole proprietors.

Let's look at an example of how your assets actually become business deductions. Jim and Sue start a small business, which has an income of $8,200 for the first year. They use their home computer 60% of the time in their new business. The cost of the computer was $3,000 and it was purchased this year. They also buy a second car, which they allocate 100% for business use—cost $16,000. They know the maximum deduction the first year is $2,860 for an automobile. Other equipment already owned, such as furniture and small machinery used in the business, has a value of $4,000 when placed in service and qualifies as seven-year property and for MACRS depreciation. How much is their total deduction?

ANSWER: The $3,000 computer can be deducted in one year using asset expensing at a business use percentage of 60%, creating an immediate deduction of $1,800 (60% × $3,000). This information is entered in Part 5 of Form 4562. See pages 351 and 352. The $2,860 maximum deduction for the automobile goes in the same section. The $4,000 equipment qualifies for a 14.29% depreciation deduction based on the MACRS method with the half-year convention amounting to $571. See both pages of the sample Form 4562 that follows for how all these pieces fit together. The total depreciation deduction is $5,031 their first year in business, saving them $1,800 in taxes!

Strategy #256
**USE PERSONAL ASSETS IN YOUR BUSINESS TO
CLAIM THE SALES TAX DEDUCTION.**

Beginning in 1987, the deduction of state and local sales taxes on personal purchases was no longer allowed. The business use percentage of the sale tax is deductible, however, if you use the

Form **4562**	**Depreciation and Amortization**	OMB No. 1545-0172
Department of the Treasury Internal Revenue Service (O)	**(Including Information on Listed Property)** ▶ **See separate instructions.** ▶ **Attach this form to your return.**	19**93** Attachment Sequence No. **67**

Name(s) shown on return	Identifying number
Jim and Sue Smart	06-204-5496

Business or activity to which this form relates
Smart Parts

Part I — **Election To Expense Certain Tangible Property (Section 179)** (Note: *If you have any "Listed Property," complete Part V before you complete Part I.)*

1	Maximum dollar limitation (If an enterprise zone business, see instructions.)	**1**	$17,500
2	Total cost of section 179 property placed in service during the tax year (see instructions) . .	**2**	19,000
3	Threshold cost of section 179 property before reduction in limitation	**3**	$200,000
4	Reduction in limitation. Subtract line 3 from line 2, but do not enter less than -0-	**4**	0
5	Dollar limitation for tax year. Subtract line 4 from line 1, but do not enter less than -0-. (If married filing separately, see instructions.)	**5**	17,500

(a) Description of property	(b) Cost	(c) Elected cost	
6			

7	Listed property. Enter amount from line 26.	**7**	4,660	
8	Total elected cost of section 179 property. Add amounts in column (c), lines 6 and 7 . . .	**8**	4,660
9	Tentative deduction. Enter the smaller of line 5 or line 8	**9**	4,660
10	Carryover of disallowed deduction from 1992 (see instructions).	**10**	0
11	Taxable income limitation. Enter the smaller of taxable income or line 5 (see instructions) . .	**11**	8,200
12	Section 179 expense deduction. Add lines 9 and 10, but do not enter more than line 11 .	**12**	4,660
13	Carryover of disallowed deduction to 1994. Add lines 9 and 10, less line 12 ▶	**13**	0

Note: *Do not use Part II or Part III below for listed property (automobiles, certain other vehicles, cellular telephones, certain computers, or property used for entertainment, recreation, or amusement). Instead, use Part V for listed property.*

Part II — **MACRS Depreciation For Assets Placed in Service ONLY During Your 1993 Tax Year (Do Not Include Listed Property)**

(a) Classification of property	(b) Month and year placed in service	(c) Basis for depreciation (business/investment use only—see instructions)	(d) Recovery period	(e) Convention	(f) Method	(g) Depreciation deduction
14 General Depreciation System (GDS) (see instructions):						
a 3-year property						
b 5-year property						
c 7-year property						
d 10-year property						
e 15-year property						
f 20-year property						
g Residential rental			27.5 yrs.	MM	S/L	
property			27.5 yrs.	MM	S/L	
h Nonresidential real				MM	S/L	
property				MM	S/L	
15 Alternative Depreciation System (ADS) (see instructions):						
a Class life					S/L	
b 12-year			12 yrs.		S/L	
c 40-year			40 yrs.	MM	S/L	

Part III — **Other Depreciation (Do Not Include Listed Property)**

16	GDS and ADS deductions for assets placed in service in tax years beginning before 1993 (see instructions)	**16**	
17	Property subject to section 168(f)(1) election (see instructions)	**17**	
18	ACRS and other depreciation (see instructions)	**18**	

Part IV — **Summary**

19	Listed property. Enter amount from line 25.	**19**	571
20	**Total.** Add deductions on line 12, lines 14 and 15 in column (g), and lines 16 through 19. Enter here and on the appropriate lines of your return. (Partnerships and S corporations—see instructions)	**20**	5,231
21	For assets shown above and placed in service during the current year, enter the portion of the basis attributable to section 263A costs (see instructions)	**21**	

For Paperwork Reduction Act Notice, see page 1 of the separate instructions.   Cat. No. 12906N   Form **4562** (1993)

Form 4562 (1993)   Page **2**

Part V **Listed Property—Automobiles, Certain Other Vehicles, Cellular Telephones, Certain Computers, and Property Used for Entertainment, Recreation, or Amusement**

*For any vehicle for which you are using the standard mileage rate or deducting lease expense, complete **only** 22a, 22b, columns (a) through (c) of Section A, all of Section B, and Section C if applicable.*

Section A—Depreciation and Other Information *(Caution: See instructions for limitations for automobiles.)*

22a Do you have evidence to support the business/investment use claimed? ☒ **Yes** ☐ **No**   **22b** If "Yes," is the evidence written? ☐ **Yes** ☐ **No**

(a) Type of property (list vehicles first)	(b) Date placed in service	(c) Business/ investment use percentage	(d) Cost or other basis	(e) Basis for depreciation (business/investment use only)	(f) Recovery period	(g) Method/ Convention	(h) Depreciation deduction	(i) Elected section 179 cost
23 Property used more than 50% in a qualified business use (see instructions):								
Automobile	5/14/92	100 %	16,000	16,000	5	MACRS		2,860
Computer	5/14/92	60 %	3,000	1,800	1			1,800
Equipment	5/14/92	100 %	4,000	4,000	7	MACRS	571	
24 Property used 50% or less in a qualified business use (see instructions):								
		%				S/L –		
		%				S/L –		
		%				S/L –		

25 Add amounts in column (h). Enter the total here and on line 19, page 1 . . . . . .   **25**   571

26 Add amounts in column (i). Enter the total here and on line 7, page 1 . . . .   **26**   4,660

Section B—Information Regarding Use of Vehicles—*If you deduct expenses for vehicles:*
- Always complete this section for vehicles used by a sole proprietor, partner, or other "more than 5% owner," or related person.
- If you provided vehicles to your employees, first answer the questions in Section C to see if you meet an exception to completing this section for those vehicles.

	(a) Vehicle 1		(b) Vehicle 2		(c) Vehicle 3		(d) Vehicle 4		(e) Vehicle 5		(f) Vehicle 6	
27 Total business/investment miles driven during the year (DO NOT include commuting miles)												
28 Total commuting miles driven during the year												
29 Total other personal (noncommuting) miles driven												
30 Total miles driven during the year. Add lines 27 through 29.												
	Yes	No	Yes	No	Yes	No	Yes	No	Yes	No	Yes	No
31 Was the vehicle available for personal use during off-duty hours?												
32 Was the vehicle used primarily by a more than 5% owner or related person?												
33 Is another vehicle available for personal use?												

Section C—Questions for Employers Who Provide Vehicles for Use by Their Employees
Answer these questions to determine if you meet an exception to completing Section B. Note: Section B must always be completed for vehicles used by sole proprietors, partners, or other more than 5% owners or related persons.

	Yes	No
34 Do you maintain a written policy statement that prohibits all personal use of vehicles, including commuting, by your employees?		
35 Do you maintain a written policy statement that prohibits personal use of vehicles, except commuting, by your employees? (See instructions for vehicles used by corporate officers, directors, or 1% or more owners.)		
36 Do you treat all use of vehicles by employees as personal use?		
37 Do you provide more than five vehicles to your employees and retain the information received from your employees concerning the use of the vehicles?		
38 Do you meet the requirements concerning qualified automobile demonstration use (see instructions)? . . .		
Note: *If your answer to 34, 35, 36, 37, or 38 is "Yes," you need not complete Section B for the covered vehicles.*		

Part VI **Amortization**

(a) Description of costs	(b) Date amortization begins	(c) Amortizable amount	(d) Code section	(e) Amortization period or percentage	(f) Amortization for this year
39 Amortization of costs that begins during your 1993 tax year:					
40 Amortization of costs that began before 1993			**40**		
41 **Total.** Enter here and on "Other Deductions" or "Other Expenses" line of your return			**41**		

*U.S. Government Printing Office: 1993 — 345-370

items you buy in your business or investments. Sales tax paid on business supplies is also deductible that year as an expense.

Sales tax paid to buy a capital asset such as a car used in a business is added to the cost basis and depreciated. For example, if you buy a $10,000 car in a state with a 6% sales tax and use it personally, the $600 tax is not deductible. If it is your second car that is used 80% for business, you add 80% of the $600 sales tax, $480, to the basis for depreciation. Since an automobile is depreciated over five years, the sales tax is deducted over the same period.

Strategy #257
TAKE DEDUCTIONS FOR REPAIRS TO BUSINESS ASSETS.

Don't forget to take deductions for repairs to VCRs, cars, computers, or other property used in your small business. Repairs to assets are deductible when the assets are used even part-time for business purposes. When you use your assets only for personal reasons, your repairs and maintenance are not deductible. You take the deduction on Schedule C, line 21, if you are a sole proprietor.

Strategy #258
TAKE A DEDUCTION FOR YOUR BUSINESS-RELATED BOOKS, MAGAZINES, NEWSLETTERS, AND TAPE COURSES.

Purchasing books, magazines, newsletters, or audio- and videotape courses that relate to business makes these items tax deductible. Much of what you already read may become tax deductible when you start your small business. Here are some examples of business-related publications that you can deduct:

MAGAZINES:

Entrepreneur	Time
Venture	Nation's Business
Fortune	Newsweek

NEWSLETTERS:

The Charles J. Givens Success InSight
Kiplinger Washington Letter
Kiplinger Tax Letter
Decker Report (Public Speaking)
Executive Wealth Advisory
Tax Hotline

BOOKS:

There are dozens of books currently available at your bookstore
in the business and social science sections that relate to starting
a business, business management, business ideas, marketing,
advertising, accounting, record keeping, and success attitudes,
including:

Megatrends	John Naisbitt
What They Don't Teach You at	Mark H. McCormack
Harvard Business School	
In Search of Excellence	Thomas J. Peters and Robert H.
	Waterman
Think and Grow Rich	Napoleon Hill
Magic of Thinking Big	David J. Schwartz

AUDIO AND VIDEOTAPE COURSES, SEMINARS, AND WORKSHOPS:

Adult education is no longer being given just in traditional
classrooms for periods spanning several years, weeks, or eve-
nings, but in one- to four-day high-impact seminars and workshops. Keeping up and getting ahead are now done at home with
audio- and videocassettes or in hotel meeting and conference
rooms. When videotape courses, seminars, and workshops you
attend are related to your business or career (or personal investments and taxes), the cost is deductible.

Strategy #259
PLAN YOUR TRIPS AND VACATIONS AROUND A LEGITIMATE BUSINESS PURPOSE AND TAKE A DEDUCTION.

Planning your trips or vacations around a legitimate business
purpose makes your travel expenses tax deductible. What better
way to travel than with your tax savings covering part of the

cost? When it comes to business travel deductions, a few simple IRS rules will keep you from being audited or losing the deductions. Although you may have as much personal fun as you wish on your trips, you must be able to show that the primary purpose of the trip was business related to make the expenses deductible.

The expenses of your spouse or other family members on the trip are deductible if they are co-owners or employees of the business and have a business purpose for being there. The expenses of your spouse or other family members are not deductible if they are simply traveling with you.

You may deduct as business travel expenses hotels, rental cars, airline fares, automobile expenses, meals, entertainment, laundry, and any other related items. The main categories or purposes of deductible business travel are:

- attending a convention or conference
- attending a trade show or association meeting
- attending a business-related educational program
- setting up distributors for your product or services
- going on a buying trip for products you intend to resell
- a stockholders or partners meeting in a closely held business
- meetings with current or potential investors
- visits and discussions with owners of similar businesses as a learning experience
- traveling to a business meeting on a cruise ship

Familiarize yourself with the IRS rules for combined business and vacation trips to insure yourself the deduction. Here are the rules.

TRIPS WITHIN THE UNITED STATES

If the primary purpose of the trip is business, you may deduct 100% of the costs of your transportation (e.g., airlines, automobile) even if you spend time playing. If the primary purpose was personal, there is no deduction for transportation but your other business-related expenses are deductible. The amount of time you spend on business during the trip is an important factor in determining deductibility. Also important is the fact that you had to be in that spot to conduct business or to attend the convention. A good rule of thumb is an average four hours per day of business, not including weekends. Even if you extend your trip for a few purely vacation days, your transportation costs are fully deductible.

TRIPS OUTSIDE THE UNITED STATES

Rules for employees:
You may deduct 100% of your travel expenses even though you vacationed provided you can show that the primary purpose was business and that you had no control over the assignment of the trip. That means that your company sent you and you neither are a managing executive nor own more than 10% of the company.

Special rules for small business owners and managing executives:
You may deduct 100% of the transportation costs if the trip outside the United States was one week or less, not counting the day you left but counting the day you returned, or the trip lasted more than one week and you spent three days on business for every one day of purely vacation time.

If you spent more than 25% of the time as pure vacation days, you may deduct the business percentage of the trip. Any day on which you conducted any legitimate business is counted as a business day.

If you conduct business on Friday and Monday, but not on the weekends, you can count the weekend as two business days. If business is conducted on Friday and Tuesday, the weekend counts as personal days.

CONVENTIONS AND SEMINARS

Travel to investment seminars is no longer deductible, but travel to business seminars is. Keep a complete itinerary of the convention or seminar as part of your records. Be prepared to show that what you learned or experienced was directly connected to your business. You must do more than just view videotapes of previous lectures at your convenience to qualify for the deductions.

FOREIGN CONVENTIONS AND CRUISE EXPENSES

To take the deduction you must be able to show the convention was directly related to your business and there was a reason for the meeting to be held outside of the United States. Conventions in Canada and Mexico are not considered foreign. You may even use the "inside the United States" rules for conventions held in Puerto Rico, U.S. Virgin Islands, Barbados, Guam, and Jamaica.

You may deduct up to $2,000 per year for attending cruise-ship conventions if all ports of call are in the United States or its possessions, and if the ship is U.S.-registered. Good examples of trips to book under these deduction rules are:

Hawaiian island cruises
U.S.-mainland-to-Alaska cruises
Mississippi River boat cruises

If you travel for business using a cruise ship as your mode of transportation to your destination, you may deduct up to twice the highest federal government per diem paid to government employees traveling within the United States. The highest federal per diem is currently $174 per day, so you may deduct up to $348 per day per person. For example, if you travel to the Virgin Islands on a cruise ship to attend a business convention or seminar in the islands, your transportation cost deduction is up to $348 per day.

If family members or others travel with you, but have no business purpose, you may still deduct full auto mileage, auto rental, and hotel expenses that you would have incurred if you had traveled alone. You may deduct only your food and airfare, not those of other nonbusiness-related family members. You may not deduct unrelated recreational and entertainment expenses such as sight-seeing, ski lifts, or theater tickets.

Keep good records and note on your receipts if the expense is related to the business portion or personal portion of your trip.

Strategy #260
CREATE A DEDUCTIBLE OFFICE IN YOUR HOME.

If you start a small business at home, use part of your home for an office, meeting, or storage area and you qualify for important tax deductions for depreciation, rent, utilities, repairs, improvements, and insurance. The rules and strategies are explained in Chapter 23, "Turn Your Home Into a Tax Haven" (see Strategy #225).

Strategy #261
MAKE LOAN INTEREST DEDUCTIBLE AS A BUSINESS EXPENSE.

Tax deductions for interest are possible when you treat interest paid as a business and not a personal expense. Business interest is deductible; consumer or personal interest is not. When you borrow money to purchase an automobile, video recorder, computer, or other asset for use even part-time in your business, the business interest portion can be deducted (see Strategy #190).

Don't forget to keep track of the interest you pay on your credit card balance that relates to items you purchased for your business but didn't pay off that month. To make the record keeping even easier, get an additional credit card that you use only for business-related supplies, equipment, entertainment, car expenses, travel expenses, and meals.

Strategy #262
CONSIDER AN "S" CORPORATION ELECTION.

Although most new, do-it-at-home businesses should be set up as sole proprietorships, what should you do if you now have a small closely held corporation? Keep it. The process of setting up the business is already complete.

Tax reform changed the rules enough for you to consider changing a small "C" corporation to an "S" corporation. An "S" corporation from a legal standpoint is not different from a "C" corporation, but from a tax standpoint the "S" corporation operates like a partnership or proprietorship. Business income and losses in an "S" corporation are taxed only once at the owner's personal tax rate. An "S" corporation cannot have more than 35 shareholders, is limited to one class of stock, and cannot have any nonresident foreign shareholders or subsidiaries.

There are two tax benefits of an "S" corporation that make the need for reconsideration clear:

1. Individual and "S" corporation maximum tax rates are 28%, except for high-income individuals, whose maximum rates are 39.6%, while the "C" corporation maximum tax rate is 35%.
2. The Alternative Minimum Tax (AMT) rate for "C" corporations is much stiffer beginning in 1987, with an increase from 15% to 20%. In addition, "C" corporations must add back to income more tax preferences before computing the AMT, which can significantly raise taxes. On the other hand, an "S" corporation completely circumvents the corporate Alternative Minimum Tax.

> ### Strategy #263
> ## CUT YOUR SELF-EMPLOYMENT TAX BY INCREASING YOUR BUSINESS DEDUCTIONS.

The self-employment tax is now a combination of 12.4% for Social Security and 2.9% for Medicare, totaling 15.3% based on *net* earnings up to $60,600. The maximum tax you can pay on $60,600 of net earnings is a frightening $9,272. The 2.9% tax continues to be paid on all of your net earnings. If you are self-employed, you pay self-employment tax rather than Social Security tax. The good news is that the self-employment tax qualifies you for Social Security payments later on; the bad news is you can probably use the money now more than later.

Those subject to self-employment tax include small business owners, independent contractors, and professionals. Members of the clergy can get an exemption. The key word in reducing your self-employment tax is *net* earnings. Only your bottom-line self-employment profit (i.e., line 31 of Schedule C) is subject to SET. Your strategy is to maximize your small business tax deductions. Each $1,000 of deductions that reduces your net profit further below the $60,600 level will save you $153 of self-employment tax. If your business net income is already in the hundreds of thousands—too much to reduce your taxable net below the $60,600 threshold—you won't miss the maximum self-employment tax of $9,272 anyway.

> ### Strategy #264
> ## USE YOUR SMALL BUSINESS TO CREATE AN INVESTMENT/RETIREMENT TAX SHELTER.

One of the greatest advantages of a profitable small business is the opportunity to create a retirement tax-shelter plan. The rules are so liberal for small business owners that as much as $30,000 to $90,000 per year can be contributed to "defined contribution" and "defined benefit" Keogh plans and excluded from current taxable income.

If your small business or profession is showing a profit, you want to contribute the maximum possible into your plan. The following chart will show you, based on your business form, which plans you are qualified to have.

QUALIFIED RETIREMENT PLANS FOR
SMALL BUSINESS OWNERS

	IRA	SEP	Keogh Defined Contribution	Defined Benefit	401(k) Salary Deferral
Sole proprietorship	Yes	Yes	Yes	Yes	No
Partnership	Yes	Yes	Yes	Yes	No
"S" corporation	No	Yes	Yes	Yes	Yes
"C" corporation	No	Yes	Yes	Yes	Yes

The more you pour into the plan, the lower your taxable income for the year.

Strategy #265
USE ONLY A SELF-DIRECTED SMALL BUSINESS RETIREMENT PLAN.

Another great advantage of owning your own business is total control of where your retirement money is invested. Most no-load mutual fund families offer retirement plans for small business owners and self-employed professionals. The use of the Money Movement Strategy in your self-directed retirement plan can earn you over 15% per year, no commissions, and no current taxes. See Chapters 30 and 31 to learn how to use the Money Movement Strategy in mutual funds. See the Appendix for which mutual funds offer retirement plans to small business owners.

Strategy #266
USE THE SEP TO MAXIMIZE YOUR SELF-EMPLOYMENT RETIREMENT CONTRIBUTIONS WITHOUT MATCHING EMPLOYEE CONTRIBUTIONS.

As your business grows, you face the problem with most self-employment retirement plans of having to pay in the same percentage for employees as you pay yourself. Under the current rules, if you want to avoid matching contributions for employees, the Simplified Employee Pension Plan (SEP) is your best bet.

TAX DEDUCTION STRATEGIES CHECKLIST FOR
SMALL BUSINESS OWNERS

Starting a small business is fun, profitable, and certainly tax deductible. Here is a summary of the strategies for maximizing your tax deductions. Check each when incorporated into your plan.

___ 1. Hire your kids to work in the business to make allowances tax deductible.

___ 2. Hire your spouse to work in the business to create a $1,750 tax deductible IRA account.

___ 3. Use your automobile in your business to create deductions through asset expensing, depreciation, gas, repairs, insurance, parking, and interest.

___ 4. Use your home computer, videotape recorder, cassette recorder, furniture, typewriter, or other assets, even part-time, in your business, and make them tax deductible.

___ 5. Set up your business office in your home so that part of your mortgage, rent, utilities, and other expenses become deductible.

___ 6. Deduct books, subscriptions, newsletters, or tape courses that relate to business in general or to your particular business.

___ 7. Deduct repairs to any asset you use in your business.

___ 8. A trip planned around a business purpose, such as staff meetings, visiting customers or suppliers, or setting up a sales organization, becomes deductible.

___ 9. Borrow the money for a business-related trip, and deduct the interest.

___ 10. Use your boat, plane, or motor home directly in a business to increase deductions.

___ 11. Interest deducted as a business expense rather than a personal expense will give you interest deductions you might otherwise lose.

___ 12. Consider an "S" corporation election if you now have a small closely held "C" corporation.

___ 13. Set up a business-related retirement tax shelter as soon as your business becomes profitable.

___ 14. Begin your business as a "sole proprietorship" instead of as a corporation.

___ 15. Use your business "paper" losses to tax-shelter job and investment income.

___ 16. Show a profit three out of five years to qualify for continuing excess tax deductions.

___ 17. Buy business equipment, furniture, computers, and tools at bankruptcy sales and auctions at less than half price.

___ 18. Qualify your spouse for Social Security benefits.

___ 19. Beat the kiddie tax with a kiddie IRA.

___ 20. Insure your car as a personal car, not a company car.

___ 21. Buy an automobile instead of leasing it for greater deductions and flexibility.

___ 22. Use the asset expensing rules for immediate deductions on assets you buy.

___ 23. Use the depreciation formula to generate big tax deductions when you don't qualify for asset expensing.

___ 24. Convert to straight-line depreciation when more deductions will be generated than by the MACRS method.

___ 25. Increase the business use percentage of your assets to over 50%.

___ 26. Use IRS Form 4562 to compute and claim all asset-expensing and depreciation deductions.

___ 27. Use personal assets in your business to claim the sales tax deduction.

___ 28. Use the simplified 90-day record-keeping method to allocate the business and personal use percentage of assets.

___ 29. Make loan interest deductible as a business expense.

___ 30. Cut your self-employment tax by increasing your business deductions.

___ 31. Use only a self-directed small business retirement plan.

___ 32. Use the SEP to maximize your self-employment retirement contributions without matching employee contributions.

Part III

POWERFUL
INVESTMENT
STRATEGIES

Chapter 26

THE SECRETS OF POWERFUL INVESTING

The man who is a bear on the future of the United States will always go broke.

J. P. Morgan
Financier
1895

OBJECTIVE

ACCOMPLISH THE THREE MAJOR INVESTMENT OBJECTIVES:

1. Up to 15% Safe Investment Return
2. No Commissions
3. No Taxes

Investing is putting your money instead of your muscle to work; yet, if there is any area of managing and making money that most people foul up, not just once, but over an entire lifetime, it is investing.

One of my personal fortunes was lost when I listened to the dubious advice of a financial salesman. At 26, after losing a million dollar idea when my recording studio burned, I decided to build my next fortune through investing. Genesco, the apparel conglomerate for which I designed computer software systems, offered a magnificent stock incentive plan to its management employees. My first 200 shares were bought for me by the company with another 200 shares on the payment-a-month plan. After I bought in at $21 per share, the stock began to split

periodically and grow rapidly in value. Being close to management computer systems, I began to see loopholes that would
legally allow me to get my hands on hundreds of shares of
Genesco stock financed totally by the company. With two thousand shares of stock, for which I had paid nothing but a few
monthly payments, I was accumulating tens of thousands of
dollars in stock equity during the company's most expansive
era, and the stock skyrocketed to $70 per share.

I was hooked on the stock market. I thought I couldn't lose.
What a learning experience I was in for! Borrowing money on
everything I owned, including my home and cars, I bought
shares in all the new stock issues of the midsixties. Margin
accounts and undercollateralized loans enabled me to run
$60,000 of borrowed capital into a stock fortune of $800,000 in
just three years. I even considered a leisurely, full-time career as
an investor. Then the roof fell in. Every morning, the newspaper
would show my newly found fortune dwindling at an ever-
increasing rate. Every afternoon, I was in contact with the
holders of my notes and margin accounts, who wanted instant
replacement for their disappearing collateral. My margin calls
seemed to have margin calls! Companies in which I had invested
heavily, such as Performance Systems (Minnie Pearl Fried
Chicken) and Continental Strategics, went bankrupt, leaving me
only memories and worthless stock certificates. I was forced to
trade my new custom-designed Cadillac for a three-year-old
Volkswagen Beetle, rather than have the car repossessed for lack
of payments. My home was finally sold with barely enough
equity to pay back most of the borrowed money. The entire
fortune was gone. I had tasted both the bitter and the sweet of
investing and vowed that I would never again risk my money
until I knew how to win without the risk of losing.

The investment principles I discovered over the next few
years were enough to build a lifetime investment fortune without investment mistakes, and these principles can do the same
for you. Powerful investing is one of the easiest of all strategies
to master, but the misinformation, lack of information, potential
for loss, and outright fraud that exist in the arena of investing
are enough to destroy any good financial plan. Traditional investing has become a mixture of storing money and legalized
gambling. Players are the usual losers, financial institutions
the winners.

Powerful investing is not like saving money. In America,
savers die broke hoping for a pitiful 3 to 10% return that is
instantly eaten up by taxes and inflation. Smart investors, on the

other hand, have learned to earn 15% per year safely often with no current taxes and no or low commissions. How? By using the ten best and safest investments in America, those you won't find at banks, brokerage firms, financial planners, or insurance agents. If the financial salesman's office is your only source of information, not only are you dealing with second-class investments, you will more than likely lose.

The ten best investments and the average yearly returns you can expect are listed below. In this section, you will learn all the strategies for successfully using each of these great investments.

Your objective as an investor is to put your money to work safely and effectively, making yourself rich instead of making financial institutions rich. Through your choice of these investments you can enjoy income, tax shelter, and maximum growth or any combination you choose.

THE TEN BEST INVESTMENTS
Average returns for 1980 to 1993*

Investment	Strategy	Average Yearly Return
1. Asset management checking account	Legal float and debit card	5–14%
2. No-load mutual funds	Money Movement	12–20
3. Mutual fund margin account	Leverage and Money Movement	15–25
4. IRA/Keogh account	Self-directed accounts and Money Movement	15
5. Your own home	Leverage and personal use	20
6. Employer's retirement plan	Money Movement and tax shelter	15
7. Self-directed annuities	Money Movement and tax shelter	15
8. Discounted mortgages	Guaranteed interest and tax deferral	20–30
9. Tax liens	Government-guaranteed interest rate	10–18
10. Rental real estate	Leverage and tax shelter	20

*Past performance is no guarantee of future performance.

THE IMPORTANCE OF INVESTING

If you don't expect to win a lottery, and you don't have the option of inheriting vast sums of money, you have only five ways to increase your wealth:

1. Putting yourself to work—employment
2. Putting other people to work—business
3. Putting your ideas to work—inventing, marketing, or consulting
4. Putting your money to work—investing
5. Putting other people's money to work—leverage

Working for someone else is the first money-making experience for most of us, beyond birthday gifts, and the tooth fairy. There are two limiting considerations when you put your financial future in the hands of the "company."

- Your success is directly tied to the success and attitude of your employer, over which you have no control.
- Your income and lifestyle are limited by your experience, age, education, the opportunity for advancement, and your ability to sell yourself on the job.

If there are any two words that no longer belong together, they are *job* and *security*. Putting together a powerful investment program will put an end to the lifelong dependency on others (employers or the government), even if you don't want the responsibility of starting your own company. In the nineties, a powerful investment plan is as essential to your lifestyle as a home or automobile. It can be your ticket to freedom, both during your working years and after retirement.

There are two approaches to investing—putting your money to work, and putting other people's money to work.

You put your money to work when you invest in:

- stocks
- bonds
- mutual funds
- certificates of deposit
- IRAs
- Treasury bills
- company retirement programs
- or any other direct investment using your own money

You put other people's money to work when you:

- buy a home with a mortgage
- use a brokerage-firm or mutual-fund margin account

- take an option on a piece of real estate
- borrow money for your business
- invest in leveraged limited partnerships
- borrow the equity on your home to reinvest
- expect any financial rewards from the use of borrowed capital

Putting your own money to work is direct and easy to understand, but limits your benefits to the profits that can be generated by your own capital. Putting other people's money to work can be more profitable, but can also be more risky and difficult to understand. The main benefit of OPM (other people's money) is that you can create profits and/or tax deductions far beyond what your own capital can generate. Using OPM is a step you will certainly want to consider once you have mastered the basics of investing your own money.

There are three major objectives of a sound investment plan that can be converted to strategies.

Strategy #267
EARN UP TO 20% PER YEAR SAFELY BY USING ONLY THE TEN BEST INVESTMENTS.

Normal investment profits can be more than doubled with knowledge and without additional time or risk when you use a combination of the ten best and safest investments. Chapter by chapter in this section we will cover them all. The last chapter will show you how to choose those that are right for your investment plan and objectives.

Strategy #268
PAY NO OR LOW COMMISSIONS BY WORKING DIRECTLY WITH GOVERNMENT AND FINANCIAL INSTITUTIONS.

You cannot split your money with everyone else and expect to end up with much for yourself. Small investors eliminate commissions by dealing directly with financial institutions and eliminating middlemen, such as brokers and financial planners. Paying unnecessary commissions is like throwing $20 bills into your fireplace to heat your home. The job will get done but at far too great a cost.

Strategy #269
USE TAX SHELTERS AND TAX STRATEGIES TO PROTECT YOUR INVESTMENT INCOME.

Most investors think the only strategies for investing without paying taxes are retirement programs or low-interest tax-exempt bonds. Any investment income can be tax sheltered. You have the choice of using automatically tax-sheltered investments, such as annuities and real estate, or creating tax deductions to match your investment income using any of the tax strategies in Part II of this book. Both methods can make your investments tax deferred or even tax free.

Whether you are a novice or a seasoned investor, you'll find all the secrets to building a powerful investment plan right here. There are no prerequisites. Your job is to organize or reorganize your investment dollars around a combination of these powerful, safe investments. Your decisions on which investments to choose will depend on your investment experience or lack of it, your financial goals, and the amount of capital you have. All ten investments are intended to remove risk and are appropriate no matter what your age.

Personal knowledge will eliminate risk and fear in your investment plan. Risk occurs most frequently when you act solely on the advice of others, without sufficient knowledge, making decisions without taking control.

THE GREATEST RISKS ARE TAKEN, NOT THROUGH THE INVESTMENTS CHOSEN, BUT THROUGH THE LACK OF PERSONAL KNOWLEDGE OF HOW TO USE INVESTMENT STRATEGIES CORRECTLY.

Chapter 27

THE TEN BIGGEST INVESTMENT MISTAKES

The trouble with the profit system is that it has always been highly unprofitable to most people.

E. B. White
One Man's Meat
1944

OBJECTIVE

LEARN TO RECOGNIZE INVESTMENT SCHEMES, SCAMS, AND BAD ADVICE.

By understanding the ten worst investments and how they earn that distinction, you will find it easier to develop your winning approach to investment wealth. Left out of the ten worst investments list are those that border on fraud or are actually fraudulent. The investments chosen for our list are considered legitimate, but have downside risks or costs that far outweigh any apparent benefits.

> **Strategy #270**
> **KEEP YOUR MONEY OUT OF VACANT LAND.**

Nondeveloped land, sometimes called vacant or raw land, will continue to be a depressed investment for the next five years. The lowered value is caused by the shift in agricultural production from small farms to major farming operations. In addition, land, unless leased, produces no income but does create negative cash flow through property taxes and loan interest. A lot in an appreciating area, or one on which you eventually intend to build, is an exception and can be a good investment.

Strategy #271
DON'T THROW AWAY MONEY IN TIME-SHARING.

Time-sharing is co-ownership of a real estate investment, usually one condominium unit, by as many as 25 investors. Each investor may personally use his unit during designated weeks, which are chosen as part of the transaction. Two unit weeks are usually sold for between $8,000 and $25,000. Owners, instead of being confined to the use of their own unit, usually have the right to trade for the use of other units in other complexes.

Time-sharing has a bad reputation because of developer defaults and bankruptcies. To combat the well-deserved negative press, developers have coined a new term, *interval ownership*, to replace *time-sharing*, but a rose by any other name is—well, you know. The latest marketing twist is the "membership" concept. The purchaser owns nothing except the right to use a unit for a week or two each year. Because the purchaser owns nothing, the price is often half of the cost of time-sharing. Is this concept sellable? Right. Is it a good value? Wrong!

There are *four* major drawbacks of time-sharing:

THE COST
A developer who sells two weeks to 25 investors for $10,000 each has generated $250,000 for one unit. The cost plus reasonable profit for building the unit may have been only $80,000, so the purchasers have overpaid by 300%. The payments at 12% interest would be $1,200 per year, plus maintenance fees of up to $1,800 per year. Renting luxury accommodations at most resorts costs far less, with no maintenance fees or headaches of ownership.

THE MAINTENANCE FEES
The developer charges yearly maintenance fees per owner of up to $1,800 per year, built in, of course, to the monthly payments. One of the developer's goals is always to sell out the project and retire comfortably on the income from maintenance fees never used for maintenance.

THE PROMISES

There are already on record hundreds of defaults because the developer wasn't able to sell enough "unit weeks." The developer goes bankrupt, the project remains uncompleted, leaving the unit purchasers holding the bag. Purchasers usually lose their down payment, plus any monthly payments already made. If the purchaser paid cash, the entire amount may be lost.

THE INVESTMENT PITCH

The salesman usually implies that the purchaser is making a good investment and that the unit weeks eventually can be sold at a big profit. Today there are thousands of unit weeks on the market that can't be sold at any price.

Strategy #272
NEVER USE LIFE INSURANCE AS AN INVESTMENT.

Buy life insurance as if you were going to die tomorrow, and invest as if you were going to live forever. Life insurance and investing, both necessary parts of a good financial plan, have little in common. Life insurance companies got into the investment business for one major reason: *There are bigger profits in selling investments than in selling insurance.*

Unlike your bank, which can tie up your money for only a few days to a few years, insurance companies have discovered methods to tie up your money for almost your entire lifetime at a low rate of return. Put $2,000 into a universal life policy and withdraw your money after one year and the surrender charge can be as much as $1,000! (See Chapter 6.)

Your strategy is to buy term insurance and build your investment wealth by choosing the correct investment and strategies yourself.

Strategy #273
STAY AWAY FROM INDIVIDUAL STOCKS AND BONDS.

Buying 100 to 1,000 shares of a stock, or pumping $1,000 to $2,500 into one or two bond issues, is eight times riskier than investing in stocks and bonds through mutual funds. Buying individual stocks and bonds also means paying commissions. You pay no commissions by using one of the more than 300 no-load mutual funds you will learn about later.

Strategy #274
NEVER INVEST IN BONDS WHEN INTERST RATES ARE RISING.

Bonds are good investments only when they are appreciating due to declining interest rates. When the prime rate is rising, any long-term bond will lose 10% of its principle value for every 1% increase in the prime rate. From March 1987 to October 1987, while the prime rate rose from 7½% to 9¼%, bond investments dropped 10% to 20% in value. Stay away from financial advisers who tell you bonds are always a good safe investment for those who want income.

Bond investments include:

Individual bonds—corporate, tax exempt, zero coupon, GNMAs
Bond Mutual Funds—high yield, fixed income, government
   securities

Strategy #275
DON'T INVEST IN INFLATION HEDGES SUCH AS PRECIOUS METALS.

Precious metals (gold and silver) are investments only for the most aggressive investors. Traditionally, gold and silver have been called a hedge against inflation. Inflation hedges are always investment losers. One hundred years ago in 1887, one ounce of gold would buy one average men's custom-tailored suit. Today at about $400 per ounce, one ounce of gold will buy—you guessed it—one average men's custom-tailored suit. With all the fluctuations in price, the real value of gold hasn't changed in a hundred years. Your loss in an inflation hedge comes when you sell your investment and pay 28% capital gains tax on your profits.

Scared investors often invest in precious metals as a hedge against economic collapse or hyperinflation, basing their reasoning on the Great Depression. The Great Depression was not even close to an economic collapse; 75% of all workers remained employed and real estate appreciated an average of 3% per year even in 1933 and 1934. Of course, no depression is a pleasant time, but it was not the end-all doom period it was painted to be. There is no impending economic collapse, no matter how many books and newsletters predict one. Therefore, all defensive investing will cause investment losses.

Strategy #276
DON'T FALL FOR INVESTMENT PHONE PITCHES.

Now you can buy your investments over the phone, but don't! Dozens of phone "boiler rooms" have been created to sell off-the-wall investments. High-pressure sales pitches are conducted by highly commissioned phone-room managers using minimum-wage telephone solicitors. The bait is the belief you are being let in on some new investment secret or opportunity not generally known to the public. Included in the wide range of these investment pitches are:

precious metals	tracts of land in desolate areas
commodities	bids on government land leases
cellular phone lotteries	industrial-grade diamonds

These schemes make big promises and deliver little, other than the opportunity to lose your money. Incredibly enough, tens of thousands of investors fall for these investment gimmicks every year.

Strategy #277
NEVER USE A COMMISSIONED FINANCIAL SALESMAN AS A FINANCIAL ADVISER.

Paying big commissions will turn almost any winning investment plan into a marginal one at best, often into a loser. Today's smart investor learns to work directly with financial institutions such as no-load mutual fund families, eliminating the need for the middleman. A commissioned investment salesman should never be used as a financial adviser for two reasons:

Bias—The salesman will always recommend as your investment solution the investments he or she sells, whether or not these are the investments you should be using.

Lack of investment knowledge—Brokers and other licensed salesmen are required to know only two things: the securities laws and how to sell investments successfully. Too many strategies recommended by investment salesmen are either too risky or 20 years out of date.

The Wall Street Journal published an article, based on a copy of a brokerage firm memo, that stated the only requirement to keep a job as a broker with the firm is to produce $100,000 in commissions for the company. A better approach would be for each firm to require its salesmen to produce a 20% after-commission return for investors and to collect commissions only on investments that actually return what the salesmen promise. Most brokers and financial planners have appalling records when it comes to making investors any real investment wealth.

Some "certified" financial planners have taken only a home-study course, and most have very little money of their own to manage. If you want to learn how to make money, you will learn the most from someone who has plenty of it.

Strategy #278
DON'T OVERLEVERAGE IN VOLATILE INVESTMENTS SUCH AS COMMODITIES.

Commodities are the riskiest of all legal investments. Greed is the commodities' drawing card. Investors can put up as little as 5% of the purchase price of the investment in order to control the entire investment. An investor can buy a $10,000 commodities contract for only $500. The leverage seems interesting until you look at the validity of the investment. The average price fluctuation in the commodities market is 1% every day. If the investor puts up only 5% and is leveraged by a factor of 20 to 1, the value of his investment will fluctuate an average of 20% per day—great news if the price goes up, disaster if the price of the commodity drops. Even if the price drop is small, the investor's capital may be wiped out. This condition in Las Vegas is known as the "gambler's ruin." Ninety-five percent of commodity players eventually lose money. There is no safe strategy for profiting in commodities. When the value of the investment drops below the 5% margin requirement, the investor is required to put up more money or lose the investment and receive a bill for the difference. These margin calls have wiped out the entire assets of many investors.

Strategy #279
AVOID OPTIONS AS A LEVERAGED OR HEDGED INVESTMENT.

An *option* is a right to buy or sell a specified number of shares of stock at a specified price on or before a specific day. A *put* is the right to sell. A *call* is the right to buy.

The investor pays a price for the option, which is forfeited if he or she does not exercise the option. The price an investor pays for the option is usually 2% to 10% of the price of the stock. Seventy-two percent of options are never exercised. The only realistic use of an option for a conservative investor would be to protect the profit on a stock already owned that could not or should not be sold at the present time.

Examples:

A. An employee is going to leave a company in six months and wants to cash in his stock, but cannot sell until he leaves. He is concerned that the price will drop during that period. He buys a put on his company stock, which gives him the right to sell at a guaranteed price. The cost of the option is like buying insurance.
B. An investor has a huge profit on a stock, is concerned the market is about to drop, but wants to sell the following year to defer the capital gains tax for 12 months. He buys a put to protect his profits from a market drop. If the market drops, he exercises his right to sell at the higher price, otherwise his risk is limited to losing the money he paid for the option.

There are now many mutual funds that use options as their primary investment or as a hedge against fluctuating prices. The mutual funds that use options as a hedge have poor overall performance records.

Strategy #280
LEARN TO RECOGNIZE BAD INVESTMENT ADVICE.

How do you really know when your broker or financial planner is just a commissioned wolf in sheep's clothing? You can tell by the statements he or she makes and the strategies you are told to employ. You should recognize the following statements as bad investment advice:

THE BIGGEST LIES IN THE INVESTMENT BUSINESS

"Stocks and bonds are a good long-term investment."
There is no such thing as a good long-term investment. The best investments change as the economy and interest rates change.

"We'll diversify into different investments—some stocks, some bonds—for safety."
Stocks and bonds are good investments at different times but not at the same time.

"Government securities are always a good safe investment for those who want income."
Government securities are bonds. Bonds drop about 10% in principal value for every 1% increase in the prime rate. Never invest in government securities when the prime rate is going up.

"Tax-exempt bonds are a good investment anytime you want a tax-free income."
Tax-exempt bonds usually pay only 7% to 8% tax-free interest. It would be better to invest in a mutual fund earning 20%, pay the taxes of about 8% maximum, and end up with a 12% profit after taxes.

"It always requires bigger risks to make bigger profits."
Only amateur financial advisers believe this. Bigger profits in the range of 20% to 30% can easily be attained using knowledge and not risk. The ten investment strategies in this section will earn you over 20% safely.

"This investment is a hedge against inflation."
If you just keep pace with inflation, your before-tax profit is zero. After you pay capital gains taxes on the phantom gains, you end up with a guaranteed 28% loss.

"By using dollar cost averaging, we can avoid the fluctuations in the market and end up with potentially bigger profits."
Dollar cost averaging is the practice of making equal investments at equal intervals in the same stock, bond, or mutual fund. This strategy violates two rules of successful investing:
1. There is no such thing as a good long-term investment.
2. Every economy has one best type of investment.

"I've got a hot tip on a good stock."
Hot tips ruin most unaware investors. Stockbrokers are always the least informed in a brokerage firm hierarchy, and their "hot tips" usually lose investors' money.

"Single-premium life insurance is one of the best tax shelters."
Single-premium life insurance is a second-class tax shelter because you must buy whole life insurance before you can make the investment. The best tax shelter, usually available from the same company, is a self-directed annuity, which allows you to invest in tax-sheltered mutual funds without the requirement of buying insurance. (See "Self-Directed Annuities," Chapter 34.) Salesmen often neglect to tell you about the annuities because they pay only a fraction of the commission earned through the sales of single-premium life insurance plans.

"Zero coupon bonds are a great investment for your children."
Zero coupon bonds are sold as investments for tax shelters and children because salesmen know you'll buy them. If not in a tax shelter, you or the kids would pay taxes on interest you do not receive. The best way to invest for children under 14 is mutual funds, averaging 15% or more, until the child earns over $1,000 a year, and then through self-directed annuities as a tax shelter. Even with a 10% onetime withdrawal penalty the child's account will average over 20% per year instead of the 10% per year earned with zero coupon bonds. (See "Self-Directed Annuities," Chapter 34.)

"Life insurance proceeds are tax exempt."
Since deceased people don't pay income taxes, there is no income tax to pay, but even insurance proceeds are subject to estate taxes. (See "Better Life Insurance for 80% Less," Chapter 6.)

"You should pay commissions because you get better financial advice."
A good financial adviser or money manager will earn you 25% per year after commissions, but those of this caliber manage portfolios of $1 million or more and spend most of their time on the ski slopes of Aspen. If you have less than a million, you won't qualify to work with the best portfolio managers. One reason this book was written is to give you the same caliber of help, even if you don't have the big dollars.

"We should make some conservative investments and then take a few risks."

No risks are necessary for a knowledgeable investor. Using the winning investment strategies in this book, even a novice investor can expect to earn 15% to 30% per year while avoiding the pitfalls and risks.

"A bank trust department should become the trustee for your estate."

Bank trust departments have the worst track records of any estate manager, often losing 50% of an estate in five to ten years. Use as your trustee an attorney, friend, or relative who will follow exactly the strategies you are learning now for building and preserving your estate.

"It is not possible to average 20% per year safely."

Nonsense. Tens of thousands of investors who have followed my strategies for two years or more have averaged 20% to 30% safely. These strategies work, work for everyone, and work all the time.

Half the battle of successful investing is ridding yourself of common false or outdated investment beliefs, most of which we have reviewed in this chapter. From now on we will concentrate on the winning investment strategies.

Chapter 28

THE 10% SOLUTION

I've been rich and I've been poor. Believe me, rich is better.

Sophie Tucker
Entertainer
(1884–1966)

OBJECTIVE

GET YOUR MILLION-DOLLAR INVESTMENT PLAN
STARTED ON A SHOESTRING.

Ninety percent of the families in America are still living pay-check-to-paycheck, always finding too much month left over at the end of the money. Paycheck-to-paycheck is a symptom, not of a lack of income, but of a lack of skills needed to build and keep wealth. You begin to feel as if there is no level of income you cannot outspend.

It is true that without the discipline to take control of your financial future there is no level of income you cannot outspend. Budgeting is certainly not the answer. The only person I've ever known to make money with a budget is the one who created Budget Rent-A-Car. The two most difficult personal promises to keep are certainly budgeting and dieting. Neither produces any instant reward or positive feedback so necessary for continued motivation. Budgeting is a plan requiring self-sacrifice now for some vague reward sometime in the not-so-foreseeable future. Budgeting never worked for me and it probably doesn't work any better for you. But there is a strategy I've discovered that allows you, without sacrifice, to build a guaranteed investment fortune for your future. I call it the 10% Solution.

Strategy #281
USE THE 10% SOLUTION TO GO FROM PAYCHECK TO PROSPERITY.

Beginning with your next paycheck, take 10% right off the top and send it to a mutual fund family (see Chapter 31). Do the same with every paycheck for the rest of your life. Write yourself the first check each month before you pay the rent, mortgage, or car payment, or even buy the groceries. We were all taught to handle obligations backward: to pay everyone else first and then enjoy and invest what was left over. The problem? There is never anything left over. To get out of that rut and guarantee yourself some real wealth, always pay yourself first, even when, and especially when, there is not enough left over to pay everyone else. Don't worry, they will still be there with their hands out next month.

Always pay yourself first. The less money you think you have, the more important the strategy. Make the 10% Solution a personal challenge. Do it now. Don't wait for it to happen.

One mutual fund family that will allow you to invest with very little money is Twentieth Century Investors, Kansas City, MO. If your account balance is under $1,000, you can have as little as $50 a month deposited from your checking account to your mutual fund account. Send 10% out of each paycheck to Twentieth Century and use the Money Movement Strategy (Chapter 30) to choose the right kind of mutual fund for the current economy. You will double your money every three to four years. Do like everyone else and put the same 10% of your check in a bank or credit union account and you will double your money only once every ten years! Twentieth Century will now debit your bank account automatically every month for the amount you want to invest—automatic wealth building.

"What do you mean, take 10% out of my paycheck?" you may be thinking. "I'm already spending 120% of what I earn!" If you are, you won't even miss the other 10%.

You can pay yourself first, and take the hassle out of monthly check writing with an automated investment program ($50 minimum monthly investment). After completing a simple authorization form, any amount you want will be transferred from your bank account or payroll check directly to your investment account. There is no charge for the automatic deduction. Such a program is offered by Wealth Asset Managers/Nelson Securities

Inc. (WAM), the recommended choice of the Charles J. Givens Organization to provide registered investment advisory services to Givens Organization members. Call WAM at **509-625-1910** for an automated investment form.

No one ever makes excuses for success. Excuses are only necessary when you forget or fail to do something. Excuses won't build wealth, action will. All successful people have discovered the same success principle: "Do it now."

Strategy #282
STORE 20% OF ONE YEAR'S INCOME AS ATTITUDE MONEY.

Have you ever noticed how directly your attitude is related to your bank account balance? The smaller the balance, the more difficult it becomes to maintain a positive, winning attitude. A positive attitude and financial self-confidence are two of the most important wealth-building tools. The easiest method of maintaining the winning attitude that comes from cash in an account is never to be without it.

Using the 10% Solution, make deposits in your mutual fund account until the balance is equal to 20% of one year's take-home pay. In writing, promise yourself you will never touch the money—not for overdue bills, emergencies, or any other logical reason. Why? As soon as the money goes, so does your attitude. You will find it far easier, attitude-wise, to have overdue bills with money available to pay them, if you wanted to, than to have your bills totally paid and be back in the paycheck-to-paycheck, empty-wallet rut.

You will always encounter tough months when the money goes out faster than it comes in. Your 20% is your attitude money, your dependable mental shelter during financial storms—never, never touch it no matter how tough it gets. Your more stable attitude will propel you past your short-term financial dilemmas.

Once you have reached the 20% quota, you won't have to deposit another dime in the account. If your goal is to double your income every five years or so, your 20% account invested correctly also will double in the same amount of time. Open a separate account for your future 10% deposits.

Strategy #283
USE THE "RULE OF 76" TO DETERMINE THE DOUBLING POWER OF YOUR MONEY.

How long does it take to double your money in an investment?—a long time in a 7% bank account, not so long if you're earning over 15% per year in a mutual fund family. But how long? The "Rule of 76" is the easiest way to determine the answer. Divide the number 76 by the expected return on your investment and the result is the number of years required to double your money if all of the earnings are reinvested and compounding. The short-term doubling power of money invested at 15% to 25% should give you the motivation to get your 10% Solution strategy started immediately.

Using investment strategies such as mutual funds, Money Movement, discounted mortgages, and tax lien certificates covered later in the book, you will soon be doubling your money every four to five years, even starting with only 10% out of every paycheck.

Let's look at it another way. For every $1,000 you invest this year at 15% to 25%, the following chart will show you how much you will have accumulated during periods ranging from 5 to 20 years. What you see in the chart can be accomplished with just $83.33 per month ($1,000 per year), the amount that someone with a net income of $833 per month would deposit using the 10% Solution. Who said you have to have big money to make big money?

THE "RULE OF 76" INVESTMENT TIME REQUIRED TO DOUBLE YOUR MONEY	
$ Invested @	*Number of years*
25%	3.0
20	3.8
15	5.0
10	7.6
9	8.4
8	9.5
7	10.8
6	12.8

| INVESTMENT OF $1,000/AMOUNT AFTER: | | | | |
Investment Return	5 yrs	10 yrs	15 yrs	20 yrs
15%	$2,106	$ 4,440	$ 9,356	$ 19,715
20	2,696	7,268	19,595	52,828
25	3,446	11,873	40,914	104,982

In my twenties, I wondered what it was I didn't seem to understand about getting wealthy. Why did some people seem to have the Midas touch, while I was still running to the bank with each paycheck to cover the personal checks I had written the previous week? I had been taught that hard work would build wealth; but I couldn't work any harder. I had been holding down at least two jobs since I was 18, and there were no more hours in the day.

Then, one day, I found an answer in "Ripley's Believe It or Not," which said:

> If you sell a five-pound bar of iron right out of the blast furnace, it will be worth $6. If you turn the iron into fishing weights, they will be worth $25. Transform your iron into fishing hooks, and they will sell for $250. Hammer the iron into hunting-knife blades and you'll get $2,500. If, however, you transform your iron bar into watch springs, they will be worth $250,000—one quarter of a million dollars.

I suddenly realized that working smarter instead of harder is what creates wealth. It doesn't matter what you are worth now, what matters is what you do with what you've got. Time and knowledge will do the work for you. Strategies such as the 10% Solution help you turn your five-pound bar of iron into watch springs.

Begin your 10% Solution with your next paycheck!

Strategy #284

SUBSTITUTE THE "RULE OF 76" FOR THE "RULE OF 72" WHEN DETERMINING THE TIME REQUIRED TO DOUBLE YOUR MONEY IN INVESTMENTS.

The formula used for years by financial advisers was called the "Rule of 72." The formula states that the number of years required to double your money in an investment is determined by dividing the number 72 by the return that you expect on that investment—not the number 76 as shown in the previous strategy.

One reason I have been so successful in building wealth, first for myself and then in teaching others, is that I begin developing all my strategies by assuming that everything I have ever been taught or heard on a subject is incorrect, and most everything written on a subject is flawed in some way.

From the time I first heard the Rule of 72 over 25 years ago, I noticed that no one ever seemed to question its validity. The rule just seemed to get passed along from generation to generation. Years ago, when I was first questioning how quickly I could double my money, I recalculated the Rule of 72 and found it was incorrect for any investment other than a bank account. Why? The original calculation seems to have been based on the assumption that the investment vehicle in which the money was to double was a fixed-interest account compounded monthly, such as a bank savings account. However, the monthly compounding assumption becomes invalid as soon as you use an investment vehicle that does not have a guaranteed interest feature, such as mutual funds, tax lien certificates, or discounted mortgages. When you recalculate based on a more logical assumption of yearly compounding—in other words, when you calculate your true earning once each year to determine the actual percentage you earned for the year and reinvest that amount—the true doubling period is better approximated by dividing the expected return into 76 instead of 72.

Although in reality the difference is small, when I first challenged and changed the cherished, established Rule of 72 to the Rule of 76, you can bet I got letters from financial folks saying that I must somehow be wrong, but none had ever bothered to check or question the mathematics themselves.

Strategy #285
GUARANTEE YOURSELF WEALTH OF A MILLION DOLLARS OR MORE WITH THE 10% SOLUTION.

The 10% Solution guarantees that you will always treat yourself and your family, not your creditors, as the most important people in your life. The 20% attitude money you accumulate will insure that your attitude never suffers due to a lack of cash. The money is in the holding account that you have vowed never to touch even when there is more month than money. Now let's combine these two strategies in a plan that will guarantee that you have $1 million to $3 million waiting for you when you quit working anytime after age 65.

No matter what financial obstacles you encounter during your working years, including layoffs, lost jobs, company closings, relocations, personal bankruptcy, or your own company going belly-up, you can still have a predetermined number of millions waiting to take care of you for the last 20 to 30 years of your life.

How? Simply by continuing to contribute 10% to your attitude money plan on a periodic, permanent basis and never touching the money through life's financial ups and downs, no matter how tough it gets.

The losing approach is to spend years accumulating money for the future only to pull it out and spend it on some so-called financial emergency. If you are willing to tap into your hard-fought, hard-bought retirement money, even if only for an emergency, chances are better than 50% that one or several times during your 45 working years you will find a reason to use the money. Although all reasons and excuses seem logical during so-called financial emergencies, you win by treating the money as if it doesn't exist. Only in that way can you guarantee that your twilight years, which should consist of the time and money for fun and travel, won't be financed with the subsistence wages of Social Security.

Tell yourself that there is no emergency great enough for you to touch that money, not even a dime of it. Every dollar you withdraw loses the opportunity for interest compounded every year until you retire. Small amounts withdrawn now become huge amounts lost in future income. The rest is up to you. The million-dollar process is simple:

- Put it in.
- Leave it in.

To help you plan your guaranteed million(s), the chart on page 388 shows you, at your current age, what you must be contributing each month to reach your objective. Surprisingly, the amounts are reasonably small. The freed-up cash from applying the strategies in this book as a coordinated plan is all you need.

APPROXIMATE MONTHLY AMOUNT TO BE INVESTED @ 15% TO
PRODUCE $1 MILLION TO $3 MILLION AT AGE 65

Your Current Age	$1 Million	$2 Million	$3 Million	Years to Age 65	Tax Rebate from Contribution Deduction per Million	Net Contribution per Month per Million
15	$ 7	$ 14	$ 20	50	$ 2	$ 5
20	15	30	45	45	5	10
25	30	60	90	40	10	20
30	70	140	210	35	23	47
35	150	300	450	30	50	100
40	300	600	900	25	100	200
45	650	1,300	1,950	20	216	434
50	1,500	3,000	4,500	15	500	1,000
55	3,500	7,000	10,500	10	1,200	2,300

Here's how to use this chart to build a million-dollar fortune.
Locate the figure closest to your current age in column 1. As you
read across the row for your age, the next three columns show
how little money you would have to invest each month to have
one, two, or three million in cash waiting for you at age 65. The
chart is based on money invested either before or after taxes in
an account such as a 401(k), SEP, TSA, or even a non-employ-
ment-related annuity, all of which allow investment earnings
to compound tax free. If your million-dollar account has tax
deductible contribution privileges like a 401(k), SEP, TSA, or
IRA, about one-third of the money you invest each year would
be returned to you in a tax refund, cutting your real-dollar
monthly contributions by one-third.

Column 5 shows how many years are left until you reach age
65, when you would stop contributing. Obviously the fewer
years you have left before age 65, the more money you would
have to invest every month to reach each million-dollar plateau.
However, if you are age 55 now and $3,500 would be required
to reach a million in ten years and that level of contribution is
beyond your current financial ability, simply add five or ten
years to the length of your plan. If you are willing to contribute
to age 70 instead of 65, you need only $1,500 a month instead of
$3,500, or if you contribute to age 75, the amount required to
bank that first million is only $700 per month.

Put the time value of money on your side and amazing things

begin to happen. Notice in particular how little is required for those who begin early and have lots of years to work their plans.

Strategy #286
LET THE GOVERNMENT FUND A THIRD OF YOUR MILLION-DOLLAR FORTUNE.

As if making and keeping a million weren't easy enough using this plan, you can also force both the federal and your state government to pick up a third or more of your total investment. Getting the government to contribute becomes automatic when you choose the right investment vehicle for producing your millions. There are no government documents to complete, no lines in which to wait, and no approvals to secure; you just put the tax laws on your side.

By choosing a company retirement-plan vehicle for your contributions, you automatically get to deduct your contribution from your taxable income. It's just like getting a tax deduction for every dollar you put into your plan. Remember the tax-deduction rule of thumb: every dollar of deduction will save you a third, or about 33 cents in taxes. Every $1,000 deduction (every $1,000 contributed to your plan) returns to you an extra $330 in your next refund check or reduces by the same amount the money you owe in taxes. Employment-related investment accounts with the contribution-deduction feature include 401(k), TSA, SEP, Keogh, 403(b), 457, and IRA. That's where you will get the most value for your money.

Although the maximum federal tax bracket is 39.6% for couples who earn over $250,000 per year, you can also add to your tax bracket, or conversely to your refund, another 4% to 10%, which is the state income tax levied by all but ten states. We've used 33% as an average figure for combined federal and state taxes.

In the chart, the last two columns indicate the net cash required to work your million-dollar plan when your contributions are tax deductible. The first of the two columns shows how much extra cash you will have because of the taxes you won't pay, and the last column shows the net you would actually be contributing each month, a third less than when your contributions are made to an investment account without the tax-advantage feature. For example, if you are age 40 with 25 years to contribute until retirement, you can build a million dollars of guaranteed wealth for every $300 per month you contribute to your plan. Make that $300 contribution into an account that generates a tax deduction from your income for the same amount and you have to contribute only $200 (last column) net per month to accomplish the same objective.

Strategy #287
**AS A SMALL BUSINESS OWNER, RELY ON THE 10%
SOLUTION AS THE ONLY GUARANTEED RETURN ON
ALL YOUR HARD WORK.**

One of the biggest money mistakes a small business owner can make is pouring every dime back into the business. But isn't that what we were taught to believe, that to make the business grow and prosper, we have to live on a little and reinvest every dime in the company? It took me many years and several businesses before I realized what a losing strategy that is. This strategy goes back to the basic fact that wealth is what is left over, not what you earned during the year.

The truth is that no matter how optimistic you are, no matter how well your business, product, or service is accepted right now, there will be good years and lousy years. Any business can be destroyed in less than a year in America by changes in government policy and regulation, tax laws, lawsuits, internal fraud, and, of course, changing economic conditions. With all that looming over your head, it is still worth the risk to be an entrepreneur instead of just another employee. However, the way to make the effort worth permanent dollars instead of becoming the potential or eventual victim of the winds of fate is to take a continual stream of money out of your business instead of continuing to put every dime back in.

The best place to invest the money you withdraw is somewhere that creditors can't touch it. Your first choice would therefore be a government- and tax-protected company retirement plan such as a 401(k) if you are a corporation, or a Keogh or SEP if you are not. Your contributions to the Keogh or SEP are limited to an amount equal to about 15% to 25% of the net income of your business. If you have employees, some plans require that you contribute an equal percentage for them.

Your strategy is to contribute as much as possible and practical to one of these tax- and liability-protected retirement plans and then contribute any balance required to reach your million-dollar goal to a self-directed, tax-sheltered annuity where at least your earnings will compound without taxes. (See Chapter 33, "IRA and Keogh Investment Superstrategies," and Chapter 34, "Self-Directed Annuities.")

Depending on your business income, your objective is to put 10% of the net or a minimum of 3% to 5% of the gross into your wealth account. That money is never to be touched, not for the business, not for personal financial "emergencies," not for any reason until you decide to extract the income in later years. Only then can you guarantee yourself and your family that your business contributes to your lifetime wealth, no matter what rocky roads you encounter in between.

Chapter 29

THE ASSET MANAGEMENT
ACCOUNT (AMA)

Most bankers dwell in marble halls, which they get to dwell in because they encourage deposits and discourage withdrawals.

Ogden Nash
Poet
(1902–1971)

OBJECTIVE ────────────────────────────────

COUPLE THE CONVENIENCE OF CHECKING WITH THE
POWER OF AN INVESTMENT.

There are 15 no-minimum checking accounts in which you can often earn twice the interest your bank will pay. These asset management accounts (AMAs) cannot be found at banks, savings and loans, or credit unions. They are national checking accounts and represent money management systems of the future that are available today.

Asset management accounts are available through brokerage firms, mutual funds, or other large financial institutions. Some AMAs require as little as a $1,000 minimum deposit, while others, such as those offered at Merrill Lynch, Fidelity, and Shearson, want $10,000 to $25,000 just to open the account. The declaration cash account (DCA) has no minimum deposit requirement. Edward D. Jones's "Full Service" account requires only a $1,000 deposit and as little as a $500 minimum balance. Additional deposits can be made at any time. Asset management accounts have no minimum check requirement or limit to the number of checks you can write. Money market funds and bank money market accounts offer only limited checking.

Strategy #288
USE AN ASSET MANAGEMENT ACCOUNT TO DOUBLE THE INTEREST YOU RECEIVE FROM A BANK CHECKING ACCOUNT.

There are two profits in an asset management account. The first is the variable interest paid on your account balance. Interest rates in asset management accounts have averaged between 6.5% and 18% since 1980 and often pay 2% to 5% more than CDs. The second profit is an additional ½% to 1% created by the daily compounding.

Strategy #289
WRITE ALL YOUR BILL-PAYING CHECKS FROM YOUR ASSET MANAGEMENT ACCOUNT.

Write all your checks from your AMA. An AMA should not be used as a place to store money unless the current interest rate is over 10½%. Deposit each month just enough to cover the checks you intend to write. Over the past nine years, you would have earned in an asset management account more than two times what you earned in a bank checking account. Here is a comparison:

	Bank Checking Account	Asset Management Account			
Year	Interest	Compounded Interest		Legal Float	= Total Interest
1986	5.50%	7%	+	2%	= 9%
1987	5.50	7	+	2	= 9
1988	5.50	7	+	2	= 9
1989	5.50	8	+	2	= 10
1990	5.50	8	+	not applicable	= 8
1991	5.30	6	+	NA	= 6
1992	4.50	5	+	NA	= 5
1993	2.50	4	+	NA	= 4
1994	2.00	2	+	NA	= 2
TOTAL	61.25%	97%	+	19%	= 116%

Strategy #290
CHOOSE AN SIPC-INSURED ASSET MANAGEMENT ACCOUNT.

Most of the asset management accounts have SIPC (Security Investors Protection Corporation) insurance. SIPC insurance is to brokerage firms, mutual funds, asset management accounts, and other financial institutions what FDIC insurance is to banks. Accounts are insured up to $2 million with additional insurance available to $5 million.

Strategy #291
CHOOSE AN ASSET MANAGEMENT ACCOUNT THAT OFFERS A DEBIT CARD.

The debit card is a plastic check that has the universal acceptance of a credit card but no end-of-the-month bill. A debit card looks like a Visa card, runs through the merchant's machine like a Visa card, but doesn't charge anything. The merchant can't tell the difference. When the merchant slip gets to your asset management account, the amount you paid is deducted directly from your account balance—a monthly bill but no check to write.

Nine of the asset management accounts issue Visa debit cards, while others, including Shearson and Smith Barney, issue American Express credit cards that cannot be used as debit cards. The debit card is too good a financial management tool to be without and should be a consideration in determining which AMA is for you.

Strategy #292
CHOOSE AN AMA WITH A LOW YEARLY FEE.

Yearly fees of $25 to $125 are charged on all AMA accounts, except the DCA, Charles Schwab, and IDS accounts, which have no fee. Charles Schwab, however, requires you to trade in other securities to keep your AMA open. A yearly fee of over $50 is unreasonable since there are alternatives. Because your asset management account is really an investment account, the yearly fees are tax deductible as a miscellaneous investment expense.

To choose your asset management account, use the comparison chart at the end of this chapter. One important decision is determining if you have the required initial deposit amount and can maintain the required balance.

After you have made your initial deposit, a much smaller minimum balance is usually required to keep the account open and earning interest. Check the chart to determine the minimum balance requirements of the various accounts. All the accounts are good. Simply pick the one that fits you best, with the convenience and services you need.

Call the toll-free telephone number listed or the local office in your area for the accounts in which you are interested. Refer to the account by name and ask for a prospectus. Contained in the prospectus is everything you need to know about the account. To open your account, simply fill out the account application card and mail it with a check for at least the minimum deposit. You will receive a checkbook similar to your bank checkbook along with your initial deposit receipt.

Strategy #293
USE AN ASSET MANAGEMENT ACCOUNT FOR YOUR SMALL BUSINESS CHECKING ACCOUNT.

Many of the AMAs also offer checking privileges to small businesses. From the Asset Management Account Comparison Chart you'll notice that those offering business accounts include the DCA account, Edward D. Jones, IDS, Fidelity, Citibank, and most of the brokerage firm accounts. You can enjoy the debit card privileges for your small business by opening a separate business account at the AMA of your choice.

Asset management accounts prove that there are always better money management alternatives if you know where to look.

ASSET MANAGEMENT ACCOUNT COMPARISON CHART

Sponsor's Name	Account Name	Information Number	Minimum Initial Deposit	Minimum Balance Required	Checks Returned	Yearly Fee	Debit/ Credit Card	Margin Accounts Available	Business Accounts Available
Declaration Cash Account	DCA	800 423-2345	100[1]	None[2]	No	0[2]	None	No	Yes
Kemper	Money Plus	800 621-1048	5,000	None	Yes	65	Visa Gold	No	No
IDS Financial	IDS Cash Mgt.	800 328-8300	2,000	300	No	0	None	No	Yes
Schwab	Schwab One	800 421-4488	5,000	None	No	0[4]	Visa	Yes	Yes
Fidelity	Ultra Service/USA	800 544-6262	10,000	10,000	Yes	0	MC Gold/ Visa Gold	Yes	Yes
Citibank	Focus	800 285-1703	100,000	10,000	Yes	125	Visa	Yes	Yes
Dean Witter	Active Asset	800 222-3326	10,000	None	No	80	Visa	Yes	Yes
Pru-Bache	Command Acct.	800 222-4321	15,000	None	No	100	Visa	Yes	Yes
Shearson	Fin. Mgt.	800 221-3636	10,000	5,000	No	50	Visa	Yes	Yes
Paine Webber	Resource Mgt.	800 937-7071	10,000	None	Yes	85[3]	MC Gold	Yes	Yes
Merrill Lynch	Cash Mgt.	800 262-4636	20,000	None	No	100	Visa Gold	Yes	Yes
A. G. Edwards	Total Asset	use local listing	20,000	None	No	80	Visa	Yes	Yes

1. Initial deposit less than $1,000; $15 opening fee.
2. Balance under $2,500: $44 annual fee deducted quarterly plus $5 fee if over 5 checks are written per month.
   Balance of $2,500–$5,000: no monthly fee, $5 fee if over 5 checks are written per month.
   Balance over $5,000: no fees, unlimited checking.
3. $85 charge for checks only; $100 with both checks and debit card.
4. $5 if account is under $5,000.

Chapter 30

THE MONEY MOVEMENT STRATEGY™

You don't buy a stock because it has real value. You buy it because you feel there is always a greater fool down the street who will pay more than you paid.

Donald J. Stockings
Securities and Exchange Commission
1925

MOVE YOUR INVESTMENT MONEY BETWEEN STOCK, BOND, AND MONEY MARKET MUTUAL FUNDS TO EARN AN AVERAGE OF 15% PER YEAR.

When *Wealth Without Risk* was first published in the fall of 1988, financial publications and financial salespeople were shocked that anyone would claim in writing that novice investors could average 15% per year in basically safe investments, mutual funds, using a strategy I call Money Movement. As a matter of fact, financial writers claimed it couldn't be done.

Unfortunately, most financial writers for magazines and newspapers know very little about money and how it really works, other than how to spell the words correctly. The reason? They are low-paid graduates of journalism school and have very little or no personal experience of the strategies required to build or preserve wealth. What these writers failed to check out or realize is that I had been teaching 15% safe investment strategies for ten years before the book was published, and over 100,000 individuals and families were already employing them successfully. Because some basically broke financial journalist doesn't believe a strategy will work only means he or she hasn't used it.

I have received thousands of letters about how well these strategies have worked for people who heretofore thought they had little chance of dealing successfully in the financial world. There is not nor was there ever really any doubt that 15% returns can easily be achieved without taking risks. Risk is more often the result of a lack of knowledge than the result of going after a greater return. That's right, anyone who ever said to get greater returns you must take greater risks was wrong.

Can you still do it in the nineties? Get returns averaging 15% per year without taking big risks? Absolutely, particularly with discounted mortgages (See Chapter 35) and tax lien certificates (See Chapter 36).

In 1993, the Givens Organization had an independent historical analysis of the Money Movement Strategy completed. Stephen Butler, managing director of World Investment Group Inc., mathematically evaluated the results of the Money Movement Strategy over the 13-year period from January 1, 1979 through December 31, 1991. Butler's conclusions are as follows:

> "Had an investor followed the strategy, and started with an investment of $10,000, based upon the criteria set forth in this report, he would have ended with the tidy sum of $61,190, which represents a total return of 15% compounded annually.
>
> "I have taken every possible step to be overly conservative in calculating the returns. I believe that the average investor who followed the Money Movement Strategy over the relevant period of time should have exceeded 15%, possibly 20% or more."

Of interesting note is that the strategy only required the average of one transaction per year, and not one transaction in the 13-year period of time resulted in a net loss.

Here are some verbatim sections of the study as written by Stephen Butler.

> The objective of this report is to examine an investment strategy known as the "Money Movement Strategy," and to determine the following issues:
>
> (1) Is the strategy, as described later, one which will over protracted periods of time return to the investor consistent profits? And,
> (2) If an investor committed $10,000 to the strategy on January 1, 1979, what would the current value of his investment be,

assuming the investor neither withdrew, nor added funds, and reinvested all income and capital gains."

In early 1979, Mr. Charles J. Givens Jr. (hereinafter the "author"), first presented a theory of investing that posits that an investor can profit from the inverse relationship between yield rates on fixed-income investments, and returns on equity investments. This theory was named "The Money Management Strategy" by the author.

The presumption is twofold, first, it is well accepted that over long periods of time equity investments far outperform fixed-income investments, particularly when other influences such as inflation are factored in, however, during certain short-term periods, particularly when interest rates are relatively high, fixed-income investments will outperform their equity counterparts. And secondly, the author felt that a timing strategy could be implemented which would allow an investor to reap the benefits of upward movements in equities, and limit the downside risks attendant to the equities markets.

The author determined that the "trigger" for allocating funds between fixed-income and equity investments should be the prime rate published by money center banks. This factor was chosen for two reasons, first because it is well published and easily determinable, and second, because the prime rate is not volatile, and reacts consistently without short-term "spikes" and "dips" which would cause erratic switches in the allocation of assets. (Note: in 1990 the author amended his strategy to allow the trigger to be the yield of the 30-year U.S. Treasury bond. The author continues to use the prime rate as the alternative method, and therefore, for consistency this report will only deal with the prime rate.)

To effectuate the switch between fixed-income and equity investments the author published what is called "The Investor Decision Line" or "IDL." The IDL is the only subjective element of the strategy.

The IDL is the percentage rate that the prime rate must achieve in order to trigger a switch. The author determines the level of the IDL by considering two factors:

(1) whether the prime rate level is relatively high or low, and,
(2) whether the direction of the prime rate is currently up or down.

The author has a fundamental belief that managing the costs associated with brokerage commissions is of paramount importance to the strategy, also that mutual funds are the most appropriate investments to be utilized in the strategy.

Therefore, the author recommends that investors using this strategy use no-load mutual funds. The author does not, however, recommend any particular mutual fund.

In the strategy, three types of mutual funds are recommended, money market funds, bonds funds, and equity funds. Money market funds are utilized during periods when interest rates are generally rising, bond funds are utilized during periods when interest rates are generally declining, and equity funds are utilized at times when interest rates are considered to be low.

THE ANALYSIS

The following analysis of the Money Movement Strategy is for example purposes only. The transactions represented in the calculations did not actually occur, and this analysis is demonstrative only of what *"would likely have"* occurred.

The purpose of this analysis is to create a model portfolio based upon the Money Movement Strategy, and to determine what rate of return an investor would have realized had he invested $10,000.00 on January 1, 1979. This analysis assumes that the investor reinvested all capital gains and income, and made no withdrawals or additional investments.

Since the author has not during the 14-year history of the strategy recommended any particular mutual fund or investment to carry out the strategy, in order to determine the return that an investor *would likely have* received during this period of time, we must look to the historical record of similarly performing investments.

For purposes of determining the yield that a money market fund *would likely have* garnered, we will use the historical record of the three-month U.S. Treasury bill. We feel that this index would actually represent an overly conservative yield since portfolio managers of money market funds may purchase investments with maturities of more than three months, and will therefore yield higher rates. Also managers of money market funds, unless prohibited, will purchase short-term corporate debt such as commercial paper which historically has yielded higher returns for like maturities.

For the purposes of determining the yield and capital gain/loss that a bond fund *would likely have* achieved we will utilize the average of Moody's Investor Services historical yields for their Aaa and Baa indexes. By averaging these two indexes we feel that we will closely duplicate the yield and capital gain/loss that a conservatively managed corporate bond fund would have achieved during the applicable periods of time. Had an investor used a "high-yield" bond fund during the same periods he likely would have garnered a higher yield and capital gain/loss, in the alternative, had an investor utilized a U.S. Treasury bond fund he likely would have realized a lower yield and capital gain/loss.

For the purpose of determining the yield and capital gain/loss that an equity mutual fund *would likely have* realized we will use the Standard & Poor's 500 stock index. This index is a broad based index of 500 domestic stock corporations. The stocks in this index have not been chosen for their dividend yields, and they are generally considered to be well capitalized, "blue chip" companies. There are two important differences between this index and the "typical" equity mutual fund. First, this index is not managed in the way an equity fund is. In other words, the manager of an equity mutual fund has the ability to dispose of poor performing stocks in his portfolio, while the Standard & Poor's 500 Index must maintain those positions. Secondly, equity mutual funds normally don't carry a portfolio of 500 different stock issuers, and are able to concentrate on specific industries which are performing well. Both of these factors would indicate that a well managed equity mutual fund *would likely have* outperformed the Standard & Poor's 500 Index.

We believe that using the indexes identified above would not only fairly duplicate the performance of a typical money market, bond, and stock fund, but it also relieves us of the obligation of having to select a particular mutual fund for historical performance, wherein our motivation for selecting a particular fund could be questioned.

Of importance to this analysis is the way in which the IDL is disseminated to followers of the strategy. Typically, it is distributed through a monthly newsletter, in this way the followers of the strategy will receive the information within one to 30 days after the IDL is changed. Therefore, in the interest of fairness in calculating returns to the model portfolio, we will calculate all purchases and sales on the 15th of each month, and at the average price of the index for the month in which the change is made.

HOW THE MONEY MOVEMENT STRATEGY WORKS

Mutual fund returns, using the Money Movement Strategy you are about to learn, should average you 15% plus over the next decade—*twice* what you could expect from a bank CD, T-bills, or leaving your money sitting in a money market fund. Almost the same 20% that was achieved in the eighties.

With the world economy stabilizing due to more and more

countries participating on a global scale, interest rates will not
fluctuate as wildly as they did in the eighties. The bigger the
fluctuations in interest rates, the greater the potential profits
from the Money Movement Strategy when used in mutual funds,
annuities, and your retirement plan. For instance, in the early
eighties money market funds were paying a whopping 18%. We
probably won't see that again in the nineties. Mutual fund
managers, however, have gotten smarter over the years and
should be able to generate bigger profits for investors for any
given set of economic conditions even without major interest
rate fluctuations.

Demand from your investment plan an average of 15% for the
next ten years and I'll show you how to achieve that goal.
Mutual fund strategies will enable you to remain a passive
investor, spending little time watching your money and still
getting high returns. If you don't mind putting in a little extra
time creating discounted mortgages or bidding on tax lien certificates, which you'll learn about later, 20% is your target.

Strategy #294
USE THE MONEY MOVEMENT STRATEGY™ TO ELIMINATE WORRY AND EMOTION FROM HIGH-RETURN INVESTING.

The Money Movement Strategy is an easy-to-use method of
maximizing profits in any mutual-fund-based investment and
takes the emotion and worry out of investment decision-making.
You can use the Money Movement Strategy successfully in:

- mutual fund families
- your 401(k) or similar retirement plan
- your IRA or Keogh plan
- self-directed, tax-sheltered annuities

One strategy does it all.

Money Movement is based on the known but underused fact
that the three most popular types of securities investments—
stocks, bonds, and money market instruments—are all sensitive
to general interest rates. That means when interest rates change
so does the value of a mutual fund group of any of these investments.

Look at the chart below and you will see the relationship
between up or down movements of the interest rates and the
values of these three different types of investments. For instance,

when interest rates go up, the value of stocks and bonds decreases, but money market instruments increase in value. The exact opposite tends to be true when interest rates go down.

THE DIRECTION OF THE STOCK MARKET, BOND MARKET, AND MONEY MARKET
based on changes in general interest rates

Interest Rates	Stocks	Bonds	Money Market Instruments
Up	Down	Down	Up
Down	Up	Up	Down

How much impact do the interest rates have on changes in the selling price of investments? Below is a chart that will show you what percentage of the increase or decrease in the price of a group of stocks, bonds, or money market instruments is the result of interest rate changes and what percentage of the change is due to other factors. Here are my estimates:

Group Of	% of Price Change Due to Changes in Interest Rates	% of Price Change Due to Other Factors
Stocks	80	20
Bonds	90	10
Money Market Instruments	98	2

As you can see from the chart, the greatest percentage of price changes, up or down, is due to changes in the interest rates. Therefore, for a smart investor who doesn't want the major risk of attempting to pick the right individual stock, bond, or money market instrument, why not make a safe, proven bet on the impact of the interest rate direction on the value of a group of such investments? That's what the Money Movement Strategy is all about.

You invest in a group of stocks, bonds, or money market instruments by putting your money into a mutual fund instead of an individual stock, bond, or money market instrument. The price of any one stock or bond is like a feather in the wind carried in nonpredictable, random directions by news reports about the company, good or bad, or rumors about the company, good or bad! Whereas 80% or more of the price changes of stocks, bonds, or money market instruments are caused by changes in national interest rates, 80% of the risk inherent in investing in them is created by buying a single stock or bond or money market instrument instead of investing in an entire portfolio or group of investments such as those in a mutual fund. Does that mean you can reduce your investment risk 80% by investing in only mutual funds and not the stock or bonds of a single company? You bet!

In Chapter 31 you will learn everything you need to know about mutual funds and how to choose and use them successfully. In this chapter, we will concentrate on how to use the Money Movement Strategy. "Why bother?" you may ask. "Why not put my money away in a good, long-term, safe investment and just let it sit in one place and work for me?"

The reason? It won't. A long-term investment won't work nearly as hard for you or return to you the kind of profits you want and deserve.

For information on a managed mutual fund account that follows the Money Movement Strategy, call Wealth Asset Managers at 1-800-487-4147.

Strategy #295
NEVER STORE MONEY.

A futile effort made by most so-called conservative investors is the search for a good long-term investment. There are good investments and there are long-term investments, but when it comes to stocks, bonds, and money market instruments, there are no good long-term investments. The best investment this year will become the worst investment next year as inflation and interest rates change. To become a successful investor, you must be willing to move your money from one type of investment to another, but only once every year or two. Fortunately, investing in mutual fund families gives you the opportunity to move your investments at the appropriate time with a simple phone call.

Strategy #296
AVOID INVESTMENT STRATEGIES THAT REQUIRE THE PREDICTION OF THE IMPACT OF IMPENDING EVENTS.

A majority of investors who have gotten beyond fixed-rate CDs often lose because they want to be part-time clairvoyants.

• "Medical stocks will rise next year because health costs are going up."

- "Invest in big agriculture companies because the emerging Eastern Bloc countries will buy more food."
- "Invest in leisure companies because Americans will have more money to spend."
- "Buy silver because there is an impending shortage."

That kind of predicting doesn't work for part-time investors. It didn't work 25 years ago when I began investing and it doesn't work any better now. You would do just as well making your decisions with a coin toss or a dart board. Why doesn't it work? Because even if your prediction turns out to be true, the changes in the prices of the investments brought on by the event have already occurred by the time you thought of it. The money has already been made, so to speak, and not by you.

Most financial salespeople play on those kinds of "insider's track" desires by listing reasons for buying a stock or other investment in the form of predictions about a company, an industry, or the direction of the economy. Those who listen lose more often than they win. The salesperson or broker, on the other hand, always wins. The percentage of commission you pay is the same whether you are winning or losing.

One advantage to the Money Movement Strategy has always been that no predictions are required. No changes in your investments are made in anticipation of changing interest rates or other events. Changes are only made after the event—the movement of the interest rates up or down. No guessing, no predicting required, and because interest rates move so slowly, you have ample time to make your changes, even 30 days or more after a change is indicated. Leave the short-term predictions and moves to the speculators. They can take the frequent losses that result from prediction strategies. You won't like them or want them.

Don't get greedy. Greed is the attempt to beat a market by doubling your money in one year or less. Like the house in Las Vegas, the market will beat you almost every time, allowing you to win just enough for just long enough to keep you interested and involved. Mentally settle for a mutual fund average return of 15%, and with the compounding of your reinvested earnings over any ten-year period, you will automatically and systematically be getting richer slowly, the safe, sure way. Because of the high earnings, your money still doubles every five years or so, instead of every ten, as it does for most investors.

Strategy #297
INVEST IN STOCKS, BONDS, AND MONEY MARKET INSTRUMENTS ONLY THROUGH MUTUAL FUNDS.

Let's look more closely at the reasons why mutual funds as an investment eliminate so many of the problems common to part-time, otherwise busy investors. A mutual fund is a group of a hundred or more different stocks, bonds, or money market instruments, all managed by the same company. When you invest in mutual funds, you own a small share of the fund's entire investment portfolio. Mutual funds give you the benefits of a diversified portfolio of stocks, bonds, or money market instruments without the risks, costs, or required expertise in picking the individual investments. Benefits of mutual fund investing are so appealing that there is virtually no reason to invest in individual stocks, bonds, or money market instruments ever again. If you are just beginning your investment plan, mutual funds get you off to the right start.

Here are the reasons that mutual funds make investment sense:

- Professional Management—Mutual fund managers are among the most knowledgeable financial people in the country. A full-time pro, not you, is responsible for evaluating the stocks, bonds, or other investments held by the fund and deciding when to buy, sell, or hold.
- Safety—A mutual fund is a group or portfolio of more than 100 stocks, bonds, or money market instruments all managed by the same company. You, as an investor, own shares in the entire portfolio. Because of the incredible diversification, a mutual fund investment is mathematically eight times safer than an investment in any one stock or bond. The safety factor of mutual funds was clearly demonstrated in the stock market drop of October 19, 1987. While many well-respected stocks dropped as much as 40%, the average stock mutual fund temporarily dropped only 16%.
- Ease of Evaluation—The track record of every mutual fund is a matter of public record. You simply check your newspaper for the previous day's closing price (NAV) just as you would for a single stock. There is currently no effective way to evaluate the recommendations or results of stockbrokers, financial planners, or investment counselors.
- Control—Only those who are willing to exercise a measure of control over their investments can safely and consistently earn big profits. Those who turn control over to a broker, financial planner, or other investment salesman generally do poorly. Mutual funds are an excel-

lent vehicle for taking control of your investments and consequently your financial future.

- Income—You can choose to receive periodic income from any type of mutual fund: stock, bond, or money market.
- Liquidity—You can withdraw part or all of your money anytime you wish and within 24 hours.
- Investment Options—Your investment options are almost limitless because there are hundreds of mutual funds. You can invest in stocks, bonds, money market instruments, overseas companies, and even precious metals through mutual funds.

Strategy #298
USE THE EXTRA PROFIT POTENTIAL OF MUTUAL FUNDS TO EARN DOUBLE THE CD RATE.

MUTUAL FUND PROFIT POTENTIAL

Type of Fund	Profit Potential		
	Dividends	Interest	Appreciation
Stock	Yes	No	Yes
Bond	No	Yes	Yes
Money Market	Yes*	No	No

* Money market dividends are actually the equivalent of the combined interest rates earned on investments.

How can you average over 15% per year in mutual funds? Because two out of three types of mutual funds pay two potential profits instead of just one. Even money market funds with only one source of potential profits paid 18% in 1981 and 14% in 1984. Average stock funds had six years of over 15% returns during the eighties. Bonds had three 15%-plus years with one year, 1982, of earning 29%—enough profit to cover two years at 15%. These results are the average performance, not the performance of the best-performing funds or the funds recommended by me during the same period. See the Mutual Fund Performance History chart, page 449.

The Money Movement Strategy has had investors generally in the right place at the right time for over 13 years, exactly what it is meant to do—and it will do the same for you.

Strategy #299
USE ONLY THE NO-LOAD MUTUAL FUNDS.

A true no-load mutual fund charges no commissions when you invest, and no commissions when you withdraw your money. Out of the over 2,000 mutual funds, about 300 are no-load.

Where does the mutual fund make its money? All mutual funds, whether they charge commissions or not, charge about 1% per year for management fees and expenses. For this low fee the mutual fund:

- does the research
- chooses the investments
- watches the markets for you eight hours a day
- keeps all necessary records of your account
- sends you periodic statements, usually monthly, about your account

No-load funds give you a great deal of investment help for very little money. The net asset value per share (NAV), quoted in the newspaper or on your statement, already reflects the deduction of the management fee.

A load is a sales commission and not a management fee. The load is paid to a broker, brokerage firm, financial planner, insurance agent, or anyone else who "sells" you the investment. A load or sales commission does nothing to increase your chances for profit. It is simply an expense. By working directly with a no-load mutual fund and eliminating the middleman, you save up to 9% in commissions. Remember, you can't be splitting your money with everyone else and end up with much for yourself.

Does paying a commission to invest in a load fund in any way earn you extra profits? The answer is no. Studies for over 20 years have shown that no-load and load funds perform equally when the sales charge is disregarded. Often there are more no-load than load funds in the list of top 20 best performing funds. When you do include sales commissions in calculating mutual fund performance, load funds earn less. If financial salespeople ever tell you something different, they are lying.

There are three classifications of load mutual funds:

High-Load Mutual Funds

High-load funds are those mutual funds that charge 4%–9% commissions that are paid from the money you invest or withdraw. The front-end load means you pay commissions when you invest, reducing your principal. A back-end load means you pay commissions when you withdraw your money, reducing your earnings. Many back-end load funds become no-load funds after your money has been invested for five years or more. Is there ever a time when your best choice of mutual funds might be a load fund? Yes, but only a back-end load fund. Let's say you want ongoing advice from a very successful financial adviser but want to avoid paying commissions for the advice. When you invest in a back-end load fund, the adviser gets paid a commission by the mutual fund instead of you. As long as you stay with the fund or the same fund family for at least five years, you pay no commissions even when you withdraw your money. If you withdraw your money during the first five years, however, you are charged a yearly decreasing commission that enables the fund to recoup some of the money it paid to the adviser as a commission.

When using the Money Movement Strategy in your employer-sponsored retirement plan, you may have no choice but to use the load funds offered in the plan. The tax benefits, however, will offset by many times the commissions you pay.

You will also use back-end load mutual funds if you invest in self-directed annuities. (See Chapter 34, "Self-Directed Annuities.")

Low-Load Mutual Funds

Low-load funds charge 3% or less when you invest or withdraw your money. There are low-load funds that do make good choices for aggressive investors, such as Fidelity's sector funds. Conservative investors should avoid low-load funds altogether. Most low-load funds do not pay commissions to salespeople but keep the money for advertising and extra profits.

12b-1 Funds

12b-1 funds are mutual funds that charge an extra 1% or so per year in addition to management fees supposedly to offset marketing costs. These funds are otherwise no-load.

Even though the Securities and Exchange Commission has permitted the 12b-1 charge for several years, very few mutual funds have actually applied a 12b-1 charge. Those who sell load mutual funds will lead you to believe that it is better to pay 6%–9% up front rather than to pay the 1% or so 12b-1 fee each year. Mathematically that is not true. When you pay an 8%

commission up front, only 92% of your money is actually invested. If you use a 12b-1 fund, 100% of your money is invested and the 1% fee is deducted from the earnings. However, you will want to avoid the 12b-1 funds, as well as the load funds, in favor of the no-load funds.

The Fund Family Fact Sheets (see the Appendix) indicate whether a fund charges a load of any type—front end, back end, or 12b-1. Those that are high-load are not in the list since there is no reason to use them.

Strategy #300
INVEST IN ONLY ONE TYPE OF MUTUAL FUND AT A TIME.

One and only one type of mutual fund is right for each set of interest rates and each economy. Interest rates and their direction are a product of and, when controlled, a cause of current economic conditions. One major mistake made by most investors, often on the advice of a novice investment salesman, is overdiversification: dividing investment capital among stocks, bonds, government securities, and money market funds. Overdiversification can cost you as much in lost profits as underdiversification. An overly diversified investment plan operates like a seesaw; when one side goes up, the other goes down. Refer to the chart on page 403.

Notice that when money market funds go up in value, stocks go down. If you diversify by putting half your money in stock and half in money market funds, the reduced profit in one can offset the increased profit in the other, getting you nowhere. When you are using the basic Money Movement Strategy, you will normally choose to keep all your mutual fund capital in just one *type* of mutual fund at a time, stock, bond, or money market. Once you learn and use the Money Movement Strategy successfully, you will be interested in the advanced strategies we teach the members of the Givens Organization that would occasionally put your money into two different types of funds at the same time.

Strategy #301
START WITH THE PRIME INTEREST RATE TO IDENTIFY THE SAFEST AND BEST MUTUAL FUND INVESTMENT FOR EACH ECONOMY.

The prime rate is the easiest of the interest rates for you to follow when using the Money Movement Strategy. Any change makes front-page headlines. The prime rate moves slowly and does not change direction as often as stock prices do. Looking at the Prime Rate Direction Changes Chart on page 421, you will notice that when direction changes of at least ½% are considered, the prime rate has changed direction only 15 times in the past 16 years. Two times during the last ten years the prime rate has continued in the same direction for more than two consecutive years. Turn to the Prime Rate Changes chart on page 421 and you can see that if you average the prime rate changes over a year, the changes tend to smooth out and flow in the same direction for long periods of time.

You must watch two components of the prime rate to know which type of mutual fund to choose:

- prime rate level—above or below the Investor's Decision Line
- prime rate direction—up or down

Refer back to the chart on page 403. Notice that two of the three choices for mutual fund investments used with the Money Movement Strategy tend to move in the same direction at the same time. When interest rates drop both stocks and bonds are on the rise at the same time. When interest rates rise, the general trend of both stocks and bonds is downward. How then do you pick which type of mutual fund will give you the greatest profit potential when interest rates are dropping?

You choose a stock or bond mutual fund based on what I call the Investor's Decision Line. Refer to the Money Movement Strategy chart on the following page. Notice that the Investor's Decision Line is at 9%. The curve on the left half of the chart represents any period in weeks, months, or even years when the prime interest rate is dropping. The upward portion of the curve on the right half of the chart represents any period when the prime rate is rising.

Also notice that there are three points during one interest rate cycle when you would move your money. At each of these points you move your money from one type of mutual fund

MONEY MOVEMENT STRATEGY™
Prime Rate Chart

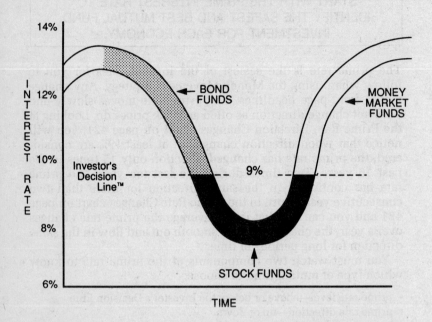

investment to another to maintain maximum safety and continued profits.

Two of these points are indicated by the Investor's Decision Line at 9%. When the prime rate is dropping and reaches 9%, you move your money from bond to stock funds. When the prime rate is increasing and reaches 9%, move from stock funds to money market funds. Finally, when the prime rate reaches a peak and changes direction from up to down, move from money market funds to bond funds. When interest rates are coming down but are still above 9%, bond mutual funds will generally grow faster in value than stocks. When the prime rate is coming down but drops below the Investor's Decision Line, 9% or less, stocks will generally grow faster in value than bonds.

To keep them straight, just remember this rhyme:

When interest rates are low, stocks will grow. When interest rates are high, stocks will die.

Does the Investor's Decision Line ever change? Yes, but only slowly over time. How is the Investor's Decision Line determined? It is determined by me by observing the general trends in the economy and interest rates. In our members' newsletter, *Success InSight*, changes in the Investor's Decision Line are always noted.

If you become a member of the Givens Organization, and I hope you do, you will be advised as all of our members are of any changes in the Investor's Decision Line. Knowing these changes can help you earn extra profits, but using the Investor's Decision Line at a fixed percentage at 9% will give you investment returns over the next few years that you may never before have dreamed possible.

Strategy #302
USE THE MONEY MARKET STRATEGY™ TO PICK THE UPSIDE OF THE MARKETS AND TO AVOID THE DOWNSIDE.

There is always one of the three types of mutual fund investments—stock, bond, or money market—that will outperform the others during any period of time. The Money Movement Strategy simply and unemotionally allows you to identify which one. In other words, by using Money Movement you have given yourself the best chance of catching the upswing or period of rising prices for stock, bond, and money market funds and at the same time avoiding the downsides. Just by moving your money every few months as shown in the Money Movement Strategy chart, you are constantly hitching your wagon to the next rising star.

Those who leave money invested long term in any one type of investment have tossed their investment future to the winds of fate, riding the stock market or bond market cycle or money market interest rates up and down like an elevator. Even though you might still end up with some profit, like the elevator, you move fast and continuously but basically go nowhere.

Two steps forward and one step backward has never been a strategy that appeals to me. Like an elevator, stocks and bonds have an up-and-down price cycle, and money market funds have an up-and-down interest rate cycle. Look at the graph on page 414 and you will see representations of these changes.

Under the best of circumstances, you would maximize your return on investment in any of the three types of mutual funds by having your money invested only during the upswing portion of each cycle. The upswings in the graphs are *a*, *c*, *e*, and *g*.

STOCK, BOND, OR MONEY MARKET FUND PRICE FLUCTUATIONS

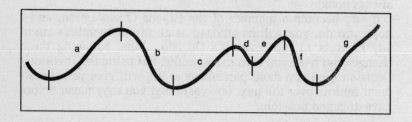

Conversely, you would not want to have your money in any one of the three mutual fund alternatives when they are in the down part of a cycle shown by *b*, *d*, and *f*. The Money Movement Strategy using interest rates as the determining factor will bring you closer to being at the right place at the right time than any other strategy, simple or complicated, that I have ever seen.

The Money Movement Strategy is not meant to get you in or out of a market or mutual fund type at the highest or lowest point in the cycle, but what it does best and most often is allow you to catch the general upswing of any cycle and avoid the period when the market or mutual fund type is in a general downswing. As soon as one type of mutual fund investment enters its general downswing cycle, you move your money to the next rising star. Therefore, your investments are growing much faster in value than they would just riding any of the markets through their normal up-and-down cycles.

The Money Movement Strategy is not meant to predict big drops in the stock market such as the one that occurred in 1987, nor when using the strategy is it necessary to concern yourself with the possibility of a big short-term drop in stock prices. Bond and money market prices don't experience big drops over short time periods.

In October of 1987 when the stock market dropped 500 points in a day, from 2200 to 1700, I was on an airplane to Hawaii to check on one of my radio stations. I only heard the news when I got off the plane and there were dozens of calls from reporters around the country.

"What should people who own stocks or stock mutual fund shares do?" was the repeated frantic question.

"Nothing," was my unemotional answer. "When interest rates are low, stocks will grow. Interest rates are low now," I said, "so the drop will be temporary and short term. The Federal Reserve will force interest even lower to increase stability and speed the recovery."

The Federal Reserve did lower interest rates and the stock market and stock mutual funds not only recovered but then set new records within a few months, turning apparent potential losses into big profits for those who stayed invested in stock mutual funds. The only losers were those who took their money out at the bottom of the short-term decline and stuck it in a bank account or money market fund. Those who were using the Money Movement Strategy profited, as always.

Emotions will make a mess out of the most well-intentioned investment plan. Money Movement removes the emotion and provides exact instructions on what to do and when to do it. Listed below are the biggest drops in the Dow Jones Industrial Average for the ten years we call the eighties. None had any lasting effect on overall stock market profits for the decade. Therefore, don't be caught up in the media-hyped term *stock market crash.*

DOW CORRECTIONS SINCE 1982

Year	Duration	Dow Begin	Dow End	% Drop
1982	Nov. 3–Nov. 23	1065	991	7
1984	Jan. 6–July 24	1287	1087	16
1986	July 2–Aug. 1	1909	1764	8
1987	Apr. 6–May 20	2406	2216	8
1987	Aug. 25–Oct. 15	2722	2413	11
1987	Oct. 19–Oct. 19	2246	1738	23
1989	Oct. 9–Oct. 13	2791	2569	8

Strategy #303
INVEST IN STOCK MUTUAL FUNDS WHEN THE PRIME RATE IS BELOW THE INVESTOR'S DECISION LINE™.

The biggest and most consistent rise in overall stock prices generally occurs when the prime rate is below the Investor's Decision Line. Why? When interest rates are low, corporations pay less interest on the money they borrow, which increases their potential profits, which in turn helps boost stock prices. Also, stock dividends look even better in comparison to other investments such as bonds, T-bills, money market funds, and

T-bill interest rates, which are all low when interest rates are down. The stock market looks more attractive and demand for stocks goes up. When you've got more buyers than sellers, prices also go up. Therefore, when interest rates are low, stocks will grow and your money belongs in a stock mutual fund.

Over the last 19 years, I have constantly worked on fine-tuning the Money Movement Strategy as the results come in. In the early eighties, for instance, the Money Movement Strategy chart showed that when the interest rate bottomed out and changed direction from down to up, that was the point to move from stock to money market funds. Many investors who have followed this strategy for the past ten years or so remember the early charts and did exceptionally well with this strategy.

You can, however, do slightly better if you wait to change from stock to money market funds until interest rates not only have begun to rise but have again risen enough to reach the Investor's Decision Line of 9%. As I write this, the prime rate is 7.75%, so Money Movement investors would wait until the prime rate reaches or exceeds the 9% level before moving from stock to money market mutual funds. Therefore, leave your money in stock mutual funds any time and every time the prime rate is below 9% or below the current Investor's Decision Line.

Strategy #304
**MOVE YOUR MONEY TO A MONEY MARKET FUND
WHEN THE PRIME RATE MOVES ABOVE THE
INVESTOR'S DECISION LINE™.**

How do you know when stock mutual funds no longer have the potential for the greatest profits of the three types of mutual funds? The answer is, when the prime rate is rising and reaches or moves past the Investor's Decision Line. At that time phone your mutual fund family and move your money out of stock mutual funds and into a money market mutual fund. Which one? Basically any one of the regular money market funds. When the prime rate is above the horizontal Investor's Decision Line, money market funds not only will give you the best return but will also be the safest investment since periods of high interest rates are when stock prices tend to fluctuate wildly and bonds decrease in value for every jump in the prime rate. On the other hand, money market fund interest rates increase with just about every increase in the prime rate.

Can you ever make money in a money market fund? Of course. Sometimes incredible returns. In 1981, with the prime rate averaging 18%, money market funds were paying as much as 20% interest! In 1984 money market funds were paying as much as 14%. However, without the prospect of capital appreciation that is inherent in both stocks and bonds, money market funds will not average the big returns you are looking for over long periods of time. Think of money market funds as your safe harbor during the storm. Instead of experiencing the wild fluctuations of stocks and the decreasing values of both stocks and bonds that occur when interest rates are high and rising, your money market fund is earning a steady 10% to 12%. You are waiting for another big opportunity in stock or bond mutual funds, which will occur when the prime rate again turns and starts downward.

Strategy #305
MOVE YOUR MONEY TO A BOND FUND WHEN THE PRIME RATE IS HIGH AND COMING DOWN.

As long as the prime rate is over the Investor's Decision Line and moving up, stay in money market funds. When the prime rate changes direction and starts downward, move your money to the third and last type of mutual fund in the prime rate cycle, a bond mutual fund.

Bond mutual funds are generally the best-paying investment when the prime rate is high and coming down. During that period you will earn two profits from bonds—interest and appreciation. The appreciation can be your big profit, averaging as much as 10% to 20% in a single year. That's in addition to the interest you are also guaranteed.

There are two principles that will help you understand why the big upswing in the bond cycle occurs when the prime rate is high (above the Investor's Decision Line) and coming down.

When the Prime Rate Drops 1%, Bonds Appreciate 10%.

Prime down "one," bonds and bond mutual funds up "ten." Ten to one is the best leverage you'll ever get in a safe investment plan. A good example was 1982, when the prime rate dropped 5%, from 16½% to 11½%, and the average bond mutual fund appreciated over 30%. Tax-free bond funds actually outperformed the regular bond funds that year.

Why are bonds and government securities a poor investment so much of the time? Because the opposite of the foregoing principle is also true.

When the Prime Rate Rises 1%, Bonds Drop 10%.

Prime up "one," bonds and bond mutual funds down "ten." Never invest in bonds, tax-exempt bonds, GNMAs, or government securities when the prime rate is going up. Your principal may be decreasing faster than you are earning interest. Yes, your interest may be guaranteed, but your principal is not. Most financial salesmen will incorrectly tell you to hold on to 7% or 8% bonds even when the value of your investment is falling because you "haven't lost anything unless you sell, and after all, you are still getting the interest payments." You have lost. What you lose with that faulty reasoning is the opportunity to reinvest your money later in bonds paying 12% to 13% when the prime rate goes up.

The Money Movement Strategy will produce the greatest profits when the prime rate is dropping, sometimes 20% or more per year in stock and occasionally bond mutual funds. When the prime rate is rising, Money Movement becomes more of a defensive strategy, but profits are still in the 10% to 15% range for the year. During these periods you can if you wish use discounted mortgages or tax lien certificates as your guaranteed source of 15% to 25% returns. See Chapters 35 and 36.

The Money Movement Strategy is not intended as a get-rich-quick scheme. It is a lifelong strategy for reducing risk and maximizing investment profits. The Money Movement Strategy will allow you to average 15% per year over any five- or ten-year period—without having to watch your money day by day or worry about its whereabouts. Money Movement is the strategy of choice for both conservative and aggressive investors, for beginners as well as more sophisticated investors. The proof is in the results, and Money Movement has consistently worked for hundreds of thousands of smart investors.

The following chart lists the prime rate history from January 1979 to May 1994. The chart also lists the correct mutual fund investments during this period according to the Money Movement Strategy. If you had made these investments, you would have profited by an average of 20% per year. The correct investments shown were based on the Investor's Decision Line published in the Charles J. Givens Organization newsletters and taught at Givens Organization workshops.

PRIME RATE HISTORY

Here's how investors using the Money Movement Strategy averaged 20% during the past 15 years.

Year	Date	Prime Rate	Correct Investment*	Year	Date	Prime Rate	Correct Investment*
1979	Jan. 1	11¾	MM		Oct. 1	13½	MM
	June 19	11½	MM		17	14	MM
	July 27	11¾	MM		29	14½	MM
	Aug. 16	12	MM		Nov. 6	15½	MM
	28	12¼	MM		17	16¼	MM
	Sept. 7	12¾	MM		21	17	MM
	14	13	MM		26	17¾	MM
	21	12¼	MM		Dec. 2	18½	MM
	28	13½	MM		5	19	MM
	Oct. 9	14½	MM		10	20	MM
	23	15	MM	1981	Jan. 2	20½	MM
	Nov. 1	15¼	MM		9	20	MM
	9	15½	MM		Feb. 3	19½	BF
	16	15¾	MM		23	19	BF
	30	15½	MM		Mar. 10	18	BF
	Dec. 7	15¼	MM		17	17½	BF
1980	Feb. 22	16½	MM		Apr. 2	17	BF
	29	16¾	MM		24	17½	BF
	Mar. 4	17¼	MM		30	18	MM
	7	17¾	MM		May 4	19	MM
	14	18½	MM		11	19½	MM
	19	19	MM		19	20	MM
	28	19½	MM		22	20½	MM
	April 2	20	MM		June 3	20	MM
	18	19½	MM		July 8	20½	MM
	May 1	19	BF		Sept. 15	20	MM
	2	18½	BF		22	19½	MM
	7	17½	BF		Oct. 5	19	BF
	16	16½	BF		13	18	BF
	23	14½	BF		Nov. 3	17½	BF
	30	14	BF		9	17	BF
	June 6	13	BF		20	16½	BF
	13	12½	BF		24	16	BF
	20	12	BF		Dec. 1	15¾	BF
	July 7	11½	BF	1982	Feb. 2	16½	BF
	Aug. 22	11¼	BF		18	17	BF
	27	11½	BF		23	16½	BF
	Sept. 8	12	MM		July 20	16	BF
	12	12½	MM		29	15½	BF
	26	13	MM				

Year	Date	Prime Rate	Correct Investment*	Year	Date	Prime Rate	Correct Investment*
	Aug. 2	15	BF	1987	Mar. 31	7¾	SF
	16	14½	BF		May 1	8	SF
	18	14	BF		15	8¼	SF
	23	13½	BF		Sept. 4	8¾	SF
	Oct. 7	13	BF		Oct. 6	9¼	SF
	14	12	BF		22	9	SF
	Nov. 22	11½	BF		Nov. 5	8¾	SF
1983	Jan. 11	11	SF	1988	Feb. 2	8½	SF
	Feb. 28	10½	SF		Aug. 15	10	SF
	Aug. 8	11	SF		Nov. 28	10½	MM
1984	Mar. 19	11½	MM	1989	Feb. 10	11	MM
	Apr. 5	12	MM		23	11½	MM
	May 8	12½	MM		June 5	11	BF
	June 25	13	MM		Aug. 15	10½	BF
	Sept. 27	12¾	MM	1990	Jan. 8	10	BF
	Oct. 17	12½	MM	1991	Jan. 3	9½	SF
	29	12	BF		Mar. 1	9	SF
	Nov. 9	11¾	BF		May 1	8½	SF
	28	11¼	BF		Sept. 13	8	SF
	Dec. 20	10¾	BF		Nov. 8	7½	SF
1985	Jan. 15	10½	BF	1992	Jan. 3	6½	SF
	May 20	10	SF		Nov. 7	7½	SF
	June 18	9½	SF		Dec. 23	6½	SF
1986	Mar. 7	9	SF	1993	July 2	6	SF
	April 21	8½	SF	1994	Mar. 25	6¼	SF
	July 14	8	SF		Apr. 20	6¾	SF
	Aug. 1	7½	SF		May 11	7¼	SF

MM = Money Market Funds
SF = Stock Funds
BF = Bond Funds
*The correct investment is based on the Investor's Decision Line published in the Charles J. Givens Organization newsletter at the time or taught at workshops.

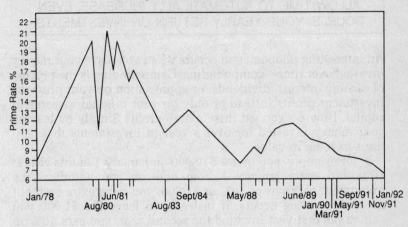

Prime Rate Changes
January 1978 – January 1992

PRIME RATE DIRECTION CHANGES CHART 1978 TO 1994

Date	From	To	Direction	# of Mos.
Jan. 1978 to Apr. 1980	8.00%	20.00%	up	28
Apr. 1980 to Aug. 1980	20.00	11.00	down	4
Aug. 1980 to Jan. 1981	11.00	21.50	up	5
Jan. 1981 to Apr. 1981	21.50	17.00	down	3
Apr. 1981 to Jun. 1981	17.00	20.00	up	2
Jun. 1981 to Feb. 1982	20.00	15.75	down	8
Feb. 1982 to Feb. 1982	15.75	17.00	up	1
Feb. 1982 to Aug. 1983	17.00	10.50	down	18
Aug. 1983 to Sep. 1984	10.50	13.00	up	13
Sep. 1984 to Mar. 1987	13.00	7.50	down	30
Mar. 1987 to Oct. 1987	7.50	9.25	up	7
Oct. 1987 to Aug. 1988	9.25	8.50	down	11
Aug. 1988 to June 1989	8.50	11.50	up	10
June 1989 to Mar. 1994	11.50	6.00	down	57
March 1994—	6.00	7.75	up	—

Strategy # 306
ALLOW TIME TO AUTOMATICALLY INCREASE, EVEN
DOUBLE, YOUR YEARLY RETURN ON INVESTMENTS.

An interesting phenomenon occurs when you leave your money invested over time—compounding. Compounding is the process of earning interest, dividends, or appreciation on your previous investment profits instead of only on your original investment capital. How do you get this "extra" profit? Simply by leaving your money invested for over a year in investments that continue to go up in value.

If, for example, you invest $10,000 on January 1 of this year at 10%, and every January 1 from now on you withdraw the investment earnings of 10% or $1,000, you have extra cash but no compounding occurs. If instead you leave the $1,000 you earned the first year invested the second year, you earn 10% on $11,000 instead of only on your original investment of $10,000. Your actual investment return is $1,100, or 11% based on your original investment, even though the stated return for the year was only 10%. The second year $12,100 is invested with the 10% return equaling $1,210 or 12.1% based on your original investment of $10,000.

That's how compounding can make you wealthy over time. In our example at a stated 10%, you are actually earning over 1% additional on your original capital for every year you leave the money invested. How's that for a self-created bonus? In fact, it is not difficult to construct a table that will show you the added percentage profit that each additional year of investment will provide (see page 423). To give you a comparison, I have used 10%, 12%, and 15% yearly returns. Your actual return on your original investment is much higher per year as time goes on.

Notice that if you leave your money invested for five years and it has compounded at 15% (see 15% column) you actually earn a 26% return on your original investment the fifth year. The time and compounding factors are also what eventually make your retirement plan worth millions.

Notice that if you have been averaging 12% in your retirement plan for 19 years, the 20th year your return on the money you invested 20 years ago is over 100%. From then on you are doubling your 20-year-old money every year, plus earning 59% on the money you put in 15 years ago and 33% on the money you put in 10 years ago. You cannot stop yourself from getting rich at those rates.

All it takes is time coupled with a strategy that earns 10%, 12%, 15%, or more. Notice how much more your real return is based on the investment return percentage you have been earning. After five years at 15%, the same money would actually earn 26% the fifth year.

Time is always on your side when your money is working for you. For those who don't choose to spend much time creating and watching their investments, mutual funds coupled with the Money Movement Strategy is the optimum winning combination. Best of all, anyone can do it!

HOW TIME ADDS TO YOUR NET RETURN

Your Actual Return by Year When Stated Return Is—

Year	10%	12%	15%
1	10%	12%	15%
2	11	13	17
3	12	15	20
4	13	17	23
5	15	19	26
6	16	21	30
7	18	24	35
8	20	26	40
9	21	30	46
10	24	33	53
Retirement Plans			
15	38	59	106
20	61	103	213
25	99	182	429
30	151	321	864

Chapter 31

MUTUAL FUND WINNING STRATEGIES

There are two times in a man's life when he should not speculate: when he can't afford it, and when he can.

Mark Twain
Following the Equator
1897

LEARN THE WINNING STRATEGIES FOR IDENTIFYING AND USING MUTUAL FUND INVESTMENTS.

There are four different investments in which you can use the mutual fund Money Movement Strategy you learned in Chapter 30 to your wealth-building advantage.

Investment	MWWR Chapter
Mutual fund families	This chapter
IRA and Keogh accounts	Chapter 33
Your retirement plan at work	Chapter 18
Tax-sheltered annuities	Chapter 34

In all four of these investment opportunities your money is self-directed. Self-directed means that you choose the investment in which you want your money placed from a list of options. In the four investment options above, most or all of your choices for investments are mutual funds.

It is important that you develop a complete understanding of mutual funds. Whether you invest in mutual funds through mutual fund families, IRAs or Keogh accounts, your retirement plan at work, or tax-sheltered annuities, the strategies, rules, and principles are basically the same. If you understand mutual funds, you will understand them wherever they are used. The names of the funds and fund families may be different, but they all operate the same way.

Three of the four self-directed mutual fund investment opportunities are tax shelters:

- IRA or Keogh accounts
- your retirement plan (401(k), 403(b), etc.)
- tax-sheltered annuities

The fourth option, mutual fund families, doesn't have automatic tax-shelter protection although some of the specific investments in a mutual fund may come with tax-exempt interest. They include:

municipal bonds—no state or federal taxes on interest
Treasury bills—no state taxes on interest

There are also money market mutual funds that invest in tax-exempt bonds that expire in less than one year. Tax shelter alone is not the reason to invest in a specific mutual fund. Let's look at the four different vehicles through which your money can end up in a mutual fund and their tax rules.

Notice in the chart on the following page that to get into a mutual fund your money is first funneled through a tax shelter or mutual fund family. In the case of the tax-sheltered options, the type of account is what provides the tax protection, whether an IRA, Keogh, retirement plan, or tax-sheltered annuity. All are governed by Congress's tax rules. The money is then invested in a mutual fund, which is usually part of a mutual fund family. In your mind, separate the tax shelter (which is simply a set of tax rules) from the mutual fund itself, which is your actual investment.

FOUR WAYS YOUR MONEY CAN BE INVESTED IN MUTUAL FUNDS

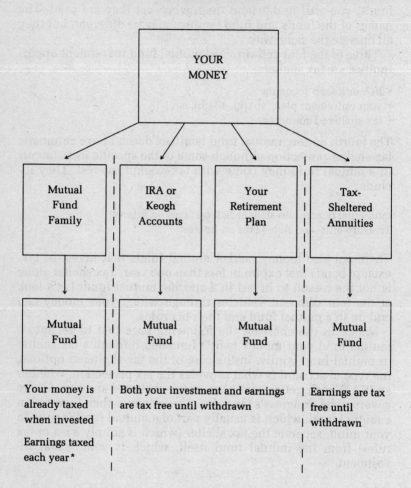

YOUR
MONEY

Mutual Fund Family	IRA or Keogh Accounts	Your Retirement Plan	Tax-Sheltered Annuities
Mutual Fund	Mutual Fund	Mutual Fund	Mutual Fund

Your money is already taxed when invested

Earnings taxed each year*

Both your investment and earnings are tax free until withdrawn

Earnings are tax free until withdrawn

* Unless the mutual fund itself has purchased tax-free investments.

Strategy #307
USE THE MONEY MOVEMENT STRATEGY™ IN ANY MUTUAL FUND FAMILY.

A mutual fund is an investment company registered with the Securities and Exchange Commission (SEC) and managed by a professional fund manager. The mutual fund uses investors' money to buy stocks, bonds, or money market instruments, and you, as an investor, own your share of the entire portfolio. If 1% of the money in a mutual fund was yours, you would own 1% of the shares. Mutual funds are open-ended; that is, they can sell unlimited numbers of shares to new investors. The mutual fund promises to redeem your shares anytime you wish (weekends excluded) at the fund's current net asset value (NAV), which is usually the previous day's closing price. A mutual fund *family* on the other hand is a group of individual mutual funds all under the same management.

MUTUAL FUND DEFINITIONS

To profit from mutual fund investments, there are 18 terms and definitions you will want to understand.

Account

Your investment arrangement and record with the mutual fund. Your account is initially the amount of your investment minus any front-end commissions. Your account increases in value when the fund's assets increase in value, when the fund pays interest or dividends, or when you invest more money. Your account decreases in value when the fund's assets decrease in value, you withdraw money, or the fund's management expense is deducted. You receive a periodic statement of your account, but the current value of a share can also be determined from the financial pages of your newspaper.

Adviser

An organization or person employed and paid by the mutual fund to give professional investment advice to the fund. You never meet the advisers.

Asked Price

The price at which you can buy shares in a mutual fund, also known as the offering price. This price is the current net asset value per share (NAV) plus any commission or front-end load.

Bid Price

The price at which the mutual fund will buy back your shares. The bid, also called the redemption price, is the current net asset value per share (NAV). Back-end loads or commissions, if any, are subtracted from the total amount you receive when you sell.

Capital Gains or Losses

Your profit or loss from the sale of your mutual fund shares. Capital gains and losses are created when investments are sold by either you or the mutual fund. When the mutual fund sells investments, the profits or losses are taxable transactions and your taxable share appears on your account statement. When you sell your shares in a fund or move to another fund, you have created taxable gains or losses. Mutual funds are required to distribute or apply their gains and earnings to each investor's account each year.

Cash Position

The amount of the fund's assets that is not invested in stocks or bonds but is put in the bank or in short-term investments. If a stock fund manager thinks stocks may go down, he will sell stocks to maintain a bigger "cash position" with the intent of buying stocks at a reduced price position, that fund will be outperformed by those funds that stayed more "fully invested."

Certificate

The printed record showing ownership of mutual fund shares, similar to a stock certificate. Because of a unique computerized record of accounts maintained by the fund, certificates are seldom issued unless the shares are going to be pledged for a loan or margin account.

Distributions

The payments to shareholders of capital gains or dividends in the form of cash or additional mutual fund shares.

CAPITAL GAINS DISTRIBUTIONS. Payments made to mutual fund shareholders representing profits earned by the fund when stocks or bonds are sold. These profits are paid at the shareholder's option, in cash or as additional shares in the fund. In the past, capital gains were distributed once per year, but because mutual funds must now distribute 90% of capital gains to avoid taxation, some will go to a quarterly distribution system. You pay taxes on capital gains distributions whether you withdraw cash or leave the money invested to buy additional shares unless your investment is made through a tax-sheltered account such as an IRA or your retirement plan at work. All mutual fund capital gains distributions are treated as long-term capital gains for tax purposes. (For a complete explanation of capital gains and strategies, see *Financial Self-Defense*, Chapter 21, "Beat the Capital Gains Tax.")

Although the total net asset value of the fund remains the same before and after a distribution, the per share net asset value (NAV) drops as more shares are issued to each shareholder equal to the capital gains per share. For example:

BEFORE DISTRIBUTION

1,000,000 shares at $11 per share = $11,000,000 net assets of fund

AFTER DISTRIBUTION

Capital gains distribution $1,000,000

1,100,000 shares at $10 per share = $11,000,000 net assets of fund

The total assets remain the same but the number of shares and the NAV per share change proportionately. The same thing happens in your account.

DIVIDEND DISTRIBUTIONS. The distribution of dividends and interest from investments to the mutual fund shareholders. The distribution methods are the same as with capital gains distributions.

EX-DIVIDEND DATE. The date on which declared distributions are deducted from the fund's assets. On that day the share price drops as shown above, but since each shareholder receives more shares, the amount in the shareholder's account remains the same until the price per share changes.

Exchange Privilege

The right of a mutual fund shareholder to transfer his money from one fund to another within the same family. The two types of exchanging are:

- telephone switching—you can move your money by making a telephone call
- mail exchanging—you write to the fund and ask for your money to be moved

You want a mutual fund family with telephone switching.

An exchange is actually the sale of shares in one fund and the purchase of shares in another. The transaction is taxable unless your investment is protected by a tax shelter such as an IRA or self-directed annuity.

Management Company

The entity that manages the fund. Often a fund family itself will have different officials than those who actually manage the individual funds. The "adviser" described earlier gives investment advice; the management company handles the business.

Net Asset Value per Share (NAV)

The mutual fund's total assets minus current liabilities, divided by the number of shares outstanding.

Net Assets

A mutual fund's total assets minus current liabilities.

Payroll Deduction Plan

A plan whereby mutual fund contributions are deducted from your paycheck and sent by your employer directly to the fund. All 401(k)s, 403(b)s, and other company retirement plans are payroll deduction plans.

Performance

The percentage change in a fund's net asset value per share (NAV) over a period of time. Performance is a method of comparing different mutual fund returns.

Portfolio

All the securities, such as stocks, bonds, and money market instruments, owned by a mutual fund.

Portfolio Turnover

The percentage of a mutual fund's investments that were changed during the year (sold and the money reinvested). The total can be from 0 to over 100%. Most aggressive funds have higher portfolio turnovers.

Prospectus

The official brochure issued by a mutual fund that describes how the fund works, how it manages its money, the objectives of the fund, how you invest and withdraw your money, and how much the fund charges in fees and commissions. Much of the information is required by the Securities and Exchange Commission. The important information from the prospectus for the recommended no-load families is in the Fund Family Fact Sheets in the Appendix of this book.

Reinvestment Privilege

The right of a mutual fund shareholder to have interest dividends and capital gains automatically used to purchase additional shares of the fund. Unless you are living off the income from your investments, you will normally choose to have your earnings reinvested.

In addition to these terms, you must know the three categories and many subcategories of mutual funds. Knowing the difference and when to use each type of mutual fund is the basic secret of mutual fund investment success.

Strategy #308
CHOOSE THE RIGHT MUTUAL FUND FOR THE MONEY MOVEMENT STRATEGY™ BY IDENTIFYING ITS CATEGORY.

All mutual funds fall into three general categories:

- stock mutual funds
- bond mutual funds
- money market mutual funds

Each category has many subcategories, which are identified by a two-letter code used throughout this chapter and in all references and charts (see pages 521–22 for key). A mutual fund category is determined by what type of investment is predominant in the mutual fund's portfolio. Of course a mutual fund could hold both stocks and bonds at the same time, and a few do.

STOCK MUTUAL FUNDS

A stock represents ownership of a portion of a company's assets. Individual stocks are bought and sold through stockbrokers, who are connected by computer to the major exchanges, such as the New York and American Stock Exchanges. Stocks not listed on the exchanges are traded broker-to-broker through the National Association of Securities Dealers (NASD). The brokers receive commissions for handling investors' stock trades. The per share price of a company's stock increases or decreases based on supply and demand. If there are more buyers than sellers, the price goes up. If there are more sellers than buyers, the price drops.

A mutual fund that invests primarily in stocks is a stock mutual fund. Stock mutual funds are classified into many subcategories and are named by their investment objectives and the type of stocks in which they invest. Since few stock funds use the term "stock" in the fund name, you, as the investor, must understand the terms that identify the type of fund.

There are years that stocks win big and other years when the stock funds lose a little. The Money Movement Strategy helps you choose those years to be in stock funds when the potential for winning is big and has you out of stock funds when they don't have the potential for performing as well.

Growth Stock Fund (SG)

A stock mutual fund that invests primarily in common stocks with what the fund manager believes is good growth potential is a stock growth fund, sometimes called just a growth fund.

		Growth %				
BEST-PERFORMING GROWTH STOCK FUNDS						
Ranked by Performance Over Last 5 Years						
Family	Fund	'89	'90	'91	'92	'93
Berger	100	48	−6	89	9	21
Twentieth Century	Ultra	37	9	86	1	22
Fidelity	Contra	43	4	55	16	21
Invesco	Strat. Liesure	38	−11	53	23	36
Fidelity	Blue Chip Growth	36	4	55	6	25

Aggressive Growth Stock Fund (SA)

A stock mutual fund that uses aggressive and sometimes volatile techniques in an attempt to increase profits. These aggressive techniques include leverage, short selling, and buying warrants and options. Using the Money Movement Strategy, you will normally do better using aggressive stock funds than any other type of stock fund, even if you are conservative.

Growth and Income Stock Fund (SI)

A stock fund that attempts to give investors capital growth and income at the same time is called a growth and income stock fund. These funds invest in stocks when they are lower in price, making the yield higher. Dividend yield is the amount of dividends paid per share divided by the price of one share. The lower the price, the higher the yield.

BEST-PERFORMING AGGRESSIVE GROWTH STOCK FUNDS
Ranked by Performance Over Last 5 Years

| Family | Fund | Growth % | | | | |
		'89	'90	'91	'92	'93
Thomson	Opp. B	31	−7	68	29	36
Twentieth Century	Gift Trust	50	−17	84	18	31
Invesco Strat.	Financial Svc.	37	−7	74	27	19
Kaufman	——————	47	−6	79	11	18
Strong	Discovery	24	−3	67	2	22

BEST-PERFORMING GROWTH & INCOME FUNDS
Ranked by Performance Over Last 5 Years

| Family | Fund | Growth % | | | | |
		'89	'90	'91	'92	'93
Berger	101	20	−8	61	5	24
Fidelity	Growth & Income	30	−7	42	12	20
Pierpoint	Equity	31	138	34	9	11
Warburg	Growth & Income	21	4	13	9	37
Gateway	Index Plus	19	10	18	5	7

The average dividends paid by the three main types of stock funds in 1990 stacked up like this:

- aggressive growth funds (SA) 0.8%
- growth funds (SG) 1.8%
- growth and income funds (SI) 3.8%

Because of the small difference in actual yield between types of funds, the better performance of growth and income funds was based on other factors. To get higher yields, (SI) fund managers look for underpriced, undervalued stocks in good, solid, well-established companies. The lower the price, the higher the percentage dividend yield. This approach creates a great potential for growth once the stock price begins to recover, but overall you will do better investing in growth and aggressive growth stock funds.

Equity Income Stock Fund (SE)

Combination stock and bond funds that have a primary goal of income and a secondary goal of growth are called equity income funds. There are about 40 no-load and low-load equity income funds whose assets on the average are invested as follows:

- 40%   high-dividend-paying stocks
- 50%   bonds
- 10%   cash

The equity income funds perform well when the prime rate is dropping because both stocks and bonds are appreciating plus earning interest and dividends. They are poor performers when the prime rate is going up because any stock gains are automatically wiped out by bond losses. Overall, equity income funds will not outperform the growth and aggressive growth stock funds and need not be used with the Money Movement Strategy. Keep it simple.

Also included in the equity income funds category are the qualified dividend funds set up for corporate investments only. Tax reform allows corporations to earn tax free 70% of dividends received from investments in other corporations (85% under pre-tax-reform rules). Several mutual funds have been created for this specific purpose.

		|	Growth %			
Family	Fund	'89	'90	'91	'92	'93
Berwyn	Income	11	0	23	22	17
Lindner	Dividend	12	−7	27	21	15
USAA	Mut. Income	16	8	19	8	10
Vanguard	Preferred Stock	19	6	21	8	13
Vanguard	Wellesley	21	4	22	9	15

BEST-PERFORMING EQUITY INCOME FUNDS
Ranked By Performance Over Last 5 Years

SPECIALTY STOCK MUTUAL FUNDS

Specialty stock mutual funds buy stocks using a special selection process, leverage, or other type of investment formula not used by the regular stock funds and are generally only for more knowledgeable and speculative investors. The following is a description of major categories of specialty stock funds.

Option Fund (SO)

A mutual fund that buys stock options instead of stocks. An option is the right to buy or sell a specific number of shares of a stock at a fixed price by a specific date. Some option funds buy stocks and then attempt to hedge against a price drop by purchasing "puts" or options to sell on the same stock. Option funds have not been particularly successful during the past ten years and should be avoided.

Index Fund (SX)

A mutual fund that theoretically owns all of the stocks in the Standard and Poor's 500 or other index. The growth, therefore, is the same as that of the index. During the past five years, the S&P 500 average has outperformed the average growth and aggressive growth mutual funds. Investors who guess at which mutual funds will be good performers often do better with an index fund. Investors who use mutual fund strategies like those in this book will normally outperform the S&P 500 and the index funds. Vanguard's Index Trust is an example of an index fund.

Balanced Fund (SB)

These mutual funds invest in a combination of stocks, bonds, and preferred stocks and violate the rule "Every economy has one best investment—stock, bond, or money market funds." Knowledgeable investors avoid the overdiversified balanced funds that are big losers when interest rates are rising.

Closed-End Fund

Closed-end funds, sometimes called "trusts," issue a fixed number of shares and are publicly traded on the stock exchanges. Unlike the open-ended funds, which are the more familiar mutual funds, closed-end funds do not issue or redeem shares from investors. Investors sell to other investors through brokers. The current share price of a closed-end fund is not the NAV (net asset value per share), but a price based on supply and demand. Poor overall performance is the best reason to avoid the closed-end funds.

Social Conscience Fund

There are three no-load funds that invest in stock of companies organized for social good, or that seek to avoid companies involved in war materials, liquor, tobacco, or gambling. The stock funds are PAX World Fund, Dreyfus Third Century, and Working Assets. These funds have had an average to poor track record and should be used only by those whose social conscience matches the objectives of the funds.

Industry Fund

Funds that purchase stocks related to only one industry are called industry funds. Some industry funds, such as the health funds, have been great performers because of the overall growth or profits of that single industry. Others, such as the high tech funds, have been at times the big losers.

Industry funds are for aggressive investors and should be used only during periods when the prime rate is dropping. Some industry funds have never done well, such as the Gaming Fund (gambling stocks) organized in 1978 and liquidated in 1982.

Industries represented by industry funds include: high tech, computer software, drugs, computers, biotech, health, chemicals, energy, financial, housing, leisure, defense, restaurants, life insurance, automotive, paper, broadcast media, banking, air transport, and industrial materials.

When these funds are hot, they are sometimes incredible performers, but they are also among the biggest losers when they are not.

Sector Fund (SS)

When you put several industry funds under one mutual fund family and allow switching between these as well as money market funds, you have sector funds. Sector fund investing allows the choosing of more specific stocks with the safety of diversification. The Fidelity family has 35 sector funds called "Select" funds and Vanguard has 5 sector funds it calls "Special" funds. Sector funds are good choices for aggressive investors when the timing is right.

Emerging Company Growth Fund

A stock fund that buys shares in new companies with good future potential. Such funds are volatile and far riskier than regular stock funds because of the unpredictability of small company performance and should be avoided by conservative investors. When the economy (usually after a recession) favors new business start-up and growth, these funds perform well.

Precious Metal Fund (SP)

Precious metal funds buy the stocks of mining companies involved in the extraction of gold, silver, platinum, and other precious metals. They are volatile funds and should be used only by aggressive investors. Overall, the performance of the gold funds has been greater than the performance of growth and aggressive growth stock funds, even with some bad years, but the swings in value from high to low are not for the faint of heart. The increase or decrease in value of precious metal funds follows the market price of the metals and not the prime rate, and makes these funds unpredictable. Invest in precious metal funds only with good, dependable advice that is hard to find.

Multifund (SB)

A multifund is a mutual fund that invests in shares of other mutual funds. An example is Vanguard's Star Fund, which invests in other Vanguard stock, bond, and money market funds. These funds have a poor track record because of overdiversification. Multifunds are sometimes classified as "balanced funds," discussed earlier.

BOND MUTUAL FUNDS

A bond investment represents a loan made by an investor to a corporation or government agency for a term ranging from 1 to 30 years at a specific rate of interest. Bonds normally pay guaranteed interest rates like certificates of deposit, but unlike CDs, bonds go up and down in value daily due to changes in marketplace interest rates. A bond may sell at a premium (more than its face value) or at a discount (less than its face value) even though the interest rate never changes. At the end of the term, the issuer guarantees to pay the investor the face value of the bond. Bonds usually come in $1,000 denominations.

A mutual fund that invests primarily in bonds is a bond mutual fund. Bond funds, like stock funds, can be classified into several subcategories.

High Yield Fund (BL)

A bond fund investing in corporate bonds with supposedly higher than usual interest rates and often lower than usual ratings.

Fixed Income Funds (BL)

A bond fund that invests most of its assets in long-term, high-grade bonds.

GNMA Fund (BG)

A bond fund that invests in mortgage bonds issued by the Government National Mortgage Association.

Government Securities Fund (BG)

A bond fund that invests in GNMAs plus bonds issued by other government agencies.

		Growth %				
Family	Fund	'89	'90	'91	'92	'93
Boston Company	ST Bond	9	8	13	5	4
Fidelity	ST Bond	11	6	14	7	9
Manager's	Bond	14	8	19	8	12
Strong	Advantage	10	7	11	8	8
Weitz	Fixed Income	9	9	11	6	8

BEST-PERFORMING BOND MUTUAL FUNDS

Ranked By Performance Over Last 5 Years

MONEY MARKET MUTUAL FUNDS

Money market funds are mutual funds that invest in short-term, super-safe, interest-bearing instruments. The maturity date of these securities is between one day and one year. The interest rate credited daily to money market fund investors is a composite of interest rates on all the investments held by the fund and has, in the last 11 years, ranged from a low of 6% to a high of 18% annually. Money market funds make good investments when interest rates are over 9% and rising, and poor investments when interest rates are low and declining.

Money market funds are not the same as money market bank accounts. *Money market account* is a fancy name for bank savings plans that pay variable instead of fixed interest. The banks use the name in an effort to confuse investors and to lure money away from the money market funds.

Money market mutual funds were originally created in 1972 with the birth of the Reserve Fund. The objective was to offer small investors the opportunity to get better-than-bank rates on money market instruments, formerly available only to investors with $100,000 or more. In 1974 the Fidelity Daily Income Trust pioneered the concept of check-writing in a money market fund. Many money market funds now allow you to write up to three checks per month, with a $250 to $500 minimum.

The per share value of a money market fund is always $1; so your principal value does not increase or decrease. The interest earned by your shares is added to your account as additional $1 shares, unless you withdraw the money. Newspapers quote the interest rates of money market funds by annualizing the daily interest rates.

Money market funds have been created by both mutual fund families and stock brokerage firms. The following descriptions center on those no-load money market funds that are part of mutual fund families.

Regular Money Market Funds (MM)

Regular money market funds, of which there are dozens, invest in:

U.S. GOVERNMENT SECURITIES. Short-term debt instruments issued by the U.S. Treasury and other government agencies that are guaranteed by the U.S. government.

BANK JUMBO CERTIFICATES OF DEPOSIT. CDs of $1 million or more that carry higher interest rates than individuals can get.

BANKERS' ACCEPTANCES. Short-term bank guarantees designed to finance imports and exports. The importer does not want to pay a foreign company until goods are received. An exporter does not want to ship the goods until he is guaranteed he will receive his money when the goods are delivered. Bankers' acceptances are the guarantees and are virtually risk-free investments.

COMMERCIAL PAPER. Unsecured but virtually risk-free short-term notes issued by large creditworthy corporations and finance companies. Maturity dates are up to nine months.

REPURCHASE AGREEMENTS. A repurchase agreement is a security sold by a brokerage firm to finance its transactions with a written guarantee to repurchase the security on a specific date, at the same price, plus interest. Repurchase agreements usually have a maturity of less than one week.

Tax-Exempt Money Market Funds (MX)

These special money market funds invest in tax-exempt municipal bonds that mature or come due within one year. The average maturity of these tax-exempt securities is 75 days compared with 45 days for a regular money market fund. Tax-exempt money market funds, because of very low interest rates, are not good investments even for those in higher tax brackets. They made sense when the top tax bracket was 45%, but not now.

Insured Money Market Funds (MI)

Some money market funds are insured, but you pay the insurance through reduced interest. Money market funds are already safe enough that the insurance is a waste of money.

Asset Management Accounts

The natural outgrowths of money market funds are the asset management accounts, which have unlimited checking and offer other financial services such as debit cards. (See Chapter 29.)

Now that you have an overall picture of the diversity of the mutual funds available, let's look at the strategies that will put these funds to work for you.

Strategy #309
INVEST ONLY IN FUNDS THAT HAVE MORE THAN $25 MILLION AND LESS THAN $3 BILLION IN ASSETS.

The size of a mutual fund should be considered in your investment strategy. If a fund has under $25 million in assets, there is a good chance it cannot afford to hire or keep the best of the fund managers. You do not want your capital used to provide the training ground for a new fund manager.

Getting too big also has a downside. If a stock mutual fund has over $3 billion in assets, it loses flexibility. Much of the success of a stock fund in beating the stock indices is created by portfolio turnover—moving money in and out of cash positions in anticipation of market drops or gains. A fund manager can't move money fast enough if the fund is too large.

A good example is the Fidelity Magellan Fund, which in 1987 grew to $11 billion. Magellan was the best-performing fund for the previous ten years, and by imposing a low load of 3% raised enough advertising capital to make itself famous. The more Magellan advertised the more capital flowed in. In an interview with *The Wall Street Journal*, former Magellan Fund manager Peter Lynch speculated that the fund would be unlikely to maintain its performance record of the past. I began warning members of my organization in the winter of 1986 that Magellan could get itself in trouble if the stock market took a sudden turn. On October 19, 1987, it happened. The Dow dropped 508 points. While the average mutual fund dropped only 16%, Magellan was a big loser with a drop of 32%. It recovered along with all of the other funds, but you don't want to set yourself up for more than a 15% swing in the value of an investment even in tough times.

Big mutual funds have an option. They can close the existing fund to new investors and start a new one with new management but an identical investment philosophy. The Vanguard family closed its supersuccessful Windsor fund to new investors when it got too big and created the Windsor II fund. Windsor II actually outperformed Windsor I in 1990.

In the Mutual Fund Family Fact Sheets (Appendix) you'll find each fund's total assets.

Funds and families with too few assets are shown in the "Not Recommended" chart on page 447 as "too small."

Strategy #310
INVEST IN GOOD-PERFORMING NO-LOAD FUNDS WITH TELEPHONE SWITCHING.

Choosing the right fund and fund family is easy once you know what you are looking for. All the information you need is in the Fund Family Fact Sheets in the Appendix. Following is a ten-step process for choosing your mutual fund.

Step 1. Choose for convenience a fund that is part of a family with at least one:
  • stock fund

- bond fund
- money market fund

Step 2. Choose only a no-load or low-load fund.

Step 3. Choose a mutual fund that has a minimum required initial deposit within your investing limits.

Step 4. Choose the right type of mutual fund for the current economic conditions by using the Money Management Strategy (Chapter 30).

Step 5. Choose a fund that has assets of more than $25 million and less than $3 billion.

Step 6. Choose a mutual fund based on its track record for the interest-rate environment in which you intend to use it, not its five-year or ten-year total performance record. (See Money Movement Strategy, Chapter 30.)

Step 7. If you want income, choose a fund that offers a periodic withdrawal plan. The minimum investment for periodic withdrawals is shown in the Fund Family Fact Sheets in the Appendix. All types of funds—stock, bond, and money market—have periodic withdrawal plans.

Step 8. If your account is an IRA or Keogh, check the Fund Family Fact Sheets, in the Appendix, for minimum required investment and yearly fee.

Step 9. Choose a fund that qualifies for a Schwab margin account if you plan to use the margin account strategy (see Chapter 32).

Step 10. If you are using mutual funds in your retirement account, you choose only the fund. Your employer chooses the fund family.

There are 21 fund families that meet these criteria. They are listed in the No-load Mutual Funds Recommended for Use with the Money Movement Strategy chart on page 448. There are 30 mutual fund families that do not qualify under these criteria for one or more reasons, and you will find these in the Mutual Fund Families Not Recommended for Use with the Money Movement Strategy list on page 447.

Strategy #311
USE THE FUND FAMILY FACT SHEETS TO CHOOSE
THE BEST MUTUAL FUND AND MUTUAL FUND FAMILY
FOR YOU.

From the Fund Family Fact Sheets in the Appendix, choose two
or three mutual fund families that meet the foregoing criteria
and your own special needs and objectives. There is no one
right choice, so don't waste time trying to find it.

If you're beginning with 10% of your paycheck, or opening a
small account for children or grandchildren, the logical choice
is to pick a fund with a low initial deposit like AARP or Invesco.
Twentieth Century is also a good choice for teaching your
children to invest correctly.

If you are an aggressive investor, looking for maximum flexibility with aggressive growth or sector funds, your choice may
be the Fidelity funds. Stein Roe and Scudder funds also tend to
lean more toward the aggressive side.

Fidelity funds are not necessarily a first choice for beginners.
If you were to call Fidelity and ask for a prospectus on every
fund the company offers, you would be reading for months.
Fidelity has over a hundred different funds.

For conservative investors, Vanguard or Dreyfus funds can be
good choices. How do you know if you're a conservative investor? Your money is probably in all the wrong places based on
what you've learned so far. Remain conservative, but remember
there are two kinds of conservative investors: conservative winners and conservative losers.

Call the mutual fund family's number and request a prospectus for each fund by name. If you don't receive it on a timely
basis, call again. All of the recommended fund families have
toll-free numbers (shown in the "recommended funds" list on
page 448). If you live in the state in which a fund is located, use
the in-state number.

The prospectus will tell you everything about the fund, including the investments owned. It is not necessary to read
through all the required technical gibberish, but read carefully
the instructions pertaining to investing, moving, and withdrawing your money. To save you countless hours of researching the
mutual fund families, you will find all of this information in the
Mutual Fund Family Fact Sheets (Appendix). To open an account, complete and send the application with your check to the

address listed in the prospectus. Specify by name the fund in which you want your money initially invested.

Although past performance is no guarantee of future performance, a mutual fund's track record should be an important factor in your choice. Use the performance histories in the Mutual Fund Family Fact Sheets along with the Prime Rate Direction Changes Chart on page 421 to compare fund performance. For instance, if you want to know what would have happened to the value of your shares in any fund during 1985 and 1986, first determine where your money should have been invested according to the Prime Rate History chart on pages 419–20. Both were years of declining interest rates and a time for stocks, so you would check only stock fund performance. The prime rate fell from a high of 11% to a low of 9% during 1985 and to 7½% by August 1986. As you might expect from your understanding of the Money Movement Strategy, one of the greatest surges in stock market history began and lasted until October 1987. When the smoke cleared, recommended stock funds appreciated 40% in 1985, 30% in 1986, and about 3% in 1987, even after the stock market drop of October 19. Stock funds then surged 15% in 1988 and over 20% in 1989.

Money market funds averaged less than 7%. Government securities funds, heavily pushed by brokers, averaged only 9% in 1985 and less in 1986, and lost 10% to 15% of principal in the first half of 1987 because of rising interest rates. International stock funds were big winners, averaging a total of 100% in 1985 and 1986 due to the declining value of the dollar. Bond mutual funds performed reasonably well during 1985 and 1986 with the prime rate dropping, but lost much of their gains in 1987 and 1988 when the prime rate began to rise.

Strategy #312
TRACK YOUR MUTUAL FUND INVESTMENTS THROUGH YOUR LOCAL NEWSPAPER.

The current value in dollars of one share of a mutual fund is known as its *net asset value* per share (NAV). You have daily access to the net asset value of any fund through the financial pages of major newspapers. The NAV is listed under "Mutual Funds" near the stock market quotes. The mutual funds are listed by family. For example, all of Value Line's funds are listed together alphabetically under "V," all of the Fidelity funds are listed alphabetically under "F."

Look to the right of the fund name and you'll find two price columns. Load funds will have a price in both columns. The higher figure is the price at which you could purchase one share, the lower figure represents the price at which you could sell one share. The difference between the two prices represents the commission charged by load funds. If the commission is 8%, there will be an 8% difference between the two prices. No-load funds have no commissions and only one column will show a price. The other column will contain a dash (-) or "NL" (no-load). (See page 451.)

If you purchased your shares at $10 each (100 shares for each $1,000 you invested), and the share price increased over the next six months to $12 per share, you have made a 20% profit on your money. When dividends are earned for one or more stocks in your stock fund, or interest is earned and reinvested in a bond fund, you will be credited with more shares unless you request a cash distribution. Make note of how many shares you receive when you first invest and check each month on your statement to see if you have been issued more shares. Even if it appears you have made only 10% on your money from the price change alone, you may discover that you now have 15% more shares and have actually earned 25% total return. The current net asset value per share (NAV) is not information enough to determine your profit or loss. Profits from capital gains distributions, dividends, and interest are usually given to investors as additional shares. On the distribution dates, the number of shares owned by each investor will increase, but if you look at NAV per share alone, your profit from distributions will not be reflected. To find the true value of your investment, multiply the number of shares shown on your last statement by the current NAV and compare to the amount of money you originally invested. On many statements, the total current value of your account is shown.

Each month, you will receive a complete statement showing your status in the fund at the end of the previous month. The statement is easy to use, easy to follow, and is one major benefit of investing through a mutual fund family.

A no-load mutual fund family investment is a must investment for everyone. Get yours started or reorganized today.

MUTUAL FUND FAMILIES *NOT* RECOMMENDED FOR USE WITH THE MONEY MOVEMENT STRATEGY

Mutual Fund Family	*Reason*
Bankers System Financial Services	Too small
Bartlett and Company	No money market fund
Claremont Company	No money market fund
Decision Funds	Not open to all investors
Depositors Investment Trust	No money market fund
Dividend Funds	Too small
Fiduciary Management	No money market fund
Flex Fund	Poor overall performance
General Funds	Not open to all investors
Gintel Equity Mortgage	No money market fund
Heine Securities	No money market fund
Horace Mann Funds	Not open to all investors
Ivy	No money market fund
Lepercq, de Neufize & Co.	Too small/No MM fund
Lindner Funds	No bond or MM fund
Loomis Sayles & Co.	S. fund closed to new investors
M.A.S. Funds	Not open to all investors
Meritor Investor Co.	Family too new/too small
New Beginnings Fund	No money market fund
Nicholas Co. Inc.	No money market fund
North Star	No money market fund
Pacific Investment Management (Pimco)	Bond funds only
Quest Advisory Corp.	No money market fund
Reich & Tang	No bond fund
Reserve Management Co.	No bond fund
State Farm Investment Mgmt.	Not open to all investors
Steadman Security Corp.	Too small/No MM fund
Unified Management Corp.	Too small
United Missouri Bank	Too small
United States Trust Co.	Too small

NO-LOAD MUTUAL FUNDS RECOMMENDED FOR USE WITH THE MONEY MOVEMENT STRATEGY

Name	# of Funds	Phone Toll-free	In State Phone	Address	City, State, Zip
1. AARP	7	800-253-AARP	800-253-AARP	PO Box 2540	Boston, MA 02208-2540
2. Babson	12	800-4BABSON	816-471-5200	2440 Pershing Rd., Ste. G15	Kansas City, MO 64108
3. Columbia	8	800-547-1707	503-222-3606	PO Box 1350	Portland, OR 97207
4. Dreyfus	40	800-645-6561	800-895-1206	144 Glenn Curtiss Blvd.	Uniondale, NY 11556
5. Evergreen	11	800-235-0064	914-894-2020	2500 Westchester Ave.	Purchase, NY 10577
6. Fidelity	88	800-544-8888	800-544-8888	PO Box 193	Boston, MA 02101
7. Founders	9	800-525-2440	303-394-4404	3033 E. Third Ave.	Denver, CO 80206
8. IAI Funds	12	800-927-3863	612-376-2600	1100 Dain Tower	Minneapolis, MN 55440
9. Invesco	18	800-525-8085	303-430-6300	PO Box 2040	Denver, CO 80201
10. Janus Capital	11	800-525-8983	303-333-3864	100 Fillmore St., Ste. 300	Denver, CO 80206
11. Neuberger & Berman	11	800-877-9700	800-877-9700	342 Madison Ave., Ste. 1620	New York, NY 10173
12. Pimco Funds	11	800-227-7337	203-352-4900	1 Statton Place	Stamford, CT 06902
13. Safeco	10	800-426-6730	800-545-5530	PO Box 34890	Seattle, WA 98124-1890
14. Scudder	26	800-225-2470	617-439-4640	160 Federal St.	Boston, MA 02110
15. Stein Roe	16	800-338-2550	800-338-2550	PO Box 1131	Chicago, IL 60690
16. Strong	11	800-368-1030	414-359-1400	PO Box 2936	Milwaukee, WI 53201
17. T. Rowe Price	29	800-638-5660	301-547-2308	100 E. Pratt St.	Baltimore, MD 21202
18. Twentieth Century	12	800-345-2021	816-531-5575	PO Box 419200	Kansas City, MO 64141-6200
19. USAA	13	800-382-8722	512-498-8000	4800 Fredricksburg Rd.	San Antonio, TX 78288
20. Value Line	10	800-223-0818	212-687-3965	711 Third Ave.	New York, NY 10017
21. Vanguard	55	800-662-7447	215-669-1000	PO Box 2600	Valley Forge, PA 19482

YEAR-BY-YEAR MUTUAL FUND PERFORMANCE HISTORY
By Type of Fund

Type of Fund	83	84	85	86	87	88	89	90	91	92	93
All											
Stock funds	21	−2	27	15	2	15	24	−14	31	6	19
Bond funds	10	11	20	14	2	7	11	2	15	6	8
Money market funds	9	10	8	6	6	7	9	7	6	4	3
Stock											
Aggressive growth	20	−10	28	11	1	15	27	−12	50	9	18
Growth	22	1	27	13	2	15	24	−10	37	8	11
Growth—income	23	6	26	15	1	15	21	−8	29	8	11
Precious metals	−1	−28	−7	37	31	−18	25	−26	−4	−15	24
International	33	−5	52	59	15	17	23	−12	18	−1	32
Bond											
Fixed income	10	11	20	14	2	7	11	2	15	6	8
Tax free	11	8	19	18	−1	10	9	2	11	9	11
Money Market											
General	9	10	8	6	6	7	9	8	6	4	3
Tax free	5	6	5	4	4	5	6	5	4	2	2

MUTUAL FUND AVERAGE RETURNS

For the Past Five and Ten Years, 1983–1993

Type of Fund	Total 5 Yrs	Total 10 Yrs	5-Year Average Return per Year	1983–1993 Average Return per Year
All				
Stock funds	43.0%	103.0%	13.62%	12.21%
Bond funds	38.5	115.0	9.95	10.77
Money market funds	36.0	92.0	5.1	7.6
Stock				
Aggressive growth	33.0	76.0	17.26	11.34
Growth	45.0	108.0	14.62	12.74
Growth—income	97.5	120.0	12.43	12.13
Precious metals	35.5	0.0	6.75	3.80
International	87.5	143.0	10.51	13.41
Bond				
Fixed income	38.5	115.0	10.45	11.57
Tax free	40.5	104.0	9.41	10.00
Income	80.0	147.0	12.05	12.42
Money Market				
General	36.0	92.0	5.1	7.6
Tax free	24.5	55.0	3.47	4.12

Chapter 32

MUTUAL FUND MARGIN ACCOUNTS

How I Made My Fortune?

It was really quite simple. I bought an apple for 5 cents, spent the evening polishing it, and sold it the next day for 10 cents. With this I bought two apples, spent the evening polishing them, and sold them for 20 cents. And so it went until I had amassed $1.60. It was then that my wife's father died and left us a million dollars.

Anonymous Capitalist

OBJECTIVE

USE OPM TO INCREASE THE EARNING POWER OF MUTUAL FUNDS.

> *Strategy #313*
> **USE A MUTUAL FUND MARGIN ACCOUNT TO INCREASE YOUR INVESTMENT CAPITAL.**

One of the most powerful uses of credit is to borrow money at a low interest rate and invest at a higher rate. The difference between the cost of the money and your investment return is your profit. Most businesses, investment fortunes, and even countries have been developed on borrowed money, and yet investing with borrowed money, or leverage, is still a foreign concept to most Americans. If your objective is to build wealth in the shortest possible time, with the least effort and greatest return, then investing borrowed money is a must.

A margin account is a line of credit with a broker or mutual fund that allows you to borrow money for investing or other purposes using your existing investments—stocks, bonds, or mutual fund shares—as collateral. The Securities and Exchange Commission recently lifted its long-standing ban on the use of mutual fund shares as collateral for margin accounts, and a new world of building bigger profits using borrowed money opened up to smart investors. A mutual fund margin account allows you to increase your mutual fund investment capital with your signature only. The important question is: How safe is a mutual fund margin account?

If shares of stocks, bonds, or mutual funds decrease in value past the legal minimum margin requirement—the amount of collateral you must maintain on your loan—you will receive a "margin call" requiring you to put up more collateral. A mutual fund margin account is actually a safer method of using borrowed money to buy securities than a broker's margin account. The stock market drop of "Black Monday," October 19, 1987, is the best example. While the Dow plummeted 23% (508 points in one day) and many well-respected stocks dropped 40% or more, the average, well-managed mutual fund dropped only 16% and still finished the year with a 3% gain.

In addition, a mutual fund must drop in price 50% before you get a margin call. The average stock mutual fund, during the worst stock market drop in history, dropped only 16%. The only exceptions were the giant mutual funds such as Fidelity's Magellan with $11 billion and no chance to move money fast enough. Magellan dropped 32%, but was already off our recommended list more than a year before, when its assets exceeded $3 billion.

The interest rate you pay on the margin account is the broker's loan rate, which is only 1 or 2 percent above the prime rate. If the margin account interest rate is 10% and you are earning an average of 25% per year in your mutual fund family, your net profit is 15% after paying the interest on the borrowed money. Your interest is also tax deductible. Under tax reform, interest on money you borrow to invest is deductible up to the amount of your total investment income. You do not have to repay the principal or interest as long as the market value of your pledged shares is within the margin limits. Interest is generally charged to your account and compounded monthly.

Strategy #314
USE A MUTUAL FUND MARGIN ACCOUNT TO FREE UP CAPITAL FOR OTHER INVESTMENTS.

If you own mutual fund shares and wish to borrow money (margin your shares) to buy more shares, you can borrow 50% of the market value of your existing shares depending on SEC margin requirements in effect at the time. For example, if you have 500 shares of a mutual fund whose NAV is $10 per share, the market value of your shares is $5,000. You may borrow up to $2,500 to buy more shares of any fund.

If you own shares of a mutual fund and want to use the shares as collateral for a personal loan for purposes other than buying investments, you may borrow up to the same 50% of the market value of your existing shares.

You cannot open a mutual fund margin account with every mutual fund, but you can through one of two discount brokerage firms that will allow you to margin shares of over 200 different mutual funds.

CHARLES SCHWAB (1-800-648-5300). Charles Schwab is a discount broker, a division of BankAmerica, and was the leader in creating mutual fund margin accounts. You may use the Schwab margin account to buy or margin any of the over 250 no-load mutual funds and fund families that Schwab represents. (See Charles Schwab Mutual Fund Margin Accounts at the end of the chapter.)

If you buy your original shares directly from a mutual fund and wish a Schwab margin account, ask the fund for the Certificate of Ownership, which you then give to Schwab for collateral. The Charles Schwab organization now has offices in most states and major cities.

FIDELITY BROKERAGE (1-800-544-6767). If you buy or own any of Fidelity's over 50 stock, bond, and money market funds, you may margin any of your shares through Fidelity. You may also margin shares of other mutual funds or fund families through Fidelity's nationwide discount brokerage service.

Here is how your profit picture develops with or without a mutual fund margin account.

Example 1:
You own or buy $10,000 worth of shares in a stock mutual fund.
The margin allowance in effect is 50%. In January, using the
Charles Schwab or Fidelity margin account, you buy an additional $5,000 worth of mutual fund shares. During the year, the
fund shares increase 28%. What is your profit with and without
the margin account if the broker's margin account interest is
10%?

With the Margin Account		Without Margin Account	
Original Shares	$10,000	Original Shares	$10,000
Financed Shares	10,000	Financed Shares	0
TOTAL INVESTMENT	$20,000	TOTAL INVESTMENT	$10,000
28% Increase	$ 5,600	28% Increase	$ 2,800
Minus 10% Interest	−1,000	Interest	0
NET PROFIT	$ 4,600	NET PROFIT	$ 2,800
Profit Percentage	46%	Profit Percentage	28%

The profit in both cases is calculated on your original $10,000
cash investment. Using the mutual fund margin account, you
have increased your net profit to 46% in a mutual fund that
returned only 28%. You earned an additional $900 or 9% on
your $10,000 investment.

Example 2:
Let's say you own the same $10,000 in shares during the same
time period, but instead borrowed 50% of the value to buy a
piece of real estate. You borrowed $5,000 and used the money
for the down payment and closing on residential real estate
property you purchased for $80,000. Tax savings from deprecia-
tion are calculated using the 27.5-year depreciation schedule for
a person in the 28% bracket. Appreciation is calculated at 5%
for the year. The appreciation of the mutual fund shares is 20%.

Mutual Fund Profits

Total Investment	$10,000
	×.20
20% Profit	$ 2,000

Real Estate Profits—$80,000 Property

Your Own Investment	$ 0
Borrowed Money Invested	5,000
Total Investment	$5,000
Tax Savings—Depreciation	$ 644
Appreciation (5%)	4,000
Real Estate Profit	$4,644

Combined Profits and Costs

Profit—Mutual Fund	$2,000
Profit—Real Estate	4,644
Minus Margin Interest (10%)	−500
Net Profit	$6,144
Profit Percentage	61%

By using borrowed money from your mutual fund margin account to buy a piece of real estate, you have achieved a 61% return on your original $10,000 capital in one year.

Mutual fund margin accounts should be considered by every investor to maximize profits in the minimum amount of time. Used correctly, they are one of the safest wealth-building accelerators.

CHARLES SCHWAB MUTUAL FUND MARGIN ACCOUNTS

AMA Advisors
Classic Growth
Income
Axe-Houghton Mgmt.
Stock Fund
Fund B Inc.
Income Fund Inc.
Money Market
Babson Funds
(not available)
Boston Co. Advisors
(not available)
Bull & Bear Group
Special Equity
Capital Growth
Equity Income
Golcorda Inv.
High Yield
Tax-Free Inc.
US Gov. Guar. Sec.
Dollar Res.
Calvert Group
Equity
Social Inv. MM
Columbia Funds
Special
Growth
Municipal Bond
Fixed Inc. Sec.
US Gov. Guar. Sec.
Daily Inc.
Dreyfus Corp.
Strategic Agg.
New Leaders
Growth Opp.
Third Century
Fund
Convertible Sec.
Mass TE Bond
NY Tax Exempt
CAL TE Bond
Insured TE Bond
Tax Exempt Bond
A Bond Plus
GNMA

Dreyfus Corp.
Pk. Ave. NY TE Int.
Int. Tax Exempt
Pk. Ave. TE MM
CAL TE Money
Tax Exempt MM
Pacific Horizon MM
MM Inst. Gov. Sec.
Pacific Horizon Gov.
Dollar Int'l.
Liquid Assets
Pacific Horizon
Fidelity
OTC
Capital App.
Growth Co.
Magellan
Value
Contra Fund
Trend
Tr. Port Growth
Growth & Income
Fidelity Fund
Health Care Del.
Equity Inc.
Real Estate
Puritan
Balanced
Qualified Div.
Tr. Equity Port. Inc.
Sel. Prec. Metals
Sel. Amer. Gold
Sel. Energy Serv.
Sel. Chemicals
Sel. Tech.
Sel. Software
Sel. Computers
Sel. Electronics
Sel. Telecomm.
Sel. BioTech.
Sel. Defense
Sel. Automation
Sel. Health
Sel. Air Trans.

Fidelity
Sel. Trans.
Sel. Automotive
Sel. Cap. Goods
Sel. Ind. Mat.
Sel. Paper Forest
Sel. Housing
Sel. Food & Agr.
Sel. Bdcast & Media
Sel. Energy
Sel. Life & Ins.
Sel. Prop. Cas.
Sel. Broker
Sel. Financial
Sel. Reg. Banks
Sel. S&L
Sel. Leisure
Sel. Rest.
Sel. Retail
Sel. Elect. Util.
Sel. Utilities
Global Bond
NY TF Yld. Municip.
CAL Free HY
Ltd. Term Municip.
Penn Free HY Municip.
High Inc.
High Yield Municip.
Agg. Tax Free
Texas Tax Free
Mass Free Municip.
Minn Tax Free
Mich Tax Free
Ohio Tax Free
Munic. Bond
NY Tax Free Ins.
CAL Ins. TF
Insured Tax Free
Short Term
GNMA
Short Term TF
Flexible Bond
Mort. Sec.
Thrift Trust
Mass TF Money

Fidelity
NY TF Money
CAL TF Money
Financial Programs
Dynamics
Industrial Fund
Industrial Inc.
Strategic Gold
Strategic Tech.
Strat. Health
Strat. Energy
Strat. Financial
Strat. Leisure
World of Tech.
Strat. Utilities
Strat. European
Strat. Pacific
Bond Sh. US Gov.
Bond Select Inc.
Tax Free Inc.
Bond Sh. High YLD.
Daily Inc. Shares
Tax Free Money
Founders
Frontier
Special
Growth
Blue Chip
Equity Income
Gov. Inv. Trust
(not available)
Lexington Mgmt. Corp.
Growth
Research
Gold Fund
GNMA Inc.
Money Mgmt. Assoc.
(not available)
Newberger
Guardian Mutual
T. Rowe Price
New Horizons
New Amer.
New Era
Growth Stock
Growth Inc.
Equity Inc.
GNMA

Newberger
Tax Free Inc.
High Yield
Int'l Bond
New Income
Tax Free Short Int.
Newton
Growth
Income
Safeco Mgmt. Co.
Growth
Equity
Income
CAL TF Inc.
Muni Bond
Scudder
Development
Cap. Growth
Int'l
Global
Growth & Inc.
NY TF
Managed Municip.
Tax Free 1993
Target General 1990
Target Gen. 1987
Target US Gov 1990
Target US Gov 1987
Select Funds
Special Shares
Amer. Shares
Stein, Roe & Farnham
Special
Farn. Cap. Opp.
Farn. Stock
Total Return
Strong Corneliuson Cap.
Opportunity
Total Return
Investment
Income
Twentieth Century
(not available)
United Services
Advisors
Lo Cap.
Growth
Good & Bad Time

United Services
Advisors
Income
Gold Shares
Prospector
New Prospect
Tax Free
GNMA
USAA Inv. Mgmt.
(not available)
Value Line Inc.
Lev. Growth
Spec. Sit.
Fund
Income
Convertible
US Gov. Sec.
TE MM
Vanguard
Naess & Thomas
Explorer
Explorer II
WL Morgan
Word US
Index Trust
Windsor
Windsor II
Trustees Commingled
Star
Word Int.
Qualified Div. I
Qualified Div. II
Qualified Div. III
Fixed Inv. HI Yld.
Bond Market
Fixed Inc. GNMA
Fixed Inc. US Treas.
Fixed Inc. Short Term
Spec. Gold
Spec. Tech.
Spec. Health
Spec. Service
Spec. Energy
Muni Hi. Yld.
Penn. Ins. FF
NY Ins. TF
CAL Ins. TF
Municip. Lg. Term

Vanguard
Municip. Lg. Term
Municip. Inter. Term
Municip. Short Term
Wellesley Inc.
Wellington
Convertible Sec.
Fixed Inc. Inv. Grade

Chapter 33

IRA AND KEOGH
INVESTMENT
SUPERSTRATEGIES

A banker is a fellow who lends you his umbrella when the sun is shining and wants it back the minute it rains.

Mark Twain
Writer
1897

OBJECTIVE ─────────────────────────────

EARN 15 TO 20% PER YEAR IN NONTRADITIONAL IRA AND KEOGH INVESTMENTS.

Twenty-three million people qualify for them, only 4.5 million take advantage. I'm talking about IRAs and Keogh accounts, which, along with company retirement plans, are the best opportunities in America to make and keep a million during your lifetime.

Even if you already have an IRA or Keogh, in this chapter I will show some exciting, nontraditional investments for your IRA or Keogh that will build your tax-free wealth two to four times faster than a bank's IRA/Keogh accounts.

First let's be certain you understand the contribution and investment rules and strategies for an IRA or Keogh account.

> **Strategy #315**
> **CONTRIBUTE THE DEDUCTIBLE MAXIMUM TO AN IRA.**

The IRA is the only retirement plan you, as an employee, may create yourself. You deposit your IRA money in investments you select, and you may contribute to an IRA any time before April

15 of the year following the year you earned the qualifying income. Your employer is not involved.

Maximum Contribution
$2,000   Self
$2,000   Employed Spouse
$2,250   Nonemployed Spouse
          (divided between spouses)

Anyone with employment or earned income of $2,000 or more may contribute the deductible maximum to an IRA regardless of total income, provided neither spouse contributes to an employer-related retirement plan. If you or your spouse contributes to a 401(k), 403(b), or other similar employer-related retirement plan, the following additional rules apply:

A. You may deduct the maximum contribution to an IRA if your adjusted gross income (AGI) is less than $40,000 (couple) or $25,000 (individual), even if you, your spouse, or your employer contributes to an employer's retirement plan.
B. If you file jointly, you lose the deduction for $200 of your possible $2,000 contribution for each $1,000 of adjusted gross income over $40,000, and so does your spouse.
C. If you file as an individual, you lose the deduction for $200 of your possible $2,000 contribution for each $1,000 of adjusted gross income over $25,000.
D. A deductible minimum of $200 may be contributed by any couple or individual whose AGI falls within $1,000 of the deduction phaseout limit.

Even with the ease of creating an IRA and the incredible tax benefits, only 20% of those who qualify have opened the account, and almost no one knows how to use an IRA effectively.

Strategy #316
BORROW THE MONEY FOR YOUR IRA OR KEOGH—EVEN IF YOU HAVE IT.

If you borrow the money for your IRA or Keogh contribution, you can end up borrowing the money free. Let's say you borrow $2,000 from the credit union or bank for your IRA. The interest at 12% for one year you would pay is $240. If you are in the 28% tax bracket, you save 28% of your $2,000 contribution, or $560, because of the nontaxed contribution. The $560 not only covers the $240 interest, but gives you an additional $320 profit. The tax-deferred earnings are also yours to keep. The interest you pay on money borrowed for an IRA or Keogh is tax deductible since IRA money is tax-deferred and not tax-exempt. Money borrowed to buy tax-exempt investments such as tax-exempt bonds is not deductible. You may deduct investment interest up to the amount of your investment income.

Strategy #317
CHOOSE AN IRA WITH A LOW TRUSTEE'S FEE, $35 OR LESS.

Your IRA is technically a trust and every IRA must have a trustee, someone certified by the IRS to be responsible for the account. If you put your IRA money in a bank, mutual fund, credit union, or other financial institution, you automatically use the institution's trustee. The required paperwork involved with your IRA is considerable, and therefore, most institutions or trustees charge an annual fee. The fee can range from five dollars to hundreds of dollars. The trustee's fee on a Keogh account is determined by whom you use and how complicated your Keogh is to set up and administer.

Avoid all IRA or Keogh accounts that charge a percentage. The percentage may seem small when your account is small, but it will amount to hundreds per year as your account grows. Many major brokerage firms and some financial planners charge a percentage. The maximum you should ever pay on a regular IRA is $35 per year. If you open a self-directed IRA with investments outside of a regular financial institution, you can expect to pay more for the extra paperwork and nonstandard transactions involved (see strategies later in this chapter for self-directed IRAs).

Strategy #318
USING YOUR 401(k) TO QUALIFY YOU FOR ADDITIONAL IRA CONTRIBUTIONS.

From your standpoint, mathematically and financially you cannot contribute too much to any tax shelter in which the contributions are tax deductible. The types of investment plans that allow for deductible contributions are now limited to employer-sponsored retirement plans discussed in Chapter 18, and the IRAs and Keoghs outlined in this chapter. These are now the best tax-shelter opportunities that exist in America. There is even a point at which the more you contribute to a 401(k) or other similar plan, the more tax-deductible IRA contributions you are allowed, upping your total potential tax-deductible investments for the year.

Once a couple reaches the $50,000 adjusted gross income (AGI) threshold (singles $35,000) and either they or their employers contribute to a company retirement plan, they no longer qualify for even a nickel's worth of deductible IRA contributions. There is a strange quirk in the regulations, however. Since your IRA contributions are based on adjusted gross income and since every $1,000 you put into an employer's retirement plan reduces your adjusted gross income by $1,000, your IRA deductible limit can go up if your AGI is near the threshold.

For example, Bill and Mary have a total income of $62,000. Their adjusted gross income is $51,000, disqualifying them from an IRA because of contributions they make to their 401(k) plans. Up to now, they have been putting very little into the 401(k)s. But this year Bill contributes $5,000 to his plan and Mary contributes $3,000 to hers, and at the end of the year they would like to contribute even more to reduce taxes. It is too late for the 401(k), but not for an IRA!

$51,000	Adjusted gross income
− 8,000	Total contributions to 401(k)s
$43,000	New adjusted gross income

Because their adjusted gross income is now under $50,000, they have qualified themselves for a total of $2,800 of optional, deductible IRA contributions, which can be made until April 15 of the following tax year.

Based on the IRA rules, you can contribute $200 as an individual or $400 as a working couple to an IRA for every $1,000 your adjusted gross income is below the threshold of $50,000 ($35,000 for singles) up to the maximum contribution of $2,000 for individuals or $4,000 for working couples. Each spouse in our example can therefore contribute an additional amount of $1,400 ($200 × 7) to an IRA and take a deduction for the entire amount contributed. The total contribution allowance for both is $2,800, saving almost $1,000 that year in taxes.

When your adjusted gross income (AGI) is in the threshold range, watch for this special opportunity.

Strategy #319
**SET UP A SELF-DIRECTED KEOGH PLAN FOR
MAXIMUM DEDUCTIBLE CONTRIBUTIONS AND
POTENTIAL EARNINGS.**

Keogh plans work similarly to IRAs. Whereas IRAs are for
individuals who work for others, Keogh plans are for people
who work for themselves. The biggest difference between IRAs
and Keogh accounts is the amount of contributions permitted
each year. IRA contributions for an individual are limited to
$2,000 for a single year, but, get this, those who are self-
employed may contribute up to $102,582 per year in some types
of Keogh plans. Of course most people just wish they made that
much each year. If your business has employees besides yourself
and you contribute to a Keogh plan, you are required to include
them in the plan.

First, let's look at the contribution rules to determine the
maximum allowable and deductible contributions per year.

There are two options for setting up a Keogh plan: defined
benefit and defined contribution. In a defined contribution plan,
you determine (or define) how much you wish to contribute to
the plan each year. You can contribute up to 20% of your net
earnings from your business to a maximum of $30,000. Of course
the 20% is the maximum. You can choose 5%, 8%, 14%, or any
other amount under 20% and you can change your contribution
amount each year.

The following chart will show you some examples of the
maximum contribution based on net income from a business
and the incredible tax savings because of the deductibility of the
contributions for someone in the 35% combined federal and
state income tax bracket.

If you own or ever plan to start your own business, the five
strategies that follow the chart will be important to you. If not,
skip to page 468, IRA or Keogh Investment Options.

DEFINED BENEFIT KEOGH PLANS

Maximum Contributions and Corresponding Tax Savings

Net Income from Business	Maximum Contribution (20%)	Taxes Saved by Contribution (35% Tax Bracket)
$ 20,000	$ 4,000	$ 1,400
40,000	8,000	2,800
80,000	16,000	5,600
100,000	20,000	7,000
150,000	30,000	10,500

The defined benefit plan is the simplest of the two Keogh plan options and is the one most commonly used. Contributions to a Keogh defined benefit plan are simple so far. However, there are actually two kinds of defined benefit plans—one is called a money purchase plan, as shown in the chart above, and the other is called a profit-sharing plan, which limits your maximum deductible contribution to 13.04%.

Strategy #320

WITH NO EMPLOYEES, CHOOSE A MONEY PURCHASE KEOGH PLAN; OTHERWISE CONSIDER A PROFIT-SHARING KEOGH PLAN.

The theoretical advantage to a money purchase Keogh plan is that you can contribute a set dollar amount each year regardless of your profits for the year. That means you can count on the amount of your contribution being set in advance without waiting to see your profit picture for the year. However, you must also contribute to your own (up to 20% of net earnings) whether or not you have a good year. Any additional contribution is not deductible.

With a profit-sharing plan, contributions are made only if there are profits, which can be important if you have employees for whom you must also contribute. Your maximum contribution to a profit-sharing Keogh is 13.04% of net income. Your maximum deductible contribution is less in the profit-sharing type plan, but you are allowed for some strange reason to set up a second money purchase Keogh plan so you can contribute the almost 7% difference in the maximums between the plans.

Your Keogh plan options therefore look like this:

Keogh Plan Options

Defined Contribution	Money Purchase Plan or Profit-Sharing Plan
Defined Benefit	Money Purchase Plan or Profit-Sharing Plan

Strategy #321
CHOOSE THE MORE COMPLICATED DEFINED BENEFIT PLAN ONLY IF YOU ARE OVER AGE 50.

A defined benefit Keogh plan is one in which you determine or define the amount of income you wish to *withdraw* each year from your plan after retirement. That's a different formula from determining how much you can or want to contribute each year in the defined contribution plan. The maximum contribution is the amount of money that would, if contributed each year until you are age 65, provide the same amount of annual income after age 65 as you have earned by averaging your top three income years. The maximum contribution limit for 1990 was $102,582.

Imagine taking up to a $102,582 tax deduction per year! With that kind of income you need all the deductions you can get. However, because employees must be included at the same percentages, if you have older employees, you could end up paying a disproportionate amount into the employees' portion of the plan. The contributions for each person included in the plan are determined by the number of years to retirement.

In order to determine what amount you must contribute each year to produce a specific retirement income, a rather complicated formula is used by the trustee of your plan to calculate the required future value of your account at age 65. For instance, if your best three years of income averaged $90,000 per year and you expect to earn 8% per year on your investments until you retire in 18 years, the question for your financial calculator becomes, "How much must be invested each year for 18 years in equal monthly or yearly installments to give me an income of $90,000 from an investment still paying 8% when I retire?"

To find the answer, first determine how much you would need in your account 18 years from now to pay $90,000 per year at 8%. The formula: $8\% \times Y = \$90,000$; $Y = \$1,125,000$. You would need $1,125,000 in the account by age 65. Next, determine how much you would have to invest per year starting this year at 8% per year to total $1,125,000. The answer, using your financial calculator, is $30,040 per year. That would be your Keogh defined benefit yearly contribution. As you can see, it is much easier to set up a defined contribution plan, unless you are within about 15 years of retirement and need to build the account quickly.

Strategy #322
SET UP A TRUST INSTEAD OF A CUSTODIAL ACCOUNT TO GIVE YOUR KEOGH MORE INVESTMENT MUSCLE.

A Keogh account, like an IRA, is technically a retirement trust. (See Chapter 17, "Whom Do You Trust?") If you choose to invest your Keogh money in bank certificates of deposit, you can simply use the custodial account form. The problem is that bank CDs are one of the worst places for your Keogh money. Don't settle for 7% or 8%. Some annuity accounts also require only a custodial account form. Banks, mutual funds, insurance companies, and some trade associations have group master Keogh plans in which you can participate so the paperwork in setting up your plan is easier and a custodian or trustee is provided.

To get real mileage and profits out of your hard-earned Keogh dollars, however, you will instead set up a trust. Either you or an independent trustee may administer your Keogh plan and make the investments. With a trust you now have the flexibility to invest your Keogh money in almost anything you wish not prohibited by law, including the unusual investments outlined in this chapter.

You can establish your plan without prior approval from the IRS, but you can also ask the IRS to review your plan by requesting a determination letter. Use IRS Form 5300. You also include Form 8717, which determines your fee for the determination letter. If you join a group master plan, the IRS work is done for you, but your investment choices are severely limited.

Strategy #323
HIRE YOUR SPOUSE TO INCREASE YOUR FAMILY MAXIMUM DEDUCTIBLE KEOGH CONTRIBUTIONS.

If your spouse is an employee of your business, he or she must by law be included in your Keogh plan, as must all employees. You can increase your tax deductions and investments by hiring your spouse to work in your business and contributing the same percentage of your spouse's salary to a Keogh as you do for yourself. The money is income to your spouse, but tax deductible to you, so the salary is a tax wash, but your spouse's contributions to the Keogh plan are totally tax deductible on your joint return. See Chapter 25, Strategy #238, for rules on hiring family members.

As long as you already have a Keogh plan in place by the end of any tax year, you can increase or make your total contribution up to the date you must file your tax return including any extensions. Once you have established your Keogh plan, the withdrawal options and strategies and rollover or account-transfer procedures are basically the same as for employee-sponsored plans as discussed in Chapter 18, or for IRAs, discussed later in this chapter.

IRA OR KEOGH INVESTMENT OPTIONS

The tax rules now give you almost unlimited options for where your IRA or Keogh can be invested. You may, in fact, invest your IRA money in anything except:

- Collectibles—e.g., art, Persian rugs, and precious metals.
- Any investment such as mortgaged rental property in which your account would be used as collateral or security for a loan. The IRS treats an IRA used as security for a loan as if you had withdrawn the money.
- A business in which you own more than a 5% interest.

These options therefore do not limit you to an account in a bank CD as many people assume. As a matter of fact, once you learn your options you will discover that an IRA or Keogh at a bank is one of the poorest. Another poor investment for your account is in a low-return tax shelter.

Strategy #324
NEVER INVEST YOUR IRA OR KEOGH MONEY IN A TAX SHELTER.

When your money is put into an IRA or Keogh, it is already tax sheltered twice—once for the contribution and once for the earnings. It would, therefore, be unwise to invest the money in your account in another tax shelter such as:

• tax-exempt bonds
• tax-exempt bond or money market funds
• tax-sheltered limited partnerships
• annuities

Why? You cannot take the tax deductions twice. Often, the return before taxes is less in a tax-sheltered investment, so you would be sacrificing your net or real return.

Where you will derive the most benefit is investing your already tax-sheltered money in potentially high-return investments where you will get maximum clout from the tax shelter—investments such as:

• mutual funds (using the Money Movement Strategy)
• discounted mortgages
• real estate options

These investments can return to you over 15% per year, but the money is not tax sheltered. Many financial salesmen, including brokers or financial planners, will sell you a tax shelter for your already sheltered money. Don't fall for it.

Now let's look at the real opportunities: how you can creatively earn 15% or more—tax sheltered.

Strategy #325
USE THE TAX-FREE ROLLOVER AND TRANSFER RULES TO TAKE CONTROL OF YOUR INVESTED RETIREMENT MONEY.

Little-known tax rules allow you to change your IRA or Keogh investments anytime you wish. Once you read this chapter you will probably want to upgrade your IRA or Keogh investment plan by getting the money out of the bank and into better investments.

Here are the rules that give you total control over where your money is invested. When you want to transfer your money to a new IRA or Keogh in a different financial institution, such as a mutual fund family, you have two options:

- Trustee to Trustee Transfer
  If you sign a transfer agreement with the new trustee or institution, the transfer of your IRA or Keogh can be handled by the institutions. There is no limit to the number of transfers that can be made each year using this method.

- IRA/Keogh Rollover
  You may physically withdraw your IRA or Keogh money and open a new IRA or Keogh with a different institution with no taxes or penalties as long as the money is deposited into the new account within 60 days after the date of withdrawal. If you withdraw the money yourself, it is subject to 20% withholding and a 10% penalty.

Strategy #326
OPEN A SELF-DIRECTED ACCOUNT TO EARN 15% OR MORE PER YEAR.

One of the major benefits of an IRA or Keogh and often the least used is the ability to choose your investments. Choosing your own investments for your IRA or Keogh is done by opening a self-directed account at a mutual fund family, brokerage firm, or independent trustee. Anyone who qualifies for an IRA or Keogh may open a self-directed account. A self-directed account puts you in control, letting you choose any investment you wish, such as stocks, bonds, mutual funds, discounted mortgages, real estate options, county tax lien certificates, mortgage pools, or even the lot next door to your home.

Every account must have a trustee. Financial institutions, such as brokerage firms, banks, or mutual fund families, have one trustee for all accounts, but you can choose from only the investments that financial institution sells. A bank usually has only one option. If you want to invest your money in real estate, discounted mortgages, or tax liens, you must find an independent trustee. Any bank trust department can legally act as your independent trustee, but many still won't. There are now a few financial planners who are IRS-registered independent trustees.

Strategy #327
LOCATE AN INDEPENDENT TRUSTEE FOR A MORE FLEXIBLE IRA OR KEOGH ACCOUNT.

The maximum flexibility in an IRA/Keogh is achieved with an independent trustee, a custodian who will allow you to invest your account in anything legal.

BANK TRUST DEPARTMENTS—Any bank trust department can act as trustee for your account and allow you to put your money in any of the investments suggested later in this chapter. You may have to check several banks before you find one that will work with you. The bank will charge you a fee per transaction of maybe $50 plus any legal fees depending on the complexity of the transaction. Any bank trust department, by law, can legally act as your trustee; some will, some won't at this point, but don't hesitate to sell them on the idea that this could mean extra business and revenue.

MAJOR FINANCIAL PLANNING FIRMS—Many big financial planning firms are now getting one of their associates registered as an independent trustee. Fees are about the same as those of bank trust departments.

Here are two suggestions:

First Trust Corporation
P.O. Box 173301
Denver, CO 80217-3301
1-800-525-2124
1-800-233-0407 (CO)
Establishment fee: $25
Annual fee: minimum $40
Limits: no real property

Providence Administration
10200 Sepulveda Blvd.
Suite 180
Mission Hills, CA 91345
1-800-282-8844
Establishment fee: $75
Annual fee: On declining scale
Limits: no real property

Some of the investment options suggested below, such as mutual funds and land lease partnerships, come with a built-in trustee; to use others, you must open your account with an independent trustee.

Strategy #328
INVEST YOUR IRA/KEOGH IN MUTUAL FUND FAMILIES.

Using a combination of a mutual fund family and the Money Movement Strategy in Chapters 30 and 31, you can average 15% or more per year by moving your money among stock, bond, and money market funds. When you open an IRA or Keogh in a mutual fund family, you automatically get a self-directed account and are assigned the fund's trustee. Most mutual fund families have IRA/Keogh options, and the low yearly trustee's fees range from $5 to about $30. The use of the Money Movement Strategy will guide you in choosing the mutual fund family that's right for you and your IRA/Keogh. The fees for IRAs and minimum investments for IRAs and Keoghs are shown in the Fund Family Fact Sheets (see the Appendix).

The following advanced strategies for IRAs and Keoghs are for those who like or don't mind doing the extra paperwork, research, and legwork required. The returns can be incredible. If you are investing IRA money, you will need to locate an independent trustee. If investing Keogh money, you can choose to be your own trustee.

Strategy #329
INVEST YOUR IRA/KEOGH IN LAND LEASE LIMITED PARTNERSHIPS.

Investing in a land lease limited partnership can produce high income and capital appreciation for your IRA/Keogh. Here's how it works. A limited partnership buys a piece of prime commercial real estate using investors' IRA or Keogh money. The investors own the real estate and then lease the land to a developer to build an office building, shopping center, apartment building, or bank. The owners of the building make lease payments to the land lease partnership representing usually 8% to 10% of the investment each year. The income to the partnership is not taxed because of the IRA/Keogh status of the invested capital. When the partnership sells the property, the investors get a share of the profits.

There are no taxes on the profitable sale of the investment as long as the profits are redeposited in the tax-sheltered account. The total return can be as high as 15% to 20% per year, all tax sheltered. The profits and original investment can be used to buy a new piece of land and the process begun again.

You can check with real estate people in your area to find these or similar partnerships, or you and a few friends can put one together yourselves. It may take some looking, but the benefits may be worth it. Check out all limited partnerships carefully.

Strategy #330
INVEST YOUR IRA/KEOGH IN VACANT LAND OR LOTS.

If you have your eye on a piece of investment land or maybe a lot in your neighborhood, you can use your self-directed IRA/Keogh money to purchase the property. You may hold the property as long as you wish, and when you sell, even at a huge profit, your profit is tax sheltered by your IRA or Keogh. You must, however, pay cash or obtain a loan that does not use your IRA/Keogh money as collateral. If your IRA/Keogh is used as collateral for a loan or mortgage, the transaction is counted as a withdrawal, triggering both income taxes and, if you're under 59½, the 10% early-withdrawal penalty.

Strategy #331
INVEST YOUR IRA/KEOGH MONEY IN REAL ESTATE OPTIONS ON LAND.

You can invest your IRA or Keogh in a highly leveraged short-term real estate option on land and enjoy huge profits without paying current taxes. A real estate option is a contract that gives you the exclusive right to purchase a piece of property at a specified price anytime within a specified time ranging from one month to several years. For the privilege, you make an option deposit of 1% to 10% based on your ability to negotiate. The option money holds the property exclusively for you during the term of the option. If you choose not to buy, the seller keeps the property and you lose only your option money. If you end up buying the property during the option term or sell your option at a profit to someone who does, your option money is applied to the purchase price. The major benefit of the option strategy is the almost outrageous profits you can generate with relatively small risk. Only your option deposit is at risk; you are not obligated to buy the property.

In 1982, my friend Don opened his $2,000 IRA at a local bank using the bank trust department as an independent trustee. He then put a 60-day option on a $1,000,000 prime 50-acre piece of land near Disney World in Orlando, Florida, where he lives. The option deposit money used was the $2,000 from his IRA. The trustee for his IRA handled the investment. In other words, Don tied up the 50-acre property for $2,000 for a period of 60 days. If he bought the property, the $2,000 would apply to the purchase and his guaranteed purchase price was $1,000,000. If Don backed out for any reason, all he could lose was his $2,000 option deposit.

Don never intended to purchase the land. Instead, during the 60-day option period, he assembled a group of investors. Per Don's instructions, investors put together a $400,000 down payment to purchase the property, not for the $1,000,000 option price, but for $1,200,000, the appraised value of the land. At closing, $200,000 of the investors' money was paid to the seller as a down payment with an $800,000 note for the balance. The balance of $200,000 of the down payment was Don's profit on the transaction.

Within 60 days, Don had taken an option on a $1,000,000 piece of property for a $2,000 cash outlay and sold the option to the investors for a $200,000 cash profit. Best of all, because the $2,000 option money came out of Don's IRA, the $200,000 profit was deposited in his IRA tax free until he withdraws the money. The moral of this story: ALTHOUGH YOUR IRA CONTRIBUTION EACH YEAR IS LIMITED TO $2,000, THERE IS NO LIMIT TO THE TAX-SHELTERED PROFITS YOU CAN EARN THE SAME YEAR.

Strategy #332
INVEST YOUR IRA/KEOGH MONEY IN REAL ESTATE OPTIONS ON RESIDENTIAL RENTAL PROPERTIES.

Another way to use real estate options to your advantage is through a two- to three-year option on a single-family home, duplex, or condo. For beginners, a longer-term real estate option on a residential property is much easier and less risky than a short-term option on a piece of land.

Using the Sunday paper or a Realtor, locate an owner who is having trouble selling his property and would be willing to give you a two-year, but preferably a three-year, option to purchase his property at today's price and lease you the property at fair market rent. The owners, even if unable to sell now, would then have the income to make their mortgage payments. You will be surprised how many options you can put together in a short period of time, because an option solves an owner's short-term problem—cash flow. Your cash flow will be neutral or positive because the owner must lease you the property at current fair market rent, the same rent you can get when you sublease to a tenant.

Two documents are required: the option contract giving you the right to purchase the property, and the lease contract giving you the right to use the property during the option period. Insert a sublease clause in the lease agreement specifying that you may rent the property to a third person. Tell the owner you will agree to be responsible for all minor maintenance and will act as manager of the property in consideration for your right to sublease.

Have the trustee of your self-directed IRA/Keogh account handle the investment of your funds. You should be able to option a $70,000 to $120,000 property for no more than a $1,000 to $2,000 option deposit. You can usually get the owner to accept the option money as the first and last month's rent, further reducing your cash outlay.

During the option period, you can sell your option to purchase at a profit to someone else. If your option deposit is $1,000 and three years later you sell your option to someone else at a $10,000 profit, you have made a 1,000% return on your money. Take your $10,000 nontaxed profit and place a three-year option on ten more properties at $1,000 each. If the profit is the same $10,000 after the next three years, you will have nontaxed profits totalling $110,000 after six years, or a return of 11,000% on your original $1,000 investment, and all tax sheltered.

An IRA or Keogh account is not required when using these option strategies, but will provide tax shelter for your big cash profits.

IRA/KEOGH WITHDRAWALS

Once you have built your tax-sheltered fortune in your IRA or Keogh account, you will eventually want to begin withdrawing all or part of your money to use as retirement income or for any purpose you choose. Here are a few of the rules:

- You may withdraw money from your IRA anytime you wish. If you are under 59½ and withdraw any part of your money, you must pay the 10% penalty on the amount withdrawn. If your account is invested correctly and earning 15% per year, however, the penalty is just nine months of interest. All withdrawals of tax-deferred money are added to your taxable income for the year. You can, therefore, successfully use an IRA as a short-term tax shelter, instead of a long-term retirement plan.
- You may begin withdrawing from your IRA in periodic payments, using the life-expectancy payout rules, at any age you wish with no penalty.
- After age 70½ you must begin withdrawing, but you can control the amounts you must withdraw using little-known options. See *Financial Self-Defense*, Chapter 19, "Build a Better IRA," for your withdrawal strategies.

Chapter 34

SELF-DIRECTED ANNUITIES

Go around asking a lot of damn-fool questions. Only through curiosity can we discover opportunities.

Clarence Birdseye
Inventor
(1886–1956)

OBJECTIVE ———————————————————————

COMBINE THE 15% EARNING POWER OF THE MONEY MOVEMENT STRATEGY WITH AMERICA'S BEST TAX SHELTER.

———————————————————————

One of the best, safest, and easiest-to-use tax shelters remaining after tax reform, and an ideal investment for the Money Movement Strategy, is a self-directed annuity, which is actually a tax-deferred mutual fund family.

Think of an annuity as an umbrella over your investment, protecting your profits from taxes. As long as you leave your money invested in any annuity, your money compounds tax free. When you withdraw part or all of your money, you add the gain withdrawn to your taxable income for that year.

The annuity tax shelters we are about to cover are individual nonqualified annuities, generally meaning that they are not employment related. (See Chapter 18 for employment-related annuities.)

477

Strategy #333
USE A SELF-DIRECTED ANNUITY TO EARN 15% PER YEAR WITH NO COMMISSIONS OR TAXES.

A self-directed annuity is a tax-sheltered mutual fund family in which you have a choice of investments. There are hundreds of annuities that have only one investment choice, a fixed-interest account, but there are only a few self-directed annuities. All of the self-directed annuities offer you at least three investment choices—stock, bond, and money market mutual funds. Because of the tax-shelter feature, you can move your money from one fund to another, with no tax liability. You may also, in most annuities, withdraw up to 10% of your money each year for whatever purpose you wish without company penalties or commissions, although you would be liable for any income taxes.

The annuity was originally a retirement program offered by the insurance companies with its origins in the pre-IRA days when most people retired broke. The insurance companies claimed that no income taxes should be paid on the interest earned until the money was withdrawn. There was no basis in tax law for that position, but because of the awesome political power of the insurance companies, Congress allowed the tax-deferred status by not specifically denying it. Congress finally decided to tackle the issue in the Economic Recovery Act of the early eighties, which not only legitimized the annuity concept, but in the process made self-directed annuities one of the best, safest, and most powerful tax shelters in America.

Few brokers or financial planners will recommend self-directed annuities because of the low commissions (or none at all) paid on the initial investment. Instead, financial salesmen recommend single-premium life insurance, a lesser investment that pays high commissions.

The first rule of annuity investments is to use them last, only after you have contributed the legal maximum into your IRA, SEP, Keogh, or other tax-deferred, employment-related retirement programs. The money you invest in an IRA or Keogh, remember, is tax deferred. In a non-qualified annuity, only the investment earnings are tax deferred; you have already paid taxes on the money you invest. (Teachers' and state employees' job-related tax-sheltered annuities are an exception.)

All of the self-directed annuities listed at the end of this chapter give you three or more choices for investing your money.

When you open your account, tell the company which of its investments you have chosen; never let the company tell you. Once you open your account, you manage your money using the Money Movement Strategy with an expectation of averaging 15% currently tax free.

You may contribute to some annuities for as long as you wish. Unlike qualified retirement plans, which require you to stop contributing when you are 70½, some annuities allow you to contribute to them year after year.

Also, you may delay withdrawals until any age. Unlike retirement plans, annuities have no mandatory age requirement to start distributions. When you withdraw, you will be given several options: cash, various periodic payments, or allowing the account to annuitize, which means the company will guarantee to pay you a monthly income for a specified number of years or even for the rest of your life. Under tax reform, there is an IRS-imposed penalty of 10% on all gains withdrawn from an annuity before age 59½. The penalty is overcome in three to five years from the tax-free compounding, so the penalty should not be a deterrent to using an annuity even as a short-term investment.

Strategy #334
DO NOT ANNUITIZE YOUR ANNUITY ACCOUNT.

Annuitizing means you agree to accept periodic payments over the balance of your lifetime. Sounds appealing until you realize the payment schedule is weighted in favor of the company. Always withdraw your money as required so no part of it becomes the property of the insurance company. I recommend that you leave your principal invested and just withdraw your gain each year until you need more income to enjoy.

Strategy #335
USE THE TAX-EXEMPT TRANSFER RULES TO MOVE YOUR ANNUITY TO ANOTHER COMPANY.

What if you become dissatisfied with one company's annuity program and wish to move to another? You may move your money to another company using the tax-exempt transfer rules without any tax penalty. You would, however, be subject to any withdrawal penalty imposed by the insurance company for early withdrawal. You may move your money from investment to investment within a self-directed annuity without becoming liable for any taxes and, in most instances, without commissions or charges.

Strategy #336
MAKE YOUR ANNUITY ACCOUNT WITHDRAWALS TAX FREE BY CREATING "EQUIVALENT" TAX DEDUCTIONS.

One annuity benefit was lost in the Economic Recovery Act: treating the first money you withdraw from your annuity as nontaxable principal instead of taxable interest. The rules now require that when you make a withdrawal, the first money withdrawn is treated as taxable profits instead of nontaxable principal. Your strategy is clear. Any year you withdraw money from your annuity, create an equal amount of tax deductions using any tax strategies you choose. One will offset the other, and, in essence, your withdrawal will be tax free.

How to Invest in a Self-Directed Annuity

Investing in an annuity is as simple as opening a bank account. Call several companies that offer self-directed annuities, or use the telephone number listed in the Self-Directed Annuities Planning Chart at the end of this chapter. Ask for a prospectus. Check the Planning Chart or the prospectus to determine your different options for investments. Be certain you have all the options necessary for using the Money Movement Strategy: stock funds, bond funds, and a money market fund (or fixed-rate investment). Determine what procedure—letter or phone call—is required to move your money from one fund to another, and how often you are allowed to change investments. Complete the application for the annuity you choose and mail it along with your check. Use the list of questions on page 483 to evaluate any annuity. For information and assistance on how to get started, call The Insurance ClearingHouse at 1-800-522-2827.

Strategy #337
**INVEST IN AN ANNUITY ONLY WITH FUNDS YOU PLAN
TO LEAVE INVESTED FOR FIVE YEARS OR LONGER.**

Annuities are commission free if you leave your money invested long enough. To discourage you from moving your money in and out, most annuities have a decreasing load or commission. If you withdraw your money the first year, the maximum commission of 5%–9% would be deducted. The commissions usually decrease by 1% each year until the withdrawal charge reaches zero. Make certain there is no commission or front-end load when you invest.

Strategy #338
**USE YOUR SELF-DIRECTED ANNUITY AS AN ESTATE
PLANNING TOOL.**

The major goal in planning your estate is to pass to your heirs as much of your wealth as possible by not letting the government and the attorneys get their hands on it. Currently, you can distribute, undisturbed by the tax collector, any amount of an estate to a surviving spouse or up to $600,000 in assets to other beneficiaries. Annuities are great estate-planning tools because they avoid probate. Annuities, like insurance contracts, allow you to nominate a beneficiary who would receive your annuity money without probate or attorney's fees. It is, however, counted as part of the estate for estate tax purposes.

Strategy #339
**USE A SELF-DIRECTED ANNUITY TO BEAT THE
KIDDIE TAX FOR CHILDREN UNDER 14.**

If you are a parent or grandparent, one of your biggest concerns about tax reform should be the low-taxed investment earnings limit for children under 14. When income from investments totals over $1,200, the child automatically pays taxes on the excess at the parents' tax rate, even though the child files a separate return. That means investment income for children can be taxed at over 30% instead of the child's rate of 0% to 15%. A child would pay in taxes more than double what an adult with the same income would pay.

The new rules make it difficult to create a college investment fund or to move some of your wealth to the lower tax bracket of children and grandchildren. A self-directed annuity is one solution to this problem. By law, there are no current taxes due on the earnings from an annuity so the earnings from even a child's college-fund investment compound tax free until the money is withdrawn.

Tax protect all of a child's income over $1,200 by using a self-directed annuity. When the child reaches college age and starts withdrawing the money, there is a 10% penalty. The tax-free compounding makes up for the penalty after the money has been invested for about three years. If the child's annuity is self-directed using the Money Movement Strategy (Chapter 30), 10% is only nine months of earnings at 15% per year.

Strategy #340
TRANSFER YOUR CASH VALUE LIFE INSURANCE, TAX EXEMPT, INTO A SELF-DIRECTED ANNUITY.

Remember, there is not a "roll over" privilege in a non-qualified annuity so DO NOT REMOVE the cash value yourself if you wish to keep the money "tax-sheltered." It must be a company-to-company transfer.

Strategy #341
ASK THE RIGHT QUESTIONS BEFORE INVESTING IN A SELF-DIRECTED ANNUITY.

Investing is an annuity is as simple as opening a bank account. Call several companies that offer self-directed annuities and ask for a prospectus. Determine your options for investments. Be certain you have all the options necessary for using the Money Movement Strategy. Determine what procedure—letter or phone call—is required to move your money from one fund to another and how often you are allowed to change investments. Complete the application for the annuity you choose and mail it along with your check.

Questions to Ask When Choosing Self-Directed Annuities:

Q: What is the minimum investment?

A: The minimum investment required must be within your investment capital range. Some annuities require a larger lump sum, others will accept monthly or other periodic deposits. Check the Self-Directed Annuities Planning Chart at the end of this chapter.

Q: Can I add money anytime I wish? What minimum?

A: It is advantageous to be able to add money to an existing account, as you do in a bank savings account. Again, check the chart.

Q: Is the annuity insured or registered in the state of New York?

A: Insurance protects you against bankruptcy or fraud of the issuing company. If the annuity is registered in the state of New York, the New York Insurance Commission has done the work of being certain the annuity is insured and you are protected no matter where you live. Otherwise check the A.M. Best rating.

Q: How often can I move my money within the annuity and what is the procedure?

A: Some annuities have telephone switching; in others you must put your request in writing. Some annuities may limit the number of times you can move your money each year, others will not. Although you will not be moving your money often, flexibility is always on your side. Check the chart.

Q: What is the load or commission charged?

A: Your objective is to find an annuity with no commission when you invest, no commission when you move money within the annuity, and a yearly decreasing commission if you withdraw. Look for a maximum 7% withdrawal commission decreasing 1% each year to zero. In addition, annuities level charges against the account including a fixed charge and a percentage amount similar to the mutual fund management fee. The total charges should be no more than 1.5% per year. Check the chart.

Q: What different investments are available with the annuity?

A: To use the Money Movement Strategy, you need a minimum of a stock fund, a bond fund, and a money market or fixed-rate fund. Check the chart.

Q: Can I withdraw 10% a year during the early years with no commissions?

A: Most annuities allow the penalty-free withdrawal of 10% a year. The money you withdraw is added to your income for the year. In that way, part of your earnings can be withdrawn for income or other purposes while the rest remains tax sheltered.

If you have been investing your money in low-interest, highly taxed bank certificates of deposit or you are considering single-premium life insurance, a self-directed annuity is a far better alternative.

Self-directed annuities are a must investment when your desire is to create safe, tax-sheltered investments for yourself, your children, or your grandchildren.

SELF-DIRECTED ANNUITIES PLANNING CHART

Definitions and Descriptions of Terms Used

GENERAL INFORMATION

Company—The name of the company that issues the annuity.

Annuity Name—The name of the annuity plan offered by the company.

Issue Ages To—The ages at which you may open or start the annuity.

Minimum Initial Deposit—The minimum investment required to open the account.

Additional Deposits—The minimum amount you can add to your account. "None" means no additional investment can be made.

Retirement Plans Available—The retirement plans that can be used with the annuity, including IRA, SEP, Keogh, 403(b), 401(k), 457.

Statements—How often you receive a statement of your account.

States Not Approved—Those states in which the company is not licensed to sell.

FEES

Mortality/Expense Fees—Represents the percentage per year charged against your account balance for expenses and mortality premiums.

Investment Fees—Charges against the fund for the investment advisers.

Administrative Fees—A flat charge assessed against your account for administrative expenses. The average is $30 per year.

Transfer Charges—The amount you are charged, if any, to move your money from one investment to another.

SAFETY

Year Company Established—The year the company began doing business.

Assets—The amount of assets in billions managed by the company.

A.M. Best Rating—The safety rating assigned by the A.M. Best Company. All companies in the charts are acceptable.

FLEXIBILITY

Investment Options—The different mutual funds or accounts in which you can invest your money.

Transfer—When, how often, and how much of your money you can move from investment to investment.

Written or Phone—The method(s) you can use to move your money from one investment to another. "Written" requires a letter or special form; "phone" requires only a phone call and gives maximum convenience.

PERFORMANCE

The percent growth for the year shown of each type of investment offered. Where more than one investment is included in a category, the average is shown.

LIQUIDITY

Surrender Fees (back-end load)—The year-by-year decreasing commission charged if you withdraw your money. *Example:* "7%-6-5-4-3-2-1" means that 7% is charged if you withdraw 100% of your money the first year; the fee decreases by one percentage point each year until it reaches zero in the eighth year and after.

Charged Against—The amount of your account against which the back-end load is charged. "Deposits" means that the load is charged against your deposits but not the appreciation. "Total" means the load is charged against your total withdrawal or account balance.

SELF-DIRECTED ANNUITIES PLANNING CHART

Company	Nationwide	Guardian	Keyport
Annuity Name	Best of America IV	Investor	Preferred Advisor
General Info			
Issue—Ages To	0–78	0–75	1–80
Min. Initial Deposit	$1,500—1st year	$500	$5,000
Additional Deposits	$10 or $25	$100	$2,000
Retirement Plans Avail.	All	All	All
Statements	Quarterly	Semiannually	Quarterly
States Not Approved	None	None	NY
Fees			
Mortality/Expense Fees	.80%/.45%—.05%	1.0%/0.1%—0.28%	1.2%
Investment Fees	See prospectus	0.5%	0.7%
Admin. Fees	$30	$35	$30
When Deducted	Contract anniversary	Contract anniversary	Contract year end
Transfer Charges	0	0	0
Safety			
Year Company Established	1929	1970	1957
Assets	$19.2 Billion	$2.5 Billion	$9.9 Billion
A.M. Best Rating	A + Superior	A ++ Superior	A + Superior
Flexibility			
Investment Options	(Portfolios) (22)	(Funds)(8)	(Trusts)(7)
	Oppenheimer	Stock	Managed Growth
	Dreyfus	Bond	Aggressive Growth
	Fidelity	Cash/MM	Managed Assets
	Neuberger-Berman	Centurion	H/Y Bond

	Strong Van Eck Twentieth Century Nationwide*			Value Line Real Estate			Managed Security Inc. M/M Cash Inc.		
General/Fixed	Yes			Yes			Yes		
Transfer	V = 100% anytime F = not <10% after 1st year			V = every 30 days F = 1st mo. ea. contract yr.			V = 5 times/yr.		
Written or Phone	Either			Either			Either		
Performance	91	92	93	91	92	93	91	92	93
Stock	37%	7%	9%	34%	19%	19%	27%	13%	7%
Bond	15%	6%	8%	15%	6%	9%	14%	6%	n/a
Money Mkt.	4.4%	2%	1.4%	4.3%	2%	1.4%	n/a	n/a	1.5%
Fixed	6.7%	5.2%	4.5%	6%	5%	4.5%	n/a	n/a	3.6%
Liquidity									
Surrender Fees	7%-6-5-4-3-2-1			5%-5-5-5-5			7%-6-5-4-3-2-1		
Charged Against	Deposits			Deposits			Deposits		
Partial Free Withdrawal	10% of Dep.			10% of Dep.			10% Acct. Val.		

*For information on the above annuities call The Insurance ClearingHouse at 1-800-522-2827
V = variable rate investment
F = fixed rate investment

SELF-DIRECTED ANNUITIES PLANNING CHART (cont.)

Company	Security Benefit	Kilico
Annuity Name	Vari-Flex	Advantage III
General Info		
Issue—Ages To	0–75	0–85
Min. Initial Deposit	$500	$2,500
Additional Deposits	$25	$500
Retirement Plans Avail.	All	All
Statements	Active—Monthly	Quarterly
States Not Approved	NY	NY
Fees		
Mortality/Expense Fees	0.7%/0.5%	1.3%
Investment Fees	Approx. 0.5%	Approx. 0.5%
Admin. Fees	$30	$25
When Deducted	Calendar year end	Calendar year end
Transfer Charges	1st free; $10 after	0
Safety		
Year Company Established	1892	1947
Assets	$4.3 Billion	$6.2 Billion
A.M. Best Rating	A + Superior	A – Excellent
Flexibility		
Investment Options	(Series)	(Sep. Acct.)
	Growth	Equity
	Growth/Inc.	Income
	World Wide Equity	Total Return
	Social Awareness	M/M

	High Grade Inc.						
General/Fixed	M/M Bond						
Transfer	Yes			Yes			
Written or Phone	V = every 30 days			V = every 15 days			
	F = min. $5,000/1 × yr.			F = min. $500/1 × yr.			
	Either			Either			
Performance	91	92	93	91	92	93
Stock	34.5%	10%	12%	57%	2%	13%
Bond	16%	6%	11%	14%	5%	5%
Money Mkt.	4.4%	2%	1.3%	4.3%	2%	1.5%
Fixed	7.6%	6.3%	5.4%	6.5%	5.5%	5.0%
Liquidity						
Surrender Fees	8%-7-6-5-4-3-2-1			6%-5-4-3-2-1		
Charged Against	Deposits			Total Funds		
Partial Free Withdrawal	10% of Deposits			10% of Acct. Bal.		

* For information on the above annuities call The Insurance ClearingHouse at 1-800-522-2827
V = variable rate investment
F = fixed rate investment

Chapter 35

DISCOUNTED MORTGAGES

A broker is a man who runs your fortune into a shoestring.

Alexander Woollcott
"Wit's End"
(1887–1943)

OBJECTIVE ————————————————————————————

EARN 30% PER YEAR GUARANTEED AND SECURED.

> ### Strategy #342
> ### INVEST IN DISCOUNTED MORTGAGES FOR A
> ### GUARANTEED 30% RETURN.

What if there was an investment that paid a guaranteed interest rate of 30% each year, in which your principal was 100% secured? There is such an investment, but you'll never find it at brokerage firms, banks, or financial planners. The investment is discounted mortgages—usually second mortgages—that you locate, negotiate, and purchase yourself.

Occasionally, an investment opportunity arises created by unusual economic conditions. During 1979 to 1984, the years of superhigh interest rates, homeowners who wanted to sell found there were not many willing buyers. High interest rates meant that the buyer's payments would be too high if a new mortgage was obtained. *Creative financing* replaced location as the most important words in real estate. In order to entice a purchaser and help that buyer avoid the costs of refinancing, the seller would allow the buyer to assume the existing low-interest first mortgage, then take back a second mortgage for a large part of the down payment. Second mortgages were most often used when the first mortgage was a fully assumable nonqualifying FHA or VA mortgage. There were thousands of properties in every area sold in this manner.

Sellers normally do not like mortgages; they want cash and as a result tire quickly of owning a mortgage that is paid in periodic payments. The seller's desire to get cash out of a mortgage creates an unequaled investment opportunity.

Strategy #343
WHEN MAKING AN OFFER FOR A MORTGAGE, BEGIN BY OFFERING NO MORE THAN 60% OF FACE VALUE.

Because there is no ready-made market for mortgages, sellers are forced to sell mortgages at a discount of 30% to 50% from the face value, and the price is determined by agreement between the seller and buyer of the mortgage. When making a cash offer for a mortgage, begin by offering 60% of the face value. You may either stick to your 60% offer or negotiate up to 75%, but usually not more. You'll be surprised by how many good mortgages you can buy for 60¢ on the dollar.

HOW YOU MAKE YOUR MONEY

If a seller sold his home two years ago and took back a $10,000 interest-only 12% second mortgage for seven years, and you purchase the mortgage for 60% of face value, you pay $6,000 for the mortgage. When the mortgage term is up in five years, you receive the entire face value, $10,000, which is $4,000 more than the $6,000 you invested. Until maturity, the interest of 12% is paid to you. The 12% interest, remember, is based on the $10,000 face value of the mortgage and amounts to $1,200 each year. Since you have only $6,000 invested, but still receive the full $1,200 interest annually, your return is 20%. Your total annualized return from the interest plus the discount is 30%.

Here is an example of how your return is earned and computed when you buy a discounted mortgage:

Face value	$10,000
Purchase price	$ 6,000
Balance of term	five years
Original interest rate	12%

Return on Discounted Mortgage as a Percentage

Your interest rate	20.00%
Earnings from discount (annualized)	10.75%
Annual return	30.75%

Return on Discounted Mortgage in Dollars

Interest ($1,200/year × 5 years)	$ 6,000
Discount	$ 4,000
Total profit	$10,000

In this example, you would have earned $10,000 during five years on a $6,000 investment or about 30% per year—guaranteed.

Once you get the hang of it, you'll wonder why every investor isn't looking for and buying discounted mortgages.

You won't buy discounted mortgages at financial institutions, nor will you normally find them advertised in the newspaper. Where do you look?

Strategy #344
USE THE COURTHOUSE AS A DISCOUNTED MORTGAGE SOURCE.

The easiest method of locating unlimited numbers of mortgages that you can buy at a discount is to go to the county courthouse.

Spend a couple of hours in the real estate records room, where you'll find all real estate transactions in date order on microfilm. Sit down at a microfilm reader and, beginning with the present and working backward, locate second mortgages on residential properties. You'll find dozens of them, ranging from $2,000 to $50,000. All the information you need is normally on the screen.

The mortgagee—person to whom the money is owed.
The mortgagor—person responsible for the payments.
The address of the property—so you can evaluate it.
The amount of the mortgage.
The terms of the mortgage—payments, interest, due date.

In many states, second mortgages are referred to as deeds of trust or second deeds of trust. You will find the people who work in the county courthouses are usually very helpful, and they will show you how to work the equipment and find the records you are looking for.

Make a list of 10 or 20 that look promising and are within your investment-capital range. Remember, your goal is to buy a mortgage at 30% to 40% less than face value. That is what is meant by *discounted*.

When you get home, let your fingers do the walking. Look up the telephone numbers of the mortgagees. If you can't find one, call the mortgagor and ask for the phone number of the person to whom he or she makes the second-mortgage payment.

Call the mortgagee and use these words to open the conversation:

"Hi, Mrs. Smith?"

"Yes."

"My name is [your name] and I understand you are holding a mortgage for $[amount] on the property located at [address]. Is that correct?"

"Yes, why do you want to know?"

"Well, Mrs. Smith, I'm an investor and I would like to buy your mortgage for cash. Does that interest you?"

Four out of five will say yes. You then set up an appointment and negotiate the discount amount by beginning your offer at about 60 cents on the dollar. For a mortgage with a $10,000 balance, you would offer $6,000 cash. The longer the mortgage has to run, the more receptive the mortgage holder will be.

Why would a person sell a mortgage to you at a discount? Because most Americans are such poor money managers, they need cash now far more than they need payments over time, even if the payments will produce more income. You'll find that one out of three mortgage holders will sell to you at a 30% to 40% discount.

Strategy #345
RUN NEWSPAPER ADS IN SEARCH OF MORTGAGES YOU CAN BUY AT A DISCOUNT.

You can spend a few tax deductible dollars running ads to search for people who want cash for their mortgages. The ads can be placed in the classified section or as larger display ads with such captions as:

"Cash for your mortgage."

"I buy mortgages."

"Investor wants to buy first and second mortgages."
"Want to sell your second mortgage?"
Most who have tried the newspaper route find it a long, slow, but eventually successful process, generating one to five calls per week and one or two mortgages a month.

Strategy #346
MAKE FRIENDS WITH REAL ESTATE PROFESSIONALS WHO WILL CALL YOU WHEN THEY LEARN OF A MORTGAGE FOR SALE.

You can cultivate a mortgage garden of real estate agents and brokers. Since there is no ready-made market for discounted mortgages, the first person a mortgage holder would think to call is someone in the real estate business. By making friends with several real estate professionals and letting them know of your interest in purchasing discounted mortgages, you'll discover a never-ending supply.

Many years ago, when I was first getting into investment real estate, I enrolled in an adult night-school course called Real Estate Financing. The people I met in that one class, mostly real estate professionals, were worth thousands of dollars to me. From friendly conversations that ensued on class breaks, I bought several properties at a bargain, found a property manager, a handyman for inexpensive repairs, got several new clients for my printing and publishing companies, and bought several discounted mortgages.

Strategy #347
WHEN BUYING DISCOUNTED MORTGAGES, EXPECT THE BEST, ARM YOURSELF FOR THE WORST, AND TALK TO YOUR ATTORNEY FIRST.

Your outside risk when buying discounted mortgages is that the mortgagor won't make the payments and you may have to foreclose on the property to protect your investment—not a problem if you plan effectively.

Before you buy a discounted mortgage, have a chat with a competent real estate attorney who is familiar with the real estate laws and practices in your area. Develop a contingency plan for how he will handle collection if the mortgagor is late with the payments. If the mortgage is in default for over one day, your attorney should serve immediate notice that you intend to foreclose. You will seldom have a real problem if you act immediately. As a holder of a mortgage, never get into the welfare business by allowing other people's problems to influence you into letting them be late with their payments. No matter how you feel emotionally, the only 100% sure method of protecting yourself and collecting every dime is to act, act immediately, and act in the strongest way possible. If you want to help people financially, do it through a contribution to your favorite charity, never by mixing business and charity; you'll always lose. Once you learn to act immediately and consistently, the mortgagor will find a way to make the payments on time because he knows you mean business.

If, in a rare case, the property does go to foreclosure because payments weren't made on either the first mortgage or your second mortgage, you and your attorney will want to choose one of three options:

1. Bring the payments current on the first mortgage to prevent the first mortgage holder from foreclosing while you are handling the situation. When you buy a mortgage, always send a certified letter to the first mortgage holder stating that you are the holder of a second mortgage and want to be notified anytime a payment is late. Although not required by law, the first mortgage holder will generally comply with your request.

2. Convince the mortgagor he should immediately deed the property to you using a quitclaim deed to avoid the embarrassment and ordeal of a foreclosure, and to preserve his credit standing. This alternative is often the best.

3. If the property goes to auction, bid an amount equal to the existing first mortgage plus the amount of your second mortgage. If someone outbids you, he or she will have to pay every cent owed to you. If you win the bid with the highest offer, you will have to put 10% of the bid into escrow and have about 30 days to produce the balance. Check the rules for your area. Your bank will help you with some short-term financing while you refinance or sell the property to get your money back. In this case, the worst that can happen is that you have purchased a property worth at a minimum 20% more than you bid at foreclosure.

Strategy #348
BUY DISCOUNTED MORTGAGES WITH NO MORE THAN AN 80% LOAN-TO-VALUE RATIO.

Every commercial mortgage company has an upper limit on how much money it will loan on a first or second mortgage. The formula for calculating the maximum loan amount is known as the loan-to-value (LTV) ratio. You will want to adopt your own LTV. I recommend you use 80% as your loan-to-value ratio, as I do.

The LTV is the maximum percentage of the market value of a property you would be willing to finance. The maximum amount you would pay for a mortgage should be no more than 80% of the market value of the property, less any other mortgage amounts. If a property is appraised at $100,000, the sum of all mortgages including yours would have to total less than $80,000 or you would not want to purchase the mortgage. If the first mortgage is $60,000 and the mortgage you are purchasing is $10,000, the total of the mortgage amounts would be $70,000. This would be perfectly acceptable because $70,000 is less than the $80,000, 80% maximum. If the mortgage on the property is $75,000 and the mortgage you wanted to buy has a face value of $15,000, the loan-to-value ratio of 80% or $80,000 would be exceeded and you would not purchase the mortgage.

Strategy #349
CHECK THE CREDIT HISTORY OF THE MORTGAGOR BEFORE BUYING A DISCOUNTED MORTGAGE.

Carefully check the credit rating and credit history of the mortgagor, the person who will be responsible for making the payments. Good credit habits are likely to continue; poor credit habits on the part of the mortgagor may come back to haunt you. Since the mortgagor has been making payments to the mortgage seller for some time, obtain proof of the timeliness of the payments. Mortgages that have a payment history are called seasoned mortgages.

If you have over $15,000 of total investment capital, discounted mortgages should be a serious consideration. You will find mortgages available between $2,000 and $50,000. Begin immediately by going through the motions of locating possible mortgage purchases even if you don't intend to buy one just now. You'll get a feel for the process without being required to make a commitment. Even if you grow to love discounted second mortgages as an income and wealth producer, invest no more than 30% to 50% of your capital in mortgages, since your investment is tied up from two to ten years.

The final step in purchasing a mortgage is to have your attorney handle the mortgage transfer and record the mortgage at the courthouse, giving you a priority claim against most other subsequent loans or mortgages.

Discounted mortgages are one of the best investment choices for reinvesting equity you have borrowed from your home (see Chapter 9).

The high guaranteed and secured investment return of discounted mortgages certainly qualifies them for our list of the "ten best investments."

Chapter 36

TAX LIEN CERTIFICATES

The art of getting rich is found not in saving, but in being at the right spot at the right time.

Ralph Waldo Emerson
The Conduct of Life
1860

OBJECTIVE

EARN 15 TO 50% GOVERNMENT-GUARANTEED INTEREST.

Strategy #350
INVEST IN TAX LIEN CERTIFICATES FOR SAFETY AND MAXIMUM INTEREST.

The highest government-guaranteed interest paid on any investment is a tax lien certificate. There are 500 government agencies, usually county taxing authorities, that issue tax lien certificates with government-guaranteed interest of 8% to 50% with an average interest of over 15%. A tax lien can be any amount from $20 to $50,000.

A tax lien certificate is an encumbrance on real estate placed by a government taxing authority and sold to an investor. Here's how the investment opportunity is created. Let's say a neighbor of yours moved away, rented out the house, but hasn't paid the property taxes. After one notice or less the county puts a lien on the property for the amount of the unpaid taxes. The lien, recorded at the courthouse, means the property cannot be mortgaged, sold, or otherwise disposed of by the owner until the back taxes are paid.

The lien gives the county some control over the property but not any money. More and more counties then sell tax lien certificates at courthouse auctions to compensate for unpaid taxes. You, as an interested investor, go to the courthouse on auction days to bid on the certificates. The amount of the certificate is usually the amount of the unpaid taxes plus costs.

The state sets the maximum interest rate. In Florida, where I live, the interest rate is 18% per year; in other states such as Michigan, interest is as high as 50%. Since the lien will not be taken off the property until the taxes plus interest are paid, your investment is virtually government-guaranteed.

Many tax liens are sold at the maximum guaranteed interest rate; others go for a lesser rate. Why? Because the hope of the bidders is that the owner won't pay the back taxes, and the investor will end up with a valuable property instead of the interest. The winning bid in most states is the lowest interest rate; in other states the interest rate remains constant but the amount of the investment is bid up.

What happens if you own a tax lien certificate and the owner never pays the taxes? That is the investor's dream. In some states, after three delinquent tax years, the property will be sold at public auction to the highest bidder; in many states the holder of the tax lien certificate simply applies for and receives a deed to the property. See the state-by-state Tax Lien Certificate and Property Auctions chart at the end of this chapter. In the case of a property auction, you show up at the auction and bid the amount of your investment (the unpaid taxes) plus all interest due you. If you are outbid, the high bidder must, by law, pay you the amount of your investment plus all unpaid taxes. If you are the high bidder, you get the title to the property. All previous mortgages and liens are wiped out except federal tax liens, if any. The appraised value of the property could be as much as 2 times to 100 times your investment.

Strategy #351
BUY A PIECE OF REAL ESTATE AT A HUGE DISCOUNT AT A TAX LIEN AUCTION.

At a tax lien auction, the property itself and not a tax certificate is sold. Maybe you'd like to buy a lot in your neighborhood or a bargain property you can fix up and live in or rent out. The courthouse steps should be your bargain-basement shopping area. In most states, properties with delinquent real estate taxes are eventually sold at auction at the courthouse. When you win a bid, you will usually have to put 10% down and you'll have 0 to 30 days to come up with the balance. If you don't have the money, it is relatively easy to get a bank, mortgage company, or investor to underwrite your liened-property purchases. Have the bank, mortgage company, or investor commit to giving you the money within the 30-day period before you bid.

Strategy #352
EXAMINE THE PROPERTY BEFORE YOU BID AT A TAX LIEN OR PROPERTY AUCTION.

Always know what you're bidding on at any auction. Before you go to a tax lien or liened-property sale, examine the property, neighborhood, and courthouse records. Buy liens or properties only in appreciating areas. The best price on the wrong property brings more headaches than profits.

Check the courthouse records for any mortgages, IRS liens, or other encumbrances. The only lien that is senior to a tax lien is an IRS lien. The recorded mortgages on a property will give you an indication of whom you will be bidding against. Normally any mortgage holder will appear at the auction to bid an amount to cover his or her mortgage plus any senior liens or mortgages. That way, the mortgage holder will either be paid off by a higher bidder or get title to the property to secure his of her investment. If the mortgage holder does not show up, and the winning bid is less than the amount of the mortgages, the mortgage holders lose all or part of their investment.

Some taxing authorities publish a description of the properties that will be sold at the next auction. Some areas will put you on a mailing list, others will only put notices in legal papers.

Strategy #353
BID NO MORE THAN 70% OF THE MARKET VALUE AT A LIENED-PROPERTY AUCTION.

Often you can buy a piece of land or even an improved property at a tax lien auction for as little as 10¢ on the dollar.

In no case would you want to bid more than 70% of the value of the property, so you can resell quickly at a profit if that is your objective. Your choices when you win a bid are to hold the property as an investment, sell it for a quick profit, or, in the case of a home, live in the property. The choice is yours.

I saw a $500,000 property in North Carolina go at a tax sale for $9,500. A property in New York was bought at an auction for $950 in unpaid taxes and sold six years later for $1.3 million! Although these incredible profits are the rare examples, you can see the upside potential without the downside risk.

Tax lien certificates give you the excitement of gambling with no chance of losing. To help you get started, the chart at the end of this chapter lists the government agencies that sell tax lien certificates or tax-liened properties. Specific information for all states is also included.

By calling your local taxing authority, you can obtain the local rules and procedures governing the sale of tax lien certificates or tax-liened properties in your area.

Some states do not sell tax lien certificates, which may necessitate your doing some traveling to nearby states in order to bid. If so, your travel expenses are deductible as a miscellaneous investment expense if you buy a certificate.

TAX LIENED PROPERTIES

Checklist for Investors

1. Check your local county or taxing authority for where and when the auctions are held.
2. If you are interested in tax certificates instead of bidding directly on properties, find the closest state where certificates are offered using the chart at the end of this chapter.
3. Find out if you can get on a mailing list, or if not, find out where and when the properties are advertised.
4. Determine the properties in which you are interested. Verify that the property is actually where it is supposed to be and is in the condition described. Most taxing authorities make plot maps available at a small charge.
5. Check with the taxing authority to determine the total amount of taxes, interest, penalties, and costs due, not just those listed in the minimum bid.
6. Check the Department of Records to be certain there are no IRS liens against the property.

7. Find out if you must preregister and put up a deposit on properties on which you intend to bid.
8. Determine the procedures and costs involved in getting title to a property you win in an auction.
9. Ascertain the minimum possible bid that can be made.
10. Decide in advance your maximum bid so you don't get carried away with enthusiasm.
11. Find out how your deed or certificate should be recorded once you win it.
12. In the case of a tax lien certificate, determine the notices and procedures you must use to acquire the property, if the owner never pays the taxes.

Strategy #354
AGGRESSIVELY ENFORCE YOUR RIGHTS AS A NEW LIEN HOLDER BY FORECLOSING ON DELINQUENT PAYERS WHO FILE BANKRUPTCY.

When a person files for bankruptcy, depending on whether Chapter 7, 11, or 13 is filed, that person may be allowed to discharge certain debts. In most states, a person would be allowed to keep his "homestead" property through a bankruptcy proceeding. What happens if you are holding a tax lien certificate on a piece of property and the owner files for bankruptcy? If the property is a homestead, and the owner chooses to keep the property, he must still make the mortgage payments and pay his property taxes, or the lien holder can force the sale.

In almost every state, real estate taxes are liens on the property, even ahead of mortgages, so tax liens are not eliminated by bankruptcy. If the property is sold, the tax certificate must be paid before anyone else receives any of the proceeds of the sale. If the owner keeps the property and still does not pay his back taxes, the holder of the tax lien certificate can still force the sale regardless of the owner's bankruptcy. However, since the bankruptcy stays or puts on hold all action temporarily, a sale may be postponed.

With these rights, investors in tax lien certificates are in a strong, secure position. Your objective is to select a profitable certificate based on value.

Following is an example of the rules for investing in tax lien certificates. Each state and county has slightly different rules.

SEMINOLE COUNTY, FLORIDA, TAX CERTIFICATE SALE RULES

1. The 1994 Tax Certificate sale will begin in Room 1628 (Bd. of County Comm. Chambers) and will continue on a day-to-day basis, until all certificates are sold. There will be a one-hour recess for lunch from 12:00 until 1:00 P.M.

2. Bidding is for the rate of interest only and may commence at a maximum rate of 18% and bid inversely to a low of zero percent. Face amount of certificate is: tax plus cost, as advertised. The advertised figure is the amount due for each certificate purchased.

3. Bidders are asked to wait until the Auctioneer has finished calling an item before bidding.

4. The first bid recognized by the Auctioneer is the official bid.

5. A reasonable deposit of 10% of the bid amount (to be determined by the Tax Collector) is required at the close of your bid.

6. Purchase of a tax certificate in no way permits the certificate holder to enter the property or intimidate the landowner. The landowner has a period of two years from the date the tax became delinquent to redeem the tax certificate. The redemption is done through the Office of the Tax Collector only.

7. In the event an error is discovered in the tax certificate, it may be canceled or corrected by Authority of the Department of Revenue. In this case 8% simple interest will be paid, except as revised by law.

8. When a tax certificate is redeemed and the interest earned on the tax certificate is less than five percent of the face amount, then a mandatory charge of five percent shall be levied upon the tax certificate. The person redeeming the tax certificate shall pay the interest rate bid or the mandatory charge, whichever is greater. This shall apply to all tax certificates except those with an interest rate bid of zero percent. Considering the exceptions mentioned, the interest rate bid shall prevail for the life of the tax certificate. Redemption is made through the Tax Collector's Office only.

9. The life of a tax certificate is seven (7) years.

10. Tax certificates must represent taxes which are two years delinquent before a tax deed application may be made. Taxes become delinquent on April 1st each year, as per Florida Statutes.

11. The name given at the sale is the name that will appear on the tax certificate, W-9 form. All redemption notices will be mailed to the address given at the sale. Subsequent changes of address must be filed with the Office of the Tax Collector only.

12. Tax certificates will be sent by certified mail after the sale is balanced and certified. Interest will be earned from the date of the tax certificate sale.

13. All tax certificates which are transferred must be recorded in the Office of the Tax Collector. There will be a $2.00 fee for transfers.
14. For further information and assignment of a bidder number, contact the Office of the Tax Collector at (407) 321-1130 ext. 638 or 641.

TAX LIEN CERTIFICATE AND PROPERTY AUCTIONS BY STATE

State	Tax Lien Certs. or Property Auctions	Certificate Interest Rate	Redemption Period	Contact
Alabama	C	12%	3 years	State Dept. of Revenue
Alaska	A		1 year	Borough Office
Arizona	C	16	3–5 years	Dept. of Revenue
Arkansas	C	varies	2 years	Commissioner's Office
California	A		none	Treasurer's Office
Colorado	C	16	3 years	Treasurer's Office
Connecticut	C	12	1 year	Tax Collector
Delaware	A		60 days	Office of the Prothonotary
District of Columbia	A		2 years	Tax Collector
Florida	C	18	2 years	Tax Collector
Georgia	C	10	13 months	Tax Assessor
Hawaii	A		1 year	Treasurer's Office
Idaho	A		3 years	Tax Office
Illinois	C	18	2.5 years	Treasurer's Office
Indiana	C	10–25	1 year	Treasurer's Office
Iowa	C	15	2.9 years	Tax Office
Kansas	A		none	Treasurer's Office
Kentucky	C	12	3 years	Sheriff's Office
Louisiana	C	27–42	3 years	Bureau of Treasury
Maine	A		3 years	Property Tax Division
Maryland	C	19–24	6 months	Treasurer's Office
Massachusetts	C	14–16	2.5 years	Tax Collector
Michigan	C	15–50	12–18 months	County Treasurer
Minnesota	A		none	Tax Forfeited Land Unit
Mississippi	C	12	2 years	Property Tax Division
Missouri	C	8	2 years	Property Tax Division
Montana	A		60 days	County Treasurer
Nebraska	C	14	3 years	Property Tax Division
Nevada	A		none	Treasurer's Office
New Hampshire	C	18	2 years	Property Tax Division
New Jersey	C	18	1.5 years	Property Tax Division
New Mexico	A		none	Treasurer's Office
New York*	C	12	2 years	Custodian of Taxes Office

State	Tax Lien Certs. or Property Auctions	Certificate Interest Rate	Redemption Period	Contact
North Carolina	A		10 days	Tax Sales Office
North Dakota	C	9–12	5 years	Tax Sales Office
Ohio	A		10–30 days	Auditor's Office
Oklahoma	C	8	2 years	County Treasurer's Office
Oregon	A		2 years	Tax Title Department
Pennsylvania	A		1 year	Treasurer's Office
Rhode Island	C	6–18	1 year	City Tax Division
South Carolina	C	8	1 year	County Treasurer
South Dakota	C	12	4 years	Property Tax Division
Tennessee	A		2 years	Clerk Master/County Treasurer
Texas	A		2 years	Tax Assessor/Collector
Utah	A		none	Auditor's Office
Vermont	C	6–12	1 year	City Tax Collector
Virginia	A		none	Department of Finance/ Tax Assessor
Washington	A		none	Treasurer's Office
West Virginia	C	1%/month	18 months	State Auditor's Office
Wisconsin	A		none	Treasurer's Office
Wyoming	C	18% 1st yr. 15% sub. yrs.	5 years	County Treasurer

* Tax lien certificate sales conducted by every county except Westchester, which handles auctions by city.

Chapter 37

POWERFUL INVESTING— HOW TO STRUCTURE YOUR INVESTMENT PLAN

He is poor whose expenses exceed his income.

Jean de La Bruyère
(1645–1696)

OBJECTIVE

CHOOSE THE INVESTMENTS THAT WILL ACCOMPLISH YOUR GOALS IN THE SHORTEST TIME.

> *Strategy #355*
> CHOOSE FROM THE TEN BEST INVESTMENTS FOR MAXIMUM GROWTH, MAXIMUM TAX SHELTER, OR MAXIMUM INCOME.

Other than safety, there are only four different objectives of a powerful investment plan. Maximum growth, maximum tax shelter, and maximum income are the three financial objectives; convenience is the fourth.

In all good investment plans safety should be the key factor and is created through your choice of investments and your knowledge of investment strategies. Maximum growth is the result of reinvesting the profits you are earning while paying no commissions or taxes or through the use of borrowed money. In the early years of your investment plan maximum growth is usually the main objective; in later years you will want to concentrate on maximizing your income. Tax shelter is always a part of any good investment plan. In structuring your investment plan, you must first determine which of the four objectives are most important to you: growth, income, tax shelter, or convenience. Safety is built into all the investment strategies we have discussed. If your objective is income, liquidity or the ability to take money out of your investments is also important.

The Ten Best Investments Rating Chart (page 509) rates each of our investments using the numbers 0 to 3. Zero means "none at all," such as "no tax shelter"; 3 means maximum, such as "maximum growth." All the investments listed are very safe when used as directed. Growth means an increase in the value of your original investment. Income means that income is available should you choose to take it, or in some cases, such as the mutual fund, the income could be reinvested. In summary, here are the reasons why these investments are the "ten best":

An **ASSET MANAGEMENT ACCOUNT** should be used as your primary checking account, offering convenience, ease of record keeping, and "legal float."

A **NO-LOAD MUTUAL FUND FAMILY** account can be used as a highly liquid, high-return investment. If growth is your objective, pump 10% of all of your net job income into a mutual fund family and reinvest the earnings. If income is your objective, you may set up your mutual fund account to send you a predetermined amount of income each month, regardless of the monthly earnings of the account. The first $5,000 of investment capital should be invested in mutual funds.

The **MUTUAL FUND MARGIN ACCOUNT** is a leveraged growth tool and can be used to the maximum by all aggressive investors, and to a lesser degree by conservative investors.

SELF-DIRECTED ANNUITIES combine high return with tax shelter, but the money should be kept invested for five years or more to eliminate commissions. All conservative and retired investors with $10,000 or more of capital should use annuities as part of their plan. After age 59½, there is no 10% withdrawal penalty. Aggressive investors with $50,000 or less will opt instead for the high returns and income from the mutual fund margin accounts and discounted mortgages, and, if adjusted gross income is less than $100,000, build tax shelter using personally held investment real estate. With over $50,000 of investment capital, annuities become a must for all investors.

If you qualify for an **IRA/KEOGH**, a **401(k)** Salary Deferral Plan, or a **403(b)** Public Employees Tax Sheltered Annuity, put every dime you can afford into the plan, even if you have to borrow money to live on. Job-related retirement programs, when used correctly, will automatically make you rich over time.

DISCOUNTED MORTGAGES should be used by everyone with more than $10,000 investment capital who desires maximum income, 20% to 30%, at a guaranteed interest rate.

Your own **HOME** is the one real estate investment you should always own because of both tax shelter and growth. You are renting mortgage money instead of renting a property.

INVESTMENT REAL ESTATE is a tax shelter alternative for those who have an adjusted gross income of under $100,000. Real estate is a great investment for those who have more time than money.

At the end of this chapter, you will find the Investment Planning Guide, step-by-step charts for allocating any amount of investment capital from $1,000 to $250,000. The Investment Planning Guide is a balanced approach to growth, income, tax shelter, and safety, all in one plan, which can easily be modified based on your personal financial objectives.

Your objective is to structure your investment plan using a combination of the "ten best investments" to earn over 20% per year. The wealth-building power of a 20% return is shown in the 20% Investment Growth Table (on page 510).

Part A shows how much you will have in 5–20 years with monthly deposits of 10% out of your paycheck.

Part B shows the results with yearly deposits as you would make in an IRA/Keogh account.

Part C shows the results you will achieve with lump-sum investments such as those in self-directed annuities or an IRA rollover.

No plan will work unless you do. Everything you need in order to profit from investing has been included in the chapters of Part III. From now on, procrastination, not ignorance, is your only enemy.

TEN BEST INVESTMENTS RATING CHART

	Growth	Income	Tax Shelter	Conven.	Safety[6]	Liquidity
Asset Management Account	0	1	0	3	3	3
No-Load Mutual Fund Family	3	3	1	2	3	3
Mutual Fund Margin Account[1]	3	3	1	2	2	2
Self-Directed Annuity	3	0	3	2	3	1
Self-Directed IRA/ Keogh	3	0	3	3	3	1
401(k) Deferred Compensation/ 403(b) Tax- Sheltered Annuity	3	0	3	3	3	1
Discounted Mortgage[2]	3	3	2	1	3	0
Your Own Home[3]	3	0	3	2	3	1
Rental Real Estate— Residential[4]	3	0	3	1	2	1
Tax Lien Certificates/ Liened Properties[5]	3	3	0	1	3	0

Notes:
1. Tax shelter in a mutual fund is the nontaxable appreciation of stocks or bonds held but not sold by the fund. Tax shelter in a mutual fund margin account is the deductible interest on the loan.
2. Growth in a discounted mortgage represents the difference in purchase at a discount and the amount of payoff when the mortgage matures. Tax shelter in a discounted mortgage is the discounted amount on which the taxes are deferred until maturity. The income is taxable in the year received.
3. The tax shelter on your own home includes deductible taxes and interest as well as the tax-deferred appreciation.
4. Rental real estate should be purchased for growth and tax shelter, not income. The income objective is neutral cash flow. The tax shelter on residential rental real estate includes depreciation and deductible expenses.
5. The growth in a tax lien certificate is represented by the opportunity to purchase property based on the taxes due if the owner does not redeem the property. The income from a liened property is the guaranteed interest paid when the property is redeemed by the original owner. There is no income on a liened property purchase.
6. The high degree of safety indicated is based on the use of the strategies covered in this book.

20% INVESTMENT GROWTH TABLE

Part A

Mthly Deposits	5 Yrs	10 Yrs	15 Yrs	20 Yrs
$ 100	$ 10,000	$ 38,000	$ 114,000	$ 318,000
200	21,000	77,000	228,000	636,000
300	31,000	115,000	342,000	954,000
400	41,000	153,000	456,000	1,272,000
500	52,000	192,000	570,000	1,590,000
1,000	104,000	383,000	1,139,000	3,181,000

Part B

Yrly Deposits	5 Yrs	10 Yrs	15 Yrs	20 Yrs
$ 1,000	$ 9,000	$ 31,000	$ 86,000	$ 224,000
2,000	18,000	62,000	173,000	448,000
3,000	27,000	93,000	259,000	672,000
4,000	36,000	125,000	346,000	896,000
5,000	45,000	156,000	432,000	1,120,000
10,000	89,000	312,000	864,000	2,240,000

Part C

Lump Sum Dep	5 Yrs	10 Yrs	15 Yrs	20 Yrs
$ 10,000	$ 25,000	$ 62,000	$ 154,000	$ 383,000
20,000	50,000	124,000	308,000	767,000
30,000	75,000	186,000	462,000	1,150,000
40,000	100,000	248,000	616,000	1,534,000
50,000	124,000	310,000	770,000	1,917,000
100,000	249,000	619,000	1,541,000	3,834,000

INVESTMENT PLANNING GUIDE

(Investment Capital = $1,000)

	Amount Invested	New or Borrowed Capital	Invest. Return	Current Income	Deferred Income	Tax Shelter
Asset Management	100	—	10%	10	—	—
Mutual Fund	900	—	15%	135	—	—
Margin Account	—	900	10%[3]	90	—	—
Retirement Program	—	2,000[1]	15%	—	300	2,300
Personal Residence	—	80,000[2]	6%	—	4,800	4,800
TOTALS	1,000	82,900		235	5,100	7,100

One-Year Investment Results

Current Income	=	$ 235	24%
Deferred Income	=	$5,100	510%
Total Income	=	$5,335	534%
Tax Savings[4]	=	$2,130	
TOTAL RETURN		$7,465	

With $1,000 of your own money and $2,000 borrowed for an IRA plus the purchase of your own home, you have created an investment return of $5,335 per year and including the $2,130 tax savings, a total one-year return of $7,465. Based on $1,000 original investment and the use of borrowed money, your total investment return is 24%. When you include real estate appreciation, your total return is 534%!

Notes:
1. The $2,000 is borrowed money for an IRA or payroll deduction for a company retirement plan.
2. The personal residence down payment and financing is made using a combination of assumable mortgages or borrowed money.
3. The return on the margin account is after interest is deducted.
4. Tax savings based on $7,100 of tax shelter is based on 30% federal and state tax bracket.

INVESTMENT PLANNING GUIDE

(Investment Capital = $5,000)

	Amount Invested	New or Borrowed Capital	Invest. Return	Current Income	Deferred Income	Tax Shelter
Asset Management	500	—	10%	50	—	—
Mutual Fund	2,000	—	15%	300	—	—
Margin Account	—	2,000	10%[3]	200	—	—
Retirement Program	—	3,000[1]	15%	—	450	3,450
Personal Residence	—	80,000[2]	6%	—	4,800	4,800
Invest. Real Estate	2,500	80,000	6%	—	4,800	7,200
TOTALS	5,000	165,000		550	10,050	15,450

One-Year Investment Results

Current Income	= $ 550	11%
Deferred Income	= $10,050	201%
Total Income	= $10,600	212%
Tax Savings[4]	= $ 4,635	
TOTAL RETURN	$15,235	

With $5,000 of your own money and $3,000 borrowed or payroll deducted for your retirement plan, $2,000 from a mutual fund margin account, and your own home, you have created an investment return of $10,600 (212%) plus $4,635 in tax savings.

Notes:
1. The $3,000 is borrowed money for an IRA or payroll deduction for a company retirement plan.
2. The personal residence down payment and financing is made using a combination of assumable mortgages or borrowed money.
3. The return on the margin account is after interest is deducted.
4. Tax savings based on $15,450 of tax shelter is based on 30% federal and state tax bracket.

INVESTMENT PLANNING GUIDE

(Investment Capital = $10,000)

	Amount Invested	New or Borrowed Capital	Invest. Return	Current Income	Deferred Income	Tax Shelter
Asset Management	1,000	—	10%	100	—	—
Mutual Fund	4,000	—	15%	600	—	—
Margin Account	—	4,000	10%[3]	400	—	—
Retirement Program	—	4,000[1]	15%	—	600	4,600
Personal Residence	—	100,000[2]	6%	—	6,000	6,000
Invest. Real Estate	5,000	100,000	6%	—	6,000	9,000
TOTALS	10,000	208,000		1,100	12,600	19,600

One-Year Investment Results

Current Income	=	$ 1,100	11%
Deferred Income	=	$12,600	126%
Total Income	=	$13,700	137%
Tax Savings[4]	=	$ 5,880	
TOTAL RETURN		$19,580	

With $10,000 of your own money and $4,000 borrowed or payroll deducted for your retirement plan, $4,000 from a mutual fund margin account, and your own home, you have created an investment return of $13,700 (137%) plus $5,880 in tax savings.

Notes:
1. The $4,000 is borrowed money for an IRA or payroll deduction for a company retirement plan.
2. The personal residence down payment and financing is made using a combination of assumable mortgages or borrowed money.
3. The return on the margin account is after interest is deducted.
4. Tax savings based on $19,600 of tax shelter is based on 30% federal and state tax bracket.

INVESTMENT PLANNING GUIDE

(Investment Capital = $25,000)

	Amount Invested	New or Borrowed Capital	Invest. Return	Current Income	Deferred Income	Tax Shelter
Asset Management	1,000	—	10%	100	—	—
Mutual Fund	10,000	—	15%	1,500	—	—
Margin Account	—	10,000	10%[3]	1,000	—	—
Self-Directed Annuity	5,000	—	15%	—	750	750
Retirement Program	—	7,000[1]	15%	—	1,050	8,050
Discounted Mortg.	4,000	—	30%	800	400	400
Personal Residence	—	150,000[2]	6%	—	9,000	9,000
Invest. Real Estate	5,000	100,000	6%	—	6,000	9,000
TOTALS	25,000	267,000		3,400	17,200	27,200

One-Year Investment Results

Current Income	=	$ 3,400	14%
Deferred Income	=	$17,200	69%
Total Income	=	$20,600	82%
Tax Savings[4]	=	$ 8,160	
TOTAL RETURN		$28,760	

With $25,000 of your own money, $7,000 payroll deduction for your retirement plan, $10,000 from a mutual fund margin account, your own home, and the purchase of $100,000 of investment real estate, you have created an investment return of $20,600 (82%) plus $8,160 in tax savings.

Notes:
1. The $7,000 is borrowed money for an IRA or payroll deduction for a company retirement plan.
2. The personal residence is already owned.
3. The return on the margin account is after interest is deducted.
4. Tax savings based on $27,200 of tax shelter is based on 30% federal and state tax bracket.

INVESTMENT PLANNING GUIDE

(Investment Capital = $50,000)

	Amount Invested	New or Borrowed Capital	Invest. Return	Current Income	Deferred Income	Tax Shelter
Asset Management	2,000	—	10%	200	—	—
Mutual Fund	15,000	—	15%	2,250	—	—
Margin Account	—	15,000	10%[3]	1,500	—	—
Annuity	10,000	—	15%	—	1,500	1,500
Retirement Program	—	7,000[1]	15%	—	1,050	8,050
Discounted Mortg.	8,000	—	30%	1,600	800	800
Tax Lien Certificates	5,000	—	20%	—	1,000	1,000
Personal Residence	—	150,000[2]	6%	—	9,000	9,000
Invest. Real Estate	10,000	150,000	6%	—	9,000	13,500
TOTALS	50,000	322,000		5,550	22,350	33,850

One-Year Investment Results

Current Income	=	$ 5,550	11%
Deferred Income	=	$22,350	45%
Total Income	=	$27,900	56%
Tax Savings[4]	=	$10,155	
TOTAL RETURN		$38,055	

With $50,000 of your own money, $7,000 payroll deduction for your retirement plan, $15,000 from a mutual fund margin account, your own home, and the purchase of $150,000 of investment real estate, you have created an investment return of $27,900, plus $10,155 in tax savings.

Notes:
1. The $7,000 is borrowed money for an IRA or payroll deduction for a company retirement plan.
2. The personal residence is already owned.
3. The return on the margin account is after interest is deducted.
4. Tax savings based on $33,850 of tax shelter is based on 30% federal and state tax bracket.

INVESTMENT PLANNING GUIDE

(Investment Capital = $100,000)

	Amount Invested	New or Borrowed Capital	Invest. Return	Current Income	Deferred Income	Tax Shelter
Asset Management	3,000	—	10%	300	—	—
Mutual Fund	20,000	—	15%	3,000	—	—
Margin Account	—	20,000	10%[3]	2,000	—	—
Annuity	20,000	—	15%	—	3,000	3,000
Retirement Program	—	7,000[1]	15%	—	1,050	8,050
Discounted Mortg.	22,000	—	30%	4,400	2,200	2,200
Tax Lien Certificates	15,000	—	20%	—	3,000	3,000
Personal Residence	—	200,000[2]	6%	—	12,000	12,000
Ltd. Partnership	20,000	—	14%	1,400	1,400	1,400
TOTALS	100,000	227,000		11,100	22,650	29,650

One-Year Investment Results

Current Income	=	$11,100	11%
Deferred Income	=	$22,650	23%
Total Income	=	$33,750	34%
Tax Savings[4]	=	$ 8,895	
TOTAL RETURN		$42,645	

Notes:
1. The $7,000 is borrowed money for an IRA or payroll deduction for a company retirement plan.
2. The personal residence is already owned.
3. The return on the margin account is after interest is deducted.
4. Tax savings based on $29,650 of tax shelter is based on 30% federal and state tax bracket.

INVESTMENT PLANNING GUIDE

(Investment Capital = $250,000)

	Amount Invested	New or Borrowed Capital	Invest. Return	Current Income	Deferred Income	Tax Shelter
Asset Management	5,000	—	10%	500	—	—
Mutual Fund	50,000	—	15%	7,500	—	—
Margin Account	—	50,000	10%[4]	5,000	—	—
Annuity	50,000	—	15%	—	7,500	7,500
Retirement Program	—	30,000[2]	15%	—	4,500	34,500
Discounted Mortg.	50,000	—	30%	10,000	5,000	5,000
Tax Certificates	15,000	—	20%	—	3,000	3,000
Personal Residence	—	300,000[3]	6%	—	18,000	18,000
Business Inv.[1]	25,000	—	20%	—	5,000	10,000
Ltd. Partnership	55,000	—	14%	3,850	3,850	3,850
TOTALS	250,000	380,000		26,850	46,850	81,850

One-Year Investment Results

Current income	= $26,850	11%
Deferred Income	= $46,850	19%
Total Income	= $73,700	29%
Tax Savings[5]	= $24,555	
TOTAL RETURN	$98,255	

Notes:
1. At this level of investment capital, tax shelter and additional income can also be achieved through directly investing in one or more small businesses.
2. The $30,000 represents a Keogh Investment assuming you own your own business or profession.
3. The personal residence is already owned.
4. The return on the margin account is after interest is deducted.
5. Tax savings based on $81,850 of tax shelter is based on 30% federal and state tax bracket.

EPILOGUE

No great thing is created suddenly, any more than a bunch of grapes or a fig. If you tell me that you desire a fig, I answer you that there must be time. Let it first blossom, then bear fruit, then ripen.

Epictetus
(c. 55–135)

Knowledge eliminates the two undesirable elements of building wealth—risk and fear. With those out of the way, you become unstoppable.

What is financial success and how do you know when you have it?

Financial success is having the money to do the things you want to do, when you want to do them, and, most importantly, the attitude to enjoy them. You must, therefore, determine through your plan and objectives what financial success means to you.

For some, financial success means having the money to pay the bills and enough left over for a six-pack and a bag of microwave popcorn. For a greater number it means living the good life with the right clothes, cars, perhaps a condominium on the beach, or even travel to exotic places. It's all available to those who are willing to take control.

The Constitution guarantees us equality of opportunity, but no one guarantees equality of results. Results are the product of knowledge and action, and that's what eventually separates financial winners from losers. Winners are those who see financial opportunities where others see only problems.

You can build your wealth under any economic conditions including inflation, recession, or even depression. It's what you

519

know and not what's happening around you that counts. Stop worrying about the economy, the deficit, and tax laws—they have little to do with your personal wealth unless fear shifts you into action.

Having a lot of money does not create problems, it solves them. Often on TV talk shows the host will ask me what the downside is to having lots of money. I've never found one.

Money is only green energy—a medium of exchange. It is what money will buy that counts, and money buys freedom—the freedom to choose alternatives not available to those without it. If you have money, you can choose where and how to live, what kind of car you wish to drive, how often you want to eat out, where you want to spend your next vacation, and when you want to quit working. Without money, the freedom to choose disappears. Your alternatives are often dictated by the thickness of your wallet. Freedom is the reason why any extra time and effort required to build your wealth is worth it.

Wealth building does not require the compromise of your principles. Greed, ruthlessness, conceit, and aggressiveness are not necessary.

You will find these positive traits among most of those with a lot of self-made wealth:

| Compassion | Discipline | Integrity | Decisiveness |
| Sharing | Caring | Sense of Adventure | Direction |

Where do you begin? You already have. Now it's a matter of applying one strategy at a time. By the inch it's a cinch. Strategies don't wear out nor are they used up. Use each strategy again and again until it becomes habit. As you put one strategy into operation, choose another and begin stacking them. You will soon be experiencing the momentum principle—producing ten units of results for each unit of effort. Your friends will comment that you have developed the Midas touch.

Guiding your momentum, and reaching the objectives you have chosen, is one of the most satisfying and exhilarating rewards of life, measurable in terms of:

"Wealth Without Risk"

My best for your success.

CHARLES J. GIVENS

APPENDIX

Fund Family Fact Sheets
Explanation of Terms and Abbreviations Used

FAMILY: The names of the mutual fund family, the company that created and manages the individual funds listed.

FUND NAME: The names of the individual funds that make up the fund family.

TYPE: The two-letter code used by the Givens Organization to identify the mutual fund type. The first letter is the major classification.

$$S = \text{Stock Mutual Fund}$$
$$B = \text{Bond Mutual Fund}$$
$$M = \text{Money Market Mutual Fund}$$

The second letter is the subclassification.

ASSET MIL: The amount of assets in millions managed by each fund.

DOW SMB: The Dow Jones computer access symbol for those who track mutual funds by computer.

MIN INVEST:
INT The initial minimum investment required to open the account.
ADD The minimum additional amount that may be added to the account at any time. "0" means that there is no minimum, any amount can be added.

LOADS AND FEES:
IN% The amount of front-end load or commission deducted from your initial investment. Shown as a percentage.
OUT% The amount of back-end load or commission deducted

from any amount you withdraw from your account. Shown as a percentage.

MGT The percentage deducted from your account each year for management fees.

12B-1 The percentage deducted from your account each year supposedly for advertising and promotional expenses of the fund.

SCWB MARG: Availability of a Charles Schwab margin account (see Chapter 32, "Mutual Fund Margin Accounts").

WITHDRAWAL OPTIONS: The methods that can be used to withdraw the money from your account.

PHONE: Indicates if your money can be withdrawn with a telephone call.

WIRE: Indicates if your money can be wire-transferred from your mutual fund account to your bank account. Other than check writing, wire transfer is the quickest way to get access to your money. Check the bottom of the page for minimum required amount for a wire transfer.

CHEK: Indicates if you can write checks on your mutual fund account. Any amount shown is the minimum amount for which a check can be written.

INCOME: Indicates if you can choose to receive monthly checks as income from your mutual fund account. Check the additional fund family information at the bottom of the page for the family's minimum investment required in order to receive monthly income checks.

ANNUAL RETURN: Indicates the percentage growth or decline in the value of each mutual fund share for the five years indicated. A dash in place of a number indicates that the fund was not in existence that year.

PHONE SWITCH: Indicates whether you can move your money from one fund to another by calling the mutual fund.

SWITCHES/YEAR: The number of times you may move your money from fund to fund during a 12-month period.

IRA MINIMUM INVESTMENT: The minimum amount of initial deposit required to open an IRA account in any of the family's funds.

IRA FEE: The amount of the trustee's fee per year for an IRA account.

KEOGH MIN. INVEST. The minimum amount of initial deposit required to open a Keogh account.

MINIMUM WIRE WITHDRAWAL: The minimum amount that can be transferred to your bank account by wire.

MIN. INVEST. FOR MONTHLY INCOME: The minimum initial investment required if you want to receive monthly income checks from the fund.

MUTUAL FUND CATEGORY CODES

Stock Funds	*Code*
Stock—growth	SG
Stock—aggressive growth	SA
Stock—sector	SS
Stock—precious metals	SP
Stock—growth and income	SI
Stock—equity income	SE
Stock—balanced	SB
Stock—option	SO
Stock—Index	SX

Bond Funds	
Bond—long-term corporate	BL
Bond—short/medium terms corporate	BS
Bond—long-term tax exempt	BX
Bond—short/medium terms tax exempt	BY
Bond—government/GNMA	BG

Money Market Funds	
Money market—regular	MM
Money market—tax exempt	MX
Money market—government	MG
Money market—insured	MI

AMERICAN ASSOCIATION OF RETIRED PERSONS (AARP)

Fund Name	Type	Asset Mil	Dow Smb	Min Inv Int	Add	In%	Out%	Mgt	12b-1	Scwb Marg	Phone	Wire	Chek	Income	89	90	91	92	93
Capital Growth	SG	718	ACGFX	250	0	0	0	.62	0	No	Yes	Yes	No	Yes	33.5	−15.8	40.5	4.7	16.0
Growth & Inc.	SI	1964	AGIFX	250	0	0	0	.49	0	No	Yes	Yes	No	Yes	26.5	−2.0	26.4	9.2	15.7
Hi Quality	BL	632	AGBFX	250	0	0	0	.49	0	No	Yes	Yes	No	Yes	12.3	7.6	15.4	6.2	11.0
Ins. Tax Free	BX	2119	ATTGX	250	0	0	0	.49	0	No	Yes	Yes	No	Yes	10.8	6.4	12.3	8.6	12.7
GNMA & Treas.	BG	6492	AGNMX	250	0	0	0	.45	0	No	Yes	Yes	No	Yes	11.7	9.8	14.4	6.6	6.0
Hi Qlty Tx Free	MM	450	AITSX	250	0	0	0	.49	0	No	Yes	Yes	No	Yes	6.2	6.2	4.8	10.0	1.6
Hi Quality MM	MM	481	ARPXX	250	0	0	0	.48	0	No	Yes	Yes	100	Yes	8.1	7.4	5.7	2.7	2.1

PHONE SWITCH—All Funds   #SWITCHES/YEAR—4   IRA MINIMUM INVESTMENT—$250   IRA FEE—0
KEOGH MIN. INVEST.—$250   MINIMUM WIRE WITHDRAWAL—No Min.   MIN. INVEST FOR MONTHLY INCOME—$10,000

BABSON FUNDS

Fund Name	Type	Asset Mil	Dow Smb	Min Inv			Loads and Fees			Scwb Marg	Withdrawal Options				Annual Return				
				Int	Add	In%	Out%	Mgt	12b-1		Phone	Wire	Chek	Income	89	90	91	92	93
Enterprise	SG	138	BABEX	1000	100	0	0	1.5	0	Yes	No	No	No	Yes	22.5	-15.9	43.0	24.6	16.7
Growth	SG	242	BABSX	500	50	0	0	.75	0	Yes	No	No	No	Yes	22.1	-9.4	26.0	9.1	10.3
Value	SG	154	BVALX	1000	100	0	0	1.00	0	Yes	No	No	No	Yes	18.2	-11.3	28.9	15.4	23.0
Shadow Stock	SG	46	SHSTX	2500	100	0	0	1.29	0	No	No	No	No	Yes	11.2	-19.3	40.0	17.4	24.2
Bab-Stew Iv Int	SG	48	BAINX	2500	100	0	0	1.75	0	No	No	No	No	Yes	27.0	-9.4	15.1	-1.7	33.5
Tax Free Inc. L	BX	32	BALTX	1000	100	0	0	.95	0	No	No	No	No	Yes	8.8	6.2	12.2	8.4	12.3
Bond Port L	BL	38	BABIX	500	50	0	0	.92	0	Yes	No	No	No	Yes	13.1	7.8	14.5	8.0	11.1
TF Inc. Short	BY	32	—	1000	100	0	0	.95	0	No	No	No	No	Yes	7.0	6.8	9.5	6.3	1.1
Bond Port S	BS	38	—	500	50	0	0	.72	0	No	No	No	No	Yes	10.8	8.1	14.5	7.0	8.4
Mon Mkt Prime	MM	104	BMMXX	1000	100	0	0	.85	0	No	Yes	Yes	500	Yes	8.4	7.3	5.4	3.1	2.3
Tx Free Inc MM	MX	27	—	1000	100	0	0	.55	0	No	Yes	Yes	500	Yes	5.9	5.5	4.2	2.7	2.0
Mon Mkt Fed	MG	24	—	1000	100	0	0	.85	0	No	Yes	Yes	500	Yes	8.2	7.4	5.3	3.1	2.3

PHONE SWITCH—All Funds   #SWITCHES/YEAR—Unlimited   IRA MIN. INVEST.—$250   IRA FEE—$10
KEOGH MIN. INVEST.—$100-$1,000   MIN. WIRE WITHDRAWAL—$1,000   MIN. INVEST. FOR MONTHLY INCOME—$10,000

COLUMBIA FUNDS

Fund Name	Type	Asset Mil	Dow Smb	Min Inv			Loads and Fees			Scwb Marg	Withdrawal Options				Annual Return				
				Int	Add	In%	Out%	Mgt	12b-1		Phone	Wire	Chek	Income	89	90	91	92	93
Special	SA	881	CLSPX	2000	100	0	0	1.0	0	Yes	Yes	Yes	No	Yes	31.9	−12.4	50.5	13.6	21.6
Growth	SA	618	CLMBX	1000	100	0	0	0.7	0	Yes	Yes	Yes	No	Yes	29.0	−3.3	34.3	11.8	13.0
Municipal Bd	BX	425	CMBFX	1000	100	—	0	0.5	0	Yes	Yes	Yes	No	Yes	9.0	6.9	11.7	6.0	10.7
Fixed Inc. Sec.	BL	291	CFISX	1000	100	—	—	0.5	0	Yes	Yes	Yes	No	Yes	14.4	8.3	16.8	8.0	10.5
US Govt. Sec.	BG	32	CUGGX	1000	100	—	—	0.5	0	Yes	Yes	Yes	No	Yes	9.6	9.3	12.7	5.8	5.9
Daily Income	MM	1004	CDIXX	1000	100	0	0	0.5	0	Yes	Yes	Yes	500	Yes	8.9	7.8	5.7	3.3	2.5

PHONE SWITCH—All Funds   #SWITCHES/YEAR—Unlimited   IRA MIN. INVEST.—$1,000   IRA FEE—$25
KEOGH MIN. INVEST.—$1,000   KEOGH FEE—$50   MIN. WIRE WITHDRAWAL—$1,000
MIN. INVEST. FOR MONTHLY INCOME—$5,000

DREYFUS CORP.

Fund Name	Type	Asset Mil	Dow Smb	Min Inv			Loads and Fees			Scwb Marg	Withdrawal Options				Annual Return				
				Int	Add	In%	Out%	Mgt	12b-1		Phone	Wire	Chek	Income	89	90	91	92	93
Strategic Agg	SA	45	DRCVX	2500	100	0	0	.75	.2	Yes	Yes	Yes	No	Yes	14.2	-7.2	32.7	15.4	24.7
New Leaders	SA	338	DNLDX	2500	100	0	0	.75	—	Yes	Yes	Yes	No	Yes	31.3	-11.9	45.4	9.4	17.0
Growth Opp.	SG	495	DREQX	2500	100	0	0	.75	0.0	Yes	Yes	Yes	No	Yes	14.7	-6.6	51.5	9.6	2.0
Third Century	SG	523	DRTHX	2500	100	0	0	.75	0.0	Yes	Yes	Yes	No	Yes	17.3	3.5	38.1	2.0	5.3
Fund	SI	2870	DREVX	2500	100	0	0	.65	0.0	Yes	Yes	Yes	No	Yes	22.5	-3.3	28.0	5.5	6.4
Convert. Sec.	SI	410	DRSPX	2500	100	0	0	.75	0.0	Yes	Yes	Yes	No	Yes	14.9	-16.7	33.1	3.8	5.0
Mass TE Bond	BX	180	DMEBX	2500	100	0	0	.60	0.0	Yes	Yes	Yes	No	Yes	7.7	6.1	9.8	7.0	12.5
NY Tax Exempt	BX	2071	DRNYX	2500	100	0	0	.60	0.0	Yes	Yes	Yes	No	Yes	8.9	5.5	12.4	9.0	12.7
Cal TE Bond	BX	1784	DRCAX	2500	100	0	0	.60	0.0	Yes	Yes	Yes	No	Yes	8.6	6.7	10.4	7.0	11.9
Insured TE Bd	BX	273	DTBDX	2500	100	0	0	.60	.02	Yes	Yes	Yes	No	Yes	8.8	7.1	11.4	7.7	12.6
Tax Exempt Bd	BX	4259	DRTAX	2500	100	0	0	.60	0.0	Yes	Yes	Yes	No	Yes	9.4	6.4	12.0	9.8	10.4
A Bond Plus	BL	633	DRBDX	2500	100	0	0	.65	0.0	Yes	No	Yes	500	Yes	14.1	4.8	18.8	8.2	15.0
GNMA	BL	1739	DRGMX	2500	100	0	0	.60	0.2	Yes	No	No	500	Yes	11.5	9.7	14.5	6.3	7.2
Int. Tax Exempt	BY	1827	DITEX	2500	100	0	0	.60	0.0	Yes	Yes	Yes	No	Yes	8.7	6.8	11.1	8.7	11.6
Cal TE Money	MX	456	DCTXX	2500	100	0	0	.50	0.0	Yes	Yes	Yes	500	Yes	5.8	5.2	11.0	6.6	2.0
Municipal MM	MX	2011	DTEXX	5000	100	0	0	.50	0.0	Yes	Yes	Yes	500	Yes	6.0	5.6	4.1	2.5	2.0
MM Govt. Sec	MG	948	DMMXX	2500	100	0	0	.50	0.0	Yes	Yes	Yes	500	Yes	8.4	7.4	5.9	3.5	2.5
Liquid Assets	MM	8042	DLAXX	2500	100	0	0	.46	0.0	Yes	Yes	Yes	500	Yes	8.7	7.6	5.9	3.5	2.6

PHONE SWITCH—All Funds   #SWITCHES/YEAR—Unlimited   IRA MIN. INVEST.—$750   IRA FEE—$10

KEOGH MIN. INVEST.—$750   MIN. WIRE WITHDRAWAL—$1,000   MIN. INVEST. FOR MONTHLY INCOME—$5,000

EVERGREEN FUNDS

Fund Name	Type	Asset Mil	Dow Smb	Min Inv		Loads and Fees				Scwb Marg	Withdrawal Options				Annual Return				
				Int	Add	In%	Out%	Mgt	12b-1		Phone	Wire	Chek	Income	89	90	91	92	93
Amer. Retire.	SB	37	EAMRX	2000	250	0	0	1.00	0	Yes	Yes	Yes	Yes	Yes	13.4	0.5	10.8	11.8	14.1
Foundation	SB	238	EFONX	2000	250	0	0	1.00	0	Yes	Yes	Yes	Yes	Yes	—	—	36.3	20.0	15.7
Evergreen Fnd	SG	629	EVGRX	2000	250	0	0	1.00	0	Yes	Yes	Yes	Yes	Yes	15.1	−11.7	40.1	8.7	6.3
GLBL Real ESt.	RE	142	EGLRX	2000	250	0	0	1.00	0	Yes	Yes	Yes	Yes	Yes	—	−22.2	13.1	9.7	51.4
Limited Mkt.	SA	103	EVLMX	2000	250	0	0	1.00	0	Yes	Yes	Yes	Yes	Yes	20.9	−10.4	51.1	10.1	9.6
Total Return	SE	1185	EVTRX	2000	250	0	0	1.00	0	Yes	Yes	Yes	Yes	Yes	16.8	−6.3	23.0	10.0	12.9
Value Timing	SI	78	EVVTX	2000	250	0	0	1.00	0	Yes	Yes	Yes	Yes	Yes	25.4	−4.5	25.8	13.8	14.4

PHONE SWITCH—All Funds   #SWITCHES/YEAR—4   IRA MIN. INVEST.—No Min. (most funds)   IRA FEE—$5 setup, $10 Maint.

KEOGH MIN. INVEST.—No Min. (most funds)   MIN. WIRE WITHDRAWAL—$1,000   MIN. INVEST. FOR MONTHLY INCOME—$5,000

FIDELITY

Fund Name	Type	Asset Mil	Dow Smb	Min Inv			Loads and Fees			Scwb Marg	Withdrawal Options			Income	Annual Return				
				Int	Add	In%	Out%	Mgt	12b-1		Phone	Wire	Chek		89	90	91	92	93
OTC	SA	1343	FDCPX	2500	250	3	0	.35	0	Yes	No	Yes	No	Yes	30.4	-4.7	49.2	14.9	8.3
Capital App.	SA	1428	FDCAX	2500	250	2	1	.30	0	No	No	Yes	No	Yes	26.9	-15.7	10.0	16.4	33.4
Growth Co.	SA	2542	FDGRX	1000	250	3	0	.30	0	Yes	No	Yes	No	Yes	41.6	3.6	48.3	7.9	16.2
Magellan	SA	31705	FMAGX	1000	250	3	0	.30	0	Yes	No	Yes	No	Yes	34.6	-4.6	41.0	7.0	24.7
Retirement Grth	SA	2848	FDFFX	500	250	0	0	.30	0	Yes	No	Yes	No	No	30.3	-10.2	45.6	10.6	22.1
Value	SA	1716	FDVLX	1000	250	0	0	.40	0	Yes	No	Yes	No	Yes	22.9	-12.8	26.2	21.2	22.9
Contra Fund	SA	6194	FCNTX	1000	250	0	0	.10	0	Yes	No	No	No	Yes	43.3	3.9	54.9	15.9	21.4
Trend	SG	1393	FTRNX	1000	250	0	0	.10	0	Yes	No	No	No	Yes	31.6	-12.7	36.3	16.8	19.2
Growth & Inc.	SI	7684	FGRIX	2500	250	2	0	.20	0	Yes	No	No	No	Yes	29.6	-6.7	41.8	11.5	19.5
Fidelity Fund	SI	1546	FFIDX	1000	250	0	0	.10	0	Yes	No	No	No	Yes	28.7	-5.0	24.1	8.4	18.4
Equity Income	SE	6641	FEQIX	1000	250	2	0	.10	0	Yes	No	No	No	Yes	18.7	-14.0	29.4	14.7	21.3
Real Estate	SI	424	FQDEX	2500	250	2	0	var.	0	Yes	No	Yes	No	Yes	13.8	-8.6	39.1	19.5	12.5
Puritan	SB	8988	FPURX	1000	250	2	0	.10	0	Yes	Yes	Yes	No	Yes	19.6	-6.2	24.5	15.4	21.5
Balanced	SB	4684	FAFTX	2500	250	2	0	.50	0	Yes	No	No	No	Yes	19.5	-0.4	26.8	7.9	19.3
Convert. Sec.	SI	3296	FCVSX	2500	250	0	0	.20	0	Yes	No	No	No	Yes	26.2	-2.4	38.7	22.0	17.8
Sel Prec. Metals	SP	550	FDMPX	1000	250	2	1	.35	0	Yes	No	No	No	Yes	32.2	-21.1	1.5	-21.9	111.6
Sel Amer Gold	SP	365	FSAGX	1000	250	2	1	.35	0	Yes	No	Yes	No	Yes	22.0	-17.2	-6.1	6.6	78.7
Sel Energy Ser	SS	82	FSESX	1000	250	2	1	.35	0	Yes	No	Yes	No	Yes	59.4	1.8	0.0	3.4	19.1
Sel Chemicals	SS	26	FSCHX	1000	250	2	1	.35	0	Yes	No	Yes	No	Yes	17.3	-4.1	38.7	8.9	12.7
Sel Equip Tech	SS	148	FSPTX	1000	250	2	1	.35	0	Yes	No	Yes	No	Yes	17.0	10.5	59.0	8.7	29.7
Sel Software	SS	164	FSCSX	1000	250	2	1	.35	0	Yes	No	Yes	No	Yes	12.1	0.9	45.8	35.5	32.5
Sel Computers	SS	61	FDCPX	1000	250	2	1	.35	0	Yes	No	Yes	No	Yes	6.8	18.4	30.8	21.2	28.9
Sel Electronics	SS	45	FSELX	1000	250	2	1	.35	0	Yes	No	Yes	No	Yes	15.7	5.8	35.3	15.3	32.2
Sel Telecomm	SS	414	FSTCX	1000	250	2	1	.35	0	Yes	No	Yes	No	Yes	50.9	-16.4	30.9	-10.4	29.7
Sel BioTech	SS	557	FRIOX	1000	250	2	1	.35	0	Yes	No	Yes	No	Yes	43.9	44.3	99.0	10.4	0.7
Sel Defense	SS	27	FDSAX	1000	250	3	1	var.	0	Yes	No	Yes	No	Yes	8.8	-4.6	27.0	11.3	28.8
Sel Ind Tech	SS	149	FSCGX	1000	250	2	0	.35	0	Yes	Yes	Yes	No	Yes	—	-15.5	26.0	22.4	19.2
Sel Insurance	SS	19	FSPCX	1000	250	3	0	var.	0	Yes	Yes	Yes	No	Yes	—	-9.8	37.0	17.5	8.2
Sel Health	SS	159	FSPHX	1000	250	2	1	.35	0	Yes	No	No	No	Yes	42.5	24.3	83.7	-8.3	27.3
Sel Trans	SS	13	FTRAN	1000	250	2	1	.35	0	Yes	No	Yes	No	Yes	26.3	-21.6	54.1	23.8	29.3

FIDELITY (cont.)

Fund Name	Type	Asset Mil	Dow Smb	Min Inv Int	Add	In%	Our%	Mgt	12b-1	Scwb Marg	Phone	Wire	Chek	Income	89	90	91	92	93
Sel Automotive	SS	231	FSAYX	1000	250	2	1	.35	0	Yes	No	Yes	No	Yes	28.5	-6.7	37.3	41.6	35.4
Sel Ind. Mat.	SS	156	FINDX	1000	250	2	1	.35	0	Yes	No	Yes	No	Yes	4.4	-17.1	35.8	12.4	21.4
Sel Paper For.	SS	72	FSPFX	1000	250	2	1	.35	0	Yes	No	Yes	No	Yes	4.0	-15.2	34.8	12.1	18.6
Sel Con. & Hou.	SS	82	FSHOX	1000	250	2	1	.35	0	Yes	No	Yes	No	Yes	16.6	-9.6	41.3	18.7	53.6
Sel Food & Agr.	SS	90	FDFAX	1000	250	2	1	.35	0	Yes	No	Yes	No	Yes	38.9	9.3	34.1	6.0	8.8
Sel Bdcst Med	SS	49	FRMPX	1000	250	2	1	.35	0	Yes	No	Yes	No	Yes	32.6	-26.2	37.9	21.5	38.0
Sel Energy	SS	145	FSENX	1000	250	2	1	.35	0	Yes	No	Yes	No	Yes	42.8	-4.5	0.0	-2.4	19.1
Sel Broker	SS	59	FSLBX	1000	250	2	1	.35	0	Yes	No	Yes	No	Yes	14.1	-16.2	82.3	5.1	49.3
Sel Financial	SS	116	FIDSX	1000	250	2	1	.35	0	Yes	No	Yes	No	Yes	19.4	-24.4	61.6	42.8	17.6
Sel Reg Banks	SS	96	FSRGX	1000	250	2	1	.35	0	Yes	No	Yes	No	Yes	26.7	-20.7	65.8	48.5	11.0
Sel Leisure	SS	105	FDLSX	1000	250	2	1	.35	0	Yes	No	Yes	No	Yes	31.2	-22.3	32.9	16.2	39.6
Sel Retail	SS	45	FSRPX	1000	250	2	1	.35	0	Yes	No	Yes	No	Yes	28.2	-5.0	68.1	22.1	13.0
Sel Elect Util	SS	23	FSEUX	1000	250	2	1	.35	0	Yes	No	Yes	No	Yes	39.0	-1.8	26.3	9.8	12.8
Sel Utilities	SS	251	FSUTX	1000	250	2	1	.35	0	Yes	No	Yes	No	Yes	—	0.5	21.0	10.6	12.4
Global Bond	BL	682	FGBDX	2500	250	0	0	.50	0	Yes	No	Yes	No	Yes	7.9	12.2	12.8	4.4	21.9
NYTF Hy Muni	BX	468	FTFMX	2500	250	0	0	.40	0	Yes	No	Yes	No	Yes	9.2	5.1	13.4	9.0	13.4
Cal Free NY	BX	290	FCFXX	2500	250	0	0	.45	0	Yes	No	Yes	500	Yes	9.6	7.0	10.1	9.0	13.4
Ltd. Term Muni	BY	1160	FLTMX	2500	250	0	0	.15	0	Yes	No	Yes	500	Yes	7.8	7.0	11.2	8.0	12.2
Spartan NY	BX	781	FPURX	2500	250	0	0	.10	0	Yes	No	No	No	Yes	9.8	7.2	34.3	21.1	21.1
Capital & Inc.	BL	3065	FAGIX	2500	250	0	0	.55	0	Yes	No	Yes	No	Yes	-3.1	-3.9	29.8	28.0	24.2
High Yld Muni	BX	2047	FHIGX	2500	250	0	0	.45	0	Yes	No	Yes	No	Yes	11.4	8.5	10.2	8.0	13.3
Agg. Tax Free	BX	932	FATEX	2500	250	0	0	.50	0	Yes	Yes	Yes	No	Yes	9.5	7.5	11.8	9.0	13.8
Mass Free Muni	BX	1314	FDMMX	2500	250	0	0	.45	0	Yes	No	Yes	No	Yes	9.3	7.4	11.3	9.0	13.0
Minn Tax Free	BX	333	FDMDX	2500	250	0	0	.45	0	Yes	Yes	Yes	No	Yes	9.5	7.2	8.5	7.0	12.4
Mich Tax Free	BX	546	FMHTX	2500	250	0	0	.45	0	Yes	Yes	Yes	No	Yes	10.2	5.1	12.0	9.5	13.9
NY Tx Fr Ins	BX	359	FNTIX	2500	250	0	0	.40	0	Yes	No	Yes	No	Yes	29.6	6.2	12.5	8.6	6.0
Ohio Tax Free	BX	441	FOHFX	2500	250	0	0	.45	0	Yes	Yes	Yes	No	Yes	10.0	7.5	11.5	8.6	12.6
Munic. Bond	BX	1211	FMBPX	2500	250	0	0	.40	0	Yes	No	Yes	No	Yes	9.6	6.9	11.9	8.9	13.3
NY Tx Fr Ins	BX	395	FNTIX	2500	250	0	0	.40	0	Yes	No	Yes	No	Yes	9.2	6.2	12.5	8.5	12.8

Fund	Code	No.	Ticker	Min Invest	Min Subseq		Fee											
Cal Ins TF	BX	290	FCTFX	2500	250	0	.45	0	No	Yes	Yes	500	Yes	8.8	7.0	10.2	9.0	14.0
Ins. Tax Free	BX	430	FMUIX	2500	250	0	.45	0	No	Yes	Yes	No	Yes	9.5	7.1	11.9	8.0	14.0
Short Term	BS	2419	FSHRX	2500	250	0	.50	0	No	No	No	No	Yes	6.3	5.8	14.0	7.4	9.1
GNMA	BG	868	FGMNX	1000	250	0	.50	0	Yes	Yes	Yes	No	Yes	13.8	10.5	13.6	6.7	6.2
Gov Securities	BG	750	FGOVX	1000	250	0	.50	0	No	No	No	No	Yes	12.6	9.4	16.0	8.0	12.5
Spartan Sht Int	BY	65	FPURX	2500	250	0	.50	0	Yes	Yes	Yes	500	Yes	7.8	6.4	8.9	6.0	5.7
Invest Grade	BL	1006	FBNDX	2500	250	0	.40	0	No	Yes	Yes	No	Yes	13.0	6.1	18.9	8.3	16.2
Mort. Sec.	BG	365	FMSFX	1000	250	0	.50	0	No	Yes	Yes	No	Yes	13.6	10.4	13.6	5.5	6.8
Select MM	MM	771	—	1000	250	0	.35	0	No	No	Yes	No	Yes	8.6	7.5	5.8	3.5	2.7
Daily Inc. Tr	MM	3918	FDTXX	5000	500	0	var.	0	No	No	Yes	Yes	Yes	8.7	7.6	5.8	3.4	2.8
Cash Reserves	MM	16142	FDRXX	1000	250	0	.50	0	No	No	Yes	500	Yes	8.6	7.5	6.0	3.8	2.9
US Gov. Res	MG	1513	FGRXX	1000	250	0	.48	0	No	No	Yes	500	Yes	8.4	7.4	5.6	3.4	2.6
Mass TF Mon	MX	791	FDMXX	2500	500	0	.45	0	Yes	Yes	Yes	500	Yes	5.6	5.2	4.0	2.2	1.7
NY TF Money	MX	614	—	2500	250	0	.40	0	Yes	Yes	Yes	500	Yes	5.3	5.0	3.9	2.3	1.9
Cal. TF Money	MX	791	FCFSX	2500	250	0	.45	0	Yes	Yes	Yes	500	Yes	5.6	5.1	4.0	2.6	2.0
Spartan PA TF	MX	412	FPURX	2500	250	0	.10	0	No	No	Yes	500	Yes	6.1	6.0	4.6	2.9	2.2
Tax Exempt MM	MX	3519	FTEXX	5000	250	0	.30	0	Yes	Yes	Yes	500	Yes	5.8	5.5	4.4	2.9	2.2

PHONE SWITCH—All Funds except Tr Fixed IAC Port LT   #SWITCHES/YEAR—Min 4—in most cases Unlimited
IRA MIN. INVEST.—$500   IRA FEE—$10   KEOGH MIN. INVEST.—$250 (Daily Inc. at $500)
MIN. WIRE WITHDRAWAL—$5,000   MIN. INVEST. FOR MONTHLY INCOME—$5,000

FOUNDERS MUTUAL DEPOSITOR CORP.

Fund Name	Type	Asset Mil	Dow Smb	Min Inv		Loads and Fees				Scwb Marg	Withdrawal Options				Annual Return				
				Int	Add	In%	Out%	Mgt	12b-1		Phone	Wire	Chek	Income	89	90	91	92	93
Frontier	SA	265	—	1000	100	0	0	1.0	.25	Yes	No	No	No	Yes	44.1	-7.5	49.3	8.9	15.6
Special	SA	437	FRSPX	1000	100	0	0	1.0	0	Yes	No	No	No	Yes	38.9	-10.4	63.7	8.3	16.0
Growth	SG	404	FRGRX	1000	100	0	0	1.0	0	Yes	No	No	No	Yes	41.5	-10.6	47.4	4.3	25.5
Blue Chip	SI	320	FRMUX	1000	100	0	0	0.5	.25	Yes	No	No	No	Yes	35.5	0.4	28.3	0.9	15.0
Balanced	SE	72	FRINX	1000	100	0	0	1.0	.25	Yes	No	No	No	Yes	25.2	-5.0	22.9	6.0	21.9
Gov. Sec. Fund	BG	29	—	1000	100	0	0	0.8	.25	Yes	No	No	No	Yes	14.1	4.4	14.9	5.3	9.4
Money Market	MM	296	FMMXX	1000	100	0	0	0.5	0	No	No	Yes	500	Yes	8.2	7.3	5.3	2.8	2.2

PHONE SWITCH—All Funds   #SWITCHES/YEAR—Unlimited   IRA FEE—$10
KEOGH MIN. INVEST.—$500   MIN. WIRE WITHDRAWAL—$1,000   IRA MINIMUM INVESTMENT—$500
MIN. INVEST. FOR MONTHLY INCOME—$5,000

IAI FUNDS

Fund Name	Type	Asset Mil	Dow Smb	Min Inv		Loads and Fees				Scwb Marg	Withdrawal Options			Income	Annual Return				
				Int	Add	In%	Out%	Mgt	12b-1		Phone	Wire	Chek		89	90	91	92	93
Balanced	SB	59	IABLX	5000	100	0	0	.65	.35	Yes	Yes	Yes	Yes	No	—	—	—	-2.1	5.0
Bond	BL	103	IAIBX	5000	100	0	0	.55	.30	Yes	Yes	Yes	Yes	No	15.9	7.1	17.3	7.0	12.3
Emerg. Grth.	SA	239	IAEGX	5000	100	0	0	.65	.35	Yes	Yes	Yes	Yes	No	—	—	23.6	22.5	14.8
Govt.	BG	40	IAGVX	5000	100	0	0	.65	.35	Yes	Yes	Yes	Yes	No	—	—	7.7	5.7	8.5
International	SW	141	IAINX	5000	100	0	0	1.00	.35	Yes	Yes	Yes	Yes	No	18.3	-13.1	16.6	-6.3	40.2
Mid-Cap Grth.	SA	50		5000	100	0	0	.65	.35	Yes	Yes	Yes	Yes	No	—	—	—	15.0	16.4
Regional	SG	634	IARGX	5000	100	0	0	.65	.35	Yes	Yes	Yes	Yes	No	31.3	-0.3	35.4	3.5	9.0
Reserve	BS	100	IARVX	5000	100	0	0	.50	.10	Yes	Yes	Yes	Yes	No	8.8	8.4	8.0	3.3	3.4
Grth. & Income	SI	130	IASKX	5000	100	0	0	.65	.35	Yes	Yes	Yes	Yes	No	29.8	-6.7	26.7	4.0	10.0
Value	SG	36	IAAPX	5000	100	0	0	.65	.35	Yes	Yes	Yes	Yes	No	22.6	-11.5	19.8	12.0	22.1

PHONE SWITCH—All Funds   #SWITCHES/YEAR—4 free per year per fund   IRA MINIMUM INVESTMENT—$2000   IRA FEE—No fee

KEOGH MIN. INVEST.—Not offered to investors   MIN. WIRE WITHDRAWAL—None   MIN. INVEST. FOR MONTHLY INCOME—$5,000

INVESCO

Fund Name	Type	Asset Mil	Dow Smb	Min Inv Int	Min Inv Add	Loads and Fees In%	Loads and Fees Our%	Loads and Fees Mgt	Loads and Fees 12b-1	Scwb Marg	Withdrawal Phone	Withdrawal Wire	Withdrawal Chek	Income	89	90	91	92	93
Dynamics	SA	319	FIDYX	250	50	0	0	.75	.25	Yes	No	No	No	No	22.6	-6.4	67.0	13.2	19.1
Industrial Fund	SG	319	FLRFX	250	50	0	0	.75	.25	Yes	No	No	No	Yes	31.4	-1.2	42.1	2.9	5.5
Industrial Inc.	SE	3905	FIIIX	250	50	0	0	.75	.25	Yes	No	No	No	Yes	32.0	0.9	46.3	1.0	16.7
Strategic Gold	SP	316	FGLDX	250	50	0	0	.75	0	Yes	No	No	No	No	+21.3	-23.1	-7.0	-8.2	72.6
Strategic Tech	SS	251	FTCHX	250	50	0	0	.75	0	Yes	No	No	No	No	21.5	8.6	76.9	11.9	15.0
Strat. Health	SS	566	FHLSX	250	50	0	0	.75	0	Yes	No	No	No	No	59.5	25.8	91.8	-13.7	8.4
Strat. Energy	SS	49	FSTEX	250	50	0	0	.75	0	Yes	No	No	No	No	43.5	-16.5	-3.5	-13.2	16.7
Strat. Financial	SS	339	FSBSX	250	50	0	0	.75	0	Yes	No	No	No	No	37.0	-7.2	74.0	27.0	18.5
Strat. Leisure	SS	304	FLISX	250	50	0	0	.75	0	Yes	No	No	No	No	38.3	-11.0	52.7	23.0	35.7
Strat. Utilities	SS	174	FSTUX	250	50	0	0	.75	0	Yes	No	No	No	No	31.4	-10.1	28.0	10.1	21.2
European	WE**	364	FEUBX	250	50	0	0	.75	0	Yes	No	No	No	No	24.2	0.7	8.0	-7.6	24.6
Strat. Pacific	SS	274	FPBSX	250	50	0	0	.75	0	Yes	No	No	No	No	20.2	-24.4	13.2	-13.6	42.6
Value Equity	SI	102	FSEQX	250	50	0	0	.75	0	.	No	No	No	Yes	21.3	-5.8	35.1	5.0	10.4
Total Return	SB	268	FSFLX	250	50	0	0	.75	0	.	No	No	No	Yes	19.1	-0.4	24.9	9.8	12.3
Int Growth	SG	113	FSIGX	250	50	0	0	1.00	0	.	No	No	No	No	16.1	-14.6	7.1	-12.5	27.9
Bond US Gov.	BG	31	FBDGX	250	50	0	0	.50	.25	Yes	No	No	No	Yes	12.4	7.2	15.5	5.6	10.6
Bond Select	BL	145	FBDSX	250	50	0	0	.50	.25	Yes	No	No	No	Yes	8.2	4.9	18.5	10.4	11.4
Tax Free Inc.	BX	319	FTIFX	250	50	0	0	.50	.25	Yes	No	No	No	Yes	11.7	7.1	12.5	8.8	12.1
Bond Sh HY	BS	316	FHYPX	250	50	0	0	.50	.25	Yes	No	No	No	Yes	3.7	-4.6	23.5	14.5	15.8
Int Gov	BG	373	FIGBX	250	50	0	0	.60	0	.	No	No	No	Yes	10.5	9.1	14.1	6.0	8.8
Cash Reserve	MM	614	FBSXX	250	50	0	0	.50	0	Yes	Yes	Yes	500	Yes	8.8	7.8	5.5	3.2	2.4
Tax Free Mon.	MX	91	FFRXX	250	50	0	0	.50	0	Yes	Yes	Yes	500	Yes	5.7	5.3	3.8	2.5	1.9

PHONE SWITCH—All Funds   #SWITCHES/YEAR—4   IRA MINIMUM INVESTMENT—$250, $50 for all Strategic Funds
IRA FEE—$5   KEOGH MIN. INVEST.—$50
MIN. INVEST. FOR MONTHLY INCOME—$10,000   MIN. WIRE WITHDRAWAL—$1,000

*In processing with Schwab
**Invests only European stock funds.

JANUS CAPITAL

Fund Name	Type	Asset Mil	Dow Smb	Min Inv Int	Min Inv Add	Min Inv In%	Loads Our%	Loads Mgt	Loads 12b-1	Scwb Marg	Phone	Wire	Chek	Income	89	90	91	92	93
Janus Fund	SG	9460	JANSX	1000	50	0	0	.75	0	Yes	Yes	Yes	No	Yes	46.3	-0.7	42.8	6.9	10.9
Janus Gr.&Inc.	SI	514	JAGIX	1000	50	0	0	.80	0	Yes	Yes	Yes	No	Yes	—	—	—	5.4	6.7
Balanced	SB	84	JABAX	1000	50	0	0	1.00	0	Yes	Yes	Yes	No	Yes	—	—	—	12.5	10.0
Enterprise	SA	271	JAENX	1000	50	0	0	.90	0	Yes	Yes	Yes	No	Yes	—	—	—	20.7	15.6
Flex. Income	BL	481	JAFIX	1000	50	0	0	.80	0	Yes	Yes	Yes	No	Yes	4.8	-4.3	25.9	11.8	15.7
Int. Govt.	BG	48	JAIGX	1000	50	0	0	.50	0	Yes	Yes	Yes	Yes	Yes	—	—	15.0	4.8	2.5
Short-tm Bond	BS	61	JASBX	1000	50	0	0	.50	0	Yes	Yes	Yes	Yes	Yes	—	—	—	0.4	6.2
Janus 20	SG	3284	JAVLX	CLSD	50	0	0	.65	0	Yes	Yes	Yes	No	Yes	50.8	0.6	69.2	1.9	3.4
Janus Venture	SA	1607	JAVTX	CLSC	50	0	0	.65	0	Yes	Yes	Yes	No	Yes	38.7	-0.4	47.8	7.5	9.1
Worldwide	SW	1268	JAWWX	1000	50	0	0	.85	0	Yes	Yes	Yes	No	Yes	—	—	24.0	9.0	28.4

PHONE SWITCH—All Funds   #SWITCHES/YEAR—4 free per year   IRA MINIMUM INVESTMENT—$250   IRA FEE—$12
KEOGH MIN. INVEST.—$250   MIN. WIRE WITHDRAWAL—$100   MIN. INVEST. FOR MONTHLY INCOME—No Minimum

NEUBERGER & BERMAN MANAGEMENT

Fund Name	Type	Asset Mil	Dow Smb	Min Inv			Loads and Fees			Scwb Marg	Withdrawal Options				Annual Return				
				Int	Add	In%	Out%	Mgt	12b-1		Phone	Wire	Chek	Income	89	90	91	92	93
Manhattan	SG	532	CNAMX	1000	100	0	0	0.7	0	Yes	No	No	No	Yes	29.1	-8.0	30.9	17.8	10.0
Partners	SG	1284	PARTX	1000	100	0	0	0.7	0	Yes	No	No	No	Yes	22.7	-5.1	22.4	17.5	16.5
Guardian Mut.	SI	2099	GUARX	1000	100	0	0	0.7	0	Yes	No	No	No	Yes	21.5	-5.8	34.3	19.0	14.5
Sel Sectors	SS	623	ENEGX	1000	100	0	0	0.7	0	Yes	No	No	No	Yes	29.8	-5.9	24.7	21.1	16.3
Ltd. Matur	BS	347	NLMBX	5000	200	0	0	0.5	0	No	Yes	Yes	No	Yes	11.2	8.7	11.9	5.2	6.8
Ultra Sht Bond	BS	111	NBMXX	2000	200	0	0	0.5	0	No	Yes	Yes	250	Yes	9.3	8.4	7.4	3.6	3.2
Municipal MM	MX	421	NBTXX	2000	200	0	0	0.5	0	No	Yes	250	250	Yes	5.9	5.5	4.1	2.4	1.8
Gov. Money	MG	516	NBGXX	2000	200	0	0	0.5	0	No	Yes	250	250	Yes	7.6	7.1	5.5	3.3	2.5

PHONE SWITCH—All Funds   #SWITCHES/YEAR—Unlimited   IRA MINIMUM INVESTMENT—$250   IRA FEE—$9

KEOGH MIN. INVEST.—$250 except Ltd Matur. at $30,000   MIN. WIRE WITHDRAWAL—$1,000

MIN. INVEST. FOR MONTHLY INCOME—$5,000

PIMCO FUNDS

Fund Name	Type	Asset Mil	Dow Smb	Min Inv		Loads and Fees				Scwb	Withdrawal Options				Annual Return				
				Int	Add	In%	Out%	Mgt	12b-1	Marg	Phone	Wire	Chek	Income	89	90	91	92	93
Equity Incm 'B'	SE	152	TQNBX	1000	100	01%/yr	01%/yr	.75	1.0	No	Yes	Yes	Yes	Yes	11.2	-15.5	33.2	7.8	21.2
US Govt. 'B'	BG	473	TUGBX	1000	100	01%/yr	01%/yr	.50	1.0	No	Yes	Yes	Yes	Yes	12.3	6.5	15.9	4.8	7.1
Growth 'B'	SG	98	TGWBX	1000	100	01%/yr	01%/yr	.65	1.0	No	Yes	Yes	Yes	Yes	27.5	0.3	41.9	2.1	9.3
Income 'B'	BL	233	TINBX	1000	100	01%/yr	01%/yr	.50	1.0	No	Yes	Yes	Yes	Yes	5.5	2.1	12.0	7.4	7.1
International 'B'	SW	271	TILBX	1000	100	01%/yr	01%/yr	.75	1.0	No	Yes	Yes	Yes	Yes	28.5	15.5	19.9	-5.8	53.5
Opportunity 'B'	SA	617	TOPBX	CLSD	100	01%/yr	01%/yr	.75	1.0	No	Yes	Yes	Yes	Yes	30.7	-7.3	68.0	28.5	36.2
Prec. Mtls. 'B'	SP	47	TPMBX	1000	100	01%/yr	01%/yr	.75	1.0	No	Yes	Yes	Yes	Yes	16.2	-25.1	-5.4	12.3	89.5
SH-Int Govt. 'B'	BG	112	TUSBX	1000	100	01%/yr	01%/yr	.65	1.0	No	Yes	Yes	Yes	Yes	12.3	6.5	15.9	2.1	2.8

PHONE SWITCH—All Funds   #SWITCHES/YEAR—No Fee   IRA FEE—No Fee

KEOGH MIN. INVEST.—Not Available at Present   IRA MINIMUM INVESTMENT—$25   MIN. INVEST. FOR MONTHLY INCOME—$10,000

MIN. WIRE WITHDRAWAL—No Minimum

SAFECO ASSET MANAGEMENT CO.

Fund Name	Type	Asset Mil	Dow Smb	Min Inv		Loads and Fees				Scwb Marg	Withdrawal Options				Annual Return				
				Int	Add	In%	Out%	Mgt	12b-1		Phone	Wire	Chek	Income	89	90	91	92	93
Growth	SG	169	SAFGX	1000	100	0	0	.75	0	Yes	Yes	Yes	No	Yes	19.2	-15.0	62.7	1.0	22.2
Equity	SI	236	SAFQX	1000	100	0	0	.75	0	Yes	Yes	Yes	No	Yes	35.8	-8.6	27.9	9.3	30.9
Income	SB	201	SAFIX	1000	100	0	0	.75	0	Yes	Yes	Yes	No	Yes	19.2	-10.8	23.3	11.5	12.6
Cal TF Inc.	BX	82	SFCAX	1000	100	0	0	.55	0	Yes	Yes	Yes	No	Yes	9.9	7.0	12.6	8.0	13.2
Muni Bond	BX	571	SFCOX	1000	100	0	0	.55	0	Yes	Yes	Yes	No	Yes	10.1	6.7	11.4	10.7	12.8
US Gov Sec.	BG	15	SFUSX	1000	100	0	0	.65	0	Yes	Yes	Yes	No	Yes	12.9	8.7	14.8	6.7	7.1
Money Mkt	MM	221	SAFXX	1000	100	0	0	.50	0	No	Yes	Yes	500	Yes	8.7	7.7	5.9	3.3	2.4
TF Money	MX	99	SFTXX	1000	100	0	0	.50	0	No	Yes	Yes	500	Yes	5.3	5.6	4.3	2.7	1.9

PHONE SWITCH—All Funds   3-WEEK HOLD ALL FUNDS   #SWITCHES/YEAR—Unlimited
IRA MINIMUM INVESTMENT—$250   IRA FEE—$5   KEOGH MIN. INVEST.—$1,000
MIN. WIRE WITHDRAWAL—$0   MIN. INVEST. FOR MONTHLY INCOME—$0

SCUDDER

Fund Name	Type	Asset Mil	Dow Smb	Min Inv Int	Add	In%	Loads and Fees Out%	Mgt	12b-1	Scwb Marg	Phone	Wire	Chek	Income	Annual Return 89	90	91	92	93
Development	SA	775	SCDVX	1000	0	0	0	1.0	0	Yes	Yes	Yes	No	Yes	23.2	1.5	71.9	1.0	9.0
Cap. Growth	SB	1422	SCDUX	1000	0	0	0	.65	0	Yes	Yes	Yes	No	Yes	33.8	-17.0	43.0	7.1	20.1
International	SI	2322	SCINX	1000	0	0	0	.75	0	Yes	Yes	Yes	No	Yes	27.0	-8.9	11.8	1.0	36.5
Global	SG	1097	SCOBX	1000	0	0	0	1.0	0	Yes	Yes	Yes	No	Yes	37.4	-6.4	17.1	4.5	31.1
Growth & Inc.	SI	1724	SCDGX	1000	0	0	0	.60	0	Yes	Yes	Yes	No	Yes	26.4	-2.3	28.2	9.6	15.6
NYTF	BX	221	SCYTX	1000	0	0	0	.60	0	Yes	Yes	Yes	No	Yes	10.1	4.3	11.4	11.0	12.9
Cal TF	BX	350	SCYTX	1000	0	0	0	.60	0	Yes	Yes	Yes	No	Yes	10.3	6.4	12.7	9.4	13.8
Managed Muni	BX	878	SCMBX	1000	0	0	0	.60	0	Yes	Yes	Yes	No	Yes	11.1	6.8	12.2	9.0	13.3
GNMA	BG	582	SGMSX	1000	0	0	0	.60	0	No	Yes	Yes	No	Yes	12.8	10.1	15.0	7.0	6.0
Income	BL	520	SCSBX	1000	0	0	0	.60	0	No	Yes	Yes	No	Yes	12.7	8.3	17.3	6.7	12.7
US Zero 2000	BS	28	SGZTX	1000	0	0	0	.55	0	No	Yes	Yes	No	No	20.5	4.6	20.3	8.8	16.0
T Bond	BS	13	SCSTX	1000	0	0	0	.55	0	No	Yes	Yes	No	No	15.7	7.3	14.3	5.5	8.2
Medium Term TF	BY	1012	SCMTX	1000	0	0	0	.60	0	No	Yes	Yes	No	No	8.0	6.6	12.6	8.9	10.9
Cash Inv TR	MM	2011	SCTXX	1000	0	0	0	.50	0	No	Yes	Yes	100	Yes	8.5	7.6	6.0	3.5	2.6
Tax Free Mon.	MX	371	STFXX	1000	0	0	0	0	0	No	Yes	Yes	100	Yes	5.7	5.3	4.2	2.5	1.9
US Treas. Money	MG	300	SCGXX	1000	0	0	0	.50	0	No	Yes	Yes	100	Yes	8.0	7.1	5.7	3.4	2.6

PHONE SWITCH—All Funds   #SWITCHES/YEAR—4   IRA MINIMUM INVESTMENT—$240
KEOGH MIN. INVEST.—$240 to $500   MIN. WIRE WITHDRAWAL—$5,000, $3.50 FEE   IRA FEE—None
MIN. INVEST. FOR MONTHLY INCOME—$10,000

STEIN, ROE & FARNHAM

Fund Name	Type	Asset Mil	Dow Smb	Min Inv		Loads and Fees				Scwb Marg	Withdrawal Options				Annual Return				
				Int	Add	In%	Out%	Mgt	12b-1		Phone	Wire	Chek	Income	89	90	91	92	93
Special	SA	1203	SRSPX	1000	100	0	0	.75	0	No	Yes	No	No	Yes	37.8	−5.8	34.0	14.1	20.4
Cap Opp	SA	177	SRFCX	1000	100	0	0	.75	0	No	Yes	No	No	Yes	36.8	−29.1	62.7	2.4	27.1
Stock	SA	358	SRFSX	1000	100	0	0	.50	0	No	Yes	No	No	Yes	35.5	0.9	46.0	8.2	2.8
Prime Equities	SI	113	SRPEX	1000	100	0	0	.60	0	No	Yes	No	No	Yes	31.0	−1.7	32.4	10.0	12.9
Total Return	SI	233	SRFBX	1000	100	0	0	.625	0	No	Yes	No	No	Yes	20.3	−1.7	29.6	7.9	12.3
High Yd Muni	BX	333	SRMFX	1000	100	0	0	.60	0	No	Yes	No	No	Yes	11.4	7.7	9.8	5.3	10.5
Inter. Muni	BY	258	SRIMX	1000	100	0	0	.60	0	No	Yes	No	No	Yes	8.1	7.5	10.7	7.6	10.9
Income	BL	163	SRHBX	1000	100	0	0	.65	0	No	Yes	No	No	Yes	7.1	6.1	17.2	9.1	13.2
Int. Bond	BL	321	SRBFX	1000	100	0	0	.50	0	No	Yes	No	No	Yes	12.6	7.1	15.1	7.7	9.2
Gov. Income	BG	53	SRGPX	1000	100	0	0	.60	0	No	Yes	No	No	Yes	13.3	8.5	15.0	6.2	7.1
Cash Reserves	MM	1114	STCXX	1000	100	0	0	.50	0	No	Yes	Yes	50	Yes	8.8	7.8	5.7	3.4	2.6
Tax Ex. Money	MX	324	STEXX	1000	100	0	0	.50	0	No	Yes	Yes	50	Yes	5.9	5.4	3.9	2.4	1.9
Gov. Reserves	MG	171	SGRXX	1000	100	0	0	.50	0	No	Yes	Yes	50	Yes	8.7	7.7	5.6	3.3	2.6

PHONE SWITCH—All Funds   #SWITCHES/YEAR—4   IRA MINIMUM INVESTMENT—$500
KEOGH MIN. INVEST.—$500   MIN. WIRE WITHDRAWAL—$1,000   IRA FEE—$10

STRONG-CORNELIUSON CAPITAL MGMT.

Fund Name	Type	Asset Mil	Dow Smb	Min Inv			Loads and Fees			Withdrawal Options					Annual Return				
				Int	Add	In%	Out%	Mgt	12b-1	Scwb Marg	Phone	Wire	Chek	Income	89	90	91	92	93
Discovery	SA	354	STDIX	1000	50	2	0	1.0	0	Yes	Yes	Yes	No	Yes	24.0	-2.7	68.6	1.9	22.2
Opportunity	SA	515	SOPFX	1000	50	2	0	1	0	Yes	Yes	Yes	No	Yes	18.5	-11.3	31.7	17.4	21.2
Total Return	SB	654	STRFX	250	50	1	0	.8	0	Yes	Yes	Yes	No	Yes	2.6	-7.1	33.6	0.6	22.5
Investment	SB	263	STIFX	250	50	1	0	.8	0	Yes	Yes	Yes	No	Yes	11.2	2.8	19.6	3.2	14.5
Income	BL	126	SRNCX	1000	50	0	0	.6	0	Yes	Yes	Yes	500	Yes	.35	-6.2	14.8	9.3	16.8
Muni Bond	BX	389	SXFIX	2500	50	0	0	.6	0	No	No	Yes	500	Yes	7.08	4.6	13.4	12.2	11.8
Gov. Sec.	BG	254	STVSX	1000	50	0	0	.6	0	Yes	Yes	Yes	500	Yes	9.9	8.7	16.7	9.3	12.8
Advantage	BS	490	STADX	1000	50	0	0	.6	0	Yes	Yes	Yes	500	Yes	9.4	6.6	10.6	8.4	8.1
Short Term	BS	1700	SSTBX	1000	50	0	0	.6	0	Yes	Yes	Yes	500	Yes	8.2	5.3	14.6	6.7	9.3
Money	MM	756	SMNXX	1000	50	0	0	.5	0	No	Yes	Yes	500	Yes	9.2	8.1	6.1	3.7	2.9
Muni MM	MX	815	SXFXX	2500	50	0	0	.5	0	No	Yes	Yes	500	Yes	6.0	6.1	5.2	3.4	2.5

PHONE SWITCH—All Funds   IRA FEE—$10
KEOGH MIN. INVEST.—$250

#SWITCHES/YEAR—5   IRA MINIMUM INVESTMENT—$250
MIN. WIRE WITHDRAWAL—$500   MIN. INVEST. FOR MONTHLY INCOME—$5,000

T. ROWE PRICE

Fund Name	Type	Asset Mil	Dow Smb	Min Inv Int	Min Inv Add	Loads and Fees In%	Out%	12b-1	Mgt	Scwb Marg	Withdrawal Options Phone	Wire	Chek	Income	Annual Return 89	90	91	92	93
Cap. Appr.	SA	560	PRWCX	1000	100	0	0	0	.70	Yes	Yes	Yes	No	Yes	21.4	-1.3	21.6	9.4	15.7
New Horizons	SA	1732	PRNHX	1000	100	0	0	0	.65	Yes	Yes	Yes	No	Yes	26.2	-9.6	52.1	10.6	22.0
Internat'l Stock	SS	5637	PRITX	1000	100	0	0	0	.75	Yes	Yes	Yes	No	No	18.1	-8.9	15.9	-3.5	40.1
New Amer	SG	629	PRWAX	1000	100	0	0	0	.60	Yes	Yes	Yes	No	Yes	38.4	-12.2	62.0	10.0	17.4
New Era	SG	821	PRNEX	1000	100	0	0	0	.50	Yes	Yes	Yes	No	Yes	24.3	-8.8	14.7	2.1	15.3
Growth Stock	SG	2022	PRGFX	1000	100	0	0	0	.50	Yes	Yes	Yes	No	Yes	25.4	-4.3	33.8	6.0	15.6
Growth Income	SI	1200	PRGIX	1000	100	0	0	0	.50	Yes	Yes	Yes	No	Yes	19.3	-11.1	31.5	15.3	12.9
Equity Income	SE	2903	PRFHX	1000	100	0	0	0	.50	Yes	Yes	Yes	No	Yes	13.6	-6.7	25.3	14.1	14.8
Tax Free NY	BX	941	PRFHX	2000	100	0	0	0	.55	No	Yes	Yes	500	Yes	10.3	7.1	11.7	9.6	13.0
GNMA	BG	883	PRGMX	2000	100	0	0	0	.55	No	Yes	Yes	No	Yes	14.0	10.0	15.0	6.5	6.1
CALTF	BX	151	PRKCX	2000	100	0	0	0	.55	No	Yes	Yes	No	Yes	8.5	5.8	12.1	8.9	12.5
Tax Free Inc.	BX	1452	PRTAZ	2000	100	0	0	0	.50	Yes	Yes	Yes	500	Yes	6.9	5.9	12.2	9.4	12.8
High Yield	BL	1623	PRHYX	2000	100	0	0	0	.62	Yes	Yes	Yes	No	Yes	-1.5	-11.0	30.9	14.7	21.8
Int'l Bond	BL	755	PRIBX	2000	100	0	0	0	.75	Yes	Yes	Yes	No	Yes	-3.2	16.0	17.7	2.9	20.0
New Income	BL	1458	PRCIX	2000	100	0	0	0	.50	Yes	Yes	Yes	5000	Yes	12.2	8.8	15.5	5.0	9.1
Tax Fr Short	BY	540	PRFSX	2000	100	0	0	0	.50	Yes	Yes	Yes	500	Yes	6.9	6.0	7.9	6.0	6.3
Short Term	BS	668	PRWBX	2000	100	0	0	0	.50	No	Yes	Yes	500	Yes	9.9	9.0	11.2	5.0	6.6
Prime Reserve	MM	6141	PRRXX	2000	100	0	0	0	.40	No	Yes	Yes	500	Yes	8.6	7.5	5.7	3.3	2.6
US Treasury	MG	926	—	2000	100	0	0	0	.50	No	Yes	Yes	500	Yes	8.0	7.2	5.4	3.2	2.5
NYTF Money	MX	89	PTEXX	2000	100	0	0	0	.45	No	Yes	Yes	500	Yes	5.1	4.8	3.8	2.4	1.8
Cal TF	MX	104	PTEXX	2000	100	0	0	0	.45	No	Yes	Yes	500	Yes	5.4	4.8	3.7	2.5	1.9
Tax Exempt	MX	799	PTEXX	2000	100	0	0	0	.50	No	Yes	Yes	500	Yes	5.8	5.2	3.9	2.5	2.0

PHONE SWITCH—All Funds   #SWITCHES/YEAR—2 in 120 days   IRA MINIMUM INVESTMENT—$500   IRA FEE—$10
KEOGH MIN. INVEST.—$500   MIN. WIRE WITHDRAWAL—$500   MIN. INVEST. FOR MONTHLY INCOME—$10,000

TWENTIETH CENTURY

Fund Name	Type	Asset Mil	Dow Smb	Min Inv*			Loads and Fees			Scwb Marg	Withdrawal Options				Annual Return				
				Int	Add	In%	Out%	Mgt	12b-1		Phone	Wire	Chek	Income	89	90	91	92	93
Growth	SG	4540	TWCGX	0	0	0	0	1	0	No	Yes	Yes	No	Yes	43.1	-3.9	69.0	-0.4	3.8
Gift Trust	SA	184	TWGTX	100	0	0	0	1	2	No	Yes	Yes	No	No	50.2	-16.9	84.9	18.0	31.4
Select	SG	4887	TWCIX	0	0	0	0	1	0	No	Yes	Yes	No	Yes	39.5	-0.4	31.6	-0.4	14.7
Ultra	SA	9318	TWCUX	0	0	0	0	1	0	No	Yes	Yes	No	Yes	36.9	9.4	86.5	12.6	21.8
Vista	SA	759	TWCVX	0	0	0	0	1	0	No	Yes	Yes	No	Yes	46.4	-15.7	73.7	-0.2	5.5
Long Term	BL	147	—	0	0	0	0	1	0	No	Yes	No	No	Yes	13.7	6.0	17.5	5.5	10.2
Tax Exempt Int	BY	94	—	0	0	0	0	1	0	No	Yes	No	No	Yes	6.7	6.3	10.1	7.2	9.1
Tax Exempt LT	BX	63	—	0	0	0	0	1	0	No	Yes	No	No	Yes	9.8	6.2	12.0	7.6	12.2
US Gov	BG	463	—	0	0	0	0	1	0	No	Yes	Yes	No	Yes	9.8	7.5	11.6	4.4	4.2
Cash Reserves	MM	1413	TWCXX	0	0	0	0	1	0	No	Yes	Yes	No	Yes	8.4	7.3	5.9	3.0	2.3

PHONE SWITCH—All except Gift Trust   #SWITCHES/YEAR—12   30-Day Hold Switches

IRA FEE—$10   KEOGH MIN. INVEST.—$0   MIN. WIRE WITHDRAWAL—$10 Fee   IRA MINIMUM INVESTMENT—$0

MIN. INVEST. FOR MONTHLY INCOME—$5,000

*There is an annual small-account charge of $10 for accounts with a balance of under $1,000

USAA INV. MANAGEMENT

Fund Name	Type	Asset Mil	Dow Smb	Min Inv		Loads and Fees				Scwb	Withdrawal Options				Annual Return				
				Int	Add	In%	Out%	Mgt	12b-1	Marg	Phone	Wire	Chek	Income	89	90	91	92	93
Agg. Growth	SA	286	USAUX	1000	50	0	0	.5	0	No	Yes	Yes	No	Yes	16.6	-11.9	71.7	-8.5	8.1
Inc. Stock	SB	1182	USAIX	1000	50	0	0	.5	0	No	Yes	Yes	No	Yes	27.1	-1.4	27.3	7.9	11.6
Cornerstone	SG	806	USCRX	1000	50	0	0	.75	0	No	Yes	Yes	No	Yes	21.9	-9.2	16.2	6.3	23.7
Growth	SG	611	USAAX	1000	50	0	0	.5	0	No	Yes	Yes	No	Yes	27.3	-0.1	27.8	10.0	7.5
Gold	SP	169	USAGX	1000	50	0	0	.75	0	No	Yes	Yes	No	Yes	18.1	-26.5	-4.4	-8.0	58.3
Tax Ex Short	BY	1008	USSTX	3000	50	0	0	.5	0	No	Yes	Yes	250	Yes	7.4	5.9	7.7	6.0	5.6
Tax Ex Int	BY	1657	USATX	3000	50	0	0	.5	0	No	Yes	Yes	No	Yes	9.2	6.7	11.1	8.5	11.5
Tax Ex HY	BX	2014	USTEX	3000	50	0	0	.5	0	No	Yes	Yes	No	Yes	10.6	6.6	12.4	8.6	12.5
Income	BS	114	USAIX	1000	50	0	0	.50	0	No	Yes	Yes	No	Yes	16.3	7.7	19.4	8.3	9.9
Money Market	MM	1312	USAXX	1000	50	0	0	.5	0	No	Yes	Yes	250	Yes	8.6	7.7	6.1	3.8	3.0
TE Money Mkt	MX	1618	USEXY	3000	50	0	0	.5	0	No	Yes	Yes	250	Yes	6.1	5.9	4.8	3.1	2.4

PHONE SWITCH—All Funds   #SWITCHES/YEAR—4, $5 FEE   IRA MINIMUM INVESTMENT—$250   IRA FEE—$10
KEOGH MIN. INVEST.—N/A   MIN. WIRE WITHDRAWAL—$1,000   MIN. INVEST. FOR MONTHLY INCOME—$10,000

VALUE LINE INC.

Fund Name	Type	Asset Mil	Dow Smb	Min Inv			Loads and Fees			Scwb Marg	Withdrawal Options				Annual Return				
				Int	Add	In%	Our%	Mgt	12b-1		Phone	Wire	Chek	Income	89	90	91	92	93
Lev. Growth	SA	292	VAIIX	1000	100	0	0	.75	0	Yes	No	No	No	No	32.3	-1.7	46.4	-2.5	16.2
Spec. Sit.	SA	94	VALSX	1000	100	0	0	.75	0	Yes	No	No	No	No	21.7	-4.5	38.1	-3.5	13.0
Fund	SG	323	VLIFX	1000	100	0	0	.75	0	Yes	No	No	No	No	31.4	-0.8	52.9	4.7	6.8
Income	SI	154	VALTX	1000	100	0	0	.75	0	Yes	No	No	No	No	22.4	2.0	28.5	1.7	8.3
Convertible	SI	52	VALCX	1000	250	0	0	.75	0	Yes	Yes	Yes	500	No	10.7	-3.8	28.7	13.8	14.8
Tax Ex Hi Yd	BX	273	VLHXX	1000	250	0	0	.50	0	No	No	No	No	Yes	8.2	6.6	12.3	7.9	11.5
Agg Inc. Tr.	BL	45	VAGIX	1000	250	0	0	.50	0	Yes	Yes	Yes	500	Yes	2.3	-3.7	26.6	12.1	19.0
US Gov. Sec.	BG	452	VALBX	1000	250	0	0	.50	0	Yes	Yes	Yes	500	No	11.9	10.3	16.4	6.3	9.8
Cash	MM	714	VLCXX	1000	100	0	0	.40	0	No	Yes	Yes	500	Yes	9.0	7.9	5.5	3.2	3.1
TE MM	MX	118	VLTXX	1000	250	0	0	.50	0	Yes	Yes	Yes	500	Yes	5.7	5.5	4.1	2.3	1.6

PHONE SWITCH—All Funds   #SWITCHES/YEAR—8   IRA MINIMUM INVESTMENT—$1,000   IRA FEE—$10

KEOGH MIN. INVEST.—$1,000   MIN. WIRE WITHDRAWAL—$1,000   MIN. INVEST. FOR MONTHLY INCOME—$1,000

VANGUARD

Fund Name	Type	Asset Mil	Dow Smb	Min Inv Int	Add	In%	Out%	Mgt	12b-1	Scwb Marg	Phone	Wire	Chek	Income	89	90	91	92	93
Sm. Cap. St.	SA	545	NAESX	3000	100	0	0	.60	0	Yes	Yes	Yes	No	Yes	10.5	−18.1	45.3	18.2	18.7
Explorer	SA	901	VEXPX	1500	100	0	0	.33	0	Yes	Yes	Yes	No	Yes	9.4	−10.8	55.9	13.0	15.4
WL Morgan	SA	1138	VMRGX	1500	100	0	0	.33	0	Yes	Yes	Yes	No	Yes	22.6	−1.5	29.3	9.5	7.3
World US	SG	1844	VWUSX	3000	100	0	0	.33	0	Yes	Yes	Yes	No	Yes	37.7	4.6	46.8	2.7	−1.5
Index Trust	SX	8479	VFINX	1500	100	0	0	6.00	0	Yes	Yes	Yes	No	Yes	—	3.3	30.2	7.4	9.9
Windsor*	SG	10922	VWNDX	1500	100	0	0	.35	0	Yes	Yes	Yes	No	Yes	15.0	−15.5	28.6	16.5	19.4
Windsor II	SG	7767	VWNFX	1500	100	0	0	.35	0	Yes	Yes	Yes	No	Yes	27.2	−10.0	28.7	12.0	13.6
Star*	SB	3662	VGSTX	3000	100	0	0	0	0	Yes	Yes	Yes	No	Yes	18.6	−3.6	24.3	10.5	11.0
World Int.	SG		VWIGX	3000	100	0	0	.33	0	Yes	Yes	Yes	No	Yes	24.8	−12.0	4.7	−5.8	44.9
Fixed Inc Hi Yd	BL	2584	VWEHX	3000	100	0	0	.25	0	Yes	Yes	Yes	250	Yes	1.9	−6.0	29.0	14.2	18.2
Bond Mkt	BL	1531	—	3000	100	0	0	varies	0	Yes	Yes	Yes	No	Yes	13.6	8.6	15.2	7.1	9.7
Fx Inc GNMA	BG	6910	VFIIG	3000	100	0	0	.15	0	Yes	Yes	Yes	250	Yes	14.8	10.3	16.8	6.8	5.9
Fx Inc US Treas	BG	968		3000	100	0	0	varies	0	Yes	Yes	Yes	250	Yes	17.9	5.8	17.4	7.4	16.8
Fx Inc Sh Term	BS	721	VFSTX	3000	100	0	0	varies	0	Yes	Yes	Yes	250	Yes	11.5	9.2	13.1	6.2	7.0
Wellesley Inc.	SB	6218	VWINX	1500	100	0	0	.25	0	Yes	Yes	Yes	No	Yes	20.8	3.8	21.6	8.7	14.7
Wellington	SB	8349	VWELX	1500	100	0	0	.20	0	Yes	Yes	Yes	No	Yes	21.5	−2.8	23.7	7.9	13.5
Convert. Sec.	SI	208	VCVSK	3000	100	0	0	.45	0	Yes	Yes	Yes	No	Yes	15.8	−8.2	34.3	18.9	13.5
Fixed Inc Inv	BL	3168	VWESK	3000	100	0	0	.25	0	Yes	Yes	Yes	250	Yes	15.2	6.2	20.9	9.8	14.5
Spec. Gold	SP	605	VGPMX	3000	100	0	1	.30	0	Yes	Yes	Yes	No	Yes	−30.4	−19.9	4.4	−19.4	93.4
Spec. Tech.	SS	92	VGTCX	3000	100	0	1	.30	0	Yes	Yes	Yes	No	Yes	14.6	−6.5	47.3	−13.5	11.3
Spec. Health	SS	69	VGHCX	3000	100	0	1	.30	0	Yes	Yes	Yes	No	Yes	32.9	16.8	46.3	−1.6	11.8
Spec. Service	SS	34	VGSEX	3000	100	0	1	.30	0	Yes	Yes	Yes	No	Yes	31.4	−15.4	34.0	10.7	12.0
Spec. Energy	SS	353	VGENX	3000	100	0	1	.30	0	Yes	Yes	Yes	No	Yes	43.3	−1.4	0.3	6.1	26.4
Muni Hi Yd	BX	1874	VWAHX	3000	100	0	0	var.	0	Yes	Yes	Yes	250	Yes	11.1	5.9	14.7	9.9	12.7
Penn Ins. TF	BX	1521		3000	100	0	0	var.	0	Yes	Yes	Yes	250	Yes	10.6	6.9	12.2	10.2	12.7
NY Ins. TF	BX	812	—	3000	100	0	0	cost	0	Yes	Yes	Yes	250	Yes	10.3	6.3	12.8	9.7	13.1
Cal Ins. TF	BX	1052	VCITX	3000	1000	0	0	cost	0	Yes	Yes	Yes	No	Yes	10.5	7.0	11.0	9.3	12.8
Muni Lg Term	BX	1057	VWLTX	3000	100	0	0	cost	0	Yes	Yes	Yes	250	Yes	11.5	6.8	13.5	9.3	13.5
Muni Lg Tm Ins	BX	2082	VILDX	3000	100	0	0	cost	0	Yes	Yes	Yes	250	Yes	10.6	7.0	12.5	9.2	13.1

Column groupings: Min Inv (Int, Add) · Loads and Fees (In%, Out%, Mgt, 12b-1) · Withdrawal Options (Phone, Wire, Chek, Income) · Annual Return (89, 90, 91, 92, 93)

Fx US Treas Lg	BG	774	—	3000	100	0	var.	0	Yes	Yes	Yes	250	Yes	13.6	8.6	17.4	7.4	16.8
Fixed Short Tm	BS	3507	VFSTX	3000	100	0	var.	0	Yes	Yes	Yes	250	Yes	14.8	10.3	13.1	6.7	7.0
Muni Inter Tm	BY	2082	VWITX	3000	100	0	cost	0	Yes	Yes	Yes	250	Yes	17.9	5.8	12.2	8.9	11.6
Muni Short Tm	BY	1512	—	3000	100	0	cost	0	Yes	Yes	Yes	250	Yes	11.5	9.2	7.2	4.7	3.8
MM Prime	MG	17142	VMMXX	3000	100	0	cost	0	No	Yes	Yes	250	Yes	9.0	8.3	6.1	3.7	3.0
MM Muni	MX	3517	VMSXX	3000	100	0	cost	0	No	Yes	Yes	250	Yes	6.2	5.8	4.6	3.0	2.4

PHONE SWITCH—All Funds except Index Treas, Sm. Cap. St., Explorer II & Gemini II   #SWITCHES/YEAR—Unlimited
IRA MINIMUM INVESTMENT—$500   IRA FEE—$10   KEOGH MIN. INVEST.—$500
MIN. WIRE WITHDRAWAL—$1,000   MIN. INVEST. FOR MONTHLY INCOME—$10,000

*Closed to New Investors:

1. Should be used by corporations seeking 70% dividend tax exclusion.
2. Star fund holds funds of other Vanguard funds which are subject to management fees.

ACKNOWLEDGMENTS

This book was originally written on all seven continents, including Antarctica. Adena, my wife, was always there with encouragement and patience. We spend two and one-half months a year exploring the world, and there is no more peaceful time to write.

For this new edition, countless hours of research and typesetting were spent by my exceptional staff, including Elaine Wilson, Steve Romeo, John Super, Marsha Shilts, Amy Detwiler, Mary Ann Swiderski, Diane Glassman, Susan Jackson, Tim Copello, and Scott Winewica.

Thanks also to Randy Reynolds, Jim Robinson, Steve Butler, David Phillips, Roger Easton, Buddy Hewell, and Mike Belton—all financial experts associated with the Givens Organization—for their assistance in reviewing the material in this updated edition.

Special thanks to my literary agent Lois de la Haba, for her recognition of the importance of the book and her zealous efforts in bringing it to print.

INDEX

About the Author

Charles J. Givens has built a business and investment empire that includes banks, brokerage firms, television production, radio stations, a quarter billion dollars of commercial real estate and the biggest financial planning and education organization in the world.

Described by one national publication as "fearless, determined, eloquent, and flamboyant," he has made it his personal mission to "stamp out financial ignorance in America," attacking the systems and policies in business and government that he feels impede the progress of individuals and families toward their dreams.

He has been featured on major television shows with Oprah Winfrey, Phil Donahue, Regis Philbin and Kathie Lee Gifford, Geraldo Rivera and Larry King, as well as The Today Show and every major radio show, and in leading magazines and newspapers nationwide.

Charles J. Givens knows about money because he learned at an early age about poverty. As a child he saw his parents' alcoholism destroy their business and family. He watched as a moving van pulled up to their home in Decatur, Illinois, and confiscated everything the family owned to be sold at auction to pay unpaid bills and taxes.

Charles J. Givens was 18 years old, earning 85 cents an hour bagging groceries, when having gone through years of depression, shyness and feeling beaten, he made up his mind to take control of his life once and for all. He began by writing a dreams list—a list of everything he would do with his life if he had unlimited time, talent and money.

Along the way he had more than his share of personal and financial setbacks. Three times in his twenties he lost everything—his home, his furniture, his automobiles, his investments—but he never lost his dreams.

So far he has seen most of those original dreams come true, including becoming one of America's wealthiest men; exploring the most remote areas of the earth—Africa, Sumatra, Borneo and Antarctica; owning a jet, a castle in Europe, a professional sports team; and, most important, developing a beautiful relationship with his family.

His wife, Adena, and sons, Rob and Charles III, are involved in everything he does and are deeply committed to the Charles J. Givens Organization. The author is based in Altamonte Springs, Florida.

CHARLES J. GIVENS ORGANIZATION

The Charles J. Givens Organization, with 650,000 members is the largest financial education and services organization in the world. By calling toll-free **1-800-333-3556 extension 1805** you will learn how to:

- Reduce your taxes by up to 50 percent

- Create a million-dollar retirement plan

- Save thousands of dollars in interest payments on your home

- Slash your auto insurance premiums by up to 50 percent

- Have better life insurance for up to 80 percent less

- Use high-powered, little-known strategies for getting out of debt and rebuilding credit

- Double your money safely every 4-5 years

- Get your next raise totally tax-free

- Protect your estate

- Cut the cost of borrowing money by 30 to 50 percent

- Make your vacations tax-deductible

- And much, much more . . .

For more information about the Charles J. Givens Organization and to get a **FREE** sample of the *Charles J. Givens Success InSight* monthly newsletter, call toll free,

1-800-333-3556 ext.1805